AF361380

Fetishizing Tradition

Fetishizing Tradition

Desire and Reinvention in
Buddhist and Christian Narratives

Alan Cole

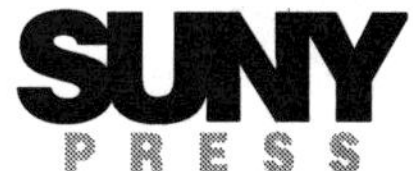

Production, Diane Ganeles
Marketing, Kate R. Seburyamo

Library of Congress Cataloging-in-Publication Data

Cole, Alan.
    Fetishizing tradition : desire and reinvention in Buddhist and Christian narratives / Alan Cole.
        pages cm
    Includes bibliographical references and index.
    ISBN 978-1-4384-5745-1 (hardcover : alk. paper)
    ISBN 978-1-4384-5746-8 (e-book)
    1. Desire—Religious aspects—Buddhism.   2. Desire—Religious aspects—Christianity.   3. Buddhism—Doctrines.   4. Christian art and symbolism.
5. Fetishism.   I. Title.

    BQ4430.D47C65 2015
    225.8'1524—dc23   2014036359

10 9 8 7 6 5 4 3 2 1

Recognizing the human condition to be one made of opposites—
stretched wide across the plains of love and war, intimacy and
formality, innocence and education—this book is dedicated, first,
to my parents, who have all along given me much and who
have probably been wondering when I would dedicate a book
to them and, second, to the NEH reviewer (a New Testament
scholar) who judged my book proposal to be totally worthless—it
is precisely for such readers that I felt most inspired to carry
through with the project.

Contents

Preface

Though the word *fetish* was originally coined to describe various religious beliefs and practices, the meaning of the term has shifted such that it now is closely associated with Freud and internet porn. Thus one can hardly mention the word in polite company without inviting wry smiles and ripples of embarrassment. However, the embarrassment or cautious bemusement likely isn't simply due to the fact that everyone immediately associates *fetish* with outrageously high stilettos heels, carefully cut leather outfits, feather boas, and messy projects with fruit and honey. Instead, I suspect the word makes us wince because its very existence stands as proof that things aren't straightforward in the world of human thought and action since, even in pursuing our supposedly most basic desires, it appears abundantly normal that people involve themselves in all sorts of complex choreography and intricate narratives of self-reinvention. In short, to recognize the enduring prevalence of fetishes is to begin to understand that human desire isn't simple or uninflected, but rather takes shape in and around culturally constructed items, events, and narratives. In fact, it is even worth wondering to what degree human desire is ever findable separate from cultural signifiers and stock narratives: flipping through any porn site suggests that background setting, sartorial selection, lighting (!), and narrative associations are perhaps as important as body and deed.[1]

Given this current understanding of the word, one can expect even more flummoxed reactions when important religious narratives are discussed within the context of the human penchant for fetishes. In particular, those who are professionally and emotionally committed to mainstream religious studies—which has for the most part avoided the problem of desire in religious narrative—surely won't be too thrilled to see a focus on the slippery and troubling topic of desire in my treatment of various Buddhist and Christian narratives. Likewise, those who take Buddhism or Christianity to be true accounts of the world—and this group often overlaps with the first group—also won't be happy to learn of this focus, and even less so when they realize that my approach coincides with a refusal to endorse the reality of the transcendental entities invoked in Buddhist and Christian narratives.

And here several lines from the well-regarded Christian studies scholar Marcus Borg clarify well exactly what I *don't* assume in my discussion of religion and religious narratives: introducing his still popular book from 1987, *Jesus: A New Vision*, he writes, "The two focal points of the book, Spirit and culture, enable us to see some of Jesus's significance for our time. For us, whether in the church or not, his life is a vivid testimony to the reality of Spirit, a reality affirmed and known in virtually every society prior to the modern period."[2] Trying to understand how such embarrassing testimony to "the reality of Spirit"—coupled with Jesus's "significance for our time"—got accepted into academia will be a continuing issue in this book, but the main thing to keep in mind for the chapters to come is that unlike Borg and the many religious studies scholars who share his assumptions, I will take terms like "spirit" or "enlightenment," to be what they have always been: words, ideas, things we long for, and so on, but which are never findable separate from culture, history (both natural history and human history), and the human body. In short, assuming existence to be a totality that has no "spirit" outside itself, I will be writing in accord with what was supposed to be the *raison d'être* of religious studies: to reflect on the nature of religion without promoting a new mode of being religious by counseling readers, as Borg and so many others do, on how they might recover some lost annunciation of Spirit.[3]

Thus, and it comes to the same thing, in this book I assume that religious discourse, like all language, is simply Being doing one of the more noisy things it does, and this noise is not fundamentally different from rain pattering on the roof or the buzz of mosquitoes.[4] But what is obviously terribly different about language is that it allows the talkative aspects of Being—us, that is—to consider ourselves to be separable from Being and to involve ourselves in all sorts of fantasies about our possible escape from Being, an escape into something we think we might like better. Coming to understand these gestures in several important narratives in Buddhism and Christianity is what this book is about, and starting with the idea of the fetish turns out to be a promising way to trace these modes of human thought.

Acknowledgments

This book grew out of a very long conversation with Brook Ziporyn (now professor at the University of Chicago Divinity School). Thinking back on this decades-old conversation, what I think was most important for me—beside all the good humor and camaraderie—was a shared sense for the strangeness of all these religious inventions, a strangeness much like the one evoked in *Le Petit Prince*: on a small, lumpy planet hung in the blackness of space-without-limit, some people came up with stories in which x figured as salvation; then, later, other people told stories that had y as the key to salvation, with y supposedly being much better than x.[5] Much later another set of people came along and tried to make sense of the stories about x and y, and though often very confused about their own relationship to those stories, realized that they could make decent money by providing endless accounts of the meaning of x and y. In my case, for some eighteen years (1994–2012), I made decent money working for the students of Lewis & Clark College who, year after year, showed up hoping to find a better way to live in America by, among other things, reading and struggling with these strange stories. In fact, it was in a large part due to their curiosity and sincerity, that I found the strength to finish this book.

I would also like to thank Prof. Kurt Fosso, of the English department at Lewis and Clark College, for being a wonderful friend and a reliable fount of good ideas. Likewise, I thank Vincent Wimbush, professor of religion at Claremont Graduate University, for being most encouraging when I presented the theoretical perspectives in this book to his Institute for Signifying Scriptures in the spring of 2007.

Charlie Hallisey, professor at Harvard Divinity School, was more than a little helpful with his trenchant but optimistic review of this book-project several years back. More recently, Monica Miller, professor of Religion and Africana studies at Lehigh University, took the time to closely review the manuscript and offer lots of advice and encouragement. I also owe a debt of gratitude to Marie-Claude Ranes, who was kind enough to twice rent me her home in Vaux, France—a quiet place by the Yonne River where in 2001–2, and then again in 2008–9, I wrote out the core chapters of this book. Back in Portland, Oregon, in the summer of 2010, Caitlin Tyler was a helpful editorial assistant, especially in terms of helping me clarify the tenor and scope of the argument. I would also like to thank Jennie Tsen for her generosity and good humor during the months in Singapore when I finished up the project in 2014.

Last but not least, I owe many thanks to Nancy Ellegate, Senior Acquisitions Editor for religious studies at SUNY, for shepherding the manuscript through Press; likewise I want to thank the SUNY staff in marketing and production for their patient work, especially Kate Seburyamo and Diane Ganeles.

Introduction

Fetishes and the Spirit of Religious Studies

A Brief History of the Term *Fetish*

Stepping back from current usage of the word *fetish* reveals that it originally didn't have the sexual connotations that it does today and, actually, used to be all about religion. *Fetish* first came into European languages as a technical term to describe aspects of *other people's* religions; in fact, *fétische* was widely used in French, in the eighteenth and nineteenth centuries, to discuss "primitive" African religions.[1] The term had come into French from the Portuguese *feitiço*, meaning "charm, sorcery," which itself derives from the Latin *factitius*, meaning "fabricated."[2] In the sixteenth and seventeenth centuries, *feitiço* had been coined by the Portuguese traders working in West Africa to refer, derogatorily, to various forms of indigenous religious practices.

Part of this discourse—Portuguese and French—appears simply to reflect a European bewilderment regarding the natives' taste in religious icons. But on another level, the term *fetish* worked as a bulwark to separate African religious practices from European Christianity. Thus, the quasi-academic discourse that began to appear in France in the mid-eighteenth century highlighted how African religions were fetishistic and altogether different from the supposedly clean, reasonable, truthful, and desire-free forms of Christianity. *Fetish*, in short, had become the pejorative term for someone else's icons, with the obvious implication being that one's own icons weren't icons in this sense of having been "fabricated"—*feitiço*, that is—but instead were the way they were because they were sanctified by the natural truths of the universe and the institution of the Catholic church. Thus, like the distinction between cults and religions, this distinction between African fetishes and "legitimate" European icons appears in retrospect to be little more than a form of cultural narcissism that insists that what we do over here when we represent the divine is wonderful, truthful, and utterly different from that demonic thing you do over there.[3]

After the term had been widely used in this manner, it was Marx who gave *fetish* a new and interesting twist. In *Das Kapital* (1867), Marx used the term in an ironic sense to point out how our participation in the capitalist economy has all sorts of magical and mythic elements supporting it.[4] Thus, next to the supposed strict rationality that was imagined to organize labor, value, and market practices, Marx insisted there was also a gigantic web of desire, fantasy, and misrecognition that held it all together. Thus, Marx introduced the religious term *fetish* into economic discussions to highlight that complex process by which humans invent commodities and set them in motion within patterns of exchange, all the while acting as though these items were not humanly created but had a life force of their own. In short, Marx used the term *fetish*, and especially *commodity fetish,* to get at the quasi-mystical modes of thought that accompany capitalist practices whereby objects are latched onto with a kind of religious fervor.[5]

In 1905, roughly a half-century after Marx's clever use of the term, Freud employed *fetish* in a manner that began to approximate how it is used in modern English.[6] For Freud, *fetish* was to be understood as desire's handmaiden since in his analytic work he had come to see how people often rely on prop-like items to orchestrate their projects of desire. Of course, in good Freudian fashion the only fetishes that really matter are those involving the penis, or, rather, the absence of the penis. In particular, Freud claimed that fetishes are stand-ins for that ever elusive item, the female phallus, that men supposedly want desperately to reattach to women in order to ward off the sobering possibility that some things are, er, in fact detachable. As he put it: "In the world of psychical reality the woman still has a penis in spite of all, but this penis is no longer the same as it once was. *Something else has taken its place, has been appointed its successor,* so to speak, and now absorbs all the interest which formerly belonged to the penis. But this interest undergoes yet another very strong reinforcement, because the horror of castration *sets up a sort of permanent memorial to itself by creating this substitute.*"[7] The logic of this passage, once liberated from Freud's hallmark hysteria over the lost penis, gets at a number of dialectical issues that are relevant to my use of the term *fetish* for reading religious narratives, especially the way that the fetish stands in for a prior object of desire and thereby is that item's "appointed successor" and yet, in a sense, is also its murderer since the birth of the fetish invariably involves the death of its predecessor, with the violence of that substitution lingering in funereal form as a kind of "permanent memorial."

While such a model of replacement and symbolization will be crucial for describing rhetorical patterns in the texts treated here, I believe it useful to point out that desire and fetishes seem to fit together in a more wholesome relationship than Freud imagined. In fact, I would say, *pace* Freud, that desire isn't something that proceeds *with* fetish assistance, but rather that desire is, by nature, fetishistic. Arguably, one can't desire anything in its totality, but only for one or more of its chosen attributes or elements. One doesn't desire someone for their knuckles, their liver functions and all the rest, just as one doesn't desire a peach for its pit or the soft thud it makes when dropped. In short, desire, by definition, is partial and preselecting, and proceeds by reinventing the desired item such that a beloved part stands in for the whole, a fetish, that is.[8] However, whereas many fetish structures maintain a basic continuity between the desired item and its choice signifying attribute/s—for instance, the sound of certain footsteps in the hallway or a long-forgotten fragrance—the gap between the desired item and its fetishized representation can grow to be quite large. Thus we need to be ready to make sense of more abstract fetishes such as national flags, brand names and logos of all sorts, zip codes, and of course, university degrees.[9] In these cases, there is a particularly high degree of abstraction as something as unthinkable as a nation is fetishized into a smallish piece of colored cloth that one is, nonetheless, supposed to be prepared to die for. In this expanded, and distinctly post-Freudian, sense of the term, fetishes can be any kind of thing, sensation, word, or idea that evokes a complex matrix that can't otherwise be represented or desired with such clarity and verve.[10]

Roland Barthes, though not employing the term *fetish* in his charming 1964 essay on the Eiffel Tower, gives us a first-rate example of how to consider the logic of fetishes in this more generalized manner.[11] Thus he demonstrates how the Tower is imagined to embody Paris and Frenchness such that seeing the Tower is a thrill because one is supposedly seeing the essence of Paris, though, arguably, real Paris is totally absent from this representation: those swooping steel girders, of course, bear very little resemblance to the other aspects of Paris that one might bump into. Thus, regardless of the mind-bending happenstances of *how* the Eiffel Tower came to be the premier icon for Paris and Frenchness—the Tower was built originally for the 1889 World Fair, with some pretense to being a weather lookout and communications relay station—the fetish function of the Tower is fairly easy to understand.

What is harder to recognize is that the construction of all identity—be it of a nation, a religion, or a person—is basically fetishistic if we grant the term this expanded meaning.[12] In the case of humans, consider that amazing process of reification whereby "sitting-up mud," as Vonnegut calls humans in

Cat's Cradle, is turned into a named someone with legal rights, a bank account, a national security card, a place in society, and of course, a Facebook page. In this hasty alchemy that renders a wandering primate into a Real Someone, we have to admit that something quasi-transcendental has been pasted on top of the bubbling biology of the body—a supposedly real honest-to-goodness identity qua Self.[13] (I will use a capitalized *Self* when emphasizing this imaginary form of the individual.) In effect, it seems we get to know ourselves and each other through the construction, and subsequent mutual recognition, of our individual Eiffel Towers, as it were. And, presumably, it is just this tension between the reified Self and the body of biology that makes death such a problem. In death, one watches the body melt back to the matrix of Being in a manner that negates the carefully constructed—and fundamentally alienated—Eiffel Tower of the Self, and hence the urgent need to construct a theory about the reified Self's timely exit from that death process. With the body beginning its descent into the great silence of the sameness of Being, we imagine that the Self flies away, attaining a new life in some postmortem land where all Eiffel Towers of the Self are happily regathered and forever set free of the threat of being reabsorbed by Being.

In order to support the fabrication of a spiritual Self over and against the physical body, it isn't surprising that we have so often invented equally reified cosmic conversational partners—divine "Big Others," as it were—to validate us and encourage us in the ongoing project of Self-exaltation. One of the standard benefits of joining in a relation with such a cosmic "Big Other" is that one can see one's Self as a knocked down version of the much grander divine Self who is, himself, fully self-sustaining and free of time and the anxiety of melting back into Being.[14] With the selfhood of God or the Buddha permanently installed *over there*, lofted up into the sphere of pure isness and eternity, we can be confident that our own final Selfhood will hold its own against the rest of Being. To further convince ourselves of this, we build up theories explaining how we are intimately related to this or that transcendental figure—usually by way of family metaphors—such that as faithful descendants of the divine we too can expect to enter into that finalized form of Self and thereby stand firm against the all-consuming matrix of Being that brooks no lasting entitiness.

Fetishizing Tradition

Understanding these modes of fetishization in the human construction of meaning and identity is useful for working on a range dynamics in religion, but they actually only lay the groundwork for what I mean by *fetishizing tradition*. With this phrase, I am suggesting that we need to see that humans have regularly involved themselves in a second-order mode of fetishization. By this I mean that at different moments in the past two thousand years, new religious discourses have emerged that, by their own reckoning, claim to be the "appointed successors" of the older religious traditions, traditions that they attempt to subsume and replace. Thus, what seems to have happened in several high-profile instances is that a well-established tradition, with its many religious techniques, rituals, and beliefs, is subject to a fetishization process whereby radical spokespersons appear claiming that the essence of the older religious tradition is *now* available via one entity—be it a name to trust in and recite, a narrative to cherish, or some other unique item or practice—that promises to single-handedly deliver the totality of the older form of tradition. In short, the term *fetishizing tradition* points out those nodes in the development of religious thought when the complex and disparate forms of prior tradition were reduced to one singular and terribly exciting Thing that supposedly subsumes and overcomes its antecedents.

What is a little harder to catch sight of is that this process of fetishizing the older form of tradition was often accomplished when *the very techniques that the (old) religion employed to fetishize the chaos of lived reality were turned back on that very religious system itself.* Seeing this involuting process at work in central texts in various traditions, we need to develop a language for describing these moments when (old) traditions were objectified and fetishized into new forms, and when their own organizing principles were turned against them.

To get a sense of this play of levels in the construction of Christianity, consider how in the gospel narratives there *is* a fleshy Covenant sacrifice performed on Passover—with Jesus's lamb-like self-sacrifice so thickly scripted with the markers of (old) tradition—and yet it is just this new story of a very peculiar Passover that provides the reason for leaving the confines of the Jewish tradition and for hoping for salvation through faith in Jesus Christ and this narrative that he lives in. In brief, it is precisely by narrating Jesus's death as a quasi-traditional sacrifice—specifically identified as an offering of Atonement—that the whole world of Temple sacrifice, with its priests, alters, and sacrificial blood, is rendered defunct and passé. Moreover, all the power, promise, and divine connectivity that Temple Judaism laid claim to is now so readily available in a new cultural form—the narrative of its overcoming, as found in the gospels. In effect, with the gospels (and the same goes for the Pauline letters), though the stories and theologizing are *about* sacrifice—the complex sacrifice of Jesus, that is—real sacrifice has disappeared, being replaced by a more linguistic form of religion in which one's primary obligations are to believe the story and to participate in a virtual "floating world" of narrative, hoping that this alone will win one the essence of (old) tradition, and, of course, salvation.

Reading early forms of Christian discourse as efforts to fetishize (old) tradition—Judaism—seems to fit the facts well, as I will argue in detail below, but such an approach becomes doubly interesting when we recognize that parallel dynamics structure some of the major narratives in Mahāyāna Buddhism. In such narratives, as found in the *Lotus Sūtra* or the *Sūtra on the Land of Bliss* or the *Diamond Sūtra*, it is claimed that there is no longer any need to join a Buddhist monastery, to meditate, to keep the lengthy list of Buddhist rules, or to actually learn something, for that matter, since salvation is promised in exchange for one's acceptance of the new discourse itself. Though in Mahāyāna Buddhism—as in Christianity—plenty of ritual forms grew up around these narratives that overcame tradition, it is still the case that these narratives represent striking moments when tradition was radically refigured since the self-articulation of tradition has jumped up a level into a linguistic medium that promises to deliver the totality of tradition via that medium itself. The importance of this aspect of early Mahāyāna literature—commonly referred to as "the cult of the text"—has, in the past thirty years, become well established in Buddhist studies, and this book is, in a general sense, an effort to bring this perspective into conversation with Christian studies.

While some might find this approach unusual, I would suggest that this reaction is largely due to the fact that many modern forms of religion are built around such tradition-consuming narratives and it is thus precisely our familiarity with such forms that makes them hard to see. Given the ubiquity of these narratives that fetishize (old) tradition, we have, it would seem, simply concluded that this is how religion naturally is, so there is nothing to be gained by pointing this out. Such a reluctance is all the more pronounced in believers of these narratives since they have committed themselves to enjoying these linguistic constructions within the confidence that they aren't simply natural, in the sense that three meals a day seems natural, but that they are divinely ordained and thus even less worthy of human scrutiny. Aware of these reluctances, this book builds its case by looking at important narratives from Buddhism and Christianity, working to show in that juxtaposition how useful this perspective on fetishizing tradition is, while also exploring why it might be that these fetishized forms of tradition have turned out to be *so* important in human history.

Central in these Buddhist and Christian narratives is a revolutionary kind of "practice" best described as *belief in belief* in which the potential convert is offered the following two-part contract: 1) believe that the totality of (old) tradition is available, *en toto*, over "here" in this newly invented narrative; and, 2) likewise believe that (old) tradition can be yours simply by believing in this account of its new locale, and *voilà*, it will be yours. In short, though the equation might be masked in different ways, one's task as a consumer of these narratives is to give the new narrative the right to purvey tradition, within the understanding that just such a gift to the narrative wins one the salvation that the narrative claims to be in charge of.[15] Thus, whether the totality of tradition is promised in the sacrificial figure of Jesus as depicted in the gospels and Paul's Letters, or in the name of the Buddha Amitāyus (Amitābha) as presented in the various Land of Bliss sūtras, or in the figure of the Chan (Zen) master Huineng (n.d.), as found in his different "biographies," there is always this two-part claim that the essence of tradition has been relocated and that it is available to those who accept this claim of relocation as fundamentally true. This might sound absurd at first, but again it would seem that our overfamiliarity with this fetishistic form of tradition-production impedes our recognition of its contours. Thus, for instance, when yet another American roadside billboard announces "Jesus Is Lord," we perhaps haven't had the wherewithal to see this statement as a perfect example of fetishizing tradition in which salvation is offered to those who both believe this statement and believe that believing this statement is the doorway to salvation.[16]

It is also the case that the call to believe in belief—in its Christian and Mahāyāna Buddhist forms—regularly validates itself precisely by comparing itself to its supposedly dim and benighted cousins of old tradition, claiming essentially: "Only the foolish and arrogant would stay trapped in that old system of physically practicing tradition, hoping for salvation." In effect, then, committing to such a new religious identity is enlivened by the fantasy of the *failed* religious identity of the Other, the Other of old tradition who is to be refuted, despised, and overcome. And yet, and this is crucial, in this complex construction, *the despised old tradition can never be abandoned.* In such a packet of desire and belief, one's religious identity isn't formed solely around a god or a truth or a practice; *rather, one's religion is, in a significant way, a theory about why someone else's religion failed.*

Coming to appreciate this dynamic means recognizing, among other things, that salvation is now promised to those who latch on to these new theories of salvation since these newly invented forms of religion take the *articulation* of salvation as the place where salvation is decided. In short, one's salvation hinges on how one receives the (new) message of salvation. Put thusly, we can begin to see why early Christian narratives look the way they do, with the same true of a variety of Buddhist texts: they aren't about content directly; they are about getting the reader/listener to move from an older zone of content and practice into this new narrative fantasy space that explains that making that very jump from the old to the new is the essence of the new content and the cause for winning salvation. In the case of Christianity, if one takes the gospels (lit: "good news") *as* good news, in the sense of being a narrative that is both true and good, then one has just become Christian.

To clarify these reflexive arrangements, let's return to the "Jesus Is Lord" assertion to get a sense for how even the simplest Christian claim involves several levels of meaning and reference. First, the statement appears to be giving new information; after all, if this wasn't news there would be no reason to announce it in elephantine block letters; and, of course, it is news—the good news. Likewise, the statement doesn't appear to be tautological, claiming that x is just x. Rather, it claims that this new thing y is actually x, with the presumption of the author apparently being that you might not have known about the reality of this equation—at your peril. In effect, the statement, while appearing as a simple assertion, implies that your prior notion of the divine needs to be overwritten with this new formulation, presumably with the starkness of the statement speaking to the gravity of the situation. Last, implicit in the claim is the basic Christian confidence that getting Jesus's identity correct—a project that is no different from accepting the narrative claims of the gospels—is the cause of one's salvation. In sum, the claim "Jesus Is Lord," however simple it might appear, actually involves one in some rather complex gestures of overcoming, gestures that deliver one into the zone where the message is about the message in a manner that parallels other early Christian narratives.

Of course, this way of reading Christian and Buddhist narratives has not, it would seem, been the norm. Most work in the fields of Christian studies and Buddhist studies has ignored these self-reflexive "media" issues and focused on trying to recover the meaning of the texts in a piecemeal manner, arguing about this or that passage, or this or that mini-theme, without reckoning these works as literary inventions quite aware of the tasks at hands: seducing audiences from one form of tradition into this newly mediatized form. However, reading for content *within* these texts without first reckoning the overall work of the narrative is like reading a recipe and forgetting that all the separate ingredients are to be combined to produce one dish. Until one clarifies how these texts were artfully constructed as recipes for conversion and conviction, discussions of the details will be of limited value.

I will, in the next chapter, say more about these texts as consciously constructed works of art—*feitiço* that fetishize tradition and themselves, that is—but for the moment I would like to suggest that the process of fetishizing (old) tradition is somewhat like that complex and interesting gap between playing real soccer and playing soccer on a video console. While in video soccer there is much that appears like real soccer—there's a field (of sorts) on the screen, with figures on it (that *look* like people), and a round thing bouncing about, and plenty of passion and disappointment, and so on—still it is true that everything is terribly different since one is alone, "kicking" the ball about with a joystick at the corner bar. Thus, despite the formal parallelism, video "soccer" exists in a very odd relationship to soccer since the electronic version seeks to *appear* as real as possible—the background "field" is green, the "players" in their colored jerseys trot about in a manner that resembles running, there are images of referees and a crowd, and so on—while also avoiding all the things that make soccer what it is: a brutally exhausting game, played in unpredictable weather, against an opposing team that will try to bend the rules at every turn, and so on. Likewise, instead of preparing to play the game by eating lightly, cleaning off one's cleats, and putting on a modicum of protective gear, one simply slips a coin into a slot and immediately loses oneself in a "sport" that is won or lost based on one's ability to become absorbed in the re-presentation of soccer such that the simulacrum is engaging and satisfying on its own terms. And, obviously, with soccer now reconstructed in this virtual form, it can be taken anywhere and played anytime. In fact, real soccer could die off, and one could still feel inspired to play video soccer, perhaps with even more verve. In short, one's old love affair with soccer is now mediated through the video presentation which promises to provide "all" future games.

While it might seem that video soccer is a most unlikely candidate to serve as a model for reading some of the more important texts of Christianity and Buddhism, I believe that the following chapters will provide convincing evidence that we need such analogies to better explain how certain Buddhist and Christian narratives cannibalized the "hands-on" traditions from whence they came as they opened up "imaginary" ways of being traditional. In these new narratives the content, logic, language, and personages of tradition are still present—and in fact these elements of (old) tradition are decisive in organizing content in these narratives—but these traditional elements are also radically refuted in the process of being refigured in new "story form." Thus, with the figures from (old) tradition put to work justifying—or rather, *traditionalizing*—these new narratives, the narratives appear ready to float free of (old) tradition and all the physical, social, and historical realities that made (old) tradition what it was. To put it bluntly, it seems clear that without thinking about the history of religions with an eye on these media shifts, one will miss the import of these developments, along with the basis for entering into a reasonable reading of these texts, just as though one took video soccer to be a traditional sport.

If one is familiar with New Testament literature, and not blinded by Christian partisanship—a rare combination, it must be admitted—one will probably already suspect that this perspective on fetishizing tradition begins to get at some of the central motifs in early Christian rhetoric as it sought to absorb and supplant the more practical forms of the Jewish tradition that had insisted on the power of rites, the unique sacrality of the Jerusalem Temple, the centrality of the hereditary priests, calendric offerings and festivals, and, of course, sacrifice.[17] However, most readers won't know that similar patterns and paradigms inform a number of important Buddhist texts. In two recent books—*Text as Father: Paternal Seductions in Early Mahāyāna Buddhist Literature* and *Fathering Your Father: The Zen of Fabrication in Tang Buddhism*—I argued that several important texts in the Mahāyāna tradition are best read with these perspectives in mind. *Fetishizing Tradition*, by putting readings of texts from the Christian and Buddhist traditions back-to-back, seeks to promote the general value of this approach, while also working to establish a platform for future comparative discussions. To this end, the first half of this book is built around analyses of early Christian rhetoric, with a focus on Paul's Letter to the Romans, and the Gospel of Mark, while the second half close reads the *Sūtra on the Land of Bliss* (*Sukhāvatīvyūha*)—an Indian text written some time before the beginning of the fifth century—and the *Platform Sūtra of the Sixth Patriarch* (referred to in an abbreviated form as *Liu zu tan jing*) from late eighth-century China.[18]

In developing close readings of each of these works, I focus on four issues: 1) the complicated dependence on prior forms of tradition that the new version of tradition carries within it; 2) the various narrative techniques that make fetishizing tradition appear plausible and desirable; 3) the role of truth-fathers in facilitating the fetishization of tradition, with truth-fathers defined as those cosmic and transcendental figures (the divine Big Others mentioned above) who supposedly own the essence of tradition and who are leaned on to ratify the new narratives; and 4) the centrality of desire in bringing about this conversion in the consumer of the narrative, a desire that is complex and regularly involved in several kinds of symbolic violence. In designing my discussion in this manner the goal is to denaturalize these moments of fetishizing tradition so as to better appreciate their gestures and genius, and to begin to shed some light on how these forms of overcoming tradition have come to inform our modern notions of the religious life.

Given my intent to denaturalize and deconstruct narratives from either tradition, I should admit that I risk insulting those readers who might be committed to the idea that Christianity or Buddhism actually provides the keys to salvation. For these readers, I would simply suggest that if they don't want to begin the work of unpacking the symbolic and psychological processes implicit in the language of these new forms of tradition, they shouldn't read this book. Or put positively, this book is written for that person—eighteen or eighty years old—who is interested in thinking about some of the ideological building blocks of the two religions that have, besides Islam, most shaped human thinking in Europe and Asia for the past two thousand years. And even if in the years to come this book is surpassed by more accurate and more attentive discussions—and this *is* the fate of academic books, isn't it?—I believe it will have served its purpose if, for the time being, it succeeds in increasing sensitivity to the truly odd frames of reference that our ancestors built for us.

A phrase like "increasing sensitivity," invites a word or two about humor. Humor, it turns out, is rather complicated, but for this discussion we only need to see that it often emerges as a happy readjustment in one's relationship to the symbolic order, signaling not just an ongoing resistance to formality, to legalism and pretense, but also the return of a sense of wholeness, bolstered by a certain kind of illegal enjoyment won by considering the demands of the symbolic order from an unexpected angle. For instance, watching Buster Keaton slip on a banana peel is (terribly) funny because it invites us to reconsider a very human reality: we are all trying to walk around properly—required to, actually—and yet we are all also rather liable to topple over for the most absurd reasons, and thus as we watch Keaton perform these ambulatory disasters, we find some grace born of the realization that our problems with the rigorous demands of gravity and normalcy aren't ours alone. One assumes a parallel paradigm at work as we enjoy the erotic catastrophes of public figures who first claim the moral high ground—such as Ted Haggard, Eliot Spitzer, and more recently George Rekers—and then nose-dive in spectacular acts of silliness that produce just that kind of recalibration in our experience of the symbolic order. In short, as the lawgivers slip on their own banana peels, religion and sophisticated society look rather different from the images given in their self-glamorizing rhetoric, and that difference is, of course, quite enjoyable to behold.[19]

If we put this perspective on humor in the terms of the reified Self discussed above, then humor's readjustment of the symbolic order often appears as the natural counterbalance to the forces that religious rhetoric musters as it works to convince us of how we ought to understand our complex lives via rarefied forms labeled "soul," "Spirit," "enlightenment," or whatever. Thus humor, in good Rabelais fashion, reminds us of the inescapable matrix of Being to which we belong, that terrifying and omnipresent matrix that we so eagerly try to turn away from with concepts such as soul or enlightenment. No surprise then that the preponderance of everyday jokes has to do with the gritty "stuff of life," such as sex, food, shit, fat, stupidity, animals, dirt, failure, and, of course, death. Put that way, humor ought to have a special place in religious studies since, like an obscene and impish gargoyle, it so regularly squats in the corner of official discourse, regularly reminding us of that process of fetishization whereby "serious" religious meaning is made out of the messy matrix of life.

For instance, the claim that God had a son is, on its own terms, a pretty funny idea—one has to ask: how did he do it, exactly? That this son is explained as the result of sexless intercourse with Mary only heightens the giggle factor. Such divine begetting without sex is certainly as funny as imagining that far to the west one finds a square place made of jewels where the residents get bombarded with perfect Buddhist discourses produced when fake birds honk at regular intervals during the day. And yet to laugh at such ludicrous claims is to invite stern chiding from those who have taken, as their life's work, the task of treating these claims seriously and therefore definitely not funny. While I am not particularly interested in eliciting the righteous rage of the believers, I am interested in returning to question that moment when humanity decided to take such claims about the reification of reality seriously. Humor naturally seems to be a useful route back to that crucial moment.

In this sense, my attempts at humor in this book aren't too different from the episodes in Peanuts where Linus sits in the pumpkin patch awaiting the appearance of the Great Pumpkin. Once messianic expectations are put in this cartoon form they are a whole lot easier to think about since one is being gently asked to reconsider one's own messianism in these knocked-down and oh-so-simple terms. The humor of the cartoon comes in doubling messianism into this wistful "kids-only" version, a doubling that naturally invites one to question how adult one's own messianism really is. Moreover, the general tenor of Shultz's piece is forgiving, and embracing—there's a distinctly "all too human" quality about waiting for the Great Pumpkin in one's most sincere pumpkin patch—and that wholesome tone offers the reader a graceful exit from those more strident, no-nonsense forms of messianism. In fact, one could argue that the humor of the pumpkin-patch sequences derives from adopting, however temporarily, a new and unauthorized gaze back on to one's messianism: it's likely nothing more than a pumpkin-patch vigil that results, every time, in disappointment and a lot of lost sleep, not to mention all that commentary from one's friends. Of course, just such ironic doubling of religious discourse provides exactly the ease and grace that religions seek to withhold, and yet that *purveyors of religion* want their claims to remain serious sounding and seemingly unassailable is just the desire of the religious and needn't be taken as a rule for the rest of us.

Another reason I have opted for the occasional joke in this book is to remind readers that religious studies is precisely that zone of modern discourse where religion *ought not be treated religiously.* While the intensity of pro-Buddhist partisanship varies significantly in Buddhist studies, in Christian studies it is clear that the vast majority of research on Christianity is conducted by authors who are also ordained clergy, and this has made the field pro-Christian by definition. There are a few notable exceptions, but a conservative estimate would be that more than 90 percent of the scholars in the field have been schooled within the dual seminary-university system which is designed to produce that curious fusion figure: the pastor (or priest) who is also an academic and who is thus poised to take a rather pro-Christian perspective into the classroom and the publication system that supports the university system. The problems generated by this arrangement, especially in terms of the formulation of research topics, are literally of biblical proportions. That these clergy-scholars insist that they are beyond any conflict of interest is hardly convincing and certainly goes against standard practice in banking, law, politics, and medical research.[20]

To counter these claims of neutrality, one only need ask: When was it decided that clergy belong to that genre of human being who can be counted on to be impartial about the very thing they have formally devoted their lives to? And, let's be very clear: to be astonished by this untoward situation doesn't mean that one is holding out for some fantasy of pure objectivity. Instead, it simply means that one recognizes that the discipline of religious studies was invented, some hundred and twenty years ago, specifically to be the place *apart from theology* where religion could be addressed without churchy assumptions regarding religion's innate value and legitimacy, and without specific goals of *reproducing tradition.*[21] And, yet, it is precisely into this zone apart from tradition that we have seen the return of the clergy, at least in American academia.[22]

Given these institutional realities, and the general pro-Christian sentiments currently reigning in America, this book will naturally appear polemical and, I suppose, rude in places. Of course, if in the chapters to come I can convince you that there *are* new and better ways to frame discussions of central elements in Buddhist and Christian narratives—and religion, in general—then my argumentativeness will, I would hope, be forgiven—and even atheists crave forgiveness. Or, and here I am hoping to share the blame, let's not overlook the fact that as long as some humans take it upon themselves to convince others of supposedly divine truths (and their dire consequences), there will always be books like this one gleefully tagging along, insisting on the thoroughly humanness of humanity, especially as seen in our quest for the transcendent.

1

Methodology and a World of Commentary

This book assumes that Jonathan Z. Smith was right when he claimed that "all religious discourse is commentary"—a statement that I take to mean that whatever is said in religion is said *back* to something that was already said and, equally important, is said with words that were already said somewhere else, in some other time, in some other situation, and with other meanings.[1] In a basic sense, language can't be otherwise since meaning is always a question of evoking something more or less already known, with words whose referents have been well established in other contexts. Within the sphere of religion, however, recognizing meaning's dependence on recycled language ruins the assumption that religious language, and the meanings it seeks to deliver, come from the transcendent beyond. Thus, Smith's claim short circuits the assumption that language of the transcendent must itself come from the transcendent, for instance, as found in the standard evangelical claim that the Bible is "the word of God," or in the faith among some Buddhists that the Mahāyāna sutras were spoken by the omniscient Buddha and not written by Indian and Chinese authors.

Smith's statement resituates religious language so that instead of appearing as a glowing reflection of divinity—and thus quasi-divine itself—it now reveals itself to be a long-term resident in the prosaic, if packed, "house of language" that humans have inhabited ever since we began to talk. In this view religious discourse is fathered not by the transcendent beyond but by the chain of ancestral linguistic precedents that, in an unthinkably dense web of articulations, stretches back to our cave-and-savannah days, and in particular, back to that moment when our grunts, moans, and shrieks turned into words that had the ability to refer to things seen and unseen. This, then, is the most interesting part of Smith's comment: the various religious claims that seek to situate their laws and truths beyond human history have a terribly thick terrestrial history.

Fetishizing Tradition as Art for the Masses

In the following close readings of Buddhist and Christian texts, I accept Smith's position that all religious discourse is commentary—and fully embedded in a specific historical context—but I also assume that the religious language in these particular texts is not the direct expression of the authors' personal convictions. Instead, I approach these discourses as *artistic creations* fashioned to produce certain effects in the listener or reader.[2] This is, of course, simply another way of saying that these texts are not diaries or "memos-to-oneself," but rather full-fledged media events, designed for public consumption.[3] Seen in this light, these texts—as artistically designed public statements—*have to be read for their management of their own consumption*, which, arguably, is one of the most basic criteria of artistic production. Thus, these texts were not composed through the simple procedure of externalizing meanings that were pre-existent *in* the authors, but rather they were produced thinking about how religious statements would look in the eyes of potential readers or listeners. Hence, in a certain sense these texts were written from the outside of the text looking in, with the text's form and content shaped by the anticipated demands of public reception. In other words, we can't avoid the conclusion that these texts *are about the people who are to consume them* since it was their desires and their notions of authority and history that were to be engaged, redesigned, and made livable in new forms.[4]

In treating these texts as art products, I naturally read the narratives for their intersubjectivity, and by *intersubjectivity* I simply mean that the authors of these works thought about how readers would think about the presentation of truth and tradition in these literary products, and organized the development of the text's contents accordingly. In short, I'm thinking about these religious discourses as determined by the place where they are to take root—in the human subject—and this seems like a wise choice since with a bit of reflection it becomes clear that the texts aren't strictly about objects of religious faith—God, the Buddha, heaven, nirvana, and so on—but rather about getting human subjects to imagine these objects in certain prescribed ways, ways that have everything to do with how they used to conceive of other sublime items that ruled their symbolic worlds before texts such as these showed up. Naturally, then, however radical these texts might have been in their rewriting of (old) tradition, their main topics, gestures, and tropes remain completely involved with (old) tradition.[5]

Switching to this art-based model of interpretation seems useful, but there is another problem to consider here since once we agree that these authors must have been thinking about how the readers would receive their work, they had to have also been thinking about how those readers *already* thought about (old) tradition, the law, history, and so on, since these were the principal religious elements that the authors hoped to reshape in the readers' imagination. Consequently, in order to move readers from the old form of tradition to the new form, as defined by the text, an author would have to get hold of the reader's confidence, the reader's desire, and the reader's current working image of (old) tradition, all in order to blend these items into the new configurations of religious meaning, as provided and sanctioned by the text. If we assume that this was the task at hand in composing these works, then each of these authors would have had to have not just a working knowledge of his anticipated reader, but also of his reader's sense of his place in tradition and history in order that that (old) package of self and tradition could be effectively overhauled. In effect, when we come across a text that fetishizes tradition, we have to prepare ourselves for engaging it in a manner that respects the interplay of five figures—author, audience, text (as new site of authority), and the two forms of tradition, old and new. In this pentagon of relay and reference, the most difficult figure to reckon is the author who has put himself in charge of handling these new modes of recognizing truth, authority, and closure against the background matrix of old tradition.

A further point worth considering is that it isn't just that such an author had to have been passably adept at objectifying images of (old) tradition and then manhandling them into new forms; he also had come to terms with the *limits of acceptability* in moving his audience from old to the new forms of tradition. In fact, we ought to say that the old law (of tradition) was rewritten under the "law" of public acceptability in the sense that the public's current appraisal of themselves and their place in history, as imagined by the author, was a defining force in the scripting of these new legal arrangements. Thus, narratives that fetishize tradition have to work not just with the elements of old tradition, and not just with the very specific kinds of desires that held old tradition fast in the imagination of his audience, but also within the horizons of what current public desire could countenance in terms of a newly formulated law.[6] In all this, the point isn't just to keep track of how items are being recycled as they are reinscribed in new narratives, but also to keep an eye on that general tissue of desire that is being tugged and twisted this way and that, as the authors moved key items around, knowing that each discourse object was always already tethered to a set of commitments and expectations.

While approaching these texts in this manner seems logical and even unavoidable, it upsets a number of assumptions that have shaped religious studies in the past century. For instance, and picking an example from Christianity that likely will be familiar to most readers, if we approach the Gospel of Mark as art in the sense explained above, then we have to jettison the pious assumption that the author was simply reporting what he had heard or what he believed to be true. And, likewise, we can't continue to imagine that he wrote his narrative with no thought given to controlling and shaping the future reception of his message, or without trying to build an image of new tradition that would overcome (old) tradition in the imagination of the reader/listener. Instead we have to treat him as a full-fledged author engaged in all the intersubjective thinking mentioned above, and, of course, intent on seducing his audience into a new view of tradition, authority, and salvation.[7]

Naturally, once we opt for treating the text as a seduction, we need to put aside the naïve assumption that the author was only reflecting a community's belief, a reading strategy that should have been abandoned long ago, once it was realized that the Gospel of Mark was designed to convince readers and listeners of things that they *didn't already believe*; thus, obviously, the narrative couldn't be a reflection of a pre-established community of believers. In place of these dead-end approaches which are more theological than theoretical, we should adopt a reading strategy that is thoroughly intersubjective and dialectical in the sense that the Gospel of Mark—and the other texts that I will be analyzing here—be read as art products, constructed by authors who expected their texts to hang in "public galleries," where random readers and listeners would have a chance to read or hear them, and, if all went well, interpret them in a manner organized and controlled, to some degree, by the author.

Perhaps because thinking about such complex modes of composition is fairly bewildering, we have chosen to imagine that our ancestors didn't take the trouble to think like this either. Or, and this seems more likely, isn't it the case that because these authors have *cleverly hid their cleverness* that we readers have opted for a most inartistic approach to their art? Whatever the case, it seems that we have more or less lobotomized these authors such that we step past the text-as-art problem to imagine, in our most naïve moments, that we are hearing Jesus, God, the Buddha, or Master

Huineng talk to us without any artistic interference. What could be more exciting? And, of course, this is exactly what each of these texts asks of us as they essentially say, "Don't look at me as an art product imbedded in a certain historical era; see me instead as a 'mere' conveyor of timeless sacred language that was produced elsewhere, an 'elsewhere' that is in fact the deepest Real of the universe." Actually, this very act of *looking away* from the art of the text is a crucial element in accepting the text and its reports of transcendental realities. Functionally, then, one's ability to leapfrog over the text as art to imagine that one has stepped into contact with the Real of the universe—receiving the voice of God, his Son, or the Buddha—is completely parallel to the hope of leapfrogging over mundane reality to win the salvation that these voices offer. That is, one can only become mystical, if one reads/listens mystically. This fact seems *not* to have been lost on the authors since the texts considered here loudly proclaim that faithfully— naïvely, that is—receiving the message about these new forms of salvation is the cause of winning that salvation.

This urge to look past the art of these texts is all the stronger given our current historical situation where these texts have won huge followings for themselves. Presumably, to treat them as curious artworks risks insulting half the world's population in the present, along with the billions of deceased people who have lived and died taking these art products as reliable, nonfabricated accounts *of* reality. In short, given all the devotion and violence that has come with these texts, it is hard to treat them as willfully constructed media gambits. And, yet, given the past two thousand years of blood and belief that happens to be our inheritance, it seems *all the more worthwhile* to read the Gospel of Mark next to, say, the Gospel of Judas, to get a clearer sense of the fully experimental and deeply contingent quality of *both* these works of art. That is, once we see how *ad hoc* the writing of tradition was, we will be in a better place to see that creativity for what it was: a rather unbridled and unsanctioned experimentation with the reinvention of tradition. Not surprisingly, all these texts explain their right to discourse on the final nature of reality, and yet this very claim of legitimacy is part of the text's lèse majesté vis-à-vis older traditions, and inseparable from the larger authorial intention of projecting an, as yet, unsanctioned account of divine law out into public space. In coming to understand these dynamics, one gradually comes to see how "illegal" the creation of the (new) law was: Who after all gave "Mark," Paul, or the Mahāyāna Buddhist authors the right, literally, to take the law into their own hands? The key obstacle blocking this vision of the invention of tradition is that *as one falls for the text's seduction, one concludes that there was no seduction in the first place,* a fact that, naturally, puts believers at a distinct disadvantage in evaluating the mechanics of these works.

That some of these new and experimental accounts of the divine law then succeeded in "living" in history, down to the present, is of course another layer of happenstance. Under slightly different circumstances, these narratives might not have survived into the modern era, or might have arrived with no more importance than the works of Mani. It just so happened that these texts took hold and that very success has made them harder to think about. While we can't duck the weight that comes with the historical success of Christianity and Mahāyāna Buddhism, we still can, in some measure, return to these texts to ask how it all got started—at least in terms of identifying the symbolic structures that organized their reinventions of tradition.[8]

Turning back to reconsider the origins of the doctrines that so shaped our notions of the reified Self appears all the more important at the beginning of the twenty-first century since it seems very likely that neuropsychology and related fields are going to completely overhaul our rather medieval notions of self, meaning, and desire. More exactly, once we are forced away from the unadmitted transcendentalism that animates most human thinking, and in particular begin to face the difficult task of making sense of human selfhood without postulating a solid core to the self, then we are going to need interpretive strategies that explore how it was that just these images of the transcendental Self were created with literature, the heady recycling of tradition, and the orchestration of enduring desires that hold such visions together. That is, as the flattering image of the reified, independent Self—an almost extraterrestrial Self, it would seem—begins to evaporate with advances in "brain psychology," we will have to go back and reconsider how it was, historically, that text and reader fit so well together as to produce just that giddy sense of the transcendental Self.

Crucial to note is the fact that while our ancestors experimented—wildly, it would seem—with rewriting the law, tradition, and modes of salvation, we latter-day readers have inherited those texts somehow thinking that they were never invented. Thus, in arguing for high levels of creativity and irony in the authors of these tradition-reforming texts, I am also hoping that we might ourselves regain a measure of those same powers and, in particular, that confidence whereby life and its meanings can be reinterpreted and resculpted as one sees fit. In sum, in granting the authors of these texts the powers of reinventing tradition, I am suggesting to my readers that we all have such powers in varying degrees.

The Doubly Present Past

To begin theorizing the creativity at work in these texts, let's return to that perspective in which we note how these narratives that repackage tradition are part of time, history, and tradition as it was developing—as all cultural items are—and yet were designed to rework the way their audiences would experience time, history, and tradition. Read this way, as they fetishize tradition, these texts both speak from within the historical sequence that is tradition and yet also try to rise "up" out of that matrix of tradition to turn around and refigure tradition for their audiences.[9] This model imagines a two-step process whereby an author *first* arrives at a practical understanding of three things: 1) recent history—the real past, as it was lived by a people that we could call "Public1"; 2) the traditional texts or stories that attempted to narratize that past in some meaningful manner for Public1; and, 3) Public1's current experience of those two elements: lived history and the traditional narratives that sought to explain that history. *Then*, the author attempts to present to Public1, in miniature form, all three of those elements—the real past, the traditional texts/stories, and the public's experience of tradition—as an incomplete arrangement, or as a patent failure, that can and should be overcome in accord with his new narrative. The author's art project succeeds when Public1 ceases to see itself within the horizons of the old paradigm, agreeing with the author that the old constellation of history-narrative-tradition—now seen in miniature in the new narrative— was a failure that can only be righted by taking hold of the author's new narrative that explains that failure. At that moment Public1 has become Public2 and is on its way to forging a new style of being traditional.[10]

Since the details can be confusing, let's go back to a foundational point: these narratives involve themselves with lots of doubles. The Christian and Buddhist narratives treated here all work in terms of presenting the reader with two images of tradition. Thus, the new mode of living history that is offered is, in part, a theory about (old) tradition and its failure to perform this basic task of rendering lived history religiously significant. In part, then, the new mode of making meaning will be generated in explaining why the old mode of making meaning wasn't sufficiently meaningful. This might seem simple enough at first, but it brings with it the implication that *the new form of religion is itself about religion* in the sense that its articulation of meaning and transcendence focuses on its precedent and rival, and consequently it is stuck finding meaning in the other's lack of meaning, or rather, making religion out of (supposedly) bad religion.[11]

If pointing out this doubling sounds unnecessarily complicated, consider if it isn't the case that the main theme in the Gospel of Mark is built around a series of personages looking at tradition in its two forms: 1) its "old" Temple form; and, 2) its new form in Jesus, and his promises of salvation-by-faith-in-the-narrative-that-he-lives-in. As the story develops, narrative personages—the voice-from-Heaven, John the Baptist, the ill, the insane, the possessed, the disciples, Moses and Elijah, the Jewish authorities, Pilate, and the Roman centurion—having been presented with either form of tradition, are shown making choices about tradition's real locale, and then, depending on the "accuracy" of their assessment, they either benefit directly or face dire and imminent threats. Thus, the entire narrative works around presenting not just two images of tradition, but also showing the reader the consequences of reading these two images of tradition correctly or incorrectly. Thus, *as one reads Mark, one learns how to read the two forms of tradition, and learning this technique of dealing with doubled tradition is presented to the reader as the essence of his or her own religious work.* Actually, each of the texts considered here works in a similar manner such that generating a "reading" of old tradition is crucial for giving birth to the new, with the audience's view of the two forms of tradition controlled by presenting, inside the narrative, figures who perform just this function of correctly distinguishing old tradition from new tradition, thereby both winning salvation and proving that this kind of reading is all it takes.

The Law of Desire and Truth-Fathers

In addition to sorting through this layered doubling in these texts that fetishize tradition, we are also going to have to pay attention to two other basic elements in these narratives: desire and truth-fathers. As for the desire, given their distance from "old" established tradition, with its well-developed social and institutional base for managing the reception of tradition, it seems that the authors of the new narratives had at their disposal but one technique in their effort to generate adherence to their new textual programs: the ability to incite and direct their audience's desires. Writing to evoke the audience's desire naturally leaves the author in a position of solicitude vis-à-vis his audience since, in the end, it is from the reader's desire that he must fashion both his new version of tradition and the reasons for its acceptability. In light of this dialectic between writing and the desire of the reader/listener, we ought to recognize that these narrative worlds emerged in such a way that the new versions of tradition and desire come wrapped around each other—an unexpected outcome since we tend to think of tradition, and its laws, as the opposite of new forms of public desire, rather than its manager or helpmate.[12] At any rate, coming to understand this play of desire and the law, as found in narratives that fetishize tradition, opens the door for a new appreciation of the "psychology of religion."[13]

The second avenue of investigation, and it turns out to be crucial for organizing the audience's desire, focuses on the presentation of images of the truth-father. The truth-father is that figure who, though distant and transcendental, supposedly owns truth and tradition—God, the Buddha, the perfect Zen master, and so on—but also supposedly has the power to pass on truth and tradition to other spokespersons. Obviously, this image of the truth-father functions to secure the desire of the audience insofar as the changes wrought to (old) tradition by these new formulations are "underwritten" by appeals to this sort of truth-father who appears above the fray and thus able, from his zone of supposed ahistorical transcendence, to validate the rewriting of tradition, the law, and history.

What is perhaps harder to see is that the truth-father reproduces more than new versions of traditions since the newly converted believer is regularly offered a new religious identity defined by winning a new familial relationship to the truth-father, for instance Paul's "sons of God" (Gal. 3:26 or Rom. 8:14) or the common enough Mahāyāna title "son of the Buddha." Given the prominence of this familial rhetoric we have to say that the truth-father is, on the one hand, imagined to *hold* tradition in a timeless manner, free of any kind of contamination by time, interpretation, and so on, and yet on the other hand is also taken to be the entity who *reintroduces* pure tradition into the mess of history, language, and interpretation such that believers feel legitimate in accepting this language and, as a consequence of accepting this new language, feel legitimate in inhabiting their new family of truth. Of course these two functions work together since there is something of a genetic sequence here in which the timeless truth-father is imagined to father the (new) tradition whose seductive rhetoric then refathers the (believing) subject, who in that act of belief gains the conviction that he or she has just now entered into the truth-father's final family. Naturally, getting the subject to believe that this is possible, and that the acting truth-father is both traditional and yet now finished with (old) tradition, is the crux of the narrative's task.

This set-up also implies that the normal reading subject is being treated as though he or she has a keyhole-like place where new tradition can insert itself and, following the metaphor, open the subject's door into a new transcendental sphere. Of course, this opening forth to the transcendental is spoken of differently in Buddhist and Christian texts, but basically the framing is the same with the new version of tradition providing the human subject with the chance to stop being an old-style human subject, cruelly ensconced in time, contingency, biology, and the house of language, in order to join or rejoin the transcendent where all such matters are resolved. All this refathering by the truth-father's gift of new tradition, then, has to be understood precisely as the means by which the subject comes to believe in a final form of his own subjectivity, a form defined by being transcendent, of and from the transcendental father, and at one with the perfect version of tradition.

Once we admit that in both Buddhism and Christianity, the truth-father, as presented in literature, has as his task the "transcendentalizing" of the human subject via the gift of new tradition, then we also are ready to admit that the truth-father and the human subject form something like a pair, with each defined by the other—a fact already made obvious by the familial language employed by either tradition to depict that rapport. That is, the truth-father functions as something like the human subject's "other half," fundamentally completing the human subject as defined within the system. Thus, we bump into a rather interesting paradox: God and the Buddha, for as transcendental and otherworldly as they are supposed to be, are defined by a very human and this-worldly orientation—they exist to serve us, to make us who we were always supposed to be.

Eyes Wide Open

In approaching these texts with the above themes in mind, what is new and presumably controversial in my discussion is that I am assuming that the authors of these texts had a fairly clear idea of what they were doing as they reinvented tradition. Previous readings of these texts have done their best to minimize the author's self-awareness in this process of reinventing tradition. My position, as just detailed, is that these authors came to understand how religious rhetoric lives with a people, and it was *only* with this knowledge that they could invent new religious rhetoric that not only could fulfill this role but also could explain why the prior mode was outdated. Crucial for this mode of reading is the assumption that the author is both part of his community's lived history—and quite aware of its historicizing apparatuses—and yet is also at some ironic distance from that shared symbolic world. Hence, it is only from such a "middle distance" that he can see the ensemble of history-tradition-public as it had been configured in the past and feel confident enough to rework it into new and creative patterns for the future. I am suggesting, in effect, that these tradition-overcoming narratives were constructed by a certain kind of "religious genius" that figured out how hands-on religions work *and* how to recreate those "realities" in the new floating world of narrative where these old functions were effectively duplicated and rendered superfluous.

Though we will see a parallel between what these authors have "seen" in the process of objectifying (old) tradition and what they ask their readers to "see" as they are taught to reread (old) tradition as a failed enterprise, we will also note that a fundamental divide exists between the vision of the author and the vision of the audience, since, while the author provides his audience with a facsimile of the skill he has learned in objectifying (old) tradition, he never objectifies this invention itself or gives his audience insight into the literary artwork that makes these new visions back onto (old) tradition appear plausible in the eyes of the reader/listener. In fact, for the readers of these texts there is an interesting dialectic between seeing and blindness since the narratives are fully mediated events intent on delivering a sense of vision onto the final nature of tradition and reality, and yet for this sense of vision to be reproduced via language, audiences need to look past the literary architecture that was put in place to give just this sense of direct vision. Consequently, as mentioned above, we have to admit that part of the art of these narratives is to disappear as art.[14]

Actually, the power of these narratives to avoid being objectified as artful creations that objectify old tradition shouldn't be underestimated since, in the case of Christian studies, it wasn't until quite recently—the late 1970s—that the narrative quality of these narratives was finally accepted and then only by some in the field. And of course, this discovery only came after two millennia during which these narratives were read as uncreated accounts of reality. To begin to think through the layers of ingenuity and intersubjectivity in these texts completely undermines their supposed sacred nature, but it begins to reveal more about the history of human thought and the crucial role that artistic creation has played in molding who we have become, a topic that I will take up again in the conclusion.

Chapter and Verse

To explore the dynamics of fetishizing tradition, I begin with a reading of Paul's Letter to the Romans—after a somewhat involved discussion regarding how best to historicize early Christian literature. Given the fairly scattered prose style in the Pauline epistles, it might be assumed that Paul wasn't relying on narrative in his explanation of how the new version of tradition supplanted—and fulfilled—(old) tradition.[15] However, closer consideration makes it clear that Paul's arguments are set within the encompassing narrative-based claim that God gave the world the gift of his only Son, Jesus, in order to enact a new covenant.[16] Thus, though his letters lack the formal structure of a story, Paul's position still is narrative-based in the sense that this new covenant is positioned as a half-completed drama that Paul is asking his audience to finalize by accepting this narrative of Father and Son as historically factual, and thus, ironically, no man-made narrative at all. Thus, when Paul claims that God reproduced and then destined his progeny to a sacrificial death, he is generating a narrative that becomes the foundation for his most basic demand on the reader: believe me when I recount this Father-Son narrative, and you will be saved because, along with giving us his Son, God also gave us the new law which explains that accepting this narrative of Father, Son, and new law, is the only way to fulfill the law qua tradition.

Chapter 2 considers the form and function of the Gospel of Mark, which is a more standard narrative with plot development, tension, resolution, and an omniscient narrator. While some of Paul's assumptions are at work in Mark, much is different too, suggesting that early notions of Jesus's death as God's sacrifice were recast, especially after the fall of the Temple in the Jewish-Roman War (66–73). In fact, though the Gospel of Mark follows Paul's fundamental claim that accepting the narrative explaining the twin arrival of the Son and the new law is the way to fulfill the new law, the author of Mark has managed to weave into his account of God's sacrificial gift a very different narrative in which it is claimed that Jesus's death was not just a sacrifice but also a murder perpetrated by the representatives of old tradition.[17] Generating an image of Jesus's two-toned death allows for the new-covenant logic to be joined with an explanation of the destruction of the Temple and (old) tradition. Thus, while we can say that Mark's narrative is relentlessly damning of the representatives of old tradition—the Pharisees, the scribes, the high priests, and the general population of Jerusalem—this damnation appears as a narrative expedient designed to make the fall of the Temple look like "just deserts," and thus not something truly catastrophic and thereby fully resistant to being folded into a history of God's covenant-based relationship with humans.[18]

Concentrating on this dual process of reconstructing tradition *in narrative* and making it fully available *via narrative* seems like a good way to develop readings of Paul and the Gospel of Mark, but in so doing we will also have built a platform for an interesting comparative discussion. Thus, chapter 3 turns to consider the case of the *Sūtra on the Land of Bliss*—a text in which the totality of the Buddhist tradition is forsaken on this planet and instead imagined fully available in another land: the Land of Bliss, located millions of miles to the west. Not surprisingly, one can only reach this land after death, provided one accepts the text's narrative and faithfully recites the name of the figure—the Buddha Amitāyus—who presides over that land. As with Paul and the Gospel of Mark, what is fascinating in this text is the play between the old forms of tradition and the text's narrative that gathers up key elements of old tradition and locates them in another zone where they are supposedly made available to the reader, provided he or she will accept the narrative as valid. What is different in this case is that this narrative seems to be working from earlier Mahāyāna narratives that, themselves, sought to fetishize tradition. Thus, this text represents a second-order fetishization of tradition that overcomes not just tradition, but also a budding Mahāyāna tradition of overcoming tradition that was already taking form in works, such as the *Perfection of Wisdom in 8,000 Lines*, that sought to promote themselves as the essence of tradition in a gesture that scholars have dubbed "the cult of the text." By following this track of literary innovation we get a more refined sense for how a tradition develops once it begins to hone the skills needed for reinventing tradition.

Chapter 4 considers the eighth-century *Platform Sūtra*. This Chan (Zen) text is particularly germane to a Christian-Buddhist comparison because in it the author has created a Chinese master, Huineng (n.d.), who claims to be a direct descendent of the truth-father of Buddhism—the Buddha—with that sonship undermining all other claims to legitimacy made by other figures in the Chinese Buddhist tradition. As with Jesus in Mark, the genealogical sameness between the truth-father and his descendent/s grounds the discourse such that the figure of Huineng can go about that familiar business of simultaneously negating prior forms of tradition and then regathering their essences into new forms, and in particular into the very text in which he is living and teaching.

This text, just like the *Sūtra on the Land of Bliss*, seems best read in a literary context wherein modes and models of overcoming past tradition had already been well explored. For instance, the narrative works hard at dethroning previous attempts to claim spiritual kinship with the Indian Buddha, just as it also works at marginalizing early Buddhist texts that sought to fetishize tradition into themselves, including the *Lotus Sūtra*, the *Sūtra on the Land of Bliss*, and the *Perfection of Wisdom in 8,000 Lines*. Thus, while modern enthusiasts assume that Chan (Zen) is the one religious tradition beyond such basic struggles with tradition, time, and authority, this chapter will present ample evidence to conclude the opposite: Chan is the tradition in which new forms for overcoming tradition are worked out on a tradition that, itself, had already developed several workable models for overcoming tradition. A key issue here will be to reflect, again, on how images of paternity, legitimacy, and old and new tradition are wound together to produce a convincing and seductive narrative about the new locale of total tradition and its availability to the believing reader/listener.

Pierre Bourdieu's Account of Religious Rhetoric

Since I rely on it in the chapters to come, I want to close out my introductory comments, with a brief description of Pierre Bourdieu's notion of the structure of religious discourse, a position that focuses on the production of the image of authority and that sums up many of my above points.[19] Bourdieu argues that the standard setup for religious authority requires three mutually reliant zones: 1) a deep origin of truth in the form of a past sage, saint, deity, or Being; 2) a means for moving that truth forward in time, be it through memory, texts, ritual practices, relics, or the regular reincarnation of the primal source in some contemporary form or body; 3) a contemporary spokesperson for that primordial truth who is sanctioned to represent it in the present, interpret it, and distribute it to a believing public, who delegate to him just this power and legitimacy. In short, Bourdieu saw religious authority always involved in a to-ing and fro-ing, shuttling back and forth as it does between its deep origins and its application in the present. Or put otherwise, in any moment of religious authority there is always an audience focused on the singular priest figure, who is expected to funnel the totality of truth forward into the group. Thus religious authority works when it performs the dual function of funneling the gaze of the audience onto the priest by convincing them that the priest funnels the fullness of truth onto them.

Bourdieu also points out that there is a certain kind of "social magic" that occurs when the audience is drawn to see this arrangement as unconstructed and natural. This social magic is that moment when those who follow a form of authority or leadership forget that authority is in the eyes of the beholder and that they themselves are in charge of deciding what is and isn't authoritative. To effect this social magic, most systems involve themselves in one contortion or another in order to appear self-verifying. Thus, usually part of the explanation about the set of three zones will be dedicated to explaining how the explanation of the three zones itself flows out of the sequence. It is no surprise then that it becomes terribly important to get self-verifying language to come out of the deep origin of zone 1 in order to explain that basic zone and, in full circular fashion, the language that explains that basic zone. Or, put in a pithier form: authority has to explain why it has the authority to claim authority. The beauty of this model is that it sketches the basic contours of a variety of religious discourses ranging from Christianity to Buddhism. In fact, it is hard to think of any religious system whose broad outlines don't conform to Bourdieu's model, and this may be due to the fact that his model articulates a fundamental antithesis between authority and time: authority is forever in need of proving itself, and to do so it creates both a timeless origin for itself and a conduit for moving that origin forward in time.

What Bourdieu paid less attention to was the fact that several religious traditions, notably early Christianity and certain "wings" of Mahāyāna Buddhism, produced texts that appear designed to deliver, in the very act of consuming a narrative, all aspects of this dialectic of authority. Hence, while I think Bourdieu's position is unbeatable for focusing a critique of any religious position, it needs to be adjusted for those special situations in which narrative and/or text come to stand as the sole purveyors of tradition. That is, we need to be ready to expand Bourdieu's position to account for those moments in religious history when we have phenomena, such as the "cult of the text" in Mahāyāna Buddhism, and what I call the "cult of the narrative" in early Christianity, when real institutions are not part of the equation defining and delivering the authority and legitimacy that Bourdieu's model predicts, and instead a new style of religious narrative emerges, one that fetishizes (old) tradition and takes on the role of moving the sanctifying past into the present.

With these issues of narrative, desire, authority, and truth-fathers briefly sketched, let's turn to the Pauline Letters to begin to see how these theoretical perspectives play out in specific readings.

2

____

Paul's Letters, or How God Became a Jewish Priest

Introduction

Reading through Paul's letters with the preceding theoretical issues in mind, it is not hard to see that his writing represents a good example of fetishizing (old) tradition since so much emphasis is put on that double motion of first summing up all of (old) tradition—Judaism—and then relocating it in new forms and practices that completely undermine the established order. To begin organizing this initial impression, and in advance of a more detailed account, let me point to four rhetorical gestures that shape Paul's efforts to fetishize (old) tradition. First, in building his new covenant logic, he metaphorizes traditional Jewish religious activities such as sacrifice, circumcision, and the keeping of Torah-based ethics.[1] Thus, the actual practice of these traditional Jewish activities is rendered obsolete and of minimal value since Paul champions salvation through belief in Jesus's divine identity. Paul's notion of belief is, of course, quite involved since it spins around itself in that manner characteristic of belief in belief: the reader is asked to believe in a salvation to be won through faith in the very discourse that explains salvation through faith.[2] Second, Paul's writing is preoccupied with two interlacing forms of the law—traditional Jewish law and Paul's new law which, while deeply indebted to Jewish law in terms of form and content, is intent on relativizing the older version in order to supplant it with a universal engine of salvation that is mobile (in terms of terrain and culture) and which, not surprisingly, stands completely free of the older forms of authority and ritual that had ensured the continuation of Second

Temple Judaism.[3] Third, Paul's rhetoric works to elicit a range of desires; in fact, one wouldn't be far wrong to read Paul's rhetoric as designed to instill something close to hysteria in his reader since he so often underscores the imminent availability of divine paternity. Thus, Paul regularly offers the stunning promise that anyone can win salvation and a place in God's family simply by embracing Paul's program of belief.[4]

Paul's fourth rhetorical gesture emerges as he works to establish the rules for securing contact with God. Here, Paul presents an extendable form of divine patriarchy that, like the segments of an old-style telescope, slides between the Father, the Son, Paul, Paul's writing, and Paul's intended audience. Thus, those who would take Paul's new theory of the Father and Son to really be *of* the divine Father—in the sense of being from him and reflecting, in language, his essence and intention—can expect to be refathered as "sons of God" (Rom. 8:14) or "children of God" (Rom. 8:16) and then rejoin the Father and Son after their deaths. In short, for Paul, the stuff of God's patriarchy first extends to the Son in some quasi-physical manner—how this came to be is never explained—and then ripples outward in a linguistic form that, though merely virtual at first, can supposedly be substantialized by all those who would believe just this language about this uncanny Something-from-the-Father. In effect, then, there is a crucial transubstantiation at work here as Paul's language describing the Father's presence supposedly turns into the Father's presence once it is wholeheartedly accepted, and, of course, this is exactly what Paul calls on his readers to do. In sum, Paul has invented a form of ubiquitously available "floating patriarchy" that lives spore-like in language, taking root anytime it is taken to be truth and not just a humanly invented narrative.

As Paul works to own and redistribute the God of Israel, he is, not surprisingly, concerned to show how his version of the Father connects to older forms of the Jewish tradition.[5] To this end, Paul provides several analogies for this relationship between the old and the new versions of God and his law—which I will discuss below—but for the moment, if we imagine that God's paternity in the older system, as the content and substance of tradition, flowed into an expanding canal system—via the Torah and God's special "genetic" bond with the descendants of Abraham, identified as God's People—then Paul cuts a sluice into that canal system, at the top of the watershed, and thereby siphons off just that paternal substance that engenders God's descendants, all in order to irrigate his own field of discourse.[6] Of course, as Paul organizes this redirection of the paternal "headwaters," the old system is still there for all to see, but, with the life- and law-giving fluid supposedly withdrawn, it appears as but a husk of its former self. And since this is a controversial point, let me say it clearly: while Paul's rhetoric of universal salvation is regularly applauded by various pro-Christian authors, we shouldn't miss that Paul has stolen "Jewishness"—in the specific sense of the Jews being God's *unique* Chosen People—from the Jews and offered it to everyone, with the result that Gentiles are now on par with Jews in God's eyes; likewise, the Jews learn from Paul that they need to convert to his system to finally gain what they thought they already had.[7]

Situating a Critical Reading of Paul and the Gospel of Mark

As obvious as these points are when one reads Paul for his fetishizing treatment of (old) tradition, it is also true that turning to such a reading strategy isn't such a simple matter since modern readers come to Paul's writing with an armload of assumptions that have been nurtured by various Christian theologies that took form after Paul. Though it has become cliché to say "Paul invented Christianity," in another sense it seems accurate to say that two thousand years of Christianity invented Paul, and thus it is hard to read his letters free of the influence of later Christian theologians, from the gospel-writers to Augustine to Luther and so on. A simple version of this problem is found whenever readers, modern or ancient, assume that there is one basic Christian message found in the New Testament (obviously yet another form of fetishizing tradition) and thus read Paul in light of the gospel narratives which were written several decades after Paul and under very different circumstances. Against this assumption, I would suggest that there is no reason to assume, a priori, that Paul's Jesus has anything to do with the later gospel versions of Jesus, and, of course, it is far from proven that either phase of writing about Jesus has anything to do with the real historical figure Jesus, a problem that will become glaringly apparent in close reading the Gospel of Mark in the next chapter.[8]

Further thwarting efforts to theorize Paul's positions is the fact that such efforts have, so far, received little support in the world of Christian studies. Hence, though there are hundreds and hundreds of books and articles on Paul, I have yet to find one that asks simple questions about the architecture of Paul's symbolic system—questions that would likely lead to the four themes just mentioned above. In short, Pauline studies has shown little interest in locating readings of Paul in wider, comparative perspectives that would clarify the basic "math" of Paul's position. Thus, for instance, a straightforward comparison of how prior forms of tradition are cannibalized and overcome, say, in the *Lotus Sūtra* and in Paul's Letter to the

Romans, has yet to be written, though such a comparison is surely worth the trouble, squarely in the zone of what scholars in religious studies ought to be doing, *and* likely very useful for understanding either text. Instead of such an approach, Pauline studies remains largely sealed off from bigger issues in religious studies, and this isn't too surprising since Pauline studies, like Christian studies in general, is overwhelmingly conducted by ordained clergy who direct their research to each other and to an equally pro-Christian public. Within this tight circle of Christians writing for other Christians about the origins of their shared Christian faith, there obviously is little motivation for wider theoretical reflections. What would be the point?[9]

To read Paul's letters critically requires stepping away from several commonplace assumptions about this early phase of Christianity. Most importantly, one needs to avoid the assumption that Jesus more or less made up the core teachings of Christianity and that the gospels can be read to learn about this foundational form of Christianity. The problem here is that, except for other gospels, there is no triangulating evidence securing the accuracy of the gospel narratives and their presentation of Jesus and his teaching—in fact, there is a fair amount of counterevidence, even in other Christian sources like Paul's letters. Despite this rather troubling historiographic problem, it turns out that assuming continuity between Jesus's life and the gospel narratives depicting his life still defines the current paradigm of New Testament studies.

To get a sense of this paradigm, let's consider statements from two leading figures in the field: Professor Paula Fredriksen of Boston University and E. P. Sanders, emeritus professor of religion at Duke University. Their various statements, though now twenty-five years old, have been rarely challenged and, arguably, still shape the basic debates in the field. As for Fredriksen, she begins her still widely read *From Jesus to Christ*, arguing for a contiguous and organic development in the construction of material about Jesus, one that flows forth from his real life and the teachings that he supposedly gave to his earliest followers. These initial followers then supposedly transmitted this information orally to others until around 70 C.E. when someone wrote the first gospel narrative—"Mark"[10]—and in so doing supposedly did no more than collect and arrange the oral material that was already in circulation. After mentioning that some of this oral material had already been written down in the hypothetical text called "Q," she sums up the process by which the Gospel of Mark was supposedly composed: "Meanwhile, other oral traditions—miracle stories, parables, legends, and so on—grew, circulated, and were collected in different forms by various Christian communities. In the period around the destruction of the Second

Temple (70 C.E.), an anonymous Gentile Christian wrote some of those down. *This person was not an author—he did not compose de novo.* Nor was he a historian—he did not deal directly and critically with his evidence. The writer was an evangelist, a sort of creative editor. He organized these stories into a sequence and shaped his inherited material into something resembling a historical narrative. The result was the Gospel of Mark."[11] The rest of her book develops around this core confidence that the material in the Gospel of Mark, and the other gospels, is no more than the distillation and organization of prior oral material that was, originally, generated by Jesus and his life.[12]

E. P. Sanders's work sits squarely in this same paradigm and assumes even more continuity between the gospel narratives and the supposedly historical events in Jesus's life that they depict. Early on in *The Historical Figure of Jesus* he claims, "There are no substantial doubts about the general course of Jesus's life." He goes on to list eleven historical events drawn from the gospels that he claims are "almost beyond dispute": "Jesus was born *c.* 4 BCE[;] . . . he was baptized by John the Baptist; he called the twelve disciples[;] . . . about the year 30 he went to Jerusalem for Passover; he created a disturbance in the Temple area; he had a final meal with the disciples; he was arrested and interrogated by Jewish authorities, specifically the high priest," and so on.[13] Apparently, Sanders considers the gospels to be reliable sources that detail historical realities such that we can safely assume continuity between events in Jesus's life, their early articulation among the disciples and others, and then their finalization in written gospel form; consequently he argues, "We should assume that part of what Jesus said and did became constitutive of Christian preaching."[14] As I will be pointing out, there are several good reasons for thinking that this is a bad approach.

And, since Sanders is regularly taken to be a giant in the field of New Testament studies, it is worth noting that though he claims to be relying on "standard methods of historical research," his position seems largely shaped by a kind of Christian nostalgia. For instance, consider the following passage that even expresses the hope of recovering the thought of Jesus: "As I indicated above, I think that we have good evidence for some of the things that Jesus thought. But inmost thoughts, even those of people whose public lives are well documented, are usually elusive. What did Lincoln really think, deep in his heart, about the emancipation of slaves? This is a difficult question, though we have a lot of material about Lincoln, and we know what he did and what the effects were. Similarly with Jesus, though our documentation is less thorough: we know some of the things he did, a fair amount about what he taught, and a great deal about the effects. We must then try to infer what he thought, deep inside. . . . The aim of this book is to lay out, as clearly as possible, what we can know, *using the standard methods of historical research*, and to distinguish this from inferences, labeling them clearly as such."[15]

Of the many problems in Sanders's methodology, let's be clear that it is only after one has consumed New Testament narratives in a certain credulous way—reading myth as factual and uninvented—that one would set out to find the historical Jesus in the first place.[16] In short, that very confidence that there is some ur-Jesus worth recovering behind all this writing results from submitting to the art of the gospels.[17] Consequently, despite his protests to the contrary, Sanders is reading Christian documents in a Christian manner insofar as he is responding to the fundamental gospel claim: the wonderful Jesus *of history* lives inside these narratives and you ought to do what you can to come "in" here, learn about him, and, in time, make him part of your reflections on history and reality. Why this approach represents "standard methods of historical research" is not explained in Sanders's work.

What I find particularly troubling in Sanders's approach is that he underemphasizes the context of the writing of the gospels which, in the case of Mark, is terribly important since it seems Mark wrote in the wake of the destruction of Jerusalem and Second Temple Judaism.[18] This catastrophe—for (old) tradition *and* presumably for the new Jesus movement/s centered in Jerusalem—appears to have shaped the form and content of Mark's narrative in a manner that is *much* more thoroughgoing than Sanders has suspected.[19] To put the problem simply: before Mark, we have next to no details of Jesus's life and teaching, and in particular, we have no evidence that his teaching or life activities were particularly at odds with the Jewish tradition/s. Then, some forty years after his death, when a portion of Jesus's life is constructed in Mark's narrative, we suddenly are told that Jesus was completely wrapped up in a conflict with the Jewish religious establishment—he's pitted against the Pharisees, the scribes, the Herodians, and even the citizens of Jerusalem—all of whom are now squarely implicated in his execution, with this execution closely linked to the destruction of the Temple. Clearly that narrative package, which so clearly defines Mark's gospel, *could not have been composed before the fall of the Temple* and thus hardly appears as an account of Jesus's real life at all. In fact, as I will be arguing in the following chapter, Mark's account of the life and death of Jesus appears fundamentally about creating an epic sin for Second Temple Judaism and the citizens of Jerusalem, a sin against God and "real tradition"—as found in Jesus—that "naturally" led to their destruction. Given the prominence of these themes that focus so intently on theologizing the end of Second Temple Judaism, it seems altogether wrongheaded to read Mark or the later gospels as reliable accounts of Jesus's real life and teachings.[20] To put it starkly, if Mark constructed Jesus's life and death to explain the fall of the Temple and the destruction of traditional Judaism—and to build a forward-looking theology around that catastrophe—then the story is more basically about that catastrophic event and not about Jesus.

Representing a position that seems to step away from the paradigm current in modern New Testament studies, consider Pheme Perkins, professor of theology at Boston College, who wisely argues that the fall of Jerusalem was crucial for gospel writing and the construction of a certain kind of anti-Judaism: "These examples indicate that the canonical Gospels have invested the fall of Jerusalem with considerable importance at the rhetorical level. . . . The evangelists have exploited the fate of Jerusalem as a powerful piece of evidence in favor of their claims about Jesus as Israel's messiah. Look what happened to Jerusalem, they say. One neglects the advent of this divinely anointed king to one's peril."[21] She follows this line of reasoning with a larger conclusion that I wholly endorse and will develop in the coming chapters: if the Temple had stood, Christianity "would not have built a heritage of anti-Judaism into its narratives or turned the ruins of God's holy place into weapons against those who did not accept Jesus as messiah—anti-Judaism would not be inscribed in Christian imagination."[22]

To get another angle on this problem, consider that Paul has no account of Jesus's struggle with the Jewish hierarchy;[23] and, most surprising, he nowhere mentions Judas's betrayal or the Passion sequence—Jesus's trial and execution at the hands of Jewish and Roman authorities on Passover—which arguably make up core narrative concerns in the four traditional gospels and which are, wrongly I believe, assumed to have been part of the early Christian tradition from the outset. In fact, Paul, writing in the decades after Jesus's death, still refers to the apostles as a trustworthy group of followers (1 Cor. 9:5 or Gal. 2:1–14) and counts them as twelve (1 Cor. 15:5), as though Judas's dastardly deed had never occurred.[24] If one insists that the basic narrative material that later shows up in the gospels was already well known and in circulation, then one has the difficult task of explaining how it was that Paul—as well traveled as he seems to have been and apparently in contact with Jesus's direct disciples in Jerusalem—ignored it all, especially given its potential for upsetting the logic of his own claims.[25] At the very least, he would have had every reason to address this material, if only to reject it.[26]

It is also worth mentioning that some mainstream New Testament studies have argued that the account of Jesus's trial doesn't look very plausible. In particular, scholars have pointed out that it makes no sense to imagine that the council of chief priests (the Sanhedrin) would have met in the night to rule on Jesus's fate.[27] In fact, that a trial and ruling would have occurred on the Passover weekend seems even more unlikely. Similarly, that Pontius Pilate is presented as flexible and concerned with dealing even-handedly with a Jewish rabble-rouser seems rather unlikely and completely at odds with other contemporaneous accounts in which Pilate appears alto-gether unsympathetic and even cruel.[28] Of course, all these problems and inconsistencies surrounding Jesus's trial make sense if we assume that the narrative isn't recounting historical fact but instead is inventing these details in order to make the Jewish authorities appear to be to blame for Jesus's death, a narrative agenda that then naturally needs Pilate and the Roman contingent to appear unmotivated and barely involved at all. Thus, the gospels' version of the trial—with its Jewish and Roman segments—seems, on its own terms, to be a very roughly hewn mini-narrative designed to generate Jewish guilt where there was none.

Now if it is true, as Paul claims, that he himself once persecuted the followers of Jesus ("the church of God"—Gal. 1:13), then we can assume that there must have been some sort of conflict over how the very early Jesus movement understood and practiced Jewish law. However, it seems to me an unfounded assumption to conclude that Paul's conflict with the early Jesus movement is evidence of the historical reality of the larger, Man-ichaean conflict between Jesus and the Jewish establishment that is depicted in the gospels. Why? First, because Paul presents himself as an unusually zealous Pharisee who, in his own eyes, outdid his peers in upholding the law. Thus, that Paul had a problem with the early followers of Jesus hardly counts as proof that there was a more general conflict between Jesus and the whole Jewish political and religious hierarchy. Second, and this is terribly important, Paul's comments about the Jerusalem followers of Jesus present them as rather pro-Torah in their religious commitments—much too pro-Torah for Paul's taste, to be sure—and this account, presumably based on his firsthand experience, is completely at odds with the anti-Judaism that so colors the gospel accounts of Jesus's teachings.[29] Consequently, until we find evidence to the contrary, it seems wisest to assume that the narrative material in the gospels regarding Jesus's conflict with Jewish authorities did not exist in this early phase of the Jesus movement, however disturbing that might be to standard Christian faith. Put more directly: the evidence as we have it suggests that the story of Jesus's struggle with the Jewish tradition, his betrayal by one of his disciples, and his unjust trial at the hands of the Jewish authorities was invented by Mark and has little, if anything, to do with either Jesus's real life and death or the early attempts—in Jerusalem and among Paul's scattered communities—to build a Jesus tradition.[30]

Arguing that Paul didn't have access to this narrative material because it had yet to be invented is also supported by the way the Passion narrative seems to have taken shape in the post-Markan gospels.[31] First, while the case of John's version of the Passion is complicated, it is clear that the two other synoptic gospels—Matthew and Luke—rely heavily on the earliest gospel, Mark, in constructing their Passion narratives, implying that they had no other sources to draw from. This fact alone undermines the standard assumption in Christian studies that the Passion narrative was already an important part of the early Christian communities in the pre-Markan period. The problem is that if Mark was simply collecting and recording currently available narratives about Jesus's trial and execution, one would expect that Matthew and Luke would have had, like Mark, access to a wide and disparate body of material, and yet that is the opposite of what a comparison of the three texts suggests. In sum, if Mark supposedly had various Passion narratives and details to draw on, why did they disappear, leaving Luke and Matthew with nothing but Mark as their definitive source?

Speculation about the Q gospel—a hypothetical text that both Matthew and Luke supposedly drew on—doesn't help in this matter because this reconstructed text also lacks the Passion sequence.[32] In fact, Q, should it prove to have existed, provides more evidence of another pre-Markan Christian spokesperson who simply didn't know of Jesus's trial and condemnation by the Jewish hierarchy.[33] And, if we agree to place the Gospel of Thomas in the pre-Markan period, then we have yet another spokesperson recounting Jesus's life and teaching with absolutely no mention of the Passion. And to consider just one more possibility: even if one accepts Dominic Crossan's argument for the "Cross Gospel" that supposedly predates Mark and is found embedded in the Gospel of Peter—and this view hasn't won many adherents—the fall of the Temple is already a key topic in this hypothetical gospel, and thus we have every reason to locate its moment of writing in the same temporal zone as Mark's. Hence, should it turn out that the "Cross Gospel" existed *and* predated Mark, it does little to move the Passion narrative any closer to Jesus's life or the earliest communities.[34]

Another painfully obvious reason for arguing against the organic development of a pre-Markan Passion narrative that passed from real history to the disciples to the early communities to the gospel writers is the fact that *the author of Mark is completely against the early disciples.* Consequently, and again modern readings of Mark have yet to fully grapple with this, Mark's rhetoric is clearly designed to undermine all those who might have claimed to have received anything directly from Jesus's closest disciples or from his family members.[35] In effect, then, Mark's new-fangled Christianity is an all-out assault on the earlier forms of faith that had taken root among those who had known Jesus, including his disciples and relatives who lived in Jerusalem and who, presumably, formed the backbone of the earliest "church"—including James, Peter, and John, whom Paul referred to as the "acknowledged pillars" (Gal 2:9). Thus, clearly, Mark is *not* summing up the Jesus traditions as they had taken form in the decades after Jesus's death; instead, Mark is completely repudiating them and, apparently, inventing all sorts of narrative material that he hopes will support his position while also providing plausible explanations for why the initial Jesus movements failed, and why it will be up to the reader of his narrative to set things right.

The key to shifting to this perspective is this: instead of seeing the form and content of Mark as the result of various religious traditions naturally moving forward and gradually clarifying their origins in ever greater detail, it seems we have good evidence to think that the author of Mark has radically redefined both proto-Christianity and Temple Judaism so that their catastrophic fates now fit into a seductive narrative in which the very account of this catastrophic past is shaped to convince the reader that he or she can become the place of final and complete tradition. What this means, then, is that our author is completely aware of his text as a platform that can move forward in time and support just this ongoing process of convincing future readers that they could be the site for real tradition to take hold, provided they accept the narrative with proper levels of faith and devotion. Put another way, Mark is essentially telling his reader this: God put Jesus into human history back in the day, and it didn't work out that great—the disciples, the public, and the Jewish authorities didn't really get it; but that's ok because Jesus is still available in story-form in such a way that he can keep coming into human history in the reading moment. In short, the narrative promises to deliver, in an ongoing manner, the plenitude of final tradition, while also explaining what happened in that first, catastrophic round in such a way that the reader feels even more inspired to accept the narrative and its free-floating promises.

When we see that *disenfranchising the earliest disciples is a basic goal* in Mark's narrative, a number of things fall into place. First, the whole problem of Jesus's confounding teaching style—the parables—now makes sense: Mark wants his reader to believe that Jesus taught in a manner such that his disciples, his family, the general public, and the Jewish authorities would *not* get truth and tradition, since the message was encrypted to ensure just that failure of transmission. For example, consider how in chapter 4,

Jesus explains the parables to the disciples in a kind of behind-the-scenes manner because, apparently, they, along with the rest of the public, didn't grasp them in the first place.[36] With the disciples privileged to receive direct, unencrypted teachings in this manner, one might think that the author is showing us the reason for their unique ability to comprehend Jesus, and yet at the end of the chapter, after Jesus has, apparently with no small amount of exasperation, explained four parables to the disciples, they seem to have made little progress toward understanding him at all. Thus, just after this explanation, and after stilling the winds and waves that threatened to sink their boat: "He said to them, 'Why are you afraid? Have you still no faith?' And they were filled with great awe and said to one another, 'Who then is this, that even the wind and the sea obey him?'" (4:40–41). In fact, the disciples' confusion and doubts continue to the end of the narrative, and thus this special teaching seems to have gone to waste, and worse, it serves as a further indictment of their dimness: even with this direct teaching, they were left unimproved.

Of course, one might be right in thinking that it really is the reader who benefits in receiving these supposedly private teachings, while also again seeing the shortcomings of Jesus's immediate disciples—a trope that repeats throughout the story and that I believe is crucial for motivating the reader's positive response to the entire narrative. (More on that in a moment.) In sum, Jesus's supposed strategy of bewildering his audience with parables is matched by the overall stupidity of the disciples since in both cases Mark wants to give his reader the impression that no one of Jesus's era—at least among his prominent devotees—correctly received his teachings or recognized his divine identity. Clearly Mark wants to convince his readers that the disciples not only did not really receive the essence of tradition, but they were also too stupid to properly interpret even the very obvious things happening around them, such as the multiplication of bread and fish or Jesus's ability to walk on water and control the weather, not to mention his supernatural talent to heal and raise from the dead.

This theme of the disciples' failure to receive tradition is, of course, underscored by the way that Mark demonizes Judas.[37] In Mark's narrative, the disciples *as a group* appear as a source of danger since supposedly one of them will, viper-like, be the cause of Jesus's demise. That is, as Mark scripts Jesus's death as the result of an "inside job," all the disciples are implicitly recast in a troubling light as the reader is naturally led to ask, "How could one of the chosen do such a thing?" And, of course, Mark makes it absolutely clear that Judas was no different from the other disciples, and that's just the point: supposedly Judas did what any of them could have done.

No surprise, then, when Jesus announces that he is to be betrayed by one of the twelve, none of them can guess who it would be because, in fact, they are all quite alike, or so Mark would like us to conclude (14:18ff).

This image of Judas is then matched by the depiction of Peter. And, smearing the character of Peter has wider implications here since if Peter, as leader of the disciples, is shown all too eager to deny his connection to Jesus (14:66ff)—even after it had been predicted to him (14:26ff) and after he had sworn unto death never to disown Jesus—then surely the other disciples would have done the same or worse; and, of course, when they flee Jerusalem after Jesus's execution and then fail to visit Jesus's tomb where the real proof of the drama is to be revealed, it is all too clear what Mark is suggesting about those who *should have known better*: they literally didn't get it.[38] In the next chapter I will develop this reading, but for now let's conclude that, given how Judas and Peter are the two disciples given the fullest "action roles" in Mark, we are left with a detailed image of the disciples as a dangerous and worthless lot who should in no way be trusted for their accounts of Jesus's teaching or his lifeworks.[39]

Then, and still within the thematic of Mark's effort to disenfranchise Jesus's most intimate followers, we shouldn't miss that Mark twice mentions that Jesus's brothers were beyond the circle of his close confidants and rudely held at arm's length *by Jesus* (3:31ff; 6:3ff). Since we have pre-Markan evidence in Paul's letters that one of Jesus's brothers, James, was known as a central leader of the proto-Christians in Jerusalem, it is difficult to imagine that these two passages disparaging Jesus's brothers were unmotivated.[40] Actually, the prominence of James, Jesus's brother, would have been particularly in view at the time of Mark's composition since according to Josephus's *Jewish Antiquities* (20:9.1), James, identified as "the brother of Jesus who was called Christ," had been sentenced and executed in 62 by a hastily organized judicial council (the Sanhedrin) for not upholding the law, a ruling that apparently outraged many in Jerusalem.[41] And, here, we shouldn't miss that Josephus's account of the public sympathy expressed for James in Jerusalem gives us another piece of evidence that pre-Markan Christianity, as led by James, was hardly locked in combat with the citizens of Jerusalem and/or the Temple traditions.[42]

Thus, it is hard to avoid the conclusion that Mark is working against all those male figures who might have been intimate with Jesus—the disciples and his brothers, that is—leaving only the women at the cross as important witnesses to Jesus's resurrection (16:1). However, since the women, too, run away and tell no one what they have seen (16:8), it would seem that they aren't positioned any better than the male disciples to play a role in the real-world transmission of the earliest Jesus traditions. Given these narrative details, Mark appears to have consistently worked to convince his readers that those very figures most associated with Jesus—his followers and his brothers, along with the two Mary figures—should not be trusted for anything. And, at least in the case of the disciples, they ought to be shunned since, besides being failed followers, they are also, in varying degrees, guilty of the very crime that Mark creates for the Jewish hierarchy: they were given every chance to "read" Jesus correctly as the Son of God, but they failed to take hold of that narrative and, in that failure, participated in varying ways in his execution.

Then, and this is to be taken as no more than an aside, let me suggest that James's trial and execution by that hastily arranged Sanhedrin in 62 might be a better place to look for the template that structured Mark's account of the Passion.[43] In short, since James's dubious trial and execution by the Sanhedrin in 62 appear to match, in a general way, the trial that Mark scripts for Jesus, one has to ask if the real historical trial and execution of James might not have been the event that Mark relied on as he scripted the new narrative explaining Jesus's death. In that light, Mark's account of Jesus's death would have gained the power of familiarity in the sense of "You saw what the Sanhedrin just did to James in 62? Well, they did the same to Jesus, too, back in 30."

Taking James's real death to be the event that was used to rewrite Jesus's death makes sense in another way: Mark's text is chock full of doubles (as has been widely admitted), and thus casting about for a well-known historical precedent—a double of sorts—for Mark's Passion narrative seems like a wise move.[44] To appreciate Mark's reliance on doubles, consider how Mark clearly worked up John the Baptist to function as a prefatory "rhyme" for Jesus, a figure who provides Jesus with some of his basic identity. John is there serving as Jesus's precedent, baptizing with water (instead of the Spirit) and publicly lauding Jesus as a superior version of himself. More interestingly, Mark mentions (1:14) that Jesus only began teaching after John's arrest, suggesting that the two figures share a kind of essence such that Jesus can only assume his leadership position when John has disappeared. Jesus as John the Baptist's doppelganger is then played up in the account of Herod's confusion over the two, even to the point that Herod thinks Jesus is John resurrected (6:14). Mark also seems to assume that the readers will find it logical that at one point (11:27ff), the Pharisees supposedly left Jesus alone in the midst of a debate about John's teaching of salvation precisely because they were afraid that saying something against *John* would start a riot. Of course, no such fear is manifest vis-à-vis Jesus, who is regularly publicly challenged and denigrated by the Pharisees and others. Apparently, Mark was working with the assumption that John's reputation figured prominently in public memory, whereas Jesus's didn't; likewise, we seem to have evidence here for thinking that even in a narrative dedicated to proving Jesus's uniqueness, John looms as the larger, more historically real figure, from whom Mark's image of Jesus was, in part, created. In short, it seems Mark thought his portrayal of Jesus would appear more believable if he explicitly linked it to John the Baptist in a manner that relies on John's identity to construct Jesus's, a strategy that I am suggesting matches my hypothesis regarding a connection between the deaths of James and Jesus.

And, insofar as I am siding with those who think that Mark was written to explain the sacking of Jerusalem, we shouldn't overlook the interesting parallel in which James's execution was held by some Jewish Christians to be the cause of the city's destruction. As Richard Bauckham puts it, "Impressed by the way the Jewish revolt and the fall of Jerusalem followed swiftly on James' death, later Jewish Christians supposed that it had been James' constant prayer for the forgiveness of the Jewish people which restrained the divine judgment until Jerusalem's guilt reached its high point in putting James to death and depriving itself of the power of his intercession."[45] Thus, the deaths of both James and Jesus appear as the result of dubious rulings by the Sanhedrin, and also share the basic parallel of being taken by some Jewish observers to be the cause of the fall of Jerusalem.

Actually, once we begin a reading sensitive to the play of doubles in Mark's writing, we shouldn't overlook that John the Baptist's execution, like those of Jesus and James, was also held to be the cause of political/military catastrophe. According to Josephus's *Jewish Antiquities*, it seems that Herod Antipas's execution of John the Baptist was taken by many to be the cause of Herod Antipas's subsequent loss in battle to King Aretas IV (father of Herod Antipas's first wife whom he disgraced by marrying Herodias) circa. 36: "Now, some of the Jews thought that the destruction of Herod's army came from God, and that very justly, as a punishment of what he did against John, that was called the *Baptist*" (18:5.2). If Josephus, writing near the end of the first century, is to be trusted with reliably recounting events that transpired half a century earlier, it would seem that in the decades prior to the writing of Mark, the unjust execution of another prophetic leader, John, was taken to have catastrophic consequences for the Jewish leadership responsible for the execution. In sum, as we look for sources for the Passion narrative, we shouldn't overlook these important parallels between the deaths of Jesus, John, and James, along with the parallel way those deaths were "read" as the cause for divine retribution.

I should add as an aside within an aside that if Josephus's ordering of events is to be trusted, Herod Antipas's marriage to Herodias—the widow of his half-brother, Philip—*seems* to have taken place circa 34, and it was this scandal that John the Baptist supposedly criticized in a manner that led to his execution, presumably before the war of 36 with King Aretas that Herod Antipas lost badly and that lead to his ouster.[46] With Jesus supposedly dead circa 30 and John not dead until circa 35, it would seem that Mark wrote up the "Herod vs. John the Baptist" mini-narrative and then, reversing the real sequence of events, tucked John's execution into his Jesus narrative as a powerful set piece supporting one of Mark's most basic narrative claims: kill a divine prophet, and expect political and military disaster.[47] Such a theory would begin to get at why John's death, presented with such detail, sits so awkwardly in the middle of Mark's narrative (6:14–29): it sits there, I suspect, as a prompt for the reader: You saw what happened to Herod after he executed John, right? Well, that was no different than what has happened to the recently savaged Jerusalem authorities who, in league with the Romans, executed Jesus.

While considering such possible links between Jesus's, John's, and James's executions and the mythologies of divine retribution that accompanied them is peripheral to my argument about the fetishization of (old) tradition in early Christian writing, this constellation of narratives about prophet executions and their political effects appears to me to be a good place to look for the elements that Mark used to create the Passion narrative. Moreover, this hypothesis works well as a litmus test: it will appear as a plausible hypothesis only to those readers who have let go of the Sunday school assumption that the Passion narrative reflects historical events surrounding Jesus's death. As I will argue in the next chapter, until modern scholarship fully accepts how Mark's narrative was essentially written in response to the fall of the Temple and the destruction of Jerusalem, speculation about the origins and motivations of this text will remain pointed in the wrong direction.

Once Mark's narrative is set squarely in the context of the disaster of 70 AD, we can begin to reconsider other aspects of the gospel's narrative as well. For instance, given that Jerusalem and Judaism, as it had been known, were completely destroyed, we can see why Mark sought to invent a whole new way to connect with Jesus and tradition—via faith in Mark's narrative itself, and in lieu of any other kind of contact with proto-Christian groups or Second Temple traditions. In short, by *inventing these crimes of the disciples and the Jewish authorities*, Mark explains both the disaster that befell the Jews and proto-Christians of Jerusalem and the reason why devotion to his narrative is the only way to move forward. Though Christian studies hasn't figured out how to make sense of this criminality shared by the icons of the Jewish tradition *and the Jesus disciples,* it is clear that this trope is the key to understanding the oldest form of the Passion narrative and, I would argue, sheds light on the question of why the narrative is so self-centered in the sense of relying on nothing but itself to push forward a revised version of tradition.

I would add, too, that the distinctly literary nature of Mark's gospel has yet to be fully appreciated in this context. As argued above, the Gospel of Mark hardly seems like a statement of a community's belief—a kind of catechism or doctrinal platform of sorts—since it is so dedicated to convincing readers/listeners of things that they didn't already believe. Thus, it seems more like a brief but urgent All Points Bulletin, put out on "broadsheet," to inform citizens of the new dire state of affairs. And though one can count a number of elements in Mark that aim to define readers' future religious obligations—for instance, the need to spread the word further and to stand firm in maintaining belief in Jesus's identity—it seems to me that there is something decidedly *unreligious* about the work in the sense that it is so free from community, ritual repetition, living authority structures, and institutional frameworks—in short, all the things that we normally assume to be elemental in religion. Instead, it seems like a one-shot news broadcast explaining: 1) what happened to Jesus as the explanation for 2) what just happened to Jerusalem, old tradition, and the proto-Christian groups and 3) what to do next in light of the coming apocalypse. Though the "good news" is all about divine matters, in another sense it is *just news*: information that you need to have to survive what comes next—the coming of the Kingdom of God.

With these problems in view it appears unlikely that current scholarship is correct in assuming that a range of proto-Christianities took form in the wake of Jesus's death, with some of them slowly morphing into the Christian communities that stood behind each of the gospel writers. Instead, we would do better to accept that the evidence, as we have it, suggests that the form and content of early Christianity was radically, even violently, overhauled by Mark after the destruction of Jerusalem and that this reinvented form had little in common with its predecessors and, in fact, was specifically designed to: 1) contradict their theological views, especially in terms of the value of the Torah; 2) void them of authority; 3) present an image of their sinfulness, which, supposedly, was then punished when they were destroyed or scattered during the war.

In sum, if we can put aside the soothing assumption that early Christianity was a stable entity invented by Jesus, and his closest disciples, that then gradually and organically developed into the Christianity that is found in the gospels, then we can read Paul in a new light and profitably ask some fresh questions about what he tried to accomplish as a writer and a theologian; then, having treated Paul on his own terms, we can turn to place those views in the context of later gospel writings which functioned in rather different ways. In doing so, we will recover a range of positions that have largely remained outside the purview of New Testament studies and likely will at first appear perplexing. In fact, when we read Paul closely we will come away with the impression that just as we have missed Mark's agenda, we have missed Paul's ingenuity as he created a very startling image of God, and his priestly actions, and an equally startling form of human subjectivity, built from recycling and internalizing a potent set of Jewish precedents.

Paul's Theory of Salvation:
A Moveable Feast of Paternal Presence

To keep my reading of Paul's theology relatively brief, I will work mainly from Paul's Letter to the Romans, which arguably represents a full statement of his notion of the new version of tradition, its relationship to the old, and, of course, its role in effecting the believer's salvation. Though I will focus on Romans, I will occasionally refer to the other letters to thicken my analysis and, in particular, to bring in useful statements about the "floating patriarchy" that holds Paul's rhetorical system together. Since Paul's letters aren't presented in narrative form—though there is a narrative holding his position together, as mentioned above—it won't be necessary to develop a step-by-step close reading of Romans; instead, I will focus on two fundamental themes.

The first theme is best defined as the genealogy that Paul gives to support his version of tradition, a narrative that moves the reader backward in time to explain the "historical" basis of Paul's position. In particular, he constructs a "history" of sacred items that have moved between God's zone and our zone. The second theme, not surprisingly, organizes the believer's motion forward in time; on this front, Paul makes a number of demands on the believing reader, including an incessant internal self-crucifixion that is to be practiced in mimicry of the sacrificed Son. As will be detailed below, Paul demands that one side with the Spirit—imagined to inhabit the believer—in a sustained attack on one's carnal desires. With this internalized self-sacrifice as the core of his practical ethics, Paul promises that the believer can fulfill this new version of tradition and, after death, join with the Father and Son.

In developing the first theme—the genealogy of the new tradition—Paul claims that God has in the recent past produced two interlocking things that change everything about human existence. First, God made a Son whom he put into human history and sacrificed.[48] Here, we have to be clear that it isn't the Romans or the Jews who are to be blamed for Jesus's death, since it is really a death that God willed, with no other agents or actors appearing important in the actualization of that death. Second, God produced and promulgated a new law, one that requires the believer to relate to that sacrificed Son—or rather the narrative of that sacrificed Son—in a certain and exacting manner. In short, with internal self-sacrifice as a key element in his practical ethics, Paul demands that one's practice of the new law be, in part, a continual rehearsal of God's original sacrifice that inaugurated the new covenant. Articulating the new law in this manner of course has major implications for the practice of the old law of traditional Judaism. As is well known, Paul's account of the new covenant is presented as the overcoming of the (old) law of traditional Judaism, or at least the overcoming of *the image of traditional Judaism* that Paul constructs for the reader.

In trying to make sense of this arrangement, especially with the gospel narratives in mind, one might wrongly think that Paul has organized a model in which Jesus was "born" of God and *then* gave a new law about obtaining salvation by leaving the confines of the (old) law—as though the new law was separate from the story about Jesus getting put into history as a sacrificial offering. Yet, this is precisely what Paul isn't saying because these two items sent by God—the Son and the new law—are in fact one functioning entity: the sacrificed Son without the new law is meaningless, just as the new law without the sacrificed Son is meaningless. One could even say that the new law and Jesus were born as something like twins, with one destined to live (the law) and the other destined to die (the Son), with the one left living essentially claiming that it has the right to live because its twin died. Thus, of the two, the twin that lives is defined by being the story of how the other twin died in order that the first twin might live. Put that way we begin to catch sight of the kind of dialectics that orchestrate Paul's writing, dialectics in which things "die" and yet continue to live in other places and in other modes.[49]

Despite their common origin in the Father and their simultaneous arrival, the new law and the Son are partially separable in a practical way since, as just mentioned, the law stays in our world after Jesus's death and return to the Father. Consequently, the new law as a mobile, timeless account of Jesus's death dangles like a rope between the transcendental Father and human history, promising that all who take up this law will, like the Son, go back to the Father.[50] Framed in this manner it is clear what Paul is proposing, at least on the level of movement between human history and the Father: there is a telescoping continuity that runs from God, to his Son, to Paul's writing, to the reader/listener and that continuity, of course, works in reverse with Paul's audience being offered the chance to climb back up to God via this interlocking set of items.

While this movement is in basic accord with the trajectory of most forms of religious "motion" which, by nature, have to articulate this kind of to-ing and fro-ing between the mundane and the transcendent, Paul's version is particularly elegant and compact since the essence of the Father that makes both the Son and the law is completely interlaced with the *narrative explanation* of both those essences, a narrative that takes the form of what Paul calls "God's gospel" and that is obviously inseparable from Paul's own writing. This means that the *narrative* of this newly invented "Father and Son" pair—God's gospel, as found in Paul's writing—is, in effect, endowed with just as much sonship as the Son that that narrative carries around within itself, since both come from the Father and since they can only be known simultaneously. The full implications of this arrangement will become clear at the end of this chapter when we see ample evidence that Paul claimed that his own writing had the power to refather believers as "children of God," as though Paul's supposedly heaven-sent narrative was some ghostly, and vastly extended, paternal appendage, ever ready to discharge its payload of paternity into any willing recipient. It is with just this self-reflexive linguistic structure in view that we can speak of Paul's language establishing a kind of perpetually fertile, "floating patriarchy."

How God Became a Jewish Priest

Setting aside for the moment the issues regarding the Son, let's consider how Paul has constructed the Father. The first thing to note is that Paul has transformed God into the *maker* of sacrifices—instead of his traditional role as the *recipient* of sacrifices—and it is in this role as sacrificer that the force of the new law is set to work in human history. Hence, if Prometheus stole fire from the gods, Paul has stolen sacrifice from the priests and given it to God. Despite conserving the preeminence of sacrifice in his version of the law, Paul's relocation and inversion of sacrifice produce some awkward results. First, Paul's God is now implicitly occupying the lower ground in the exchange since he is in effect the supplicant—the one with a gift to give that will put the world to right. Hence with God's reliance on gift giving and his choice of blood sacrifice, God is implicitly assigned the subaltern role. Worse, it would seem that God is now an agent who takes his cues from the Hebrew Bible such that instead of "authoring" or fathering that tradition—as he does in Torah narratives—he and his more recent actions appear to take form in imitation of that tradition. Or more exactly, God is now shown conforming to rules of purity and sanctity that he had in the past dictated to Israel and the Temple priests.[51] In short, in terms of ritual action and intention, Paul's God has become an upside-down figure—as if the king entered the kitchen, and not only washed up and put on an apron in accord with kitchen etiquette, but also went about the business of serving regal meals for the chefs and busboys.[52]

Second, not only has Paul turned the old sacrificial system on its head, he has also repositioned the play of particulars and the universal. Thus, whereas Temple Judaism was organized around a multitude of particular meat sacrifices being regularly sent up to God-the-universal, now God-the-universal is making a very singular sacrifice *downward* that serves as the basis of a new universal covenant that ruins the old system of sacrifice even as it mimics it, albeit in an inverted and displaced manner. Christian readers accustomed to the rhetoric in the gospels, such as, "For God so loved the world that he gave his only Son" (John 3:16), might not at first perceive what an odd reversal of standard Jewish sacrifice this is, but it might have been rather stunning to a first-century reader/listener familiar with traditional Judaism.

Besides reversing the flow of sacrifices that structured traditional Judaism, Paul also scripted a priestly role for God in the sense that God's sacrifice wasn't simply a "free gift," but rather was in some measure designed to demonstrate God's holiness and righteousness. Paul explains, "But now, apart from law, the righteousness of God has been disclosed, and is attested by the law and the prophets, the righteousness of God through faith in Jesus Christ for all who believe. For there is no distinction, since all have sinned and fall short of the glory of God; they are now justified by his grace as a gift, through the redemption that is in Christ Jesus, whom God put forward as a sacrifice of atonement by his blood, effective through faith" (Rom. 3:21–25). Here, Paul seems to be saying that it is not just that God made a sacrifice to create a new covenant—bizarre in its own right since it had been man's job to sacrifice to God to preserve the covenant—but also that God is making a blood sacrifice of atonement that mirrors the form and function of the priestly sacrifices that were performed to placate God. Put this way, it is clear that Paul has demoted God to a *mere sacrificer*—a sacrificer who, without making this sacrifice, would find himself not just bereft of sanctity and proof of his righteousness, but also lacking a mode by which to establish a covenant with humans. Reversing the claim in Genesis that God made man in his own image, Paul has made God a Jewish sacrificer who sacrifices in just such a way as to effect new relations between God and man.[53]

In understanding how Paul's God submits to priestly guidelines in traditional Judaism, we shouldn't miss one other double at work here: Paul presents God working from the old template of offering the firstborn, as found either in the narrative of *aqedah,* in which Abraham agrees to offer Isaac to prove his devotion to God, or in the Passover offering that replaces the offering of the firstborn with the sacrifice of a lamb or goat.[54] Consequently, in Paul's narrative of Jesus's birth and death, the Hebrew Bible has been brought to life in a quasi-historical manner since God is now acting out basic narratives that had, previously, been received simply as literature. Likewise, the past has become present since in Paul's writing God's blood sacrifice appears terribly current in comparison to the hoary story of Abraham and Isaac in Genesis 22 and the travails recounted in Exodus 12 that explained the origins of Passover.

Relying on recycled images and logics to explain God's treatment of his Son might seem straightforward enough except that Paul also makes clear that his new version of the law spells the end of the sanctity and finality of the traditional form of the law, the very law that Paul relies on to justify his new law. Near the end of his Letter to the Romans he states, "For Christ is the end of the law so that there may be righteousness for everyone who believes" (Rom. 10:4). Clearly, Paul is using Jewish precedents—in the form of scriptural passages and the sacrificial system—to construct a symbolic system that is noticeably at war with its parent system. Arguably this goes a good bit beyond what the phrase "robbing Peter to pay Paul" implies about the futility of in-house exchanges, since Paul is essentially stealing the logic and logos of the prior system in his efforts to convince his readers to leave just that system. In all this, Paul's law rhymes with the old law even as it fundamentally kills it, and kills it with the story of a sacrificial killing (Jesus's death) that relies on the symbolic power of the old law long enough for this singular blood sacrifice to appear legitimate in killing off traditional blood sacrifice and initiating a new covenant.[55]

In sum, Paul is arguing that if you believe that God performed this Jewish-style sacrifice, then you've just become a Christian, and in particular, a Christian who has no more *practical* use for Judaism and its sacrificial system. Or more exactly, since the term "Christian" was not in use in Paul's era, we should say that as one comes to believe that God made this Jewish-style sacrifice, one has accepted the brand new "gospel of God," which is none other than Paul's gospel and which annuls all that made Judaism unique and meaningful.

In this aggressive recycling and inversion of tradition, we should not be surprised to find Paul claiming that the life-giving spirit of tradition is to be found uniquely in his own theology. In his Letter to the Galatians, Paul makes the divine origin of his own writing absolutely clear when he claims, "For I want you to know, brothers, that the gospel that was proclaimed by me is not of human origins; for I did not receive it from a human source, nor was I taught it, but I received it through a revelation of Jesus Christ" (Gal. 1:11–12). In fact, he begins the letter writing, "Paul an apostle—sent neither by human commission nor from human authorities, but through Jesus Christ and God the Father . . ." (Gal. 1:1). Clearly, as Paul worked to redefine, monopolize, and relocate (old) tradition, he had to open up conduits between himself and the fount of tradition so that his writing would appear to flow directly from that already established supreme origin.[56]

How Does He Do It?
Paul's Six Techniques for Rewriting Tradition

In arranging for this deadly birth of the new law from the old, there are at least six rhetorical strategies that Paul relies on in his Letter to the Romans. In the first and perhaps most obvious maneuver, Paul cherry-picks passages from the Hebrew Bible to support his reinvention of tradition. Hence, Paul uses a reading strategy that itself is fetishistic in nature since he takes it upon himself to select parts of the (past) whole to represent a new whole. As is well known, Paul selects passages that he finds useful from the massive Hebrew Bible, wrenches them from their context, and then sets them and their cachet of sacrality to work supporting his own version of the law which, of course, is designed to kill off the final sacrality of that very body of literature that he just drew from. Thus, with select passages from Genesis, Isaiah, or the Psalms, he borrows the familiarity and sanctity of the old for his presentation of the new law, a law which, obviously, involves the practical renunciation of just these books, along with the tradition that had preserved them.[57]

Looking more closely at Paul's recycling of language, one sees two formats. In the first, passages from the Hebrew Bible, introduced with the phrase "as it is written," are explicitly cited in order to shore up parts of his argument. Thus, on and off throughout his writing he provides full quatrain-length quotes when such passages can be made to support his positions. A particularly good example of how far he could stretch this reading technique is the claim in Galatians 3:13 that Jesus's death, in a certain sense, was a "curse for us" since Deuteronomy explains, under "Miscellaneous Laws," that "anyone hung on a tree is under God's curse" (Deut. 21:23). In the second form of recycling language, Paul's borrowed rhetoric seems to work on a more unconscious level, with half-visible traditional phrases and idioms sprinkled throughout his text, giving the vague impression that Paul's rhetoric is legal because it is written, to some extent, with the linguistic flavor of the old law. Obviously, this kind of borrowing is harder to prove but needs to be kept in mind for understanding some of the more subtle modes of fetishizing tradition.

In either mode of recycling material from the Hebrew Bible, Paul, as reader of (old) tradition, has placed himself above the plane of traditional literature, with his unimpeded movement from one selected passage to the next proving his freedom from tradition, even though his gesture of finding authority in just this objectified and picked-over version of tradition reveals an ongoing dependence on (old) tradition. In these gestures, Paul rises above the controlling function of the (old) law and makes the (old) law "suffer" his own choices about what is to be read as the law, and yet despite this symbolic violence that he wreaks on (old) tradition, he remains completely involved in the language of the old law.[58] Put metaphorically, Paul has constructed for himself, and his reader, a "reading platform" that circles the planet of the (old) law, but now is immune to the particulars of that world's geography as it orbits in a jubilant free fall that, though still locked in perpetual orbit around the (old) law, nonetheless flatters itself with the sense that it is above it all. In a moment I will follow Paul's other efforts to co-opt the (old) law for his own purposes, but for now it is more important to see that Paul passes on to the reader just this right to judge the (old) law. Consequently, the (old) law now lies below the reader since it has been transformed into an object of evaluation and, at times, an object of derision.[59] This point is crucial because the other texts considered in the following chapters also work like this in their overcoming of tradition: the reader is set up as a judge of (old) tradition and the (old) version of the law.

In drawing his readers into passing judgment on the (old) law, Paul has also effaced the dividing line between priests and ordinary believers. In fact, as Paul grants the ordinary believer the right to judge the (old) law, we have every reason to speak of the "priestification of the masses." Actually, just such a graduation of the ordinary believer into priestly functions will be matched by Paul's insistence that each believer be in charge of sacrifices—metaphoric and internal though they be—with these virtual sacrifices turning each individual's body into a temple of sorts. In such refigurations, the whole landscape of (old) tradition is now found within the believing individual who imagines these sacred powers and locales to be properly within his or her own purview. Clarifying how this now democratized and universalized essence of tradition works within each human body, he writes, "Or do you not know that your body is a temple of the Holy Spirit within you, which you have from God, and that you are not your own? For you were bought with a price; therefore glorify God in your body" (1 Cor. 6:19–20).[60]

Next to Paul's strategies for rewriting and relocating tradition, we see the parallel gesture of treating the (old) law to a logical critique—the second of his six techniques, which, arguably, is really a corollary of the first. Here, Paul again assumes the higher ground vis-à-vis the (old) law and applies different forms of logic in his treatment of the (old) law. Thus, in critiquing traditional legal obligations regarding diet, adultery, or circumcision, Paul claims that the essence of the (old) law is, in fact, outside the (old) law—a point that of course ruins the old version of the law. For instance, in the case of circumcision, a particularly sensitive topic for his communities, Paul argues that circumcision without faith and commitment is meaningless. Pushing on this logic that it is the will-to-obedience that is paramount in being lawful, Paul offers the reader a kind of interiorized circumcision: "For a person is not a Jew who is one outwardly, nor is true circumcision something external and physical. Rather, a person is a Jew who is one inwardly, and real circumcision is a matter of the heart—it is spiritual and not literal" (Rom. 2:28–29).[61]

In metaphorizing circumcision in this manner, Paul is arguing that everyone should become "Jewish" in this internalized sense, even though such a gesture is, obviously, undermining Jewish identity as it had been defined by tradition, with its long-standing emphasis on real circumcision to mark in-group status. Thus, as with his other arguments, Paul is overcoming (old) tradition by transforming its key elements into linguistic forms that first take up the power and promise of the prior form, and then deliver them to the believer of Paul's rhetoric. In this transformation of a physical practice—such as circumcision—into language and belief, Paul finds a way to lay hold of (old) tradition and then extract from it a "spiritual" form of the practice, leaving the original command and practice looking quite useless and emptied—the veritable dead letter of the law. However, the (old) law as dead letter turns out to be endlessly productive; or, rather, *that gap between the (old) law and its new "spiritualized" form turns out to be endlessly productive.* For, regardless of how universalizing and anti-Torah Paul's version of the law turns out to be, his law is only what it is in overcoming the (old) law. In short, it is precisely the (old) law and its supposed finitude that provides Paul with the material for his universalism and his offer of free access to the Spirit. Or, and it comes to the same thing: the reality of Jewish practices remains the basis of Paul's "spiritualized" forms that are now but metaphors of their former selves.

Among his six rhetorical ploys, the third is Paul's insistence that despite the obvious antagonism between the old law and the new, there is also a continuity between them—a claim that he supports by evoking various family metaphors. In one passage, he treats the new law like the new husband of a widow whose previous husband was the old law (Rom. 7:1–6). Thus, just as one wife could have two husbands, serially, provided one first died, so too could one *legally* step from one form of the law into a new form of the law—from the Torah, to Paul's version of the law, that is.

Working along another track of family affiliation to justify the new law, Paul claims that Jesus is descended from David (Rom. 1:3), with the obvious implication being that this patrilineal heritage renders Jesus and his involvement with the new dispensation of the law fully traditional.[62] This seems to be an odd claim and is supported by nothing else in Paul's discussion. The claim is particularly odd because Paul specifies that this mode of inheritance is "according to the flesh" (Rom. 1:3). Apparently, then, for Paul there are two kinds of patriarchy at work in Jesus's identity: one supposedly of the flesh, the other of the Spirit. One problem in doubling Jesus's paternity in this way is that even "fleshy" patriarchy is, arguably, a spiritual matter since the connection between father and son remains invisible and only communicable in language and supported by faith in the entire superstructure of patriarchal identity, a problem I will explore in the chapters ahead. Strictly speaking, then, patriarchy "according to the flesh" is an oxymoron, since inheriting one's identity from one's father rests on faith in that invisible essence that is supposedly passed between father and son as patriarchy moves through the crucible of the mother who, of course, has to be negated in establishing the son's identity as from the father.

The more obvious problem with putting Jesus in David's lineage, though, is that Paul is providing Jesus with *two tradition-making fathers.* Clarifying this surplus of fathers goes a long way to figuring out how Paul is trying to situate his new version of the law. He wants the new law to appear totally traditional—hence Jesus is of Davidic origins—and yet this would be of little consequence without the higher, non-Jewish, fathering that Paul imagines for Jesus as the Son of God, a God who is no longer to be imagined as Jewish. The counterintuitive aspect of this arrangement is that the Davidic lineage, though judged useful for legitimizing the new divine lineage claim, has in the process been identified as flesh-like, and thus something to be superseded by Jesus's supposedly direct spiritual inheritance from God.

Paul's fourth rhetorical ploy is to claim that the new law is, in fact, older than the old law and thus not new at all. Hence, with a convoluted close reading of God's covenant with Abraham in Romans 4, Paul produces the conclusion that a version of his faith-only system was present before (old) tradition was enacted.[63] In making this argument, Paul insists that his version of the law—the faith-based covenant with God—was actually the foundation for Abraham's reception of the action-based covenant. Thus, with some rather careful parsing of the story, Paul forces the conclusion that God only gave Abraham transmission of the (old) law based on Abraham's performance of Paul's (new) law of faith, thereby making Paul's law the older of the two dispensations and discoverable at the earliest moment of (old) tradition.

In rehistoricizing the origins of tradition in this way, Paul has hollowed out the form of old tradition—defined by the twin inheritance of Abraham's seed and the transmission of the law/covenant first given to Abraham—since these items are now imagined to flow in the wake of Abraham's commitment to Paul's version of the law, which supposedly was the reality that held Abraham to God and allowed for this mix of legality and fertility to pass from Abraham to all the people of Israel. Consequently, Paul is hijacking tradition by claiming that wherever you see (old) tradition, you should know that this is nothing more than the external appearance of this deeper form of Paul's tradition that was in place before (old) tradition got started and that now, in Paul's writing, is simply being returned to its properly ascendant place.[64] In his Letter to the Galatians, Paul makes this distinction all the clearer as the (old) law is identified as a second-rate item and merely prophylactic in nature—given by God due to human transgressions (Gal. 3:19) and set in place to function until the real promise of God could be delivered in the form of Jesus's sacrifice. As Paul puts it, "Now before faith came, we were imprisoned and guarded under the law until faith would be revealed. Therefore the law was our disciplinarian until Christ came, so that we might be justified by faith" (Gal. 3:23–24).

The final two techniques that Paul uses to rewrite the law circle around sacrifice and patriarchal reproduction and have been discussed above. In sum, Paul's argument assumes that there really is only one way of ratifying the law, and it is in accord with (old) tradition's notion of establishing law, identity, and covenant through blood sacrifice. What is clearly so new in Paul's position is that this new form of the covenant can now be established through *belief* in one particular sacrifice—Jesus's.

Given the above details regarding how Paul established the genealogy of his new law, it would seem impossible to avoid the conclusion that Paul's position is deeply involved with negotiating a productive relationship between the old and new forms of the law, and on three levels. First, as discourse, Paul's proto-Christianity appears as a fetishized form of Judaism that retains—in iconic, metaphoric, and linguistic forms—the key signifiers of (old) tradition: sacrifice, paternal reproduction of the law, covenant logic, and so on. Second, all these traditional elements have been rearranged in Paul's discourse such that the force and promise of old tradition can now be taken hold of and internalized as a kind of personal practice that involves a complex form of symbolic self-sacrifice to be conducted in the "temple" of each believer (more on this below). And, finally, it is the very figures of meaning and value from (old) tradition that are invoked to explain and legitimize this tectonic shift in the locale and practice of tradition. Thus, in Paul's account, God has in effect killed the Jewish sacrificial tradition with a Jewish sacrifice—the blood sacrifice of Jesus—and *that is precisely* what makes Paul's position legitimate.[65] Or phrased more succinctly: God killed tradition in accord with tradition, and that's how we got (new) tradition.

Tradition on the Inside

This obsession with the interface between the old law and new law is equally in view when Paul claims that versions of the two laws are found within each believer—and here we turn to take stock of what I termed the second major theme in Paul's rhetoric: the forward-moving aspect of his theology that explains how the new law is to be internalized and practiced in order to produce a new subject who can move into the future. Before entering into this discussion, which is going to be complicated and multi-sided, let's remember that Paul has argued, in unambiguous terms, that the entirety of tradition is present and available within each believer. This position is summed up in the call that everyone should take his body as a temple, presumably in the sense of a mini-version of the Temple of Jerusalem, and find therein the Spirit of Jesus, sent from God, with whom the believer can commune in such a way that this Spirit, in effect, takes over the believer and finalizes his or her identity, thereby completing the entire drama that God initiated when he sacrificed his Son. This interior temple is, not suprisingly, animated by sacrifice—a style of sacrifice that turns out to be rather involved and that, at bare minimum, brings together four elements: 1) the basic affirmation that sacrifice, quite literally, makes something sacred, and thus the death of something, even in metaphoric form, is the cause of power, purity, and access to things divine; 2) a commitment to practicing a form of internal sacrifice that replays Jesus's sacrificial death, the death that underwrites the legality of this kind of internal sacrifice; 3) a framing of internal sacrifice that makes it a sacrifice of the old law, a metaphoric killing off of old-style killing which is to give birth to the new law, the law that demands just this kind of interiorized sacrifice; and 4) the articulation of a kind of psychological sacrifice in which a "spiritual" version of the self sacrifices what it takes to be a lower, libidinal version of itself.

To clarify these four elements of internal sacrifice, let's begin by noting passages in which the believer is invited to participate in a facsimile of Jesus's death. Paul writes, "Do you not know that all of us who have been baptized into Christ Jesus were baptized into his death? Therefore we have been buried with him by baptism into death, so that, just as Christ was raised from the dead by the glory of the Father, so we too might walk in newness of life" (Rom. 6:3–4). Slightly later, the believer's metaphoric dying, which had first been linked to baptism, is marked as a killing—a crucifixion, in fact: "We know that our old self was crucified with him so that the body of sin might be destroyed, and we might no longer be enslaved to sin. For whoever has died is freed from sin. But if we have died with Christ, we believe that we will also live with him" (Rom. 6:6–8). In this passage one is not simply passively baptized "into his death" but participates in an enhanced mimesis of Jesus's death in which "our old self was crucified with him." The fullest statement of this internalization of Jesus's sacrifice comes near the end of Romans when Paul writes, "I appeal to you therefore, brothers, by the mercies of God, to present your bodies as a living sacrifice, holy and acceptable to God, which is your spiritual worship" (Rom. 12:1). In this line, Paul has brought the various doubles together such that the internal dying is to be conducted as a self-sacrifice that rhymes with Jesus's death-as-sacrifice but not simply because it too is a crucifixion, but also because it is explicitly a sacrificial gift, a "living sacrifice," to be offered to God.

As the strange phrase "living sacrifice" suggests, advocating these metaphoric sacrifices has powerful implications for how Paul's system will define one's participation in time.[66] The key is to see that Paul is asking his believers to get involved in a mode of self-articulation in which one part of the self sacrifices what it takes to be a lower form of itself, labeled in the above passage as "body of sin" or the "old self." Apparently with the same logic of a bifurcated self in view, but preferring the term "flesh" for "body of sin," he argues in Galatians, "Live by the Spirit, I say, and do not gratify the desires of the flesh. For what the flesh desires is opposed to the Spirit, and what the Spirit desires is opposed to the flesh; for these are opposed to each other, to prevent you from doing what you want" (Gal. 5:16–17). These carnal desires, it would seem, are in fact the "body" that Paul is asking the believer to kill. This means, basically, that Paul's religious program is not just a call to avoid acting on these desires, but to judge them as exterior to one's Spirit Self. Then, with that Spirit Self set clearly apart from the body of sin, Paul is asking that one kill those desires that arise that have as their object anything but the Spirit, with the killing of those desires functioning as a mimetic sacrifice that finalizes the entire program by joining one to Jesus, and his trajectory of resurrection, such that Paul can write, as cited above, that those who kill their own carnality in this manner can live with Christ (Rom. 6:8). The power of killing carnal desires is spoken of in a similar way in Colossians (3:2–5): "Set your mind on things that are above, not on things that are on earth, for you have died and your life is hidden with Christ in Lord. When Christ who is your life is revealed, then you also will be revealed with him in glory. Put to death, therefore, whatever in you is earthly: fornication, impurity, passion, evil desire, and greed (which is idolatry)."

Fully articulating this Self-within-the-self which is at war with its baser desires, Paul famously writes, "For I delight in the law of God in *my inmost self*, but I see in my members another law at war with the law of my mind, making me captive to the law of sin that dwells in my members. Wretched man that I am! Who will rescue me from this body of death? Thanks be to God through Jesus Christ our Lord! So then, with my mind I am a slave to the law of God, but with my flesh I am a slave to the law of sin" (Rom. 7:22–25, italics added). Put this way, one might simply assume that the "old self" that lives in the body's members is simply an evil "slave to the law of sin" which is to be killed off by the more central "inmost self," the self that, once separated from this swampy matrix of desire, will gain entrance into the life of Christ. However, a little more reflection on this paradigm would suggest a much more tangled arrangement. First, if this internal killing of desire qua "old self" really is to be a sacrifice, then these carnal desires are in fact essential to the project, since presumably in their absence there would be no way to perform the internal sacrifice that Paul sets up as the sine qua non of salvation—the sacrifice by which one kills one's old self-of-flesh in order to live with Christ. Ironically, then, though Paul has nothing good to say about these desires, they still are the fuel that drives the entire project of Spirit reclamation, providing it with an endless stream of "sacrificial victims" that will be pleasing to God and secure the believer in covenant with God by means of making one's life a "living sacrifice."

Asking the believer to re-enact this paradigm of God's sacrifice of Jesus, however exciting as a mode of intimacy with things divine, nonetheless implies that Jesus-the-sacrifice is to be aligned with the believer's flesh and, of course, with those carnal desires that the believer is supposed to execute. In this sense, it isn't that one's desires are imagined to be Jesus-like, but rather that pre-resurrection Jesus is implicitly taken to be flesh-like, and especially flesh-like in Paul's sense of that which has to die in order to give birth to the new. Given this logic, perhaps we shouldn't be surprised at how little Paul has to say about Jesus as a teacher, hero, or spiritual reality.[67] In fact, we ought to expand this point to say that Paul's theology is almost exclusively God-centered—it is God's actions, not Jesus's, that matter. Thus, the reader is invited to act much more like God than Jesus as he performs his internal sacrifice, with the believer's body-of-sin serving as a Jesus-like "animal" that will die properly and produce not just the Spirit but a deep rhyme between believer and God, with both figures now similar in having purposefully cast off some elemental aspect of their being. Presumably it is in this context of the power of the post-sacrificed Jesus that Paul wrote in 2 Corinthians, "always carrying in the body the death of Jesus, so that the life of Jesus may also be made visible in our bodies. For while we live, we are always being given up to death for Jesus's sake, so that the life of Jesus may be made visible in our mortal flesh. So death is at work in us, but life in you" (2 Cor. 4:10–12).

However we decide to parse the parallel between sacrificing one's own fleshy desires and God's sacrifice of Jesus, we have to admit that in either case Paul is promising that *one can make Spirit with flesh*, its opposite. That is, in Paul's gospel, the fundamental magic of making Spirit is still locked within the Jewish model of killing animals to communicate with God—the first of the four elements of internal sacrifice mentioned above. Or, more exactly, Paul is arguing that God performed a Jewish blood sacrifice of his Son in such a manner that humans could gain access to that incalculable power of sacrifice provided that they perform a parallel sacrifice inside themselves, a metaphoric sacrifice to be sure, but one that still took the flesh as the basis for making the Spirit. In a fully circular manner, then, Paul gave

Jewish sacrifice to God so that, via the gift of the "twins"—Jesus and the new "gospel of God"—sacrifice could, in this metaphorized form, be given back to people. In sum, according to Paul, everyone now is required to mimic God's fundamental sacrificial gesture, even as God's gesture mimics old-style Jewish sacrifice.

In fact, looking at how important internal sacrifice is for Paul's spiritualized subject, we have to ask if we haven't misunderstood Paul's hatred of the flesh. It is often said that Paul represents a particular puritanical version of Jewishness, visible in his harsh statements regarding the dangers of flesh and desire. While it may be that Paul's theology has behind it a very negative assessment of the body, it may also be that he was drawn into such an assessment by the logic of the sacrificial system that is providing the form and content of his message. In this light, the will to demonize the flesh was not the cause of Paul's discourse but rather the effect of it, with the cause to be found in Paul's reorganization of the sacrificial system that now took carnal desires to be its sacrificial meat. That is, Paul's metaphorical sacrificial system needed a bloody victim, and Paul, in casting about for such a victim, landed on carnal desire, which then had to suffer the killing that would be so productive for all the other values Paul is offering.

Of course, the brilliance here is that Paul has inserted resistance to his new law into the very practice of the law, arguing essentially: "take all those motives that are not directed toward the new law—the motives tending toward the flesh and not the Spirit—and 'kill' them, confident that it is with that very 'action' that one is fulfilling the law." Thus, if we bracket the basic Father-Son narrative, and the longing that it produces in the believing subject, the content of Paul's law is the claim that the practice of the new law is no more and no less than the murderous—and doomed—enforcement of the law that one should only live for the law. The circularity of his system advocating perpetual private civil war is perhaps attenuated by the possibility that there are three subject positions at work here: the carnal, the Spiritual, and the one who watches the battle, hoping the Spirit wins. Put that way, Paul's new law involves one in various modes of self-alienation, self-observation, and self-fetishization as one learns to reenact, over and over, in a kind of home theater, that moment when the new law was initiated by God's sacrifice of Jesus.

It is in working to understand just this complex structure in which the contents of "old religion" turn into both the form and content of "new religion," albeit now metaphorized and redeployed as a mode of self-understanding, that I believe the theoretical perspective of fetishizing tradition has the most to offer.

Choosing One's Parents

To develop my suspicion that there are actually three subject positions in play in this form of internalized sacrifice, let's consider how Paul explains the believer's practice. He argues that the believer has a fundamental reoccurring choice, a choice that arguably is the essence of Paul's program: the believer can chose to follow the body qua flesh, its passion, and the old law, and thereby win death;[68] or, the believer can focus on the Spirit, renounce carnal desire, and thereby win that Spirit which takes one to God after death: "For those who live according to the flesh set their minds on the things of the flesh, but those who live according to the Spirit set their minds on the things of the Spirit. To set the mind on the flesh is death, but to set the mind on the Spirit is life and peace" (Rom. 8:5–6). This setting of the mind on the flesh or the Spirit marks, then, that bifurcation in the destiny of the believer and, of course, the place where one decides to commit to Paul's theology, or not. That is, Paul is asking for a self to appear who can take in Paul's rhetoric, visualize these two potential selves—of the flesh and of the Spirit—and then decide to go with the Spirit, within the confidence that with just this choice the Spirit and its heavenly destiny have been won.

The complications involved in siding with the Spirit (and with Paul) against the flesh (and the old law) multiply when Paul then explains that siding with the Spirit wins one a new self. In effect, one doesn't just choose to follow the path that parallels Jesus's, the path that returns one to the Father. Instead, Paul argues that the choice to set the mind on the Spirit, and to "Put to death, therefore, whatever in you is earthly," brings about a new identity, as though the choice of the new path turns one into a new self. Thus he writes slightly after the above passage, "[F]or if you live according to the flesh, you will die; but if by the Spirit you put to death the deeds of the body, you will live. For all who are led by the Spirit of God are children of God (lit. "sons of God"). For you did not receive a spirit of slavery to fall back into fear, but you have received a spirit of adoption (lit. "adoption as sons"). When we cry, 'Abba! Father!' it is that very Spirit bearing witness with our spirit that we are children of God and if children, then heirs, heirs of God and joint heirs with Christ—if, in fact, we suffer with him so that we may also be glorified with him" (Rom. 8:13–17).[69] Looked at closely, this passage suggests that Paul wants his audience to imagine that practicing the internal sacrifice of one's flesh-oriented desires generates not just the presence of the Spirit, but a kind of refathering of the practitioner who now is to be known as a "son of God." Of course, since this chain of events is generated by one's *choice* to follow the Spirit and not the flesh, one is, in effect, fathering oneself by engaging in the course of action that will manifest this new self, based on this newly won paternity.

Here we have reason to return to that interesting play of paternal narratives and imagined essences that I mentioned above. If one chooses to follow the Spirit, believing it to be a real internal essence, then one hopes to win another essence—being a son of God—an essence that will ensure one's future ability to follow Jesus back to the Father. The problem is, and I will explore this more fully below, that paternity, for as substantial as one might hope it to be, is never anything but a narrative product. The passing on of an essence from father to son—forget about promises of their future reunion—is obviously a narrative progression in which sameness is imagined to continue over time and space, as it jumps from one subject to another in the development of their "history." As argued back in the methodology chapter, this fantasy of sameness is always one in which a narrative about essence hopes to be taken as proof of that essence. Thus try as one might to make paternity appear to be a substantial nonlinguistic reality—a fixed reality that could serve as the basis of a new personhood such as "son of God," for instance—it will continue to reveal itself as the effect of a story. That we now live in a world with DNA testing that can reliably determine paternity doesn't shift the real problem, which is simply the tension between *claiming* a connection between father and child (paternity as narrative) and pinning that claim on an imagined shared substance (paternity as essence). Lurking here is the obvious point that patriarchal forms of identity are particularly fetishistic since they require finding a reified Self above and beyond the matrix of the physical and mental modes of the individual, even as this Self is put forward as the final essence of that individual, with that essence supposedly deriving from a patriline, however that patriline might be construed.

Before embarking on the problem of paternity-as-narrative, let's note that in multiplying internal agents, Paul allows that the believer's choice of the Spirit is in fact aided by the Spirit. In this sense, one's choice of one's Self (and one's destiny) is imagined to be the result of a kind of infiltration of the choosing-self by the Spirit. Thus not only do we have the Spirit helping the believer cry, "Abba! Father," as in the above passage, but Paul also insists that the Spirit can take over and essentially instruct one in one's practice: "Likewise the Spirit helps us in our weakness; for we do not know how to pray as we ought, but that very Spirit intercedes with sighs too deep for words. And God, who searches the heart, knows what is the mind of the Spirit, because the Spirit intercedes for the saints according to the will of God" (Rom. 8:26–27). In this passage we get a sense of Paul's notion of conversion and practice in which the believer comes to understand his interior as a rather complicated place since it is there that the Spirit arrives and contests with the carnal forces in order to determine the believer's fate. In fact, the Other-based quality of this kind of Spirit-invasion is brought to its fullest form when Paul speaks of how God chose, in advance, those "predestined to be conformed to the image of his Son, in order that he might be the firstborn within a large family" (Rom. 8:29). Put this way, one's "choice" to follow the Spirit seems completely overdetermined by God's earlier definitive choice in the matter of who will and will not belong to this large family of those who conform to the "image of his Son."

While explaining God's selection of the predestined family members might *logically* discourage effort and desire on the part of the believer, I think as a rhetorical figure the opposite is the case. Apparently, the predestined nature of one's salvation is to be understood as a supposed "fathering" that is anterior to Paul's discourse and yet now, with Paul's discourse, is available for recovery, and it is in this sense that Paul writes of that "large family" "predestined to be conformed to the image of his Son." Consequently, the always-already established reality of this family presumably makes it all the more attractive as one goes about the somewhat ironic business of selecting one's identity and one's final parent, but within the confidence that this identity is already existent and recoverable, and certainly not the *mere* illusory effect of participating in a discourse on the Father and his children.

The point here is that Paul seems focused on one thing: winning the desire of his readers, for it is only desire that will drive the choosing-self to pick his Spirit-Self instead of the body of sin. This all-consuming play of desire is clear every time Paul tempts the believer with the promise that this act of desiring the Spirit will result in infinite life, even as it is won in killing off the desires of the flesh that would lead to death. Of course, the final piece of seduction is that Paul also offers a new body to the believer who chooses the Spirit-Self—a body that is to be inhabited after resurrection. So the current overcoming of the body by Spirit is, ultimately, activated by the promise that one gets one's body back later, after death. And, equally ironically, one wins family precisely in the extirpation of sexual desire— the very thing that normally makes family. Arguably these two ironies go together under the shared fantasy of having Father-only reproduction—the basis of Paul's entire program—in which the will to believe in Father-only reproduction is taken to be the very thing that will, ultimately, make such a wish a reality, albeit in another world.

Summing up Paul's notion of internalized sacrifice, it is clear that the sacrifice and sacrificer of the traditional system have been collapsed into a single agent—the Christian subject—who is defined as one who understands that he has to carry on the Jewish mode of flesh sacrifice but now vis-à-vis his or her own body, in mimicry of God's sacrifice of Jesus. In establishing this model for Christian practice, the believer's identity is organized around a dialectical procedure in which part of the self is taken to be old, base, and sinful, and yet it is to be taken hold of and "killed" in such a manner that it will convincingly produce the presence of the transcendental Spirit-that-is-of-God that will serve as one's final self, and in a manner that will eventually return one to God as a "co-inheritor," with Jesus, of God's paternity. So it is with just this complex self-spiritualization that the believer imagines to have lodged himself or herself in God's "large family" that has Jesus as its firstborn.

Not to be missed here is that this gesture of turning to sacrifice part of one's self in order to take hold of the Spirit matches the fetishizing procedure that Paul inflicts on the Jewish tradition. That is, Paul asks the believer to conclude that vastly complex things—such as the human subject or the Jewish tradition—can be easily summed up, owned, and controlled, provided one gets hold of their spiritual essence, an essence which supposedly stands "behind" the organic and unthinkably diverse matrix of the individual and tradition and which, when correctly accessed, brings all three—spiritual essence, the individual, and tradition—together, while excluding all that is not Spirit. In short, the entire Pauline system rides on this fetishizing gesture, a gesture that has everything to do with fantasies about the ubiquitous essence of the truth-father, found in the self and (partially) in old tradition, and, most importantly, in Paul's rhetoric, which is the house of the new tradition that explains how to access just that essence of the truth-father in one's own "house" qua temple.

Standing back from the mechanics of Paul's seduction it seems fair to say that we have been slow to understand this dialectical self-overcoming of (old) tradition and the (old) subject. That is, we haven't gotten very good at objectifying and judging systems of objectification, judgment, and essentialization. Thus, though Paul teaches us how to do this to ourselves and to the Jewish tradition, we haven't taken the next step to do it to Paul. Likewise, we haven't gotten very good at seeing how his system of transcendence arrives in *complete* dependence on prior forms, the very forms that he disparages. That is, it would seem that few readers of Paul come away with a sense for how the Spirit and the new covenant are only what they are precisely in their dependence on the right combination and re-presentation of the old and "physical" aspects of Jewish traditions. Instead, two millennium of readers have delighted in this system for producing transcendence precisely by misrecognizing its embeddedness in its opposite: the Jewish sacrificial tradition, flesh, language, metaphor, memory, family, and so on. In effect, it took the exact combination of all these "earthy" items—items that are fundamentally the opposite of Paul's offer of sudden, no-fault, preapproved redemption—to give the impression of just that kind of sudden transcendence.

In short, for one to participate in a system of fetishizing tradition (and fetishizing oneself), one has to practice a similar fetishization of the origins of such a system. Such a gesture of fetishizing the fetishization of tradition is, of course, prepared for within Paul's system so that one immediately turns to God as the origin of the overcoming of (old) tradition, instead of seeing that Paul's position for overcoming tradition is based on a traditional gesture (sacrifice), now performed *on* tradition, and held in place by traditional markers (Hebrew Bible citations and priestly logics) that signify how traditional all this killing of tradition really is.

A Death in the Family That Remakes the World

In coming to understand Paul's overcoming of tradition and his call that the subject practice a facsimile of this overcoming on him/herself, we need to get more clarity regarding Paul's use of the family motif as the relay between the mundane and the transcendent. To begin appreciating this side of Paul's theology we should note that with Paul's writing, God has become a family man of sorts—a man on whom time, history, and loss can function. Or perhaps we ought to say God is shown to be a risk-taker, perhaps even a gambler, and he is gambling with his most precious possession: his Son. The basic problem is that, while Paul makes it clear that Jesus returned to God after the resurrection, the whole journey into time involves the possibility of failure since there is the distinct possibility that the world will ignore God's gesture and, thereby, annul its value.

More exactly, Paul has set up a kind of indeterminacy in God's sphere of action: God takes the trouble to inject elements of himself into time—via his Son, his love, and his new version of the law—and yet this heavenly work is only finalized by the reader's response to the whole project, a response that is really defined by the reader's reaction to Paul's explanation of the whole situation. Thus it is revealed that God's gift, which arrives with such a wondrous promise of universally available divine kinship, could dangle meaninglessly in the breeze of time should Paul's audience turn away from Paul's theology. Put this way we can see more clearly that God's vulnerability vis-à-vis the Other who might not recognize his work mirrors Paul's vulnerability vis-à-vis his own reader. Naturally, then, God is only freed from the risk of having sacrificed in vain when the reader sides with Paul's theories about God's sacrifice. In a certain sense, when one begins to read Paul with faith, the sacrifice of Jesus, which is *what is inside* the narrative, starts to appear real *outside of the narrative* in just such a way to make you feel more obliged (and eager) to accept Paul's narrative of that sacrifice.

Besides these issues, it is worth mentioning two other emotion-eliciting elements wrapped up in Paul's narration of God's sacrifice. First, Paul presents God's sacrifice as the most impressive and heart-rending sacrifice possible. Thus, in terms of rhetoric, God's loss is designed to apply pressure on the reader who is invited to think: "With God accepting such a huge personal loss on my behalf, wouldn't it be all the more awful if I didn't respond as commanded?" The irony is, then, that it is by invoking God's *private* suffering that Paul can best take his message to the public. As usual, public propaganda works best when it masters the personal touch.

Second, we have to reckon how Paul's promise of reconstituted paternity works against the backdrop of several interlocking forms of patriarchy in ancient Jewish culture. Before Christian writing there was the patriarchal family, the patriarchal lineage of priests (Aaron's lineage that represented all other Jewish families to God), and the nation of Israel under God the Father who considered Israel to be his firstborn son (see, for instance, Exodus 4:22). Thus, as with Chinese dolls, there was an interlocking set of patriarchal relationships that held these various strata of Jewish society in sacrificial relationship with God. However, with God's sacrifice of his Son, readable on one level as the death of God's lineage, Paul asserts that all other previous sacrificial arrangements are annulled. According to Paul, after this sacrifice one can only find one's proper relationship to the ultimate source of patriarchy by believing that he killed his sole descendent, and thus his future, just for you. Accept that horrifying fact, and divine patriarchy not only will live again, but will live *in you* because, according to Paul, in that act of recognition you have refathered yourself and extended God's family. Thus, and at the risk of sounding more Lacanian than I am, it seems fair to say that with Jesus as sacrifice, Paul has put a hole in God's identity—a hole that, at least in one phase of the narrative, predicts the ruination of God's lineage, his happiness, and his well-being—and then claims that this divine hole will be filled once the reader properly understands this hole. That is, insofar as one takes it as one's business to acknowledge this breach in God's lineage, then one is ironically doing the very work that will close it back together.[70]

Though the following quote comes from what now is understood to be a pseudo-Pauline letter it seems to articulate the logic present in Paul's argument in which the believer's faith in this narrative of God's sacrifice is taken to be the act that reconstitutes Christ's body and presumably thereby reestablishes the Father-Son lineage. In the Letter to the Ephesians we learn how the community of believers must work "building up the body of Christ, until all of us come to the unity of the faith and of the knowledge of the Son of God, to maturity, to the measure of the full stature of Christ" (Eph. 4:12–13). Here, there is both a thrill and terror for the reader because his or her actions are now, in a sense, intimately involved in the ongoing process of fathering Jesus since, again, it is human belief in the destruction of Jesus's body that brings the spiritual "body of Christ" to completion. And, of course, if the reader should turn away from the project, he would effectively kill Jesus again and end God's lineage for good.[71] In sum, we have here another version of fathering one's self, since both God and the believer are restored through the singular action of the believer who finds his own wholeness in believing that his own belief in this sacrificial process will also return wholeness to God, his Son, and their lineage, a lineage which, it shouldn't be missed, is now poised to be the lineage of the believer.

A somewhat similar dialectical process of reconstituting Christ's body appears when Paul explains the Eucharist rite. In the classic passage from 1 Corinthians, Paul first clarifies how the sacrifice of Jesus delivers the items that are to be shared—the "blood" and "body" of Christ—promising that consumption of these items, in faith, will produce a body whose wholeness reflects the totality of believers and their oneness with the resurrected Christ and his Father, through baptism into "the one Spirit." Paul writes, "The cup of blessing that we bless, is it not a sharing in the blood of Christ? The bread that we break, is it not a sharing in the body of Christ? Because there is one bread, we who are many are one body, for we all partake of the one bread" (1 Cor. 10:16–17). Then, in a slightly later passage, Paul emphasizes the same point: "For just as the body is one and has many members, and all the members of the body, though many, are one body, so it is with Christ. For in the one Spirit we were all baptized into one body—Jews or Greeks, slaves or free—and we were all made to drink of one Spirit" (1 Cor. 12:12–13). Then, after developing a long riff on the totality of the human body that unifies its various parts, Paul concludes his characterization of the body of believers by saying, "Now you are the body of Christ, and each one of you is a part of it" (1 Cor. 12–27). Thus, the body of Jesus was singular as the Son of God, but then, after his execution and resurrection, his Christ-body became divisible but precisely in a manner that allowed for the reconstitution of his body via the metaphoric fusion of believers into the one body of all those *baptized into this very belief* regarding the mode of joining Jesus's/Christ's body, which, of course, is a body reconstituted in some kind of living form. Thus, as the believers' belief becomes unified in the shared conviction regarding *how* to return unity to Jesus's body, they have in fact accomplished the work of putting Jesus back together, and back with his Father, just as they have performed the deed that will also join them to this Father.

One last thing to say on this point about drawing humans and God together in the double-jointed act of refathering Jesus *and* the believer: by scripting God's ultimate action as the sacrifice of his Son, Paul has done to God what the Jews kept fearing God was going to do to them. Thus, back in Exodus 12, the Jews are shown in Egypt fearing a nocturnal assault from God—in the form of the angel of death—who would pass through their houses and take their firstborn. Faced with this threat, the Jews were instructed to slaughter a year-old male lamb and to smear the blood on the doorframes of their houses, thereby clarifying that a parallel gift had already been offered to God, thus releasing the household from the obligation of delivering up the male infant. This substitution works, though God's proxy, the angel of death, still kills the infant sons of the Egyptians, thereby both proving the reality of the divine threat and clarifying that substitution-sacrifice is necessary and, consequently, that those who don't provide suitable replacements will lose their firstborn sons.

On one level, the point of this story of murder, sacrifice, and substitution is to draw family-based patriarchy into a larger societal whole since all Jewish families are to perform it, on the same date and in perpetuity. The overarching Jewishness of each individual family is likewise underscored with the rule that visiting foreign males can eat of the Passover meal provided that they are circumcised (Exodus 12:48–49), thereby attesting to a certain pan-Jewishness that is undergirding the logic of the at-home ritual. On another level, the story seems designed to "prove" that the life of the at-home patriarchy lives or dies according to the will of the grand patriarch—God. Thus, the narrative implies that all births are, ultimately, God's doing, and as such, *can be taken back* from the "small" version of the patriarchal family at any time. By offering a first-year male sheep as a substitute, the sacrificial equation is maintained since God collects the first fruits of the season thereby proving, after a fashion, that all fertility is his to begin with, be it animal or human.[72]

As usual with Paul's rhetoric, this logic has been inverted such that humans are, in effect, collecting God's firstborn—Jesus. Putting it this way reinforces my claim above that Paul puts humans in charge of God's reproductive fertility, but it suggests something else as well. As Paul visits on God this loss of the firstborn, we might do well to ask if traditional Jewish readers might not have been confronted with the possibility that whereas the Jews of Exodus figured out how to duck this sacrificial requirement, God apparently hadn't. Thus, God finds himself facing a sacrificial demand that parallels the one he gave his Chosen People but ends up with a catastrophe precisely because he didn't figure out how to do a substitute covenant offering to avoid that obligation of sacrificing his firstborn. Put this way, traditional readers of Paul are going to be doubly eager to do anything to get the Son back to the Father, and right a ritual wrong that, according to Exodus, really should never be permitted—human sacrifice, and, in particular, the sacrifice of one's first son.

Fetishizing the World

In this heady swirl of fathers and sons we shouldn't overlook that Paul also claims that all of creation has been waiting for this paternal law to arrive, *and be received,* so that the Spirit-Self can be birthed—after a fashion—and then "adopted" into God's family. Thus Paul writes, "We know that the whole creation has been groaning in labor pains until now; and not only the creation, but we ourselves, who have the first fruits of the Spirit, groan inwardly while we wait for adoption (more literally, "to be made sons,"), the redemption of our bodies" (Rom. 8:22–23).[73] Here, Paul appears to be arguing for a thorough-going fetishization of the universe, claiming that "the whole creation" is at work supporting Paul's system and simply can't wait till we convert to Paul's position since our conversion, and the redemption that it produces, is the singular destiny of Being. In short, existence has no other purpose than this birth of the Spirit that is of the Father and takes one back to the Father as one of his sons. The logic of this mode of birthing the Spirit from the matrix of creation might not resolve in a straightforward manner, but at the very least we ought to see that Paul imagines that the transcendental Father has, after a fashion, already impregnated the mother-creation and now both mother-creation and Father-spirit are waiting for us to acknowledge this situation so that we can: 1) win our paternity as "heirs of God and joint heirs with Christ" (Rom. 8:17) and 2) end our time in the womb of the world where paternity wasn't recognized and consequently gain, first, a spiritualized version of ourselves in this life, and then, after death, a resurrected version of ourselves in God's family; and, at the same time, 3) release mother-creation from her long and painful pregnancy as "she" waited for the individual's conversion and salvation.[74]

Summing up the promise of personal and cosmic rebirth, Paul writes, "For the creation waits with eager longing for the revealing of the children of God (lit: "sons of God"); for the creation was subjected to futility, not of its own will but by the will of the one who subjected it, in hope that the creation itself will be set free from its bondage to decay and will obtain the freedom of the glory of the children of God" (Rom. 8:19–21). What such a statement implies is that Paul is casting the entire universe as nothing more than a vast patriarchal project with all of creation simply doing its best to play out the story of the great Father-and-Son reunion, a reunion to which all are invited, provided we are ready to see the world in this fashion.[75] In short, just as Paul turned God into a family man, with the believer positioned to be a heir to that family, so too is the whole of Being nothing but a family member—a mother, it turns out—doing her part to produce the sons of God who will, like Jesus, make it back to the Father.

While it is clear that Paul is working to thoroughly domesticize reality—by insisting on the patriarchal Spirit behind it all—we can't help but notice various forms of symbolic violence at work here. First, the world is essentially owned by the Father and has no meaning or destiny apart from this Father. Moreover, Paul doesn't clarify how the mother of creation fares at the end of the process since he only allows that she "will obtain the freedom of the glory of the children of God" (Rom. 8:21)—a decidedly vague and subsidiary fate. And, remembering the role of Jesus's death in the project, there is a kind of violence of suddenness in which the normal organic growth and development of Being is brutally refigured in the sacrifice of Jesus, with this violence then transferred to all believers who, as seen above, are encouraged to commit similar kinds of violence on what has been identified as the non-Spirit portions of themselves. Put simply, the Father-Son-believer reunion comes with knife-like certainty in which Spirit is cut away from non-Spirit, within the understanding that all that is not-Spirit is of no value other than providing useful props in Paul's singular play of divine patriarchy.

What I hope is reasonably clear from this discussion is that reading Paul for his fetishizing of (old) tradition isn't simply a good hermeneutical choice; it also takes us closer to understanding how it is that humans came to inhabit a symbolic order of lived transcendentalism in which mundane reality is imagined to be in contact with the divine paternal law, presented as a kind of omnipresent patriarchy that can supposedly complete the self and the world, but in the process also nourishes a substantial fear of the body, Being, history, and women, all of which will have to be, in one way or another, pushed aside in order to deliver the believer into perfect communion with the ultimate patriarch.[76]

Conclusions

Gathering up these arguments, it seems clear that Paul's symbolic system is animated by the fantasy of an endlessly available "floating patriarchy" that legitimizes his promise of the new law, guarantees the believer's rebirth as a son/child of God, and delivers the universe from its uncomfortable "pregnancy." Clarifying the construction of this kind of patriarchy reveals a coherency in a number of Paul's positions and will also work well for organizing comparisons with the Gospel of Mark and with Buddhist literature. To sum up Paul's notion of floating patriarchy in slightly different language, we can focus on Paul's mapping of two trajectories. The first is defined by divine reproduction that "swoops" from a transcendental zone down into human history, and then back into the transcendental, with Jesus identified as the item that makes this voyage. Obviously, by arguing for such a sonship-in-motion, Paul has already created a kind of floating patriarchy that doesn't stay at home and that is on the road precisely to make itself available to the random Other. The second trajectory is defined by Paul's claim that all humans can, if they believe Paul's account of this first swoop, follow the same trajectory and arrive "back" with the Father, as Jesus supposedly did.

These two trajectories are supported by three narratives: 1) God produced a Son—a simple narrative about the doubling of the deepest form of patriarchy in the system, a doubling that then sets in motion everything else that Paul promises; 2) this Son moved into human history to die in a certain manner to make floating patriarchy available to all—a more complicated narrative about the contact between the divine and mundane, and about how the ritual power of sacrifice was supposedly at work behind what otherwise would have appeared as an unimportant historical event (Jesus's execution by Roman authorities); and, 3) the unfinished narrative of seduction that claims that accepting narratives 1 and 2 completes the entire sequence. That is, when one believes in narrative 1 and 2, then one finalizes not just one's own destiny in the Spirit and the Father; one also finalizes narratives 1 and 2 by rebuilding Christ's body and making that "body" the one that subsumes all those who would believe in these narratives. *Christ's body is put back together, then, by all those who believe in the divine reason that determined why it had to come apart in the first place.*

Framed this way we can draw several other basic conclusions regarding Paul's notion of floating patriarchy. First, and most obviously, Paul has created a kind of "promiscuous" paternity that is available to all, regardless of origin. Of course, given that paternity is a system for creating singular identities and securing exclusive legal privileges—it is this boy, here, that is my son and inheritor, and not the other two hundred boys in the village—arranging for a ubiquitous, and totally public form of sonship might seem a little illogical. And yet Paul insists that this deepest of paternities is available to all, with *the mode* by which one relates to this claim of *ur*-paternity providing the magical spark that unleashes paternity's reproductive power. Hence, Paul argues that believing the patriarchal narrative is the magical deed that turns the descriptive language of the Father into the real essence of the Father's presence. Here, as mentioned above, we have to admit that Paul is not too far from claiming that one is fathering oneself insofar as one's belief is the trigger that effects the dissemination of that identity, or, rather, finalizes that identity that was already preestablished by the Father. Thus, once the believer becomes convinced that Paul's language is really attached to the divine patriarchy, he has, in effect, attached himself to divine patriarchy and thereby rescued him- or herself from time, history, the old law, the body, sin, and so on. Likewise, in the act of taking Paul's instructions for living and reliving God's sacrificial deed, the believer participates in a blood sacrifice—the sacrifice of Jesus qua firstborn son—with that participation sealing the legitimacy of the believer's new patriarchal identity. Of course, the big difference is that this sacrifice is now available to the believer in a virtual form with the entire project of refathering-by-sacrifice occurring in language and in the believer's consciousness.

With Paul's theology read as a multi-form program for refathering, we can make sense not only of the abundant paternal rhetoric that explains the process whereby belief turns one into a son/child of God, but also that rather telling moment in 1 Corinthians where Paul articulates the full telescoping function of his patriarchal language. He writes, "I am not writing this to make you ashamed, but to admonish you as my beloved children. For though you might have ten thousand guardians in Christ, you do not have many fathers. Indeed, in Christ Jesus I became your father through the gospel (lit. "begot you through the gospel"). I appeal to you, then, be imitators of me" (1 Cor. 4:14–16). In this procession of fathers, Paul seems to be saying that as God delivers the gospel to Paul, and as Paul delivers the gospel to his followers in Corinth, *Paul fathers them*, with the gospel as the tool that effects this refathering precisely by being the mobile mediator between God, Paul, and the believer—the mediator that renders floating patriarchy "concretely" available as the reality behind the language of fathering, even though it is precisely by language that it arrives and remains. This is, then, that moment when we see that "the ghostly, and vastly extended, paternal appendage" responsible for all this fathering is none other than Paul's rhetoric.

The second basic conclusion is implied in the first: Paul's system of promiscuous patriarchy domesticizes reality. Thus, in believing that with belief one can attach oneself to that swoop that moved the Son in and out of history, one has given oneself an ultimate Self and thereby turned mundane history, time, being, and radical contingency into nothing more than meaningless static that can be cut through simply by tuning into the frequency of floating paternity that promises that it can, at every moment and at every place and for every human being, deliver the pure essence of the Father that refathers the believer and brings him or her back to that transcendental zone, free of history, time, and meaninglessness. In short, in offering each believer a place in this transcendental patriarchal family, Paul has rendered the rest of reality a wasteland of Otherness, a zone of nonfamily to which one is only tangentially related, as in the case of in-laws. Obviously, to gain this kind of father is to lose the world, and that is, for Paul, a good thing. In fact, Paul extends his notion of mimetic crucifixion such that it defines his relationship with the world: "May I never boast of anything except the cross of our Lord Jesus Christ, by which the world has been crucified to me, and I to the world" (Gal. 6:14).

The next conclusion is more subtle but also clearly implied. Paul's system of floating paternity only works when it can hide its own place in human history—that is, when it can deny its complete reliance on the borrowed symbolic order of Judaism and its literature, not to mention its dependence on historical developments in first-century Mediterranean culture. In short, Paul's transcendental paternal truth only functions to explain origins and destinies when it can effectively deny the vast plume of productive forces that effectively fathered this theory of the universally available Father. Thus, when one asks about one's origins, Paul's theory of floating patriarchy directs one's attention to the supposedly always-already-present universal and transcendental Father and *completely away from the historical origins of this theory of origins.* Thus, there arguably is another alchemy at work here: once this theory of transcendental origins takes hold in a believer's imagination, an understanding of the various historical causes and conditions that fathered just this theory of transcendental paternity becomes unthinkable.[77] Consequently, Jonathan Z. Smith's comment that

"All religious discourse is commentary" becomes a major problem for such a believer.

Put this way, and without factoring in the more glaring examples of anti-Judaism in the gospels, we can see why Christianity bears within its symbolic order an awkward relationship to the Jewish matrix from whence it grew: the Jewish traditions represent the real historical father that Christianity wishes it never had, and in fact can't have if it is to claim to have a transcendental Father, even though this transcendental Father is nothing more than a fetish form of the Jewish tradition/s.[78] It is just *this unavoidable dependence in the making of the image of independence* that, presumably, has been so hard for Christians to get over. And for those who might think such symbolic struggles between Christianity and Judaism are over, let me note that when I was writing this chapter in the Fall of 2008, a debate was still simmering within the Catholic Church over how to articulate a new version of the Good Friday Prayers, one that preserves some expression of the traditional plea that God convert the Jews to Christianity, while also not drawing the ire of Jewish communities from around the world. Presumably this ongoing debate reflects the difficulties inherent in negotiating Christianity's discomfiting symbolic debt to the Jewish tradition.[79]

Conclusions, Part II:
An Outsider's Reflections on Recent Pauline Studies

For someone looking in from the outside, Pauline studies in the last thirty years appears rather odd. The quantity of publications is truly amazing, but the discussions are limited to a handful of topics that, if you are not Christian, aren't very interesting and, in general, don't join up with wider discussions in the history of religions. Within these flattened horizons, one reads over and over that we need to admit that Luther misread Paul, and thus we need to get around Luther and return to Paul with new eyes. In a sense that seems reasonable enough, but who, except Lutherans and other Protestants, reads Paul with Luther as a guide?[80] And if the take-home point in the wake of the work by Sanders, Dunn, and Wright is simply, "Ohmygosh, tradition misunderstood tradition," that is, that Luther's reading of Paul is altogether idiosyncratic, then that is hardly news for anyone used to thinking about how religions develop in history.

I should add, parenthetically, that before beginning this book-project, I regularly bumped into the opinion, widely held by my colleagues in Buddhist studies, that New Testament studies was a well-oiled, high-tech research machine that had developed modes of analysis and interpretation that were well in advance of those found in the other subfields of religious studies, such as Buddhist studies. What I came to see in several years of reading in New Testament studies, however, was that the field has a terrible track record for establishing sensible research agendas and little appreciation for some of the basic hermeneutical issues that have evolved in the other humanities during the twentieth century. One can find here and there a book or article on "deconstruction and the gospels," but many issues that have become foundational in related fields such as literary studies, history, and film studies have remained largely unexplored in New Testament studies.

In the case of Pauline studies, the problem, it would seem, is that almost all the scholarship on Paul is written by those who have been living "under" Paul's law themselves, and in many cases, in a manner inflected by Luther. Thus, a discussion about the imprecision of Luther's Paul is terribly important as it shifts the parameters of one's notion of God, life, ethics and so on. In short, many of these authors have given themselves the task of recalibrating—against Luther's reading—the Pauline message for themselves and their Christian readers, while also working to finesse a connection between this newly redefined "core" of tradition and the practices ordained by the church institutions with which they are affiliated. In this sense, then, the "New Paul" publications not only are theological in the fullest sense of the word, they are also acutely aware of their place in the Christian tradition and eager to find an acceptable accommodation between New Testament studies and modern Christian practice.

Thus, even if we are right in thinking that E. P. Sanders and others really wanted to take a strictly historical approach to rethinking early Christian writing, the result of this effort hasn't led to a full historicization of Paul's letters. To do so would require at least three more steps that are, as far as I can tell, generally lacking in Pauline studies. In the first step one needs to objectify Paul's symbolic system to understand, in a structural sense, how this *form* of discourse works. Until one figures out the formal features of Paul's discourse (as I have tried to do in this chapter), then debates about the content of this or that phrase are of next to no value. That is, if one is still debating what Paul meant by "faith in Christ" versus "faith of Christ" (a beloved topic in Pauline studies), without figuring out that Paul made God into a Jewish priest, internalized sacrifice so that the individual was the Temple and so on, while rerouting the law through his own writings, then one doesn't have a leg to stand on if one wants to speak, write, and think non-theologically about Paul's theology.

In the second step one needs to ask about the wider historical forces at work shaping Paul's discussion. Here, one begins (and it is going to take a while for this perspective to really come into view) to approach Paul's writing with a sense for something like the organic life of a tradition in which one expects that sooner or later this kind of fetishizing fold in tradition is going to make an appearance when conditions x, y, and z are present. In particular, I suspect that one needs to ask about the role of literature in Paul's theology. Given Paul's subtle notions of mimesis and metaphor, we need to locate his writing within something like an evolutionary history of logic and articulation in which his overall flexibility with doubles and transpositions likely has much to do with his place in an increasingly literate and multicultural setting.

In the third step, one looks for useful parallels to Paul's inventions. Arguably, making sense of Paul's deft folding and refolding of elements of tradition into new forms that float along in unmarked waters, and beyond preordained cultural horizons, has to be understood as the result of his particular place in thoroughly Hellenized Mediterranean culture. However, it also seems true that to understand this it would help to see another example, say, for instance, in Mahāyāna Buddhism where the cult of the text in *some* sūtras also offers believers the fullness of (old) tradition, via literature, without any reliance on place, race, formal training or institution. Thus, just as Paul's believer learns that he or she is the Temple, that is, the center of the world and the chosen place to make sacrifices (albeit in metaphoric form), so too the reader of Mahāyāna sūtras learns that wherever the text is, that place is sure to have the virtual presence of the Buddha and all the protector gods.[81] Until one learns to read each system in light of the other, one won't really appreciate what is in front of one and likely will rest in a comfortable zone defined by, "Oh, it just happened like this." Or the harder to dislodge, "Oh, it happened like this because this is a heaven-sent arrangement."

On another front, we have to say that modern Pauline studies hasn't settled into a reliable assessment of the role of Jewish law in Paul's writing. Here the debate circles around questions such as: Is Paul really against circumcision and all the other Torah commandments, or is he much more tolerant of the law? Or, as some have suggested, might he not have even been an advocate of (old) tradition? This debate has, at least, the advantage of being close to the heart of Paul's writing, and yet there are two pressures on this topic that have inhibited a fuller discussion from emerging. First, current reflection on Paul has come with a vague sense that Christianity is partly responsible for the Holocaust. The weight of this realization is obviously quite terrible, but it is also true that this weight appears doubly burdensome when the nature of the problem is only half understood. In short, appreciation of the full tragedy of the situation won't develop as long as modern Christian writers continue to labor under the illusion that the Christian-Jewish interface can be rehabilitated with just a little bit of cleaning up here and there, and, in particular, by minimizing lines such as the one in Matthew in which Jewish guilt for Jesus's death is squarely announced (Matt. 27:25).

This motivation to find more congenial Christian-Jewish connections is, of course, altogether commendable. Likewise, it is all to the good that Christian thinkers have gotten around to questioning how it was that Christianity, as the dominant religious ideology in Europe in the 1930s and 40s, was so easily drawn into anti-Semitic fascism.[82] And yet this urge to reconciliation seems to lead on to bad (in the intellectual sense) interpretations of Paul and, as we will see in the next chapter, Mark. In short, if one, in hoping to ease the tension between Christians and Jews, fails to point out that Paul's entire program is dedicated to ending the salvific hegemony that justified traditional Judaism, then one surely has missed the point of his letters. Thus, instead of facing the evidence that Paul appears completely absorbed in the task of single-handedly undermining the Jewish tradition, many authors try to soften Paul's position, arguing that he wasn't really against the Torah, or that he wasn't really intent on rendering it superfluous and/or passé, and so on.[83]

Should one have any doubt about Paul's effort to overcome tradition, just ask where it is that Paul gives credence to any site of authority in tradition that he doesn't then try to dominate and absorb? Worse, the items that previously made Second Temple Judaism sensible to Jews—the genealogy of Abraham, the Israel-exclusive covenant, the Temple sacrificial system, and identity-marking via circumcision—have all now been appropriated and put to work in Paul's system where, in metaphorized form (the only form that counts for Paul), they are the proper concern of all peoples, Gentiles as well as Jews. Until modern scholarship reads Paul's program as a play of levels which is totally aggressive vis-à-vis old tradition, *and dependent on it*, we will continue to get long, misguided discussions claiming that Paul couldn't have been against the old law since he relies on it so thoroughly to build his new system.

The case of circumcision makes this play of levels clear. In a sense, Paul is procircumcision, but now it is a metaphoric and invisible "circumcision of the heart" that both replicates the old system and completely undermines it since, after all, the whole point of circumcision is that it be visible so that it can thereby serve as the mark of Jewish difference. In short, Paul is saying what you do to your flesh is of no consequence as long as you learn to play this other "game" whereby you internally "mortify your flesh" by sacrificing your body of sin continually in a metaphoric duplication of God's supposed sacrifice of Jesus. For Paul, if you think circumcision of the penis is of use for developing this kind of internal sacrifice, which is the real cause of salvation, you are as confused as the person who puts on cleats and shin guards to play video soccer. Even though on the screen one can still see figures with such gear on (like the ongoing presence of the language of circumcision and sacrifice within Paul's presentation of interiorized practice), that in no way justifies actually wearing it oneself. In sum, until Pauline studies gets a dialectic-of-overcoming in view (one in which the worked-over item is both destroyed and re-presented in symbolic form), nothing very sensible is going to be said about Paul's treatment of (old) tradition.

Put that way we have to admit that it looks like, on the level of the symbolic, there can be no Christian-Jewish reconciliation, since for Paul, being saved is defined specifically in terms of a way of not-being-Jewish, with the negation and reappropriation of the Jewish tradition fundamental to everything Paul argued for. Thus, it does no good to argue as Sanders does that first-century Judaism wasn't at all like the flat, and altogether unflattering, profile that Paul sketches.[84] What matters for Paul is simply that this *image* of (old) tradition appear worthy of being overcome *in the eyes of his audience*. That is, Paul, and Christianity in general, is fundamentally *a way of looking at Judaism*—disparagingly, of course—and thus proving that real Judaism doesn't really resemble that image generated in Christian literature doesn't change the problematic structure of Christian-Jewish relations. Likewise, it doesn't help to argue that Paul's position is really deeply indebted to prior currents in Jewish thought where a God of grace and forgiveness can be found. All Paul cares about is convincing his audience not to look *over there* for value and salvation, and instead to make the jump into his own rhetorical system, which, though loaded with elements borrowed from *over there*, is only to be regulated by Paul's own notion of the law.

In this light, Christian meaning and identity appear terribly derivative. Thus, in line with all the trouble it took to convince nineteenth- and twentieth-century Christians that Jesus was Jewish, now the challenge is to realize that Paul's "Christology" is a form of Jewish thought turned on itself—that is, the isness of Christianity is to be found precisely in the folding of Judaism back onto itself, and yet from the Christian point of view, Judaism was the very thing that one thought one was renouncing (or simply avoiding) in order to get at the new glorious law—the gospel of God/Christ. Likewise, if one has *already learned,* in accord with the basic dynamics of Christian identity, to disparage those supposedly insufficient Jewish origins, then to see the second giving of the law as a play of those disparaged origins *on themselves* would, by definition, represent a collapse of Christianity into the very item that one had learned to dismiss in the hope of attaining higher value. In short, I don't think one can "ride" the dialectic up (that is, maintain a Christian identity) and see the dialectic and its self-consuming mode for what it is.

In the following chapter on Mark, I explore other forms of anti-Judaism that appear foundational in Christian theology, forms that unavoidably need to be addressed in coming to a religious studies understanding of the situation. The reason I am pursing this angle of the analysis isn't to smother Christian readers with evidence of the symbolic violence that organizes their system of faith, but rather to get at the building blocks of the Christian system that have been largely unexplored, presumably in part because they point to rather uncomfortable conclusions about what Christian faith is made of.

3

The Gospel of Mark, or
Narrative as Floating Patriarchy

Introduction

With a sense for Paul's treatment of the Jewish tradition in the construction of his theology, the structural logic of the Gospel of Mark is a good bit easier to sort out. In fact, one wouldn't be far wrong in thinking that the Gospel of Mark is a clever dramatization of *some* of the basic elements of Paul's theology outlined in the previous chapter. Thus, like Paul, the author of Mark claims that divine patriarchy swooped into human history—as Son and the narrative about the Son—promising that in accepting the narrative about the Son's arrival, from the Father, and his subsequent return to the Father, one would fulfill one's religious obligations, obtain the totality of tradition, get refathered, and follow the Son's trajectory back to the Father. And, as in Paul's theology, the efficacy and legality of this newly offered law is said to have been actualized with the blood of a sacrificial death—Jesus's. However, in the Gospel of Mark, this sacrificial death is now explained as occurring on Passover, and at the hands of evil Jewish authorities—a particularly potent enhancement, as we will see.

Significantly more challenging to understand are the involved narrative strategies that characterize Mark's presentation of this newly available form of divine patriarchy. These strategies are challenging in their own right, but the narrative also offers several troubling themes that modern readers might be reluctant to acknowledge, even when they are quite clearly established in the story. For instance, Mark, unlike Paul, promotes an uninflected hatred of (old) tradition—Second Temple Judaism, that is—even as Mark's narrative, like Paul's theology, borrows so many of its constitutive elements from that tradition. Thus, Mark's gospel reads as an apocalyptic struggle of the good—Jesus and his few helpmates—against the bad, with the bad squarely identified as: 1) the representatives of (old) tradition—the Pharisees, the scribes, and the chief priests; 2) the people of Jerusalem who called for Jesus's execution and then taunt him during his final moments; 3) the dubious and complicated figures of Judas and Peter, who both turn against Jesus; and, finally, 4) the remaining disciples who prove to be dim, arrogant, and weak.[1] Taking stock of these elements in the narrative will take us far from the saccharine things often said about Christianity—especially the standard claim that Christianity is first and foremost a religion of love—for surely hatred, disgust, and disappointment are the more prominent ingredients in the story. In fact, and this is the most troubling element in the package, should the reader come to love the image of Jesus that Mark presents, then it has to be said that this love comes hand in hand with hatred for (old) tradition and its representatives, who, of course, are shown despising Jesus and then murdering him.[2] In effect, then, the narrative works hard to evoke hatred for those who *supposedly* hated Jesus.

Despite its prominence in Mark's narrative, I believe we have to say that there is little chance that this hatred of Jesus reflects some real conflict between Jesus and traditional Judaism; instead it appears best read as a *literary invention* that Mark created to explain recent history—the fall of the Temple and the destruction of Jerusalem—and, presumably, to generate a more gripping narrative.[3] More exactly, as I argued in the previous chapter, it seems that after the destruction of the Temple, Mark wrote his narrative calling for conversion to this new form of tradition by, among other things, demonizing the already defunct tradition of Temple Judaism and by using the fall of the Temple as the final piece of evidence proving Jesus's divinity. Hence, Mark's narrative seems to be built around the following logic: the crime committed by (old) tradition and Jerusalem must have been of epic proportion, given the severity of the retribution visited on them, and that crime could have been none other than the murder of God's only Son. As Burton Mack puts it, "Thus we can see the viciousness of Mark's narrative plot in which the destruction of the temple serves as the sign for Jesus's innocence and God's vengeance upon the Jews."[4] In short, Mark made the destruction of the Temple appear as divine retribution, meted out to (old) tradition, for their persecution and execution of the divine Son.[5]

Thus, though this call to hate traditional Judaism would in time contribute to various forms of real-world anti-Judaism, in its infancy it was but a narrative contrivance in which random historical events were turned into elements in a new, and one suspects, totally panicked religious "equation." This means that without the fall of the Temple, there would have been no reason to invent the Passion narrative explaining the evil choices of the Temple authorities; and, of course, without the Passion narrative, there would be no Gospel of Mark and no Christianity as we know it. Coming to appreciate this play of happenstances strikes me as one of the more important rewards gained by working through the narrative logic of the text. Ironically, then, we need to understand how it was the very randomness of history that pushed an author to pen a story that so thoroughly insisted on God's role in shaping history.

Mark and the Cult of Narrative

Reading the Gospel of Mark for its narrative logic took off in the 1980s and 90s with the publication of good literary analyses from the likes of Joanna Dewey, Robert M. Fowler, Donald Juel, Werner Kelber, Elizabeth Struthers Malbon, Norman Perrin, Norman Petersen, David Rhoads, Robert Tannehill, and Mary Ann Tolbert.[6] With these publications we finally get coherent discussions of the narrative's dynamics, its reliance on iconic characters, its use of intercalated events, its construction of the audience's point of view, and so on.[7]

Thus, after some hundred and fifty years of research, New Testament studies finally came to terms with the basic fact that the Gospel of Mark is a well-wrought story and needs to be treated as such if it is to be understood. While it is encouraging to see this development, it is also the case that several key aspects of the narrative have remained little explored, and these aspects are none other than the themes that make up this book: establishing belief in the narrative as the sole criterion for salvation; fetishizing the totality of (old) tradition into a mediating figure who orchestrates the overcoming of the (old) law; and, creating an image of floating patriarchy that holds the whole arrangement together and promises to bring the believer to God, the alleged origin—and author—of this new version of tradition, and, as we'll see, something like the "deep" author of this very narrative.

Another shortcoming in recent scholarship on Mark is a lack of clarity regarding the role that narrative itself plays in offering the reader a new form of tradition. As I'll argue below, it's not just that the narrative explains that the totality of tradition is to be found in a new zone—in the person of Jesus, Son of God—but also that the narrative presents itself as *the means by which the reader can get at that totality of tradition* since belief in just this narrative about Jesus is identified as the means to salvation.[8] Hence, the text is a religious drama designed to effect its meaning in a processual manner that takes place in the reader as he or she sides with Jesus against (old) tradition and its supposedly evil patrons. Framed in this manner, the story isn't strictly about Jesus but rather about just this process of doubling tradition in a manner that 1) flatters the reader with the promise of gaining the totality of past tradition, while, also, 2) promising a new covenant in which the reader's own salvation will be granted based on his or her reception of this narrative and its demands.[9] In effect, then, the Gospel of Mark works somewhat like a chain letter: according to the narrative, what you do with this narrative determines your future. Likewise, in a rather sophisticated manner, the narrative works as something like a "pop-up" book since when the story is read as a historically reliable account, the characters seem to leave the page and come before the reader, perpetually eager and willing to give instructions regarding how the reader ought to relate to the narrative's salvific message.

With this kind self-reflexivity built into the narrative, Mark's gospel can't be read as a Greek biography, nor can it be read as a wisdom tale or an inspiring example of a good death, since the narrative is, in effect, something like a religious institution in Pierre Bourdieu's sense of the term.[10] (See the final section of chapter 1 for a discussion of Bourdieu's position.) Thus, the narrative seems designed to perform, in a minimalist way, all the tasks that any tradition must accomplish: it establishes a perfect origin for tradition (still basically the God of Israel, but now acting in a new way), shows how that tradition moved forward in time (via the Son who redelivered tradition into history), and then delivers that content of total tradition to the believer in a convincing manner that connects the dots of the past and offers up an ever-available conduit to tradition to those who would believe this set-up. In other words, while we need to take Mark as literature, we can't understand the text's structure and strategies without also identifying it as a very odd kind of literature, *a literature that takes itself to be the sole item necessary for delivering the totality of tradition to its audience.*[11] One way to become convinced that the narrative functions like this is to ask: Does the narrative offer any other means, besides faith in its story, as the ticket to salvation? The answer would seem to be "no," since no other institution, text, ritual, or authority is identified as a possible alternative. According to the narrative, the reader's destiny is determined, solely, by how he or she decides to relate to the narrative.

Presumably, the reason that we haven't recognized how the text is built around a newly invented "cult of the narrative" is that we have assumed that it must have been an already-functioning religious community that brought the text into existence. That is, it has been assumed that the text records a religiosity that was already in existence, when in fact a better reading of the text shows that it is designed to *generate* a new style of religiosity based on its own presence and supposedly divine origins.[12]

A Flair for Drama

Since Paul's letters do not operate with this degree of drama and self-reflexivity, this chapter will have to develop a reading strategy that is sensitive to Mark's ability to present "live" events to the reader, and, after a fashion, to bring the reader on stage to participate in key judgments about events and identities. In short, we will have to figure out how to make sense of the way that the narrative requires the reader to repeatedly look at figures in the story who, themselves, look at Jesus and offer assessments, with the effects of correct and incorrect assessments made abundantly clear to the reader. Given how the narrative is designed such that vision leapfrogs from characters inside the narrative to the reader, it is not surprising that the reader finds himself unavoidably implicated in the narrative, its development, and its apocalyptic threats and promises.[13] The key to building this kind of reading is to see that, with no direct dialogue between author and reader regarding the legitimacy of Jesus and his teachings on the new covenant, the author of Mark works to generate *the image* of a reliable history of other people's assessments of Jesus, his identity claims, and his teachings. This "history," then, does the author's work as he slyly disappears behind the characters he creates and has them do all the heavy lifting, especially in terms of establishing the validity of his narrative and the reliability of its various promises. In short, Mark's narrative operates as a complex seduction, with the trusting reader gaining confidence in the possibility that one can, in effect, "read" one's way to heaven by correctly reading about how others correctly read Jesus.

Obviously, a trusting reading of the narrative, in which one comes to believe in the salvific power of belief in the narrative, is only possible when the narrative is misrecognized by the reader as history and thus no narrative at all. If a reader begins to recognize the seductive nature of the gospel and, in particular, its wily efforts to put itself forward as the ticket to heaven, the entire presentation naturally loses its appeal.[14] Hence the narrative is doubly about itself since hiding its narrative nature is part of its narrative nature; or, rather, *teaching the reader to read the narrative in a mode of misrecognition* is a fundamental element in the plot. Hence, though the Gospel of Mark is literature—with characters, a plot, a climax, and so on—it is literature that manages to hide its literary nature behind a façade of supposed historicity, with just that literary sleight-of-hand absolutely key for turning the text into a virtual religious institution that encapsulates, represents, and delivers the essence of tradition.[15] Put another way, we can see that the narrative is designed so that one thinks that one is seeing what is on the other side of the narrative—historical events, unshaped by a crafty author—with these events then being taken as proof of how God's basic plan for Jesus's life and death worked itself out in history, as planned. Naturally, the text can effect this kind of seeing as long as it can maintain a misunderstanding of how these "visible" events were generated by the author, in narrative form, for the reader, with one of the specific authorial goals being to organize just such a blind reaction to all of this seeing.

Thinking more carefully about this, it would seem that the structure of the Gospel of Mark requires that there be three parallel narratives at work in the reader's assessment of the situation. First we have God's narrative in the sense that Jesus's life in human history—or more exactly, his death—was first "composed" as His plan, and it is one that Jesus speaks of three times (8:31, 9:30, 10:32). Second, there is the flow of supposedly historical events that make it seem like Jesus's life and death closely conform to God's original plan. Finally, there is the supposedly reliable account of those supposedly historical events, given from the point of view of the text's omniscient narrator, that makes it seem like this flow of events was never constructed by a worldly author. This awkward assemblage of layered narratives, then, is none other than the Gospel of Mark, which provides a stable vision in which one "sees" that real history and God's narrative for Jesus coincided in Jesus's life and death.

In some sense the most mysterious version of these three narratives isn't God's, but rather the author's, for the author's narrative is the one that holds the other two within itself and that in a basic sense remains invisible and unexplained, as is the case with most omniscient narrators. Reading through the various scenes in the text, one has to ask: Who could have known all this? Who could have had access to Jesus's clairvoyant thoughts as our author does? (2:8). Likewise, how could the author have been with the disciples, receiving the private instructions that Jesus gave them, while actually not being a disciple? And surely, given how the narrator presents the disciples as unreliable and dimwitted, the author would have had no interest in being associated with them. And, speaking simply in terms of narrative detail, the author can't be a disciple since he narrates the resurrection scene after having clarified that there were no disciples there, only the various women who had been following Jesus, all of whom then ran away, telling no one. Thus, with a little reflection, the omniscient narrator appears as an uncanny figure whose presence isn't usually noticed but who nevertheless has to be reckoned as a crucial player in the narrative since his voice is the voice that comes from seeing and understanding all. Perhaps we even ought to say that the knowledge, vision, and confidence of the omniscient narrator of the gospel rivals God's, an important point to keep in mind for determining the authorial irony required in the invention of Christian narratives.

Actually, there is a trickier theoretical problem to consider here, and it has to do with generating the image of a certain kind of objectivity in which it would seem that "the facts speak for themselves." More exactly, we have to speak of a kind of immaculate perception accorded to the narrator *and* the reader, both of whom now seem endowed with the ability to see these supposedly historical events free of narrative, free of the limits of normal human perception and distortion, free of desire and ideology, and so on. Giving birth, in the art of narration, to this kind of mimetic objectivity is particularly interesting when we remember that the Father-Son relationship that is the *raison d'être* of the narrative is, itself, a play of mimesis, with the Son appearing to be no more than a doubling of the Father, moved forward in time and out into public. Thus, the author's talent for "immaculately" reproducing the events of "real history" in narrative form becomes the basis for securing that other most important reproduction: Jesus's fathering by God. Putting all the pieces together: the theology of Mark, and Christianity in general, is a narrative claim about Jesus's origins in the Father—their mimetic relationship, that is—and this claim can only be "demonstrated" when it is constructed in a narrative that rides on the illusion of historical verisimilitude that, too, is based on a perfect mimesis. The crucial point is that our author seems to have understood this and composed a story in which the Father-Son mini-narrative appears to be objectively true and self-standing—no mere narrative—because it is demonstrated in the larger narrative of the whole gospel that also appears to be objectively true and self-standing. Thus, if our author had posed as anything less than God-like in his ability to perceive and narrate supposedly historical events involving God and his Son, then the entire operation would lose its appeal and collapse.

While objectifying the narrative's bid to appear objective compromises the seductive powers of the text, it is also true that this kind of close reading is essential for revealing the overall creativity of the text. Moreover, once we put this reading next to readings of Buddhist texts that reveal similar patterns, we will be in a good position to reflect anew on the nature of religion, and in particular this odd turn toward fetishizing tradition that seems to have been so powerful once it was initiated two thousand years ago.

Two Principal Themes

Since the publication of Martin Kähler's *The So-Called Historical Jesus and the Historic Biblical Christ* in 1896, it has been common to note that Mark's gospel is basically an account of Jesus's death preceded by a long introduction.[16] These two sections of the text are joined at 8:27–30, where the topics, tone, and geographic centering shift noticeably.[17] The minimalism of this two-part framing is a good way to begin a reading of the text, but to get at a more comprehensive reading, I suggest we follow two themes that together shape the entire narrative. I choose these themes because they cover the content of the narrative well, and because they reveal how the two parts of the text are equally crucial in coercing the reader's conversion to this new version of tradition.

The first theme circles around the claim that it is correct to believe that Jesus is the Son of God: this theme opens the narrative, and it is this theme that underwrites the two basic activities in the first half of the narrative: Jesus's healing of the sick, and his overcoming of older, established versions of tradition.[18] Hand in hand with establishing Jesus's divine identity is the important subtheme that seeks to prove that belief in Jesus's identity as Son-of-the-Father is the sole activity required of the audience.[19] Thus, in short, while eliciting belief in the Father-Son connection is fundamental to the gospel, that belief had to be supplemented by the next demand: believe that it is by believing in Jesus as Son of God that one will win salvation. This claim runs throughout the text and of course is believable precisely because it is made by the Son of God whose paternal "inheritance" presumably makes him a legally reliable source for reinventing the rules for fulfilling tradition's demands and winning salvation.

The second major theme revolves around Jesus's death which, as mentioned, is presented as part of a divinely orchestrated plot. The reality of this pre-established narrative is supposedly known by Jesus, and he announces it three times to his disciples, while also citing scripture that suggests that all the visible events in the story are happening in accord with divine intentions. But more than simply playing out a divinely wrought script of sorts, Jesus's death is designed as a sacrifice that activates the salvific power of belief in that divine sonship.[20] So, as with Paul's theology, the new law needs to be sanctified with a blood offering, one that is also made from the top of the symbolic order downward, and from the universal to the particular. Thus in the "Last Supper," supposedly organized at the beginning of the Passover festivities "when the Passover lamb is sacrificed" (14:12), Jesus says to his gathered disciples, "This is my blood of the covenant, which is poured out for many" (14:24), thereby leaving little doubt that his death has been shaped in the narrative to have covenant-forming functions.[21]

The importance of placing Jesus's death on Passover has been little appreciated in New Testament studies, which, by and large, assumes that this is simply what happened in history, an assumption that, of course, requires submitting to the most basic seduction of the text: it's not a craftily designed narrative, but simply a telling of historical facts. A better way to read this crucial detail in Mark is to see that it is an excellent example of working elements and aspects of (old) tradition into a narrative of pseudohistorical events, events that appear to have the power to redesign tradition precisely because they involve elements of (old) tradition. Thus, just as Jesus's actual execution was made into a divine sacrifice in Paul's writing, this sacrificial motif is further enhanced in Mark by placing Jesus's death on Passover, the most significant covenant-building ritual in (old) tradition.[22]

Bart Ehrman and other well-respected New Testament scholars are willing to admit that in the Gospel of John, Jesus's death was likely shifted up a day to make it coincide with the slaughter of the paschal lambs.[23] Thus, in a limited way they are prepared to admit that a gospel writer likely shaped the presentation of a historical event in order that it might conform, in a more meaningful manner, with a traditionally established ritual sequence. In short, they are allowing that symbolism is trumping historicity in this small detail in John's narrative. My position is that this suspicion regarding John's handiwork needs to be expanded such that the entire combination of Jesus's death and Passover be seen as an artistic invention—the invention of the author of Mark, to be exact. If this is true, then the author of John is simply refining a literary strategy that he recognized in Mark's gospel.[24]

In Mark's account of the Last Supper, Jesus offers symbolic versions of his body and blood—the bread and wine—as part of the Passover meal, and thus it would seem that this symbolic death is standing in for the paschal lamb that, normally, would have been the key blood offering clinching the Passover promise of atonement. Looked at this way, in Mark, Jesus dies twice—first, symbolically, to provide the Passover meal: "Take; this is my body. . . . This is my blood of the covenant which is poured out for many" (14:22–24). Then, on the next day, when he is killed on the cross, his blood isn't mentioned in the narrative since his blood had been, as it were, already given. In short, Mark juxtaposed Jesus's symbolic death with his actual death in order to lock in a huge theological claim: Jesus's death, besides being an evil murder, was also a divine Passover sacrifice—that moment when a new covenant was offered to humanity, one in which the blood of God's only Son was offered as a traditional-looking, if upside-down, offering of atonement on the occasion on which (old) tradition required that just such an act of atonement be performed. The near simultaneity of the two deaths consequently functions as an unannounced metaphor in which all that Passover traditionally stood for is gently pushed onto the historical death of Jesus.

John's account follows the same logic but improves on the arrangement by making Jesus's execution coincide more exactly with the Passover sacrifice and by making the linkage between Jesus and the paschal lamb more obvious. No surprise then that we find that detail in John that clarifies that Jesus's legs weren't broken during the crucifixion in order that his body would conform to Passover regulations regarding a suitable offering (Exodus 12:46), with just that line from Exodus cited in the narrative—John 19:26. Looked at that way, we have a better reason for explaining why John doesn't need to provide "Eucharist" language in his account of the Last Supper (John 13:1ff) since he has collapsed the two nearly simultaneous "deaths" in Mark into one event, "on the day of Preparation for the Passover" (John 19:14), when paschal lambs were traditionally slaughtered. In short, John, apparently unsatisfied with Mark's more metaphoric use of Jesus's blood (and death), moved Jesus's execution up one day so that, in his history, Jesus's actual blood from the crucifixion would be the blood of the new covenant.[25] Thus, John gets a whole lot closer to claiming that Jesus *is* a paschal lamb, whereas for Mark, Jesus was to be read as lamb-like in a vaguer way. Standing back from the two narratives, it hardly makes sense to argue which one is to be trusted as more historically accurate since to do so is to miss the big picture in which it is clear that both scenes have been sculpted to have the same narrative effect of making Jesus's execution appear as a Passover sacrifice of atonement.[26]

Summed up, it isn't just that Jesus must die for the new version of tradition to be effective, nor is it enough that (old) tradition be responsible for this death, but rather that Jesus must die *in the midst of the most sacred ritual of (old) tradition.* Thus, Mark's author not only enlists the representatives of the (old) law to act out the details of his narrative—serving as they do as the villainous figures of (old) tradition—he also takes up their ritual system and sends Jesus through it in a manner that seems to benefit from its assumed ritual power, even as that very act of inserting Jesus in the system promises to destroy that entire ritual mechanism and its attendants. Jesus's death, then, is the effect of the (old) tradition on several levels: he dies due to (old) tradition's incorrect evaluation of his identity, and he dies in accord with (old) tradition's ritual mechanism for making death into a covenant—the Passover blood sacrifice—and he dies in such a way that explains why (old) tradition had to be destroyed later in history, in the Jewish-Roman War.

An End Run

Next to these two major themes, we need to keep track of another crucial subtheme: the effort to disenfranchise the direct disciples of Jesus, a trope that I introduced in the previous chapter. Below I will argue that the failure of the disciples to fully recognize Jesus's divinity—a failure that they share with the Jewish hierarchy which was supposedly punished so terribly for just this crime—has important implications for the reader's reaction to the narrative, but for now we ought to see that Mark's narrative lodges itself in history in a manner that effectively says: "Don't worry about what Jesus might have said to the disciples, they were completely dim and hopeless. Instead just accept this narrative that jointly explains: 1) why the Jewish tradition *and* the proto-Christians received the wrath of God; and, 2) how you can join 'the elect' and avoid just this fate."[27]

Once one sees how the narrative works to set itself up as a completely independent conduit to Jesus and the Father, one that does an end run around both traditional Judaism and the early followers of Jesus, we get a sense for why the text refuses to associate itself with a specific holy place, a living lineage descending from Jesus, a proto-Christian community, or even a clear set of ethics, and why, in the end, it relies simply on itself and its relationship with the reader in order to deliver tradition. Likewise, this reading makes sense of the supposed secret nature of Jesus's teaching and the explicit claim that Jesus taught in confounding ways, since both these tropes generate the image of an esoteric reality behind the publicly perceived events, a secret reality that the text obviously lays claim to and reveals to the reader. In effect, the narrative works up a conspiracy theory in which the reader learns not just the inside story about Jesus but also why so few on the outside got it right.[28]

In sum, Mark's narrative is designed to "consume" tradition in all the forms—Jewish and proto-Christian—in which it had been generated. After reading Mark, one has no other task but to secure one's relationship to the narrative in such a manner that this very narrative turns into a reliable "vision" of the ultimate truth-father at work in history: Jesus, as Son of God, lives out the narrative of sacrifice that his Father had imposed on him, and along the way he explains that believing this narrative of sacrifice is all that it takes to be saved.[29] To securely link oneself to God's gospel— and thereby fulfill the law that the text commands—one must take up this narrative with such enthusiasm that its narrative nature evaporates into the conviction that paternal essences are to be found on either side of the narrative: in its origination in the Father, and in its ability in the near future to take one to the Father. Of course, just such a reading gesture is another act of fetishization, since the sprawling details of the narrative are boiled down to a singular faith in a cosmic form of paternity that is available in and through the narrative—an ultimate paternity that will supposedly solve all problems of meaning, identity, suffering, tradition, history, and being.

Why this peculiar form of floating patriarchy appeared and then seduced billions of people is, arguably, one of the key questions that hasn't been properly asked in Christian studies. It is also the question that promises to tell us some rather important things about who we are as linguistic creatures who apparently crave, or can be induced to crave—and that difference is important—just such a connection to a paternal transcendental Something that will supposedly put an end to our days of wallowing around in language, time, interpretation, and history.

The First Theme: Establishing Jesus as the Son of God

Without clarifying exactly what Jesus's divine identity might mean, or how it came about, the author of Mark begins his account with several startling mini-narratives designed to prove that Jesus was the Son of God. Before presenting these supposed historical encounters that confirm this identity, the omniscient narrator identifies Jesus, saying: "The beginning of the good news of Jesus Christ, the Son of God" (1:1). This opening claim is then followed by Jesus's baptism by John the Baptist, a supporting ritual moment that also legitimizes Jesus for the reader and all the more so when John explicitly identifies Jesus as the one who will henceforth baptize with the Holy Spirit. In identifying their respective powers in this way, the author also makes clear that John understands his own version of baptism as but a prelude to the real one, the one of Spirit. Consummating this initial sequence of recognition, the narrator recounts how this preliminary, water-based form of baptism was, nonetheless, effective since the baptism moment occasions a miracle in which just as Jesus "was coming out of the water, he saw the heavens torn apart and the Spirit descending like a dove on him. And a voice came from heaven, 'You are my Son, the Beloved; with you I am well pleased'" (1:10–11).

In sum, the author decided to open the gospel with these supposedly real voices testifying to the fact that Jesus is the Son of God. These voices come from: 1) the omniscient narrator who proclaims Jesus's divine sonship at the outset, and then cites a passage from Isaiah to support the claim, thereby making it appear that (old) tradition stands in support for this new claim about the locale of perfect tradition; 2) John the Baptist, who ratifies Jesus's identity—and here again a version of (old) tradition is made to endorse the new version, though in this case "old tradition" refers to John's popular baptist movement and not traditional Judaism and its sacred literature; and, finally, 3) when John baptizes Jesus, God adds his endorsement with his statement—"You are my Son." This kinship claim is then made visible with a rending of the heavens, which are "torn apart," presumably in a gesture reflecting the removal of the barriers that would separate a heavenly father and an earthly son, with the descending spirit-dove making that connection all the more visible. Interestingly, this public statement from heaven and the vision that supports it aren't registered by the audience inside the narrative—John certainly isn't shown reacting—suggesting again that these events are for the reader's benefit. In short, with these straightforward claims functioning as a foundation, the rest of the narrative will work to convince the reader/listener of the reality of this divine sonship and what the presence of God's Son in history implies for accessing a new and perfect form of tradition.

But how, really, should we think of this divine sonship? The key, I would suggest, is to understand sonship—in any situation—as a double. The son, as he legally inherits all or some of his father's identity and patrimony, represents a moment of formal duplication in which the son, identified as the one who is different and further along in time, is understood to be the same, in some basic sense, as the paternal figure that is posited as his origin. Thus, legal sonship functions to ward off the corrosive nature of time, difference, and death since the son is to be, on the plane of things legal, no different than the father in a way that overcomes the impermanence of Being. Put this way, it shouldn't be surprising that sonship would figure as such an important trope in organizing the fetishization of tradition since, in effect, the two gestures function in very parallel ways: they both claim that the essence of a predecessor is "here," en toto, in a legally defendable manner, even though this newly celebrated locale is so different and so distant from that origin.[30]

As we will see, reading Mark well depends on seeing how these two basic tropes of duplication work together: tradition is legally doubled in the figure of the Son who, by being the double of the Father, can claim that he and his new dispensation of tradition are both *of* the Father and thus are completely legitimate in their claim to surpass and replace (old) tradition. What is a bit disorienting, though, is that the new law that the Son offers in the Gospel of Mark (as we'll see below) is none other than the promise that accepting this claim regarding his divine sonship represents the fulfillment of new tradition. Put this way, we can see that the arrangement basically calls for the public to accept not just the reality of the private Father-Son transmission, but also to accept the Son's claim that accepting the reality of just that private transmission will bring the public to the Father and thereby fulfill tradition's deepest promise. In short, not only do we have here that standard kernel of belief in belief, but we also have something like the democratization of patriarchy insofar as the Son of God is offering everyone a facsimile of divine sonship provided that they in turn grant Jesus his divine sonship and the legal right to make divine sonship publicly available to those who "correctly" recognize his own divine sonship. A similar bargain was, as noted in the previous chapter, central to Paul's construction of "sons of God."

The Public Nature of Personal Identity

To make sense of this bargain that links acceptance of Jesus's divine paternity with winning access to a kind of public sonship to God, we need to keep in view the fact that normal sonship, though supposedly reflecting a private father-son transmission, is itself only "effected" via public recognition. Thus, in general, for patriarchal father-son reproduction to occur, the public must: 1) formally recognize this particular relationship between the two figures; and 2) uphold a general mythology that explains that such father-son transmission is in fact *not socially constructed*. In this paradoxical situation, the father-son connection—which is otherwise invisible since the son comes from the mother and since the father's role in the matter was always disputable before DNA testing—is jointly recognized by the public who agree to impute to this boy the essence of the father while also disavowing that his being and identity were made, in no small part, by his mother, in conjunction with just this social process of identity-recognition.

Thus, even in the most basic forms of paternity, the essence of the father arrives, ironically, through external public assent in the form of the generic statement: "Yes, we agree that that boy there is yours and that what you have—your name, your rights, your property—is to be his when you will it to be so. We also agree with you that identity arrives from the father and not the mother, and thus your ancestors are his ancestors, and his descendants are your descendants."[31] Of course, the alienated and dialectical form of this recognition—the public now seems elemental in establishing family identity—is obscured with a rhetoric of essences such as the standard claims that the son is the "flesh and blood" of the father, the "seed" of the father, or a "chip off the ol' block," and so on. In sum, patriarchy is itself basically structured as a fetish: the son is supposedly the totality of the father and his lineage, while all the other nonpaternal elements that went into him are to be disavowed so that he can simply be the son of his father.[32]

On one level, then, the basic structure of the Gospel of Mark appears to be an extended dramatization of this essential paternal problem: getting the public to acknowledge a son. Why it turned out that one can basically make a new form of tradition out of a narrative dedicated to proving the reality of a final and essentially ever-present form of patriarchy is a rich and fascinating problem, one that will, again, tell us much about who we are as linguistic, social animals, hoping to solidly establish the reified Self and secure its final reunion with the identity-granting Father.

Society at Large

With Jesus's divine sonship attested to by four supposedly reliable sources—the narrator, the passage from Isaiah, John the Baptist, and God's voice from heaven—the narrative turns to report how this new form of divine sonship was assessed by other less easily convinced figures in history. Since moderns read this narrative with the assumption that the author is simply remembering real events and presenting them in a sensible way to the reader, they fail to see that the series of events that follow this opening scene are provided to support just those introductory statements and are presented solely for the reader's benefit. Consequently, these encounters—with representatives of (old) tradition, the insane, the possessed, the ill, Moses and Elijah, the disciples, Pontius Pilate, and the Roman centurion—are best defined by the author's concern that his primary claim regarding Jesus's sonship be accepted by his reading/listening audience. Hence, besides supporting my above comments regarding the logic of socially produced sonship, these repeating encounters within the narrative are miniature versions of the reader's own encounter with the narrative, a narrative that is of course fundamentally about installing this divine sonship in the reader's imagination in such a way that it no longer appears socially or symbolically constructed—that is, to install this sonship in the reader's imagination in such a way that it no longer seems to have been installed, for it is only in that way that it can appear divine and unconstructed.[33]

Assuming this play of levels where one is essentially being taught to read a narrative of sonship by "seeing" how others *inside the narrative* have conducted parallel readings of their own needn't be taken to be a postmodern perspective. In fact, it is quite obvious that our author is very comfortable with this gesture of condensing his narrative and representing it to figures *within his narrative*. Thus, for instance, not only is Jesus thrice made to articulate the nature of the narrative that he is in—destined, as he is, by the Father to a painful death at the hands of (old) tradition—but the author also gives as one of Jesus's fuller teaching moments the Parable of the Tenants (12:1), which is a near perfect condensation of the Gospel of Mark, with the father and owner of the vineyard sending different representatives to a recalcitrant group of renters who resist his entreaties until he decides to send his son to deliver his message, resulting in the son's death and the father's destruction of the group.[34] In sum, it is quite clear that Mark is a text designed to represent itself within itself to several kinds of internal audiences, and this leaves little doubt that this talent is also being applied in representing the entire text to its reading/listening audience.

Ask Anyone

In these repeating encounters between Jesus and the yet-to-be-convinced public *inside the narrative*, several interlocking objectives are advanced. First, these encounters generate a vast system of triangulation in which spokespersons from various walks of life are brought on stage to confirm the author's fundamental claim that Jesus is the Son of God. In a certain sense this is a bit humorous since, by implication, God's declaration of Jesus's sonship at the outset ends up appearing to be of minor value since it is obviously in need of this troupe of decidedly mundane witnesses. Thus, for reasons that presumably have to do with the author's estimation of who would appear more believable to the reader, the narrative spends its time canvassing a series of rather ordinary, and in some cases unsavory, witnesses. Presumably it is their apparent disinterest in things religious and political that makes them reliable witnesses in a narrative about things religious and political.

In these encounters a standard sequence plays out. An unsuspecting somebody has an interaction with Jesus and concludes instantaneously, and with no argument, that he really is the Son of God. This moment of instant recognition comes in some cases after Jesus magically heals the person—physically or mentally—and in some cases comes with the forgiveness of sins. Within the narrative, each one of these moments represents how Jesus's sonship is naturally "found" by the Other, as the Other effortlessly and instantaneously recognizes that divine sonship. The author's reliance on this trope is obvious, but it is important to see that this trope of sudden recognition is set against a backdrop of: 1) the disciples' reluctant and partial recognition of Jesus's identity; and 2) the hostile and total resistance to such recognition by the representatives of (old) tradition. Of course, what we have to keep in mind is that the entire arrangement is proposed to the reader whose reaction to the claim of Jesus's divine sonship is what the text is really trying to manage.

The first real narrative action described after Jesus has gathered together his disciples (1:16) and sets out into the social world involves a healing encounter in which the standard exchange is enacted: Jesus effortlessly controls the situation, he heals the person, and the healed person declares his divine identity. In this case, the unclean spirit who has just submitted to him cries out, "What have you to do with us, Jesus of Nazareth? Have you come to destroy us? I know who you are, the Holy One of God" (1:24). Jesus, then, in another gesture that he will repeat in other situations, immediately closes out the encounter by commanding the spirit to silence.

To read this encounter of healing and recognition well requires noting that it is set within the context of public amazement over Jesus's dominance of (old) tradition. Thus, after the unclean spirit has been exorcised, those in attendance—presumably it is the disciples—"were all amazed, and they kept on asking one another, "What is this? A new teaching—with authority! He commands even the unclean spirits, and they obey him" (1:27).

In this public assessment of the healing event, Jesus's dominance over the unclean spirit is blended with his domination over (old) tradition since he supposedly has this new teaching that is taken to be so impressively authoritative.[35] Without showing how it was that Jesus's *teachings* healed the man—something that will never be said—we, in the audience, are invited to assume that the power behind the new teaching was also the power behind the healing, and this power has been squarely recognized by the one healed, who knew not only Jesus's earthly identity as "Jesus of Nazareth" but also his heavenly identity as "the Holy One of God"—and, presumably, if he got the earthly one right, he got the other one right, too. That is, as the man correctly identified Jesus, he found himself healed, with the visibility of the healing proving to the reader the correctness of his assessment of Jesus's identity.

There is an interesting twist here: Jesus's divine identity is only powerful and effective at solving a problem when it is recognized as such, a fact that wouldn't make much sense unless we locate the entire narrative within the scope of the problematic dialectics inherent in establishing any kind of sonship, as discussed above. That is, if sonship wasn't structured in this circuitous and social manner, presumably the narrative could simply have had Jesus, as God's Son, go around magically effecting whatever changes he wanted, and, in particular, making people believe in his divine sonship. But, in fact, the text works in the opposite manner with Jesus essentially wandering around looking for those who would have faith in his divine sonship, a fact that makes Jesus's problem of legitimacy no different from the narrative's problem of legitimacy. Or, more exactly, Jesus, as supposed Son-of-the-Father, is a story hoping to be accepted as naturally true and definitely not invented in language.[36] In short, our author seems to be fully aware of the problems involved in establishing sonship and has organized a seduction for the reader in which the reader becomes increasingly interested in granting Jesus his divine sonship since the narrative promises that that very gesture of recognition insures that all sorts of healings, both mundane and otherworldly, will suddenly be available.[37] In effect, then, the narrative has invented a figure inside itself who needs exactly what the narrative needs—to be recognized as divine issue—and the narrative arranges for a series of events where Jesus gets recognition in just the right doses that *ought* to make the reader grant Jesus, and his supporting narrative, suitable recognition. Lurking here, then, is that most interesting play between sonship and narrative since *our author uses narrative to prove Jesus's sonship and then uses that sonship to guarantee the narrative's validity.*

Also not to be missed in this initial encounter is the disciples' *partial* understanding of what is going on. They consider his teaching to be inexplicably impressive, and they see that he has conquered the unclean spirit, and yet they don't register what the unclean spirit so explicitly said: "I know who you are, the Holy One of God." This perfectly clear articulation, which Jesus doesn't deny or refute—he simply silences the spirit *after* his identity has been announced—lingers on stage as the piece of the puzzle that needs to be set in the right place for all the pieces of the scene to make sense. Now the reader, of course, has all the needed information and can plug in this piece of information from the testimony of the healed man to solve the on-stage doubt and befuddlement generated by the disciples' partial comprehension. In effect, it would seem that the author has shaped this encounter so that the reader feels impelled to finalize the reading of the scene, and of course, winning just this kind of participation in this set-piece lines up with the narrative's basic agenda of winning the reader's assent for the claim of Jesus's divine sonship. In short, even in Mark's first chapter, the reader is being led into actively drawing conclusions about Jesus's divine sonship based on observing partial and fully correct readings of Jesus's identity and wishing that the partial readings would turn into the full readings—a dynamic that will continue to the end of the text.

Finally, we need to remember that this healing scene is actually the second part of a sequence that had been set up in the previous passage in which Jesus had been teaching at a synagogue where those in the audience "were astounded at his teaching, for he taught them as one having authority, and not as the scribes" (1:22). It is in leaving the synagogue that the healing takes place, and it is after observing this healing that the disciples *again* comment on the awesome quality of Jesus's teaching, a teaching which has, for them, some as yet unexplained authority behind it. Thus in sandwich form, there are two moments of public recognition of Jesus's power over (old) tradition—his awesome teaching—placed around this healing moment, a moment when the "deep background" reason for that mastery over (old) tradition is revealed by the healed man. Thus, *the reader* concludes, "Oh, right, he's the Son of God, so this dominance over the scribes and over unclean spirits and his ability to teach with inexplicable authority *in the synagogue* make total sense because, evidently, he is/has the final version of tradition."[38]

That these individual moments of healing and recognition-of-identity repeat so often in the rest of Mark suggests that the narrative is essentially functioning to *stockpile* these proof-texts to more solidly establish Jesus's identity in the eyes of the reader who, reading over the shoulders of the bumbling disciples, sees and hears enough to draw the conclusion that the disciples never really get a grip on. In short, what is taken to be the long introduction in the narrative—up to 8:27—works at "proving" what the introduction claimed—Jesus is the Son of God—by showing over and over how this claim was recognized in "real history," in a manner much more convincing than simple claims by an omniscient narrator, even when he is wielding that "voice from Heaven."[39] And, as Jesus's divine identity gains solidity, it will be brought into closer contact with (old) tradition until the apocalyptic conclusion of the narrative in which all the "debates" about correct and incorrect readings of Jesus are finalized.

Thus, though the metaphor of seed and soil is given (4:3ff) by Jesus to describe reception of the gospel—and is clearly aimed at describing and shaping the reader's reaction to the narrative—these moments of sudden and total recognition by figures *inside the text* appear like sparks that leap from Jesus to land on these various figures, setting them ablaze with this new and total knowledge of his divine identity. The seemingly simple nature of this spark that jumps between Jesus and his interlocutors, however, turns out to be a bit complicated since what successfully jumps from Jesus to the healed person is really a double of the spark that jumps from God the Father to Jesus the Son. That is, what is transmitted in this moment-of-recognition is recognition of the moment-of-transmission between divine Father and Son. Thus, if we label as "B" the interaction between Jesus and the healed, and then label the interaction between God the Father and Jesus the Son "A," then it is clear that we are to believe that B happened only because A happened, and it is for this reason that we keep hearing about how B happened, all in order that we will gain confidence in A. In a certain sense, while the narrative is all about proving A, it can only work with the B elements, and thus the narrator gives us scene after scene of B. And, in an equally paradoxical manner, the author of the narrative seems to believe that gradual, plant-like, growth of confidence in Jesus's identity can only be produced with a series of these sudden spark-like moments.

Did You See What I Saw?

Understanding this literary set-up has another complication to it since the spark that jumps from Jesus to the healed person is being watched by three different types of observers: (old) tradition, the disciples, and the reader who sees all this, including the very seeing performed by the various figures on stage. Put schematically, the situation looks like this:

$$\text{(Old) tradition} \rightarrow \text{the healed} \leftarrow \text{the disciples//the reader}$$
$$||$$
$$\text{Jesus as Son of God}$$

In this complex figure, not only do the members of (old) tradition lack the spark of recognition in their own assessments, they also remain unconvinced even as they see the spark of recognition visibly manifest in those whom were healed; thus, they are doubly immune to the Jesus spark. The disciples, for their part, have a very ambivalent reaction: they don't receive the spark directly—and below I will explore why it is crucial that the narrative never allows that they be directly healed or touched by the Jesus spark—but they begin to gain some confidence in what they are seeing as they watch the spark jump to the out-group others—the sick, the insane, the handicapped, and so on. Despite this at-a-distance quality that characterizes the disciples' understanding, it is also important to note that the narrative provides for their *slow* seduction into faith in Jesus's divine sonship. Thus they are shown witnessing such scenes roughly ten times before the narrative has them directly confront Jesus about his divine sonship in chapter 8, in a moment that represents the climax of the introduction.

In sum, the author has arranged for three levels of conversion to work in concert: 1) the perfect and instantaneous conversion of the ill; 2) the slow and partial conversion of the disciples (they have after all decided to follow Jesus, even if they don't manifest the sudden and unequivocal conversions that the ill provide); and 3) the reader whose conversion remains to be produced by observing all these other conversions. Thus, again designating A for the normally invisible Father-Son link and B for the recognition of A by various invalids, then we obviously need category C to identify the observing reader for whom these A and B sequences are demonstrated.

$$\text{Father} \rightarrow \text{Son} \rightarrow \text{Healed-person} \; || \; \text{Reader-who-believes A because of "seeing" B}$$
$$\quad\;\; \text{A} \qquad\qquad \text{B} \qquad\qquad\qquad \text{C}$$

Hence the narrative keeps driving A into B, hoping to thereby drive A into C. And, naturally, when C really "gets" A, B will become unimportant and even hard to recognize as the way that A got into C. Thus, the narrative that constructs this motion of A into B and then into C will become increasingly difficult to recognize once it has done its work. Maybe we even ought to say that as the reader comes to believe A, all those healing events that constitute B might begin to appear somewhat dubious, invoking not just a time and a world when A wasn't believed, but also representing something like a trail of crumbs along the path marking how B turned into A when, in the eyes of C, A should have never needed this gradual "insemination." Thus, and leaning a bit harder on this aspect of the narrative, I wonder if it might not be the case that all these B events also appear, after one's conversion to the narrative, as disturbing and distracting nuggets that suggest that the perfect sonship of Jesus is actually fathered by social recognition, generated first within the narrative and then transferred to the reader in a metastatic process of recognition organized by someone—the author!—who understood what it takes to produce divine sons. At any event, just as one has no patience for the recipe after learning how to cook the dish, it is hard to see how a reader, once convinced of Jesus's divine sonship, would be that interested in this aspect of the narrative.

Halfhearted Disciples

Noting how these categories of observers function in the set pieces demonstrating Jesus's divine sonship gives us a clue about a puzzling problem. Why is it that those who are healed in a moment of sudden and unmediated recognition of Jesus's identity don't join the group of disciples? Logically, this would be an expected result since, after all, who would want to leave the presence of a living deity once recognized as such? And, yet, even when they don't specifically leave the scene after their interaction with Jesus, as most do, these healed figures are never let into the group of disciples.[40] That is, oddly, the group of disciples is never strengthened by the addition of members who, again logically, would have every reason to be in this group. One might first think that the author wants to show the healed person heading off to alert others to the possibility of being healed, and in some cases something like that is suggested. However, I think the better explanation of this conundrum involves noting that the narrative has positioned the disciples to be structurally most like the reader—observing the healing and yet still at a distance from that moment of perfect sparking. Thus, the disciples, as a category, must remain defined as semi-converted: they "saw" everything, just as the reader did, but they, again like the reader, have to take it all on faith without a direct "zapping" from Jesus. Naturally, then, if the category of disciples accepted into its midst those healed figures who no longer have a faith problem, having been directly "zapped," the parallel between reader and the disciples would break down. For this parallel to hold, the disciples have to remain suspicious readers lacking exactly what those who were so perfectly healed have—unmediated and unimpeachable knowledge of Jesus's divine sonship.

Equally important, and Markan studies has partially admitted this, it seems clear that within this parallel, the author has given the reader the upper hand vis-à-vis the disciples. Thus, as we saw above in the example of the first healing encounter, the reader seemed placed to finish what the disciples only started: full acceptance of Jesus as divine Son and, as such, the legally justified owner of tradition. What this means is that though the reader is poised to read "through the disciples," this reading only fully actualizes itself when the disciples are disparaged and "jumped over," as the reader moves into a more intimate appreciation of Jesus, one full of confidence in his divine identity. Given this enticing dynamic, if the category of disciples included those healed directly by Jesus, then there would be no way for this trope of overcoming-the-disciples to play out since the disciples would now include those whose conviction in Jesus's sonship was supreme, unsurpassable, and unavailable to the reader. In short, there is a "feel-good" ploy tucked in here: the reader is invited to think that he can do what the disciples never quite accomplished.

This trope in which a faithful reading of the text involves jumping over the disciples to secure a better relationship with Jesus requires that we recognize another important parallel in the text: "jumping over the disciples" rhymes with the more basic trope of jumping over (old) tradition. In both cases, the disciples and the representatives of (old) tradition have received sufficient information to convert, and yet they have failed, and now it is up to the reader to make sure that the message "gets through," or rather, that the Jesus spark really lands somewhere and generates fire. That is, it is by watching repeating instances of the spark's failure to ignite that the reader is most inspired to be the dry kindling for the Jesus spark. Given their parallel failures to receive the "spark," it is no surprise then that the author explicitly accuses (old) tradition and the disciples of the same crime of having hardened their hearts in their reluctance to accept Jesus as Christ (6:52; 8:17).

When we put these pieces of narrative evidence together we see a coherent logic at work in the management of the reader's reaction, and likewise see coherence in otherwise inexplicable details in the text. Moreover, by seeing how the author has fired up the reader's desire for conversion by dramatizing failed conversion inside the narrative, we can better understand the ongoing Christian obsession with getting the Jews to convert to Christ since, at least in terms of Mark's narrative, one becomes Christian through submitting to a narrative-ploy that involves, among other things, the specific hope that the reluctant Jewish disciples on stage convert to Jesus as Christ. Except for the Syrophoenician woman, Pilate, and the Roman centurion, everyone on stage is presumably Jewish, and thus the narrative works around building the reader's own conversion out of the wish that the partial conversion of the Jews in the text be finalized.

Innocence in Denial

Jesus's reaction to the various public announcements of his divine identity warrants special attention. After each of these encounters that results in someone recognizing his divine identity, Jesus commands the person not to announce this understanding to others, but of course Jesus doesn't deny the identification. Thus *the reader* is left with the specific sense that a truth has been recognized—by the person and by Jesus—and that though this truth originally was not intended to be shared with the public, it has nonetheless slipped out into plain view. Obviously, then, even though Jesus commands the various persons he has directly touched not to share this knowledge with others *in the narrative*, the sharing has already been effected *for the reader*. To get at what I take to be the logic of this construction, and its rhetorical power, we ought to see that the reader is given the sense that this crucial world-shaking truth is not coming at him as a seduction, since after all, Jesus apparently didn't want anyone—reader included—to know about this. That is, each time Jesus calls for a moratorium on announcing his identity, it is as though we have a loud on-stage whisper which announces to the reading audience the truth of exactly what is to be kept quasi-secret in the drama.

Once we read this arrangement as a narrative technique, we can also see that just this supposed reluctance to propagate his divine identity will likely produce a desire in the reader who thinks, "Whaaaat? This was known at the time and not widely and openly proclaimed?" Likewise, repeatedly showing Jesus's lack of desire to convince the public produces a kind of innocence in the text, since the reader has the impression that there never was any intention to prove just this point about Jesus's identity. In short, dramatizing *Jesus's lack of desire* to publicize his identity works very handily with the author's basic goal of publicizing this identity, just as Jesus's dramatized reluctance to draw the public into this process of verifying his identity helps to solidify his identity as supposedly independent of social recognition.

Living outside the Law

Next to these numerous encounters which reveal Jesus's identity and transcendental powers to heal and to forgive sins once that identity is recognized, there is a category of scenes in which Jesus is shown overcoming what we could refer to as "natural law," for lack of a better term. Thus by showing Jesus stilling a storm (4:35), walking on water (6:47), and twice magically multiplying bread and fish (6:30ff and 8:1ff), the author again makes clear that Jesus isn't a mundane figure, and consequently, the realities of gravity, math, and weather don't apply to him.[41] Implicit here is the argument that, since for Jesus even the laws of life—like gravity and conservation of matter—are optional, we ought to accept that he has a similar right and power to rewrite cultural law as he sees fit. Once again the logic of this rhetoric is developed from doubles, with the visible overcoming of "natural law" setting up expectations for the invisible overcoming of cultural law—traditional Judaism, that is. Actually, in the first occurrence of such an encounter with "natural law," the disciples' reaction mirrors exactly their reaction to his first healing encounter since they say after Jesus calms the storm, "Who then is this, that even the wind and the sea obey him?" (4:41). Thus, there is an obvious parallel in view in which observers inside the narrative react to Jesus's power to heal in just the same manner that they respond to his power to control "nature," and in both cases it is a matter of asking the question: "Who is this?" Of course for the reader this question has been technically answered from the beginning of the narrative, and thus he or she is reading, watching others slowly learn to read Jesus correctly, a process that presumably is very enticing since it comforts the reader in the dual sense of thinking he or she knows more than those on stage and, second, thinking that the language given at the outset is now being confirmed over and over.

A Motherless Child

It might at first appear as another minor point in Mark, but it is worth pointing out that the mini-narratives that work to position Jesus beyond natural law are matched by two scenes in which his identity is located beyond the scope of his natal family. Thus, although Mark has no mention of Jesus's immaculate conception, in both these scenes there is a clear effort to break Jesus's connection with his birth mother and his "biological" family. In the first scene Jesus's mother and his brothers come to visit him and, standing outside of the dwelling where he is, ask to see him, but he refuses. Then, speaking to non-family members grouped around him in the house, Jesus declares, "Here are my mother and my brothers! Whoever does the will of God is my brother and mother" (3:34).[42] The implication in this encounter isn't simply that Jesus is no longer owned by his natal family, but also that his now unhinged identity provides the basis for a new family constituted by submission to God's will—the final father around whom "family members" are to be ultimately grouped. Or put in terms of a dialectic of overcoming, as Jesus "dies" to his biological identity and family, he also gives birth to a new kind of family born of the law in which submission to the law of the Father—as wielded by the Son—generates identity, kin, and inclusion.

A similar point is made, but in reverse, in the scene depicting Jesus's return to Nazareth. Here his identity is demonstrated as per the usual—he presents amazing teachings at the synagogue—but those who know his mundane identity and continue to locate him in his natal family refuse to accept his divine identity, even as they admit to having seen signs of just that otherworldly power. Thus they take offense and say, "Where did this man get all this? What is this wisdom that has been given to him? What deeds of power are being done by his hands? Is not this the carpenter, the son of Mary and brother of James and Jose and Judas and Simon, and are not his sisters here with us?" (6:2–3). Apparently taking this objection seriously, Jesus explains: "Prophets are not without honor, except in their hometown, and among their own kin, and in their own house" (6:4). The point of the exchange seems to be that as long as "readers" inside the narrative keep Jesus attached to his local, biological identity, he can in no way serve as the gateway for contact with the divine, which, though universal by definition, also promises a kind of in-group family formed by those who accept that such a divinity has these reproductive, family-forming powers, and dispenses them through Jesus and the narrative that he lives in.

Dramatizing Jesus's separation from his natal family is, of course, completely parallel to the basic effort to generate an image of his divine sonship, but it also opens the door to a better reading of the later rhetoric in which Jesus promises that accepting his message and thereby winning the kingdom of heaven is to be effected in a child-like manner. "People were bringing little children to him in order that he might touch them; and the disciples spoke sternly to them. But when Jesus saw this, he was indignant and said to them, 'Let the little children come to me; do not stop them; for it is to such as these that the kingdom of God belongs. Truly I tell you, whoever does not receive the kingdom of God as a little child will never enter it'" (10:13–15). That joining in the new Jesus family might involve breaking off ties to one's natal family is directly stated slightly later: "Jesus said, 'Truly I tell you, there is no one who has left house or brothers or sisters or mother or father or children or fields, for my sake and for the sake of the good news, who will not receive a hundredfold now in this age—houses, brothers and sisters, mothers and children, and fields, with persecutions—and in the age to come eternal life'" (10:29–30).

In short, once the trope of being reborn in the symbolic sense of finding kin in those who submit to God's will has been defined, early in the narrative, the ground has been prepared for a more powerful use of this rhetoric when, within the death portion of the narrative, Jesus explains the logic of converting to his law in a manner that will overcome one's old family identity and win one the kingdom of heaven. Not to be overlooked here is the, now familiar, dynamic in which this refathering is only promised to those who accept Jesus's own refathering. In short, if one accepts the narrative of how Jesus was refathered—that his *real* father is God and not some man who was Mary's partner in Nazareth—then one is ready to be refathered by Jesus and the narrative he lives in.[43]

Who Do They Say I Am?

The steady accumulation of these encounters proving Jesus's divine sonship comes to a head in chapter 8 when Jesus, for the first time, asks his disciples who the public takes him to be (8:27). The disciples respond with a number of interesting and flattering answers—John the Baptist, a prophet, or Elijah—but it is Peter's answer that satisfies Jesus. Peter proclaims, "You are the Messiah," and Jesus, in line with the pattern already established in parallel encounters, "sternly ordered them not to tell anyone about him" (8:30). This scene functions not only to finalize the prior scenes of identifying Jesus as the Son of God, but it also works to put this knowledge directly in the hands of the disciples in an act that both gives the reader full confidence in this assessment—Jesus accepted Peter's statement of his divine identity in full view of the other disciples—*and* sets the stage for the guilt of the disciples who were directly informed of Jesus's identity as the messiah qua Son of God, but didn't really believe it. In short, it seems that this is the point in the narrative where the various vignettes supporting part one of the text's agenda—proving Jesus's divine sonship—are brought to a climax and harvested in Peter's uninflected declaration of Jesus's divinity.[44] Noting this gradual, cumulative conversion of the disciples suggests that the author estimated that *outside the narrative* people would likewise convert to his narrative in a gradual, piecemeal manner. And, as mentioned, it also seems fair to say that the author has provided the reader with an extra incentive for converting to his narrative since by doing so, and especially by doing so in a wholehearted manner, he or she can complete the disciples' partial conversion *in* the narrative, and thereby right the wrongs of their casual reactions to Jesus and the various kinds of "proof" of his divine sonship that he provides.

Though after this climatic section of chapter 8 there will be several more healing encounters in which Jesus's divine identity is revealed, the motion in the narrative henceforth is taken over by a steady march to Jerusalem and Jesus's execution. Preparing for this death is the passage that immediately follows Peter's recognition of Jesus's divinity in which Jesus, for the first time, explains to the disciples what is going to happen. Switching to identify himself as the Son of Man, Jesus explains that there is a certain nonhuman narrative at work in the moment and that, in fact, the history that they are currently living has already been written. By having Jesus clarify the divine origin of these layered narratives, the author is implicitly rejecting the potential accusation that he himself has sculpted all these events, and their supporting logic, ex post facto. This discussion also underscores that even Jesus has a very basic narrative problem: the story he is living has already been written, and now it is up to him to live it. Jesus's struggle to live the Father's narrative, of course, has major implications for the reader, who, in the course of the narrative, learns that he or she too should become Christ-like in becoming a committed follower of the narrative, and in that way win a place in the Father's family.

The Transfiguration, or Tradition in Three Huts

Before turning to recount the details of the special death that will fulfill what the author, via Jesus's comments, presents as the divine narrative prepared for Jesus by the Father, the author first briefly returns to again prove Jesus's identity in the passage known as the "Transfiguration." Here, we learn of a quasi-secret revelation in which Jesus took Peter, James, and John up "on a high mountain apart, by themselves" (9:2) and presented them with a magical vision of himself, a vision that seems designed to prove Jesus's divine sonship and to inscribe him, however awkwardly, in the Jewish tradition. In this vision, the chosen disciples, and the reader, see Elijah and Moses talking with Jesus, presumably thereby affirming their mutual affinity and, more importantly, demonstrating that Elijiah and Moses recognize Jesus's place in *their* tradition. Peter is shown interpreting the scene in just this way, and he then suggests that three huts be built, one for each of the three figures, thereby emphasizing the suitability of their living together, and perhaps even suggesting a lineage of sameness in which they live together in timeless unity. Then, leaving nothing to chance, the author abruptly brings in the voice from heaven who declares in an echo of his statement in the first chapter, "This is my Son, the Beloved; listen to him!" (9:7).

This scene, a key one for clarifying the narrative's logic of fetishizing (old) tradition, matches the other scenes of recognition but betters them in several important ways. First, it shows that our author is again working up a faux secrecy in which he creates scenes that are supposedly set apart and out of sight but are, of course, completely in view for the reader. Second, the author has provided the reader with a "miniature" version of tradition since Moses and Elijah presumably represent key nodes of (old) tradition. Third, we have a perfect kind of father-son pairing with the Father telling the audience to listen to his Son, while of course a moment before the Son had been talking about his relationship to the Father (8:38). Thus, at this point in the narrative there is, fully in view, mutual recognition between Father and Son, and both figures are urging the internal audience to accept their claims. And this entire package is being made altogether visible to the reader—even though it was supposedly a secret revelation—thereby heightening its appeal while also explaining why the general public, the other disciples included, might not have gotten the message.

Also in this scene we get clearer confirmation that the divine patriarchy behind Jesus is the same one that is/was behind Moses and Elijah, even though it is only Jesus who is the real Son, the Beloved. That is, the voice from heaven appears here as the "deep background" for tradition, old and new, and makes his preferences perfectly clear: he has nothing to say about Moses and Elijah, and instead again declares his special kinship with Jesus, his beloved Son. Of course, too, with the return of the voice from heaven at this midpoint in the narrative, the reader gains more confidence that the narrative, as it has been developing, was in fact divinely ordained. Once all this has transpired, the author gives Jesus his standard line in which he commands this inner circle of disciples not to tell anyone what they just saw, with the caveat that they can reveal this later, after he has risen from the dead, an anticipated reality that was announced in the preceding passage when Jesus "began to teach them that the Son of Man must undergo great suffering, and be rejected by the elders, the chief priests, and the scribes, and be killed, and after three days rise again" (8:31).

With the Transfiguration sequence set in the context of statements made on either side of it, we have a clear example of that trope of divine patriarchy swooping into history since the narrative explains Jesus as laden with divine paternity *and* total tradition, while also explaining that this fact of divine sonship needs to be publicized *after Jesus's return* to the Father, presumably so that the public can benefit from getting tradition *out of Jesus* by believing that just that essence of tradition had been put into him, and, of course, believing that belief in just that presence is all that it takes to regain it. This focus on belief in belief becomes even clearer when we recall that the Transfiguration follows directly from that teaching passage where Jesus explains that his disciples are those who will follow him in name and deed: "If any want to become my followers, let them deny themselves *and take up their cross and follow me.* For those who want to save their life will lose it, and those who lose their life *for my sake, and for the sake of the gospel,* will save it. . . . Those who are ashamed of me and of my words in this adulterous and sinful generation, of them the Son of Man will also be ashamed when he comes in the glory of his Father with the holy angels" (8:34–38, italics added).[45]

Here, the bargain tendered to the reader is crystal clear: believe the identity of Jesus as the Son of God, and believe that this belief is paramount for one's salvation, and then rest assured that salvation will be yours. And, conversely, understand that reading with disbelief—and maintaining disdain for the One who explains the consequences of good and bad reading of his identity—will result in catastrophe when the narrative comes full circle with the return swoop of Father and Son.[46] Explaining the power of reading, believing, and following also comes with a rather clever double in which it is explained that those outside the narrative should understand that holding to the gospel with faith, unto death, is the very thing that, after a fashion, will take them "inside" the narrative since their faithful maintenance of the narrative is defined as a cross that is to be borne unto death.[47] In short, it is in one's faithful reading of Jesus that one becomes Jesus-like oneself. Or, in a fuller sense: one becomes Jesus-like by believing the narrative of how Jesus followed his own Father-given narrative. In sum, life *without* the narrative of the Father and the Son is to be traded for life *with* the narrative of the Father and the Son, within the expectation that holding that narrative will lead on to a final reunion with the Father, albeit after death, or, and it comes to the same thing, on the day of the Second Coming. Arguably, this is the backbone of the Gospel of Mark, and all the other themes and details support this structure.

With Jesus's command that the reality of the Transfiguration—the most visual revelation of his divine sonship—be publicized after his resurrection, we have good reason to read the intervening chapters before that resurrection is recounted as a long, parenthetical interlude. That is, in terms of the structure of the promise made to the reader, everything is now in place, and it is just a question of waiting to see if Jesus really is to be resurrected and returned to the Father in a "historical" reality that will, once and for all, prove the facticity of the narrative about patriarchy swooping into history and then returning to itself. In a funny sort of way, just as the narrative relies on nondivine figures to shore up claims of Jesus's divinity—the lepers, the cripples, the insane, and so on—so, too, here it seems that the brute facticity of "history" is taken to be the final arbitrator of claims about divine narratives.

Of course, what happens in those intervening chapters between 8:27 and the narration of the supposedly historical resurrection is no more and no less than the complete demonization of (old) tradition, assisted by various mini-narratives that increase the supposed culpability of the representatives of the Jewish tradition—and the disciples (!)—and that climax in the specific prediction that the destruction of the Temple will follow in the wake of the Jewish authorities' evil treatment of Jesus.

A Clean Getaway

Jumping over the details of the execution, which I explore below, the resurrection is managed in a minimalist manner that works again around "visual" evidence that is given to the reader under the veil of a kind of faux secrecy, a gesture that is exciting for several reasons. For instance, we learn that a certain Joseph recovered Jesus's corpse from the cross—after Jesus was pronounced fully dead by the centurion—and lodged it in a "tomb that had been hewn out of the rock" (15:46), presumably thereby clarifying that there was but one entrance to this tomb. Then, as Joseph "rolled a stone against the door of the tomb" (15:46) sealing in Jesus's body, the conditions for judging the reality of Jesus's resurrection appear fully established, given the tomb's hermetic structure and this heavy stone. Thus, as though observing a science experiment, we are led to believe that if the narrative reports that Jesus's body has disappeared, it can only be due to divine intervention, as predicted by Jesus back in 8:31. This set-up for proving the resurrection concludes when Mary Magdalene, Mary (mother of James), and Salome come on the day after the Sabbath to anoint Jesus's corpse. Upon arrival they find the stone moved, the corpse gone, and a very odd spokesperson explaining what has supposedly happened. This unnamed spokesperson, a "young man, dressed in a white robe," finalizes the narrative by explaining, in detail, where the body had been, whose body it was, and what in fact has happened to that body: "Do not be alarmed; you are looking for Jesus of Nazareth, who was crucified. He has been raised; he is not here. Look, there is the place they laid him" (16:6).

Apparently knowing all the details of Jesus's resurrection, this curious figure even seems to speak like Jesus in that he alone knows what is to occur next in the Jesus-narrative, a power previously restricted to Jesus alone.[48] He thus instructs the women to go tell the disciples what has happened and to specifically inform them that Jesus will reappear to them in Galilee: "there, you will see him, just as he told you" (16:7). Despite the utter confidence with which this prediction is made—and clearly the youth in white knows that this event was promised by Jesus too—this promised appearance that would seal the deal and reveal the final truth of Jesus's identity to the disciples *inside* the narrative is short-circuited as the women flee, "and they said nothing to anyone, for they were afraid" (16:8). That the message is lost to those *inside* the narrative, however, in no way threatens its transmission to those outside of the narrative since the reader, if s/he has been believing these details about the tomb and this odd spokesperson, has all he or she needs to know about the finalization of the narrative's promise: the body was gone, the promise fulfilled, and thus he or she should be quite ready to set about the task of believing in belief, aware that this will be a cross-bearing enterprise, and convinced that in this enterprise he or she will have the chance to recover tradition in its fullest form and follow Jesus back to the Father.

Clearly, the resurrection narrative parallels rather closely the structure of the earlier mini-narratives in which Jesus's divinity was recognized by someone. Here, as with those moments of recognition, there is a clear declaration of the reality that is supposedly in front of us (this time it's the missing body, instead of a visible healing) and, as usual, we learn that the publication of the revelation is at risk. In this case, instead of Jesus's usual command not to tell anyone, the figures in the narrative flee from the task of transmission that the youth had entrusted them with. However, this is far from being a tragic ending. Everything has happened as promised, and the various narrative details push the reader to conclude that the observed events match the divinely inspired narrative that supposedly generated those events. For instance, as Jesus dies there are three details given to further prove that the narrative is on track: 1) there is darkness at noon, which covered "the whole land," leaving little doubt about the cosmic nature of the events underway (15:33); 2) this point is driven home when, magically, "the curtain of the temple was torn in two, from top to bottom" presumably symbolizing that his death directly ends the sacredness of the temple (15:38); and, 3) the Roman centurion in charge of his death, positioned as a perfect witness "who stood facing him," draws the conclusion that the narrative has pushed from the outset: "Truly this was God's Son!" (15:39).

With everything happening as planned, the failure of the women to transmit to the disciples the message containing the "proof" of Jesus's resurrection along with the promise of his imminent return to Galilee is of little consequence other than to explain again why the disciples never figured out who Jesus was. The reader knows, now, what has happened, and the reader has received this message from a spokesperson—the youth in white—who seems to know everything about Jesus, his deeds, and his plans. Thus, this final moment of failure works much like Jesus's command to those who recognize his divinity not to spread the word: the negation simply heightens the reader's desire to involve himself or herself in just that project of spreading the word which is so clearly "true" and yet which has been pumped into less-than-reliable receivers and transmitters. In sum, the "science" experiment is now complete, the results have been squarely announced and, most importantly, the reader has learned that this perfect closure to the narrative has been lost on those in the narrative, and thus there is every reason for the reader to want to make that jump *from his or her own place in history into the narrative*—to take a stand as the final reader of events and then take on the task of being the purveyor of the narrative that no one on stage could absorb and handle correctly.

In this final event, we can "see" that all the narrative frames match up: the Father made the Son and a narrative-of-sacrifice for that Son, put the Son in human history to live that sacrificial narrative, *and then, from a point of view never revealed,* the final narrative emerges—the Gospel of Mark—that documents how "real" history and the divine plan qua narrative-of-sacrifice coincided perfectly. The only problem is that the Gospel of Mark, while establishing this perfect parallel between the divine plan (for Jesus) and its historical enactment (by Jesus), also shows that this parallel and all its implications were missed by most people in the world. While this arrangement works as a handy incentive for the reader's conversion to the narrative, it also means that the Gospel of Mark has presented God as one who sent his Son into the world to live out a preconceived plan but without planning carefully enough to control the reception of this cycle of events. In this sense, the author of Gospel of Mark is trying to fix this key flaw in God's plan—its reception by the world. Our author manages this fix by doing what God didn't think to do: show the world, in this "higher" narrative (characterized by what the Gospel of Mark provides), the reality of the situation and in such a manner that the world will want to acknowledge what has happened precisely because the world will know all the details of this Father-Son drama, while *also knowing that without this additional gospel perspective,* nothing would work out. In sum, our author positions himself to be the PR man that neither God nor Jesus ever figured out how to be, which naturally suggests that our author has taken it upon himself to be God's supplement. There is, of course, every reason to believe that our author hoped that the transcendental-looking origins that he gave to this Father-Son drama would completely cover over his own role as the author of the story that holds that Father-Son drama within itself. Like many well-wrought things, once it is put before us in a just-so manner, we fail to see how much ingenuity went into its construction.

With some understanding of the narrative's structuring of the reader's "vision" of the Jesus-of-history that proves his divinity and the validity of the narrative that he lives in, we need to go back and retrace the narrative's account of new tradition's conflict with (old) tradition.

Legal Problems

Interspersed among the set pieces in which Jesus's identity is explicitly recognized by those whom he heals are a series of encounters with figures best defined as representatives of (old) tradition. These encounters, like the healing encounters, circle around the question of the ownership of tradition: Is tradition to be found in the scribes, the Pharisees, the Temple authorities, or the Torah? Or, instead, is tradition rightfully the property of Jesus of Nazareth who can legitimately redefine it as he likes since he is, in fact, the Son of God, and God is, of course, assumed to be the author of any form of tradition? Read in this light, these mini-debates over practical matters regarding Torah injunctions are, like the healing encounters, set pieces whose content isn't *in* the debate, but rather in the implications of the framing of the debate and its outcome. Thus, the point of having Jesus declare revolutionary rulings regarding Sabbath laws or purity issues isn't that these particular legal matters are important to the narrative. Instead, what is important is demonstrating to the reader that Jesus, as the Son of God, has the right to sit in judgment on what is and isn't legal in tradition. That is, just as the reader isn't asked to read the healing encounters hoping to learn how to heal with mud, spit, and certain phrases—as though *that* were the point of the healing episode—so too the reader doesn't appear to be invited to ruminate on the legal details regarding the Sabbath, purity, divorce, and so on. These encounters happen very quickly, their content isn't developed in an ongoing manner in the narrative, and thus these joustings over the law appear as beguiling examples of a master-at-work, with the divine Jesus easily overcoming the rather pathetic-looking representatives of (old) tradition who, it should be added, are also presented as craven, vicious, and conniving.[49]

A good example of how the author presents these legal encounters occurs at the beginning of chapter 2, a case which combines the two tropes of healing and legal rulings in a manner that shows how parallel they are as narrative inventions. Here, Jesus is shown healing a paralytic by saying, "Son, your sins are forgiven" (2:5). Conveniently, there are some scribes at the scene to offer commentary, a somewhat odd situation since this healing is supposedly happening while Jesus "was at home" (2:1). At any rate, the presence of the nameless scribes allows for the scene to develop into a confrontation between the old and new versions of tradition. Watching Jesus heal the paralytic, the scribes think to themselves, "Why does this fellow speak in this way? It is blasphemy! Who can forgive sins but God alone?" (2:7). Jesus clairvoyantly hears this critique and, after a brief debate about the phraseology he used to effect the healing, puts the matter to them bluntly: " 'But so that you may know that the Son of Man has authority on earth to forgive sins'—he said to the paralytic—'I say to you, stand up, take your mat and go to your home.' " Then, the paralytic stood up and walked out, and everyone was "amazed and glorified God, saying, 'We have never seen anything like this!' " (2:10–12).

In this encounter it is pretty clear what the author is doing: Jesus's power to heal is showcased as illegal in the eyes of the representatives of (old) tradition—the scribes—and they chastise him for blasphemy and in particular for doing what only God is supposedly allowed to do: forgive sins. Then, with the legality of Jesus's version of tradition in question, the author has Jesus vanquish (old) tradition by both healing the paralytic in their presence and then explaining to them that this healing is for *their* benefit—"so that you may know that the Son of Man has authority on earth to forgive sins." In short, as the reader watches this healing event unfold, he or she learns that Jesus's new version of tradition is both fully legal and underwritten by God, and that (old) tradition is seriously out of touch with things divine.

Moreover, we should note that Jesus's attack on (old) tradition follows the *logic* of tradition since he is effectively saying, "Yes, you scribes were right in claiming that only God can forgive sins, but what you didn't know is God had a Son, and this Son has the same rights as the Father." In short, even though Jesus refers to himself as "Son of Man" and not "Son of God," his divine legal rights are confirmed by the intertwining of two sorts of laws, since (old) tradition's legal notion that only God had these rights to forgive sins is being extended or appended by the application of patriarchal law in the sense that the Son can do what the Father does, and thus what at first appeared to be an extralegal healing ought to be seen not just as legal in its own right, but also proof of Jesus's divine sonship.

Put in other terms, in the very act of supposedly breaking the laws of tradition, Jesus's legal status as the Son of God is confirmed since it is only God, and apparently his Son, who can step in to reverse the normal functioning of the law by forgiving sins, sins which, presumably, accrued from failing to uphold the (old) law. Then, to more fully mark all this overcoming of (old) tradition as legal and God-based, the author has the scene conclude with everyone on site rejoicing to God, saying "We have never seen anything like this." This final comment presumably has to be read as a further indictment of (old) tradition since when the new version of tradition and its new representative are recognized as both legal and from God—after all, the paralytic *was healed,* thereby proving that his sins were forgiven, and presumably with God's approval—(old) tradition thereby appears radically diminished and of little consequence, a position that will be developed more explicitly in later encounters.

Besides seeing that these legal confrontations match the surrounding narrative context that is devoted to proving Jesus's identity, and match the basic agenda of the text as well, we have four solid pieces of evidence to support treating these confrontations as set pieces presented to encourage the reader's conversion to the text. First, in several of these encounters Jesus is made to articulate this logic in which the outcome of the debate is none other than the proclamation that Jesus has the truest form of tradition, based on his special identity, and that the other traditional authority figures have something smaller, usually defined as a human tradition in contradiction to Jesus's divine tradition. For instance in the debate in chapter 2 over Jesus's disciples plucking grain on the Sabbath, Jesus is first shown defending this action by evoking a story from 1 Samuel (21:3–6) in which Sabbath bread is eaten in a technically "illegal" manner that is, nonetheless, still acceptable to God. Then, Jesus turns from this argument by the book to the more basic issue at hand, which is the question of his identity, and concludes: "The Sabbath was made for humankind, and not humankind for the Sabbath; so the Son of Man is lord even of the Sabbath" (2:27–28). Though this set of statements seems a bit convoluted, it still seems clear that Jesus is claiming that his identity trumps tradition and allows him to rule on the law of the Sabbath and presumably (old) tradition in general. In short, since he is none other than "the lord even of the Sabbath," he is symbolically "bigger" than the Sabbath and, by implication, bigger than all of (old) tradition. And, as with the healing of the paralytic, it is precisely by the act of transgressing the established law of tradition that the narrative reveals: 1) the legality of the new form of tradition; 2) its dominance over the old; and, 3) the divine sonship that makes all of this possible.

A version of this scene is repeated in the next encounter as Jesus is shown healing a man with a withered hand, again on the Sabbath (3:1). Here, however, the narrative moves Jesus closer to the center of (old) tradition since while the prior healing was located outside the synagogue, this one occurs inside the synagogue, in full view of the authorities, now labeled "Pharisees." Jesus's argument this time is that healing is more important than keeping the injunction against working on the Sabbath. The conclusion to this encounter with (old) tradition is equally revealing because the author takes us, again, inside Jesus's head where we learn that he interprets the Pharisees's reaction to his Sabbath-healing as the result of that fundamental "hardness of heart," the crime that is specifically identified in other passages as the inability to accept Jesus as the Son of God. (See for instance, 6:52 and 8:17, where it is the disciples who are charged in this manner.) In brief, then, the legal encounters are really no different from the healing encounters since they too revolve around the acceptance or rejection of the basic claim of Jesus's divine identity.[50]

Key here is that the rejection of Jesus—due to that hardness of heart— cuts across categories of people in a surprising manner. Thus, the disciples are guilty of this crime, just as the scribes, Pharisees, and chief priests are. The negativity of those who would reject Jesus is underscored by Jesus's characterization of his era as "this adulterous and sinful generation" (8:38), suggesting that the author isn't simply setting up a Manichaean struggle between old and new versions of tradition, but wants to give the reader a supposedly divine assessment of the reader's current historical situation, a situation that, with only (old) tradition to rely on, would be basically evil.[51]

Jesus's characterization of the current generation as "adulterous" warrants more reflection. He presumably could have charged them with other, much more egregious, crimes—especially given that they are soon to participate so enthusiastically in his execution. Keeping in mind that the whole symbolic structure of the text is dedicated to proving the legitimacy of a particular father and son relationship—God and Jesus—and then offering inclusion in that patriarchal family to all those who would consent to this newly established father-son pairing, this charge of "adulterous" seems to function to carve a deeper "hole" of illegitimacy in the reader, a hole that will be filled in by exactly what the text is offering: a publicly available hyper-paternity that reconnects the believer to the Father. That is, it seems sensible to read this charge of illegitimacy within the wider scope of the seduction organized by the entire narrative, a seduction based on providing the reader with access to a transcendental form of patriarchy that will, one expects, resolve all issues regarding paternal legitimacy.

In the case above of the faithful man with the withered hand versus the hard-hearted Pharisees, we shouldn't miss that the final line sets this encounter within the larger narrative regarding Jesus's fate. Thus, after the healing we learn, "The Pharisees went out and began to plot with the Herodians how to destroy him" (3:6). In adding this detail, the author is implying that it was just these legal encounters, and the identity issues packed into them, that would lead on to the biggest of such encounters—Jesus's trial by the chief priests of the Sanhedrin where, again, the issue of Jesus's identity as Son of God was the sole item that mattered (14:60). In sum, we have compelling evidence of a solid thematic unity structuring Mark's narrative since these set pieces of healing and overcoming (old) tradition appear as miniature versions of the final episode of judgment in which (old) tradition fully rejects Jesus, organizes his execution, and thereby fulfills God's narrative by committing the crime that will warrant their own destruction later in the Jewish-Roman War. Given this thematic unity dedicated to establishing Jesus's divine identity and his rights over tradition, I think we would be quite mistaken to read these legal encounters as somehow revealing any specific content in Jesus's teaching. That is, once we see that the text is dedicated to organizing, for the reader, a series of good and bad reading of Jesus, we have good reason to understand these mini-conflicts as fractal in nature: they are miniature versions of the larger agenda that shapes the entire narrative.

The second reason for thinking that the legal encounters are performative is that when Jesus is given more developed discourses in which he explains how salvation is won or lost, the question of specific ethical or ritual action—Torah-based or otherwise—largely disappears. Thus, Jesus normally explains salvation to be won or lost solely in terms of one's relationship to his identity-claims, as presented in this narrative.[52] Hence when the text provides its own definition of legitimate tradition, these particular issues surrounding Jewish law have no place in the discussion. If there is ethical content in the debates over the Sabbath, fasting, and purity rules, it is simply in the promise that real ethics are to be found elsewhere. Or, more exactly, we find the promise that real ethics are found in the act of *leaving the details* of the Torah, along with the authority figures that directed submission to those details, in order to accept Jesus as the new figure with authority, the one who has the right to direct just this shift. Thus, just as learning the details of healing isn't the point of the healing stories, so too learning to interpret the Torah "correctly" isn't the point of the legal encounters. In sum, we ought to take both the healings and the legal rulings on the Torah as but proof-texts designed to underscore the transcendence of this new form of tradition and its representative, Jesus.

Thus, and put in the idiom of the narrative, in Jesus's rulings on various legal matters, the emphasis isn't on *what* comes out of Jesus's mouth, but rather that it is *Jesus's mouth* from whence real tradition can be learned. That is, these mini-scenes of overcoming (old) tradition are put forward to prove a kind of non-linguistic and completely unthinkable connection between Father and Son. Read in this manner, each time Jesus-as-tradition encounters and overcomes (old) tradition, it is as though another piece of testimony is added to the bewildering claim of Jesus's divine sonship. Put schematically, and in parallel with the healing episodes, as the reader watches B, he gains confidence in A.

A: God made Jesus as his Son

B: Jesus convincingly overcomes the representatives of (old) tradition

The third reason why these disputes over the law appear performative in nature is much more straightforward. Given that the text concludes by locating itself in a time just before the apocalypse, it is hard to see how rulings on comparatively mundane affairs such as the Sabbath, dietary concerns, or even marriage law could have any relevance. In fact, in chapter 10, when the conditions for salvation are clearly explained, we get a good sense for how ethics, in the most general sense, have condensed into one's relation to the narrative-claim regarding Jesus's identity, with an emphasis on the renunciation of family in all its forms as seen in Jesus's tough comment to Peter regarding the coming apocalypse, "Truly I tell you, there is no one who has left house or brothers and sisters . . ." (10:29).[53] Given these terms for salvation through faith in Jesus's divine identity and his "good news," ethical laws concerning practical realities, especially those related to family life—calendars (Sabbath), food (purity), and physical reproduction (marriage and adultery)[54]—seem fundamentally distant and at odds with what the narrative is promising: that the end of time is near and that there will be one final reckoning made based on one's relationship to this narrative which is none other than the Gospel of Mark. And those who accept Jesus's divine identity are thrice described as "the elect" since they are the lucky ones who will be spared God's wrath at the end of time (10:40, 13:20 and especially 13:22, which makes clear that the "elect" are those who take Jesus to be the Messiah). Given this supposedly imminent judgment of one's relationship to the narrative, how could consideration for specific ethical concerns have any place in the "bargain" that the author is offering the reader?

The Parables: Do You Know What Am I Talking About?

The final reason for taking the legal encounters to be set pieces has to do with the way other moments of teaching work in the text. If we look closely at what Jesus is made to preach, we see that a good deal of his teachings are self-referential and thus little interested in exploring practical content. The parables, which are often taken to be paradigmatic of Jesus's teaching style, provide a good example of this self-referentiality: as we consider the parable of the old and new wine, the two parables on the seeds and the earth, the lamp under the bushel basket, and then the parable of the wicked tenants, it is clear that each parable has Jesus giving *teachings about receiving his teachings*. Thus, in each case, the reader learns that Jesus's message is focused on clarifying how one ought to relate to his message. Thus, with the parable of the wineskins, one learns that the new wine, like the new version of tradition, can't be properly held within the old containers. With the seed parables, one learns that the gospel is just like a seed that only can fructify if the soil is fertile. With the parables of the lamp and basket, the promise is made that the final meaning of Jesus's teaching will, eventually, be revealed, and hence should be accepted now. The parable of tenants then sums up the entire narrative that Jesus is living in, with an emphasis on the horrible destiny in store for those renters who chose, first, to disregard the messages of the vineyard's owner and then murdered his son whom he had sent to them to deliver his final message.[55] Since so much of Jesus's teaching is presented as self-reflexive commentary regarding how to relate to his teaching, it would seem, in a visible and manifest way, that the gospel has little or no use for straightforward ethical discourse—real laws about daily life, that is. Likewise, this absence of ethical detail seems sensible since specific rulings regarding the Sabbath, or food, or marriage would undermine the more important narrative agenda of presenting the narrative as the sole cause for one's salvation, an agenda that presumably determined the choice to make Jesus's teachings focus on the absolute value of accepting him and his teaching.

Put in the language of fetishizing tradition, it would seem that the Gospel of Mark's discourse is working to establish two new *containers of tradition*: 1) Jesus as the container of the perfect and final version of tradition; and, 2) the gospel's narrative as the container of Jesus such that "having" the narrative means having Jesus, and having, thereby, reliable access to his perfect version of tradition. In seeking to establish convincing images of these containers, specific ethical rulings wouldn't just be secondary and incidental; they would be a fundamental hindrance since they would generate a zone of legality independent of the narrative's primary goal of persuasively lodging total tradition in Jesus, and in itself, and then offering that fetishized version of tradition to the reader. Thus, like Paul's fury over the return of interest in real circumcision in the Galatian community, Mark's author presumably has no practical use for specific ethical arrangements since they would represent a falling back to the level of real-world legality that the narrative is working to overcome as it establishes a kind of salvation-by-belief.

Lurking here is a troubling idea, encapsulated in the phrase "belief in belief," that the Gospel of Mark circles around a big zero, or perhaps more exactly, a very big, but utterly vapid, divine Father who gives the law about accepting the (new) law that he just gave. That is, the text takes as its fundamental content the promise that there is a truth-father in the universe and that believing the discourse about that truth-father as *from the truth-father*, regardless of however empty of content and self-referential it might be, is the cause for salvation and eternal at-one-ment with just this truth-father. In sum, in this paradigmatic gesture of fetishizing tradition, one is left with the language-of-transcendence promising transcendence to those who take just this language to be transcendental.

The Guilt of (Old) Tradition

To begin to close out this reading, and to further demonstrate the Gospel of Mark's effort to promote the overcoming of (old) tradition, we would do well to focus on several remaining tropes that work to highlight the culpability of (old) tradition in Jesus's death. First, the author of Mark goes out of his way to accuse the totality of (old) tradition. Thus, in preparation for the nighttime trial of Jesus, we learn, "They took Jesus to the high priest; and *all* the chief priests, the elders, and the scribes were assembled" (14:53, italics added). This emphasis on the active participation of the whole of (old) tradition, appearing assembled here as a group, reappears slightly later with the account of the release of Barabbas. At that point, the narrative makes clear that one prisoner could be released and that it was up to the priests and the crowd to decide whom it would be, with the clear offer that Jesus could be released (15:6–15). However, the crowd, stirred up by the chief priests, chooses Barabbas and screams for the crucifixion of Jesus, a brief detail that suggests to the reader that the general population of Jerusalem was as guilty as the chief priests in the death of Jesus.

Second, the Jewishness of this guilt also appears behind the choice to have one of the twelve disciples betray Jesus and thereby initiate the trial and execution sequence. Since *now* Jesus's death appears to be the result of an inside job, responsibility for his death is, again, to be found within the sphere of the Jewish people; in fact, it is to be found in the very group of those closest to Jesus, and *not on the outside* in the oppressive Roman legal system that managed the occupation. The contrived nature of Judas's crime is visible as the narrator has to awkwardly explain, just prior to the beginning of the Passover-execution sequence (14:10), how Judas had gone to the chief priests in order to betray Jesus. Judas's inexplicable action, introduced apropos of nothing in the narrative, sits at the top of the Passover meal, like a locomotive on the wrong track, promising to deliver a series of horrible events that will, nonetheless, fulfill the narrative's agenda of transforming Jesus's death into: 1) a ransom sacrifice; 2) a covenant offering; 3) a murder committed by (old) tradition; and, 4) a betrayal by one his most intimate disciples.

The third trope of guilt is found in the various ways that the narrative explains the actions of the high priests who tried Jesus and turned him over to Pilate for execution—they acted out of jealousy and bad faith. Thus their practice of traditional law was decidedly illegal, and even Pilate supposedly knew this, "For he realized that it was out of jealousy that the chief priests had handed him over" (15:10). More serious is the fact that the chief priests and all concerned *knew* of the narrative that explained Jesus's divine identity and yet failed to believe it. Thus, during the trial, the sole charge against Jesus is simply the very claim that the narrative is putting forward: that he is/was the Son of God. Hence, when the Jewish establishment killed him, they did so knowing full well what they were risking: they had been informed of the divine narrative that explained Jesus's identity, and they turned away from it. It was, then, not just that Jesus was a nuisance or a political liability or disliked. Rather, it was that, presented with the narrative of his identity, the old law and its supportive public chose to read him and his narrative as a lie. In short, *what is fundamentally on trial in the trial of Jesus is this very narrative of the Gospel of Mark.* The trial, then, is the fullest version of that repeating trope in the first half of the narrative in which various figures are presented with Jesus and invited to read him, with good and bad readings recorded in order that the reader learn to trust the positive reading and to fear the effects of the negative reading.

Once we read the trial as the consummation of the narrative-ploy of showing split-screen readings of Jesus's identity, we are in a good place to understand the trope of mockery that seems so important to the author in the final phase of the execution.[56] In the process of killing Jesus, everyone concerned—the guards, the chief priests, passers-by, and the two other men being crucified with him—evokes the core of Mark's narrative but in a degraded manner that dismisses its promise of transcendence, the very promise that Jesus's coming resurrection will prove. In parodying the narrative, these malevolent figures perform three functions. First, they prove their basic nastiness—a man is dying, and they take pleasure in making fun of him. Second, they prove, by taunting him with his titles of Messiah and King of the Jews, that they are familiar with his identity-claim and the narrative that supports it, and yet have chosen not to take it as true. And third, their mockery seems joined to a subtle claim about the truth of Mark's narrative. To see this linkage note that the bad readers of Jesus focus on the supposed laughability of: 1) Jesus's divine kingship; 2) the coming destruction of the Temple; and 3) Jesus's ability to save himself from death.

Now, given that the author clearly assumes that the reader already knows of the destruction of the Temple, he is as usual setting up a clever split-screen situation in which he demonstrates that since (old) tradition specifically taunted Jesus regarding his prediction regarding the destruction of the Temple—*and it came to pass*—readers ought to also expect that those other two claims that were ridiculed—regarding Jesus's divine kingship and his coming resurrection—would likewise be utterly vindicated. Thus, reading in the wake of the fall of the Temple that "[t]hose who passed by derided him, shaking their heads and saying, 'Aha! You who would destroy the temple and build it in three days, save yourself, and come down from the cross!'" (Mark 15:29–30), one would be ready to believe that other promises that were made fun of were, in fact, also reliable. Of course, as the reader finishes the narrative he or she will "see," narratively at least, that Jesus's resurrection also in fact occurred, so that leaves only Jesus's identity as the Messiah as the one claim that was ridiculed that needs final confirmation, though now it is set in the good company of the other two scorned claims that were proven to be "historically" accurate. Of course, that Jesus was "seen" by the believing reader to have been resurrected would, of course, go a long way to making the claim of his divine sonship an established fact.

Standing back from this arrangement, it seems fair to say that the author of Mark has harvested the historical fact of the destruction of the Temple for some rather spectacular narrative claims, claims that both explain that destruction but also fold it into an intricate narrative of fetishizing tradition whereby the destruction of the Temple serves as a terrible threat to those who would refuse the narrative, while also offering proof of the enormity of the situation that the reader now finds himself in: the Temple fell because of the misreading of *this* narrative, and that proves that this narrative is the one from God that controls the life and death of tradition, new and old.

In sum, while this narrative would turn into the basis of a distinctly non-Jewish tradition—Christianity—which, once sufficiently distanced from its original Jewish context, would regularly reinterpret this Jewish guilt in a very deadly way, we still ought to see that the story is about how tradition killed itself, traditionally, on Passover that is, in order to live again. Or, rather, in the rampant play of doubles that structures the narrative, it is as though tradition gave birth to a double of itself that it, unwittingly, killed in an act of misrecognition that led to its own death, a death that occurs in such a way that tradition lives again, but with that dead version of itself always there to sacralize the new covenant. Thus the key to a good reading of the narrative is to see that the two deaths—Jesus's and (old) tradition's—go hand-in-hand, with Jesus as the bright and lovable fetish of the death-of-old-tradition, a death qua execution-by-God that underwrites Jesus's death and his message in every way. Everything, after all, turned out as planned. In short, just as Paul made Jesus's death at the hands of the Romans the basis of a new form of salvation, so too has the author of Mark woven the Temple's "death" at the hands of the Romans into a new form of salvation, and in fact Mark's narrative ties the two deaths together so that they explain each other *and* give birth to the promise of new tradition.

Where's the Love?

While it seems sensible to see Mark's narrative providing a rather Jewish solution to a Jewish problem, we need also to admit that the narrative works to evoke some rather strong anti-Judaic emotions in the reader as he learns that it is divinely sanctioned that he should come to despise (old) tradition, the inhabitants of Jerusalem, and, though it's rarely admitted these days, Jesus's disciples as well. Thus, from early on in the narrative the doubters of

Jesus's identity—mostly figures of (old) tradition, but the disciples too—are presented as reprehensible: they are jealous, selfish, foes of truth, nit-picking, lacking contact with real tradition, greedy, and of course, murderous. Then, at the apex of demonstrating this hatred toward Jesus, we see the high priests and the Jerusalem community screaming for Jesus's crucifixion and then mocking him with his own narrative claims—a most ugly scene.

As we have seen, the Jewish authorities' supposed hatred of Jesus works hand-in-glove with the basic plot since this hatred needs to be in place to explain their supposed execution of Jesus, the act that fulfills the plan that God had for Jesus, and sets in motion the destruction of the Temple and the imminent Second Coming. Thus, for Mark's author to turn Jesus's happenstance death into the truly dastardly murder that it has to be in order to explain God's destruction of the Temple, he had to cast the Temple authorities in the worst light. Hence he needs them to appear thoroughly base, jealous, and vicious, all in order to generate the weight of guilt that will match the gravity of the destruction of the Temple which the author is trying to shoehorn into the standard crime-punishment schema that the Hebrew Bible regularly relies on to explain the historical catastrophes that so often befell Israel.

Thus, there is a rather unfortunate conjunction of hate and love built into the narrative: as one learns to love Jesus as the Son of God and the good-news narrative that he lives in, one also learns to hate those Jews of (old) tradition who supposedly received the narrative but rejected its claim to be truthful and of ultimate consequence. Once we recognize Mark's creation of a "Jewish sin" in this manner, then we also ought to say that this is a sin that the reader could commit. Or, in a certain sense, this is a sin that the reader has already committed, as he might have, like the figures in the narrative, doubted what he was reading early on in his experience of the narrative. Framed this way the "Jewish sin" generated in the text represents an image of the reader's own relationship to the text in the sense that even if one ultimately converts to the text's narrative, there would, presumably, be phases of doubt along the way. If I am right about this, then we have some important clues not just about Christian anti-Judaism, but also about the Christian need to convert others to this narrative since with each act of successfully pushing this narrative onto a new reader/listener, one might think one has, yet again, triumphed over that initial (lingering?) "Jewish sin" that was present (and enduring?) in one's original relationship to the gospel narrative.

All of this is to say that insofar as modern commentators like to repeat the claim that "Christianity is a religion of love," a close reading of the

Markan narrative suggests something much more complicated and troubling regarding the quality of the believer's belief, for it appears that becoming convinced of Jesus's divinity is inseparable from buying into a hatred of (old) tradition and then building—structurally, at least—one's faith upon it. Of course, with time and with more direct statements in the later gospels, Christians found even more reasons to hate the Jews for killing "their" deity.

Conclusions: An Empty Double, or Religion as Narrative

Standing back from this reading a number of important conclusions are in view, conclusions that aren't very cheerful but also aren't avoidable. First, we see a narrative that is essentially about itself in the specific sense that its content is directed toward arranging the reader's relationship to the narrative. Thus, save for some very sparse lines given to Jesus about the importance of loving God and your neighbor (12:29ff)—hardly news to a Jewish audience since these lines are taken from Deuteronomy 6:4–5—the encounters, the teachings, the parables, the debates with the old law, and most important, the Passover trial, are basically no more than miniature versions of the reader's own relationship to the narrative and its claims about Jesus's divine sonship. Thus one would be hard pressed to find much content in Jesus's teaching here—apart from the promise that believing the narrative is all one needs to do in terms of ethics. In a similar way, though the narrative is completely dedicated to proving that (old) tradition has been overcome—making the visible death of (old) tradition into a compelling story about the locale (and legitimacy) of new tradition—the content of new tradition is left decidedly vague. New tradition seems to consist of little more than believing a story about what happened to (old) tradition when it met new tradition and didn't believe that new tradition was heaven-sent.

Then, what maybe is less clear is that by offering salvation to those who believe the narrative, the text has made solving its own problems of legitimacy the doorway to heaven. Thus, the narrative's own needs have been prepared for by making them identical to the reader's needs such that belief in the narrative solves the reader's problems and the narrative's problems at the same time.[57] Put this way, religion and salvation are taking form around the medium that they *now* live in—narrative. Or rather, the medium is overtaking the message since, in the end, salvation is promised to those who respond in the way that will make the narrative live in time. As mentioned above, given how key figures in the narrative—in particular, the disciples and the women at the cross—turn away from the narrative, it is hardly surprising that the text specifies that one's religious work is to be focused on cherishing the narrative and broadcasting it, thereby accomplishing what all the other supposedly trustworthy figures in the narrative failed to do. Moreover, in gaining confidence that salvation is found in devoting oneself to the story explaining salvation, one is also tempted with the possibility of mimicking Jesus since all can "take up their cross" (8:34) to follow Jesus by believing in the good news of the newly revealed Father-Son connection and believing unto death that it is just this belief that takes one back to the Father.

Finally, given this dependence between form and content in which the practice of salvation takes form around the medium by which the discourse of salvation was offered, might it not be that belief became the essence of newer, "reactive" religions—such as Christianity—precisely because they "came second" and thus needed belief in order to get started, given that they had neither a ritual tradition nor an institutional basis? That is, might not the move away from the primacy of purity concerns, community, and ritual toward a focus on belief and interiority be the unintended consequence of the evolution, not of humanity, but of discourse systems in which later contestants would have clearly benefited from privileging belief, conversion, and interiority?

These conclusions and questions rest within the general conviction that we haven't thought enough about what this narrative, at the heart of Christianity, is made of. In particular, we haven't noted that there are four things about it that help to explain why it would go on to have such worldwide success. First, as just mentioned, it is totally mobile, cut free as it is from anything physical that one would need to rely on to accomplish the religious goals offered. Second, it is a recipe for powerful emotions, emotions that would increase the mobility and durability of the narrative. As one reads or listens with faith, one is generating the convictions that would lead one to push the narrative forward in time and onto others. Third, the emotional reactions organized by the narrative are likely enhanced by the democraticization of salvation: anyone who consumes the narrative with faith finds that all hierarchies are flattened, with only two identities left standing: those who believe the story (the elect) and those who don't. Thus, we can speculate that there is a certain thrill of sameness encoded in the text since all humans are rendered equal before the single question: Do you believe that this is what happened to Jesus, Son of God?

And, last, it seems clear that Mark's narrative, in its most basic sense, is built around securing the eternal sanctity of human identity against the vast and uncaring matrix of Being. Thus, once Jesus's natural and uninvented sameness with the divine Father is "proven" to be real—a sameness beyond time, death, language, and so on—the mechanism for all humans to find a final semi-divine identity is *also* firmly established. In this sense, one of the reasons why this narrative—and those that it spawned—was so successful has to be that, in trying to preserve some slim remnant of the Jewish tradition, after the destruction of Second Temple Judaism, it rather accidently set out a self-perpetuating paradigm for solving the most basic problem that language and culture seem to have given us: how to have confidence in the permanence of the symbolically manufactured Self when it seems to disappear so completely with the body at death.

The tragedy of this situation, though, is that in trying to explain the fall of (old) tradition and its rightful replacement by the new, the narrative generated a rather evil image of the Jewish tradition, an image that would go on to bedevil what remained of the Jewish tradition as it rebuilt itself and endured into the present. In short, the author of Mark built something like a *memorial* to Temple Judaism by lodging the essence of tradition in the new form of Jesus and the narrative that he lives in, so that, even with its death, (old) tradition could move forward into a new item that would serve as its successor—to borrow Freud's language for describing the function of a fetish. Unfortunately, it was in turning the death of (old) tradition into a just punishment that Mark's author also accidentally built a narrative that would in time come to incite hatred for traditional Judaism, and Jews in general, a hatred that completely fails to see the dialectical and fetishizing process that is behind the invention of this form of Christianity. In sum, until we see that Mark is art and not history, we will be stuck with a logic and a set of desires that can only be described as anti-Judaic, even though it seems clear that Mark's author was Jewish and was, in a most basic sense, trying to save a sliver of tradition, in reliance on some very traditional themes and gestures.

With these issues in view, let's turn to see how Buddhist authors worked with similar strategies for fetishizing tradition.

4

The *Sūtra on the Land of Bliss*, or
That Place between Tongues and Texts

Introduction: Buddhism, Off in the Distance

What is called "the Shorter" *Sūtra on the Land of Bliss* (*Sukhāvatīvyūha*) is indeed a short text, likely composed in Sanskrit, in India, some time before the beginning of the 5th century, when it was first translated into Chinese.[1] Since it presents itself as a record of a discourse that the historical Buddha gave, no author is indicated; likewise, no mention is made of how the Buddha's supposed oral discourse was turned into text. Setting the *Land of Bliss* next to Paul's Letters and the Gospel of Mark seems appropriate because this text is also built around a series of gestures that fetishize tradition into new icons-of-desire that promise to deliver the totality of (old) tradition to the believing reader. In this case, the normal truth-father of the Buddhist tradition, the Buddha Śākyamuni of India, introduces a double of himself—the Buddha Amitāyus—who, we are told, is in charge of dispensing a perfect form of the Buddhist tradition in some very unconventional ways.[2] According to the Buddha of (old) tradition, Buddha Amitāyus presides over a wondrous land called the Land of Bliss (*sukhāvatī*), a faraway place where perfect tradition can finally be won, with the only drawback being that one must die to get there. On the bright side, the text promises that admission to the Land of Bliss is easy, since one need only believe this text and then recite, with pure faith, the name of the Buddha Amitāyus, in order to win rebirth in that land after one's death.[3]

In a basic way it isn't hard to see that, from the name of this magical land on down, the text is designed as a careful and persistent seduction in which readers or listeners committed to (old) tradition are gently led to the conclusion that they should take this text as the sole guide for winning authentic tradition. One's religious task in this life, then, is to believe this text and then *wait for tradition* in a specific sort of way defined by the text. Actually, instead of saying "wait for tradition" we should say "long for tradition," since it is precisely the desire for this postponed form of tradition that the text identifies as essential for gaining entrance to the Land of Bliss. Given this focus on a rendezvous with tradition after death, it isn't surprising that there is nothing in the text that suggests that one has any reason to seek out (old) tradition in this world: be it in the monasteries, in the presence of living monks, in other Buddhist texts or discourses, or in the performance of standard Buddhist practices—such as meditation and ethics.[4]

Essential to drawing the reader into this particular form of longing for tradition is an elaborate description of the Land of Bliss: it turns out to be a magnificently constructed landscape remarkable for the way it blends an array of somatic pleasures with intimate contact with tradition. The pleasures begin with the architecture of the place: the Land of Bliss is said to be clean, orderly, and completely fenced in. Within this geometric precision, various elements have been installed to please the inhabitants; for instance, there are trees and lotus-flower ponds, and they are all made out of seven kinds of precious jewels: gold, silver, beryl, crystal, sapphire, rosy pearls, and carnelian. Likewise, the ground is a golden hue and pleasant to behold, and heavenly music is also always playing. And, as we will see, this well ordered and wondrously alluring landscape is but a backdrop for the inhabitants to receive and absorb, in a most direct and pleasurable manner, the totality of traditional Buddhism.

While the beauty of the land is manifest in these static features, the dispensation of tradition involves two curious activities: three times a day and three times at night, inhabitants receive the essence of Buddhism when magically produced birds show up to sing in a delightfully harmonious manner that directly installs tradition in the minds of the inhabitants. A similar transmission of tradition occurs when, apparently in a more continuous manner, the wind blows through the gem trees and makes the nets of bells hung in those trees tinkle, thereby sounding as though there were a heavenly orchestra playing and, again, making the inhabitants think of the essence of Buddhism. The surviving Sanskrit version of the *Land of Bliss* includes the detail that these magically produced sounds are so efficacious that they even produce a physical effect in the inhabitants' body, making them feel as though the Buddha, his teachings, the Buddhist community were fully present: "When human beings in that world hear this sound, they remember the Buddha and feel his presence in their whole body, they remember the dharma and feel its presence in their whole body, and they remember the sangha (the Buddhist community) and feel its presence in their whole body."[5] Apparently, our author wants to emphasize that this highly unorthodox mode for transmitting tradition—however pleasurable and inexplicable—nonetheless works perfectly as a stand-in mechanism for delivering tradition, since it even gives inhabitants a physical sense of the presence of the most basic building blocks of old-style tradition.

The regular transmission—and perfect reception—of tradition via natural sounds is balanced by one other major activity given to the inhabitants of the Land of Bliss: every morning they travel to billions of other Lands of Bliss in order to offer flowers to the buddhas who reside there. Despite the distances involved, these whirlwind tours don't last all that long, and one returns in time for a pre-noon lunch, as stipulated by the Buddhist monastic code—a nap follows. Thus, the day's activities blend the flawless and automatic reception of tradition with the worship of billions of cosmic buddhas, the figures who presumably constructed these lands that so wonderfully deliver tradition. Given this description, the Land of Bliss seems to be a blending of a magical monastery with an exquisite Indian garden, a possibility that we will return to below.

Though the text claims that Amitāyus's Land of Bliss is unsurpassed for its ability to maintain and reproduce perfect tradition, much in this fantasy would have surprised traditional Buddhists. For instance, besides the very idea of such a Land of Bliss—a idea whose strangeness seems to be assumed, given the author's slow and detailed explanation of the place—this newly revealed Buddha Amitāyus would have been a shock for old-school Buddhists who typically assumed that only one buddha lived per cosmic era. Though the buddha of our epoch, the Buddha Śākyamuni, was thought to have had several predecessors in eons past, never was it said that the universe was populated by other buddhas, living at the same time. That there might be billions of buddhas out there, presiding over their individual lands of bliss, would have, no doubt, been quite shocking to traditional Buddhists.[6]

Presumably even more disturbing to traditionalists would have been the way that the text marginalizes the Buddha Śākyamuni's place in tradition. As is probably already obvious, the text effectively demotes Śākyamuni to being a mere signpost for Amitāyus and, thus, in place of performing his traditional role of revealing truth and tradition, in this text the Buddha Śākyamuni's discourse focuses on the techniques for leaving this world and winning a place in Amitāyus's land.[7] Consequently, instead of fathering tradition and installing it in various practices and institutions so that believers could, in our world, replicate Buddhist truth and find salvation—as he does so often in the discourses taken to be traditional—Śākyamuni is now gently pushing his audience away from him in order to guide them to Amitāyus who is identified as the one who will, henceforth, serve as the truth-father delivering tradition to believers. In this sense, Amitāyus is presented as a crucial guardian of tradition, with Śākyamuni's responsibilities now limited to getting his own followers to long for this singular place where, after death, perfect traditon can finally be accessed.

Even as Śākyamuni is reduced to advertising this postmortem form of tradition, he also is given the task of legitimizing Amitāyus and the Land of Bliss. Hence, as often happens with texts that fetishize (old) tradition into new forms, the text has made the older version of the truth-father, the Indian Buddha Śākyamuni, explain why his newly introduced double is to be taken as the ultimate site for winning tradition. Apparently following the logic that it takes a buddha to know a buddha, the author has Śākyamuni Buddha and a host of other recently invented buddhas provide testimony in support of the claims regarding Amitāyus and his land, and, of course, the text that is currently explaining all this. In effect, then, the text relies on the authorizing elements of (old) tradition to nullify (old) tradition, while also relying on those prior forms of authority to promote the text and its discourse as the way to win tradition on the other side of death.

Though Śākyamuni is shown finding a better version of himself in Amitāyus, we can't help but notice that Amitāyus's version of tradition functions in a rather unusual manner, to say the least. To counter the reader's likely impression that Amitāyus's form of tradition is alarmingly bizarre, the text claims that it is Śākyamuni who is, in fact, the odd-man-out since Amitāyus is supposedly identical to every other cosmic buddha in the universe, all of whom supposedly reside in similarly structured Lands of Bliss. To make this distinction absolutely clear, the text has Śākyamuni Buddha explain, at the end of the text, that he himself is unique in having to live and teach under the rude and unfortunate conditions that characterize our world. Thus, we learn from Śākyamuni Buddha that (old) tradition, as we know it in our world, is a cosmic anomaly and is, obviously, far from being exemplary. In particular, living as we do in a world of "five afflictions"—in a time of cosmic and human decay, when humans have relatively short lifespans, many passions, bad views, etc.—we have to receive teachings about the distant Land of Bliss and then hope to get there after death, whereas other beings already live there and practice that delightfully easy form of bird- and wind-based tradition.[8] In an additional piece of cleverness, the text mentions that it is these very afflictions, the ones that mark our world as unique and difficult, that will make it hard for people to accept this very text and its teachings on, among other things, our afflicted condition.[9] Stringing together these claims, we can see that the text explains itself as the Thing that will allow the hapless sentient beings of our hopeless world to get over their bad views and thereby cross over the gap that exists between our degraded world and the Land of Bliss, even as the text also explains why people in our world—presumably readers of this text—might resist the whole explanation of doubled tradition, and reject the text that promises to overcome just that gap.

Even though there are other Mahāyāna texts that promote similar visions of these Lands of Bliss, there are good reasons for thinking that this text, which so concisely balances this double tableau of perfect and degraded forms of tradition, is one of the more important religious texts ever written.[10] Though this text, and those several others like it, seems to have had little impact on religious life in India, it would not be an exaggeration to say that East Asian Buddhism was, in time, largely shaped by faith in the Land of Bliss.[11] Somewhat ironically, then, it was just this image of tradition postponed, lodged in the distant zone of the Land of Bliss, that proved to be a very stable element in organizing the East Asian Buddhist traditions.[12]

An Introduction to Literary Reinventions of the Buddhist Tradition

To explain the structure and logic of the *Land of Bliss*, I have broken my analysis into two sections. In the first section I close read the narrative to show how it conjures up an image of (old) tradition, overcomes it, and then relocates its essence in a fetishized form that it promises to deliver to the reader—provided that the reader believes the narrative—once they are reborn in the Land of Bliss. In the second section, I consider several textual precedents that seem to have provided both the details of the *Land of Bliss* and the impetus to consolidate tradition into belief in belief. In particular, I explore the possibility that the *Land of Bliss* has reworked material taken from the final section of an earlier Mahāyāna text, the *Perfection of Wisdom in 8,000 Lines* (*Aṣṭasāhasrikā Prajñāpāramitā*), a text that also fetishizes tradition and works to convince the reader that tradition is now to be found in itself, as text. To that end, the finale of the *Perfection of Wisdom in 8,000 Lines* describes a wonderful and exciting *city* called Gandhavati that closely resembles the Land of Bliss in terms of form and content, but which is nonetheless supposedly located in our world, far to the east. At the center of this city is a magnificent gold version of this very text—the *Perfection of*

Wisdom in 8,000 Lines—along with an incomparable teacher who regularly gives an oral version of the text when he is not enjoying his sixty-eight thousand consorts. Thus, set within another carefully established double tableau of two radically different forms of tradition—found in and outside of this city—the *Perfection of Wisdom in 8,000 Lines* promises that devoted readers of this very text will, ultimately, end up in just this city where they can receive an oral, and particularly effective, articulation of the text that they are currently reading, while also enjoying the massively pleasurable elements of this cityscape. That is, in the *Perfection of Wisdom in 8,000 Lines*, the reader is encouraged to devote himself to the text within the fantasy that just such a devoted reading will, in time, result in a most pleasurable kind of engagement with the text, in this magical city of Gandhavati.

If we hypothesize that the author of the *Land of Bliss* worked up his vision of paradise at least in partial dependence on the account of this perfect city in the *Perfection of Wisdom in 8,000 Lines*—and they share a remarkable number of details—then, insofar as the *Perfection of Wisdom in 8,000 Lines* promises the reader access to a zone where one receives tradition *orally* and with maximum bliss, the *Land of Bliss* goes a step further and tries to interest the reader in a paradise where even oral versions of texts—given by human teachers, that is—are surpassed, since one receives tradition via the music of birds and wind. Put that way, we might wonder if the Land of Bliss isn't, itself, something like a huge magical text since, once inside it, it serves as a stable, impersonal source from whence tradition flows, effortlessly, and in a kind of uncanny, surround-sound manner, in the complete absence of a living teacher. Given that the Land of Bliss has these "literary" powers, it is no wonder that the author chose not to mention a teacher or book within this Land of Bliss—what would be the point? In sum, while the *Perfection of Wisdom in 8,000 Lines* presented itself, as text, to the reader as the timeless container for tradition, the *Land of Bliss* presents the Land of Bliss as a text-like thing that can, too, be relied on to timelessly preserve *and* deliver the essence of tradition. In that sense the Land of Bliss is a wondrous text in the sky that takes the earlier Mahāyāna forms of reader seduction to the next level.[13]

To understand why the Land of Bliss likely represents a "post-literature" paradise—in the sense that it was designed in reaction to earlier Mahāyāna attempts to fetishize tradition into texts—I need to back up and clarify several general historical points regarding the writing and rewriting of tradition in early Mahāyāna Buddhism.[14] The key here is to realize that writing was only introduced into the Buddhist tradition some several hundred years after the Buddha's death, roughly at the beginning of the Common Era. In the earliest phases, the Buddhist tradition was literature-free, with the Buddhist elite—monks and nuns, that is—representing something like a resilient guild of practitioners who took it as their responsibility to remember, practice, and transmit the Buddha's teachings. In time, this elite group of Buddhists came to consolidate themselves into monastic communities—in the centuries before the Common Era—in which the legacy of the Buddha's message could be lived out with a minimum of distractions. Roughly at the beginning of the Common Era these communities began to take on a much more institutionally developed presence, while also constructing their buildings and grounds in more enduring ways. At some early point in this process, Indian Buddhist monasteries came to speak of themselves as gardens or pleasure groves and seemed to emphasize—in terminology, design, and architecture—parallels between the classical Indian garden and the monastery.[15] This important double needs to be kept in mind as we try to make sense of the way that the *Land of Bliss* constructs the transmission of Buddhism as a completely natural affair, free of all human interference, even as it lodges this "natural version" of the Buddhist tradition in a completely manicured and controlled space—a garden of sorts, that is.

Next to the professional form of Buddhism established in the monasteries, there was a "spectator" kind of Buddhism in which lay Buddhists had but a rudimentary understanding of Buddhist doctrine, and essentially limited their practice of tradition to living productive and ethical lives in order that they could bolster their karmic accounts and provide the monastery with the resources it needed. And, of course, for the system to work generation after generation, the lay families had also to produce the future monks and nuns—those select persons who would renounce the lay-life to join the monasteries.[16]

In the absence of writing, the content of Buddhism, along with all the rules for practicing Buddhism, were delivered orally and via highly ritualized conduits. Thus, tradition repeated itself through sustained person-to-person contact such that the "life of tradition" essentially piggy-backed on the lives of its most devoted practitioners in the sense that tradition had to be re-created and lived, generation after generation, *through the human body*. Once writing was introduced into India, and the earliest evidence points to this occurring in first half of the 3rd century BCE, Buddhist teachings and the details of the monastic system were soon written down. Not surprisingly, this writing effort resulted in several very large collections of Buddhist works taking shape in quasi-canonical form in India and Sri Lanka. In general, it seems that this writing of tradition was conducted within the hope that doubling tradition in textual form would give it a better chance of surviving the vicissitudes of history.

Presumably at the time few Buddhists worried that in opening up this new literary form of tradition they were also opening up a major threat to maintaining the content of tradition as it had been known. While it seems very likely that all along the oral tradition was flexible and inventive, it had some very sturdy bulwarks in place to keep its contents relatively uniform. Thus, monks and nuns were to meet fortnightly to recite the list of monastic rules, an occasion for reaffirming at least one crucial element of tradition. Too, there appears to have been various well-developed mnemonic practices, practices likely borrowed from the Vedic system of memorization, to ensure that oral texts were remembered intact. Thus, for instance, the Buddha's teaching were often put into verse and put to melodies that aided memorization and that made it more obvious if something was missing or deformed. However, once the master-to-disciple mode of transmitting tradition was doubled by the written text, the door was open to all sorts of innovation, since it became very difficult to tell which texts were legitimately written as simple doubles of the oral tradition and which texts had only recently been invented.

In thinking about this inventive re-writing of the Buddhist tradition, it is worth distinguishing two different styles. One was the straightforward effort to maintain tradition by writing new Buddhist teachings to resolve specific problems that hadn't been imagined or addressed by the Buddha. For instance, the literature detailing monastic practice—the Vinaya—grew steadily as newly appearing institutional issues were addressed and resolved by first inventively narrating how the problem supposedly had arisen during the Buddha's lifetime, and then having the Buddha-in-the-text address the matter with some specific ruling. These vignettes, though clearly fictional, stayed within the broad outlines of monastic Buddhism. And, equally important, these texts "lived" next to the mass of other Buddhist narratives that had been written and consolidated by the monastic institution. In short, there was a fairly high degree of institutional control over what new material was to be accepted as traditional and housed with other works deemed traditional.[17]

In the second form of re-writing tradition we find a body of texts that must have been written outside the control of the monastic tradition since they appear to be at odds with the monastic tradition on several fronts. First, though they pretend to be traditional *sutras* representing the voice of the Buddha, they often attack standard forms of Buddhist teachings and the monastics that sought to practice those teachings. These attacks also include charges that the real Buddhist tradition isn't, in fact, held by the monastics but must be sought elsewhere. In this vein, quite a few of these texts—such as the *Perfection of Wisdom in 8,000 Lines*—have the Buddha-in-the-text explain that the text itself is the perfect purveyor of tradition and thus should be worshipped accordingly, thereby instituting what Gregory Schopen dubbed "the cult of the text."[18] Not surprisingly, as these texts sought to generate the impression that they were containers of real tradition, they completely redefined the essence of tradition and then made that essence of tradition available in new and unexpected ways that basically revolved around the worship and maintenance of the text itself. Though many Buddhist ideas remain in force, foundational monastic practices were put in question, and in their place we find the promotion of belief: belief in new buddhas, belief in new narratives, belief in new practices, and, of course, belief in the powers of belief.

To give a sense of how explicit these texts could be in presenting themselves as the essence of tradition, consider the following passage from chapter ten of the *Lotus Sūtra* which is representative of this promotion of the "cult of the text" in early Mahāyāna Buddhism. In this passage the Buddha is made to explain how this text is, in effect, the container of tradition and a suitable buddha replacement:

> Again if there are persons who accept, read, expound, and copy the *Lotus Sūtra of the Wonderful Law*, even only one verse and look upon this sūtra with the same reverence as they would the Buddha, presenting various offerings of flowers, incense, necklaces, powdered incense, past incense . . . then you should understand that such persons have already offered alms to a hundred thousand million buddhas and in the place of the buddhas have fulfilled their great vow. . . . [And,] if someone should ask what living beings will be able to attain buddhahood in future existences, then you should show him that all these people in the future existences are certain to attain buddhahood. Why? Because if good men and good women accept, read, expound, and copy the *Lotus Sūtra of the Wonderful Law*, even one phrase of it, offer various kinds of alms to the sūtra, flowers, incense, necklaces, powdered incense, etc . . . then these persons will be looked up to and honored by all the world. Alms will be offered to them such as would be offered to the Tathāgata (the Buddha). You should understand that these persons are great bodhisattvas who have succeeded in attaining unsurpassed enlightenment."[19]

Exaggerating only slightly, this text, and others like it, promise that one becomes a legitimate Buddhist by reading and believing these newly penned narratives that explain: 1) how the "real" Buddhist tradition isn't in the monasteries, or in the recognized body of rituals, codes, and practices that shaped Buddhism since its inception; and, 2) that tradition is fully present in the text that is accomplishing this rhetorical overcoming of tradition and that this full version is, of course, available to the believing reader. In short, the text has become the container of the specific language that the reader supposedly needs to accomplish all the goals of (old) tradition.

Consequently, salvation is no longer defined as the straightforward Buddhist task of overcoming desire and ignorance by seeing the true nature of reality. Instead, salvation is predicated on one's devotion to these new textual narratives that, among other things, completely redefine tradition.[20] Putting aside the standard assumptions about Mahāyāna Buddhism—its supposed emphasis on emptiness and compassion—I think a careful and balanced reading of these texts leaves little doubt that salvation was, in some key instances, defined not as the function of a view on reality, but a view back on tradition. That is, one's salvation is said to be won through a change in allegiances—from traditional Buddhism to textualized Buddhism—and not as the effect of a straightforward grappling with existence. In a fully circuitous manner, then, these texts promise that one becomes a buddha by reading and assenting to particular theories about how one becomes a Buddha.

The *Land of Bliss* most likely figures in this literary revolution, though I expect it belongs in a second or third wave of Mahāyāna writing. The reason it makes sense to locate the *Land of Bliss* in this literary movement is that the Land of Bliss functions just like one of these early Mahāyāna texts that fetishizes tradition into itself, since the Land of Bliss, too, presents itself as a newly revealed container of tradition which can, endlessly, dispense the language of tradition in the absence of any human teacher. Moreover, there are good reasons for thinking that the *Land of Bliss* sought to fetishize not just the old monastic tradition, but also those older Mahāyāna texts that had, in earlier phases of writing, sought to fetishize tradition into the "cult of the text." For instance, as the *Land of Bliss* fetishizes the "practice" of tradition in our world into belief in the name of the Buddha Amitāyus, the older "cult of the text" appears overcome and improved. Likewise, with the promise that the language of tradition will be lovingly injected into the inhabitants of the Land of Bliss via the birds and wind through the trees, it would seem that the *Land of Bliss* has designed a post-literature paradise where the frustrations of both reading and human orality are replaced by these luscious, pleasurable, and infallible forms of communication.[21] As we will see, it seems sensible to conclude that the *Land of Bliss* offers a rarefied form of Buddhism dedicated to convincing believers that they will get the essence of Buddhism without all the various encumbering realities that prior form of tradition had relied on.

Part I: Faith and the Power of Submission

The *Land of Bliss* is quite short in comparison to other Mahāyāna sūtras and is usefully divided into four parts. The first section introduces the "listening" audience present when the historical Buddha Śākyamuni supposedly gave this discourse. These details, provided by an omniscient narrator, create the image that the discourse to follow really was given by the Buddha at a specific historical moment, even though, of course, these details are in fact exterior to the Buddha's discourse and thus naturally appear as proof of an author at work. Thus, it was only with this supporting narrative framework that the author thought he could make the discourse appear fully "oral," and therefore reliable. As in the case of the Gospel of Mark, the talent on display here is to make art appear to be non-art, and in that manner most appeal to the reader who mistakes the text as the result of an uncontrived historical event. With the text thereby generating an image of its own innocent origin, it can pose in front of the reader saying, essentially, "This is what the Buddha taught one day, and since the Buddha is both omniscient and a reliable narrator, this text must be true, and thus you have no choice but to believe this." After the narrative has established the on-site audience, the text moves to establish a two-person dialogue, a format common in early Mahāyāna texts. In this case it is a "conversation" between the Buddha and Śāriputra, the disciple most favored in traditional, pre-Mahāyāna Buddhism, a choice that again gives the text a traditional-looking veneer. Curiously, Śāriputra never gets to speak and, consequently, he seems simply to be an ear for the delivered discourse, and thus, presumably, he serves as a proxy for the reader who listens through him.

In the following discourse delivered to the silent and docile Śāriputra, we find the remaining three sections of the text. Here, the Buddha first describes the form, content, and function of the Land of Bliss. This section of the text is full of details regarding the gems, flowers, and ponds that make up the landscape of the Land of Bliss, along with those magical birds and winds that preach the essence of Buddhism to the inhabitants of the Land of Bliss. The section closes with a very brief explanation of Amitāyus's name, followed by a short passage on the requirements needed to gain rebirth in this land. In this crucial statement we learn that one needs simply to hear and faithfully retain the name Amitāyus, single-mindedly, for one day or two days or three, and so on, and then, when one dies, Amitāyus and his retinue will arrive to take one to the Land of Bliss.

In the next section the author shifts topics to have the Buddha list, formulaically, other buddhas like Amitāyus who have their own Lands of Bliss and can be found in each of the cardinal directions, including up and down. This comparatively lengthy section presents a cosmic overview of the various buddhalands in the six directions, but it also serves as a gallery of voices validating the author's own discourse since it turns out that these buddhas are presently looking back at our world, encouraging beings here to believe this very text. Here, then, we find an interesting fold in the text, a place where it talks about itself in such a way that it gains the appearance of having been confirmed from outside itself, through the eyes and assurances of reliable narrators—these cosmic buddhas—who were, of course, nevertheless produced within the discourse by the author. This literary technique closely matches strategies in other Mahāyāna works and reveals the kind of literary self-consciousness that I assume to be essential to their composition.[22] Naturally, too, having such a large number of cosmic buddhas ratify the text helps solidify the text's position that its version of tradition is, in fact, the default mode of tradition in the universe, whereas (old) tradition in our world is a weird and sad aberration.[23]

Following this section that legitimizes and hypes the text, the narrative moves to closure by explaining the benefits of accepting this discourse on the Land of Bliss: not only will all the buddhas remember and protect such a reader, but the aspiration to be reborn in Amitāyus's land will be the sufficient cause for actually taking rebirth there. Then, and in a slightly convoluted passage, the Buddha claims that simply by hearing the name of this sūtra—now referred to by its secondary name "Embraced By All Buddhas"—and the names of the buddhas within it, one can win rebirth in the Land of Bliss, provided one has the aspiration to do so.[24] The final section, as mentioned above, turns to talk about the difficulty in believing this discourse, given the decadent state of our current world, with the Buddha explaining why the other buddhas praise him for preaching in this world characterized by lack of faith, a gesture that again shows the text commenting on itself in a self-justifying manner.

Put schematically, there are three zones of language that work through one another in the text's construction of itself: 1) the Buddha's orality, as he supposedly preaches the *Land of Bliss* to that audience at Rājagṛiha in North India, with the implicit claim that if he preached it, it must be true; 2) the reliable replication of that orality into the *textual* form of the *Land of Bliss*, a form that the author objectifies and makes the "speaking" Buddha promote; and, 3) the distant Land of Bliss's reliable replication of the buddhas' orality in the birds and wind that now are the mouthpieces of tradition in that postmortem paradise. Put this way, the text is essentially saying to the reader that if you assent to the claim that 2 (text) was purely produced by 1 (the Buddha's orality), you will win 3 (the Land of Bliss with its incomparably perfect "orality"). Thus, what looks at first to be a simple seduction involving 2 (text) and 3 (Land of Bliss) turns out to be equally involved in the tension in moving from 1 (the Buddha's orality) to 2 (text), since 3 (the Land of Bliss) seems to be a perfected form of 2's relationship to 1, with the birds and winds acting like a text in the sense of presenting the Buddha's orality in his absence, just as the text itself presents the Buddha's orality in his absence. In its fullest form we should see that both 2 and 3 are zones for re-presenting a buddha's orality, and 3 is the perfect version of 2 that is won from believing that 2, also, is perfect in its representation of 1.

But Where Is Amitāyus?

Near the beginning of the text, the author has the Buddha say, "To the west of us, Śāriputra, a hundred thousand million buddha-fields from where we are, there is a world called the Land of Bliss. At this very moment, the Tathāgata, arhat, perfect and full buddha called Amitāyus lives in that buddha-field; he abides and remains there, and even now continues to teach the dharma in that field."[25] However, after this statement we never are given any more information about how Amitāyus lives in the land, how the inhabitants worship him, or how he teaches the dharma. Thus, one might rightly wonder in what manner he is actually present there. Actually, once it is clear that the text cares only to explain the Land of Bliss's teaching powers in terms of the birds and the wind, the better question is: Why is it that, in this sublime landscape, birds and winds have been set forth as teaching agents more suitable than a buddha? And, likewise, why is there absolutely no cultic interest in the Buddha Amitāyus when the text describes the form and function of this land?[26]

In addressing this conundrum, the first thing to clarify is that the author *could* have easily insisted that the Land of Bliss was governed by a wonderful buddha who, himself, taught a most perfect and irresistible form of Buddhism. But instead of offering the reader a vision of the Land of Bliss in which the traditional form of Buddhism would be recoverable in a traditional manner—for instance, having a chance to sit at the Buddha's feet and listen to all the original sūtras—the author has depicted a radical alternative for the transmission of Buddhist teachings and truth. In brief, with the narrative focused on this strange, dislocated form of perfect communication in the Land of Bliss, we would do well to ask why the text is trying to interest the reader in participating in a world where communication arrives from "natural" sources, yet still gives one the sense of the presence of the original speaker who, nevertheless, is nowhere to be seen. Obviously, in this sense, the text has opted for a paradise in which human orality is replaced by something stranger and distinctly more alienated.

The Birds

With these problems in view, let's consider more closely the daily appearance of the singing birds in the Land of Bliss:[27]

> Furthermore, Śāriputra, in that buddha-field wild geese, curlews, and peacocks gather three times every night and three times every day to sing in chorus, each singing with a different voice. And as they sing, one hears that their voices proclaim Buddhist virtues, such as the five spiritual powers, and the seven elements of awakening. When human beings in that world hear these sounds, their thoughts turn to the Buddha, their thoughts turn to the Buddha's teaching, the dharma, and their thoughts turn to Buddha's order, the sangha.

As the birds are tasked with transmitting the essence of Buddhism in this manner, it would seem that the author has effectively cleansed Buddhism of itself. With human teachers, practices, texts, sects, and rule-bound organizations out the picture, one still receives what are known as the Three Jewels of Buddhism—the Buddha, the dharma, and the sangha—along with "seven elements of awakening," which is basically another list of elemental items customarily taken to contain the whole of traditional Buddhism. In short, the beauty and sonic charms of the birds is matched by their functional ability to provide the essence of Buddhism in the absence of human or institutional mediation.

What the text next says about these birds is telling. Given that rebirth as an animal is understood in Buddhism as a form of punishment, and since there can't be, by definition, any pain or negativity in the Land of Bliss, the author has the Buddha explain to Śāriputra that in fact these birds aren't real birds, but instead are magically created by Amitāyus himself: "Rather, those flocks of birds gather there to sing with the voice of the dharma only because they have been created magically by the buddha who presides in that field, the Tathāgata Amitāyus."[28] Thus while the fantastic jewels and flowers are left to be real in the Land of Bliss, the birds had to be hollowed out and explained as no more than magical emanations of Amitāyus. With this passage, one senses a bit of awkwardness since, apparently, the author very much wanted birds in the Land of Bliss, but he also wanted it truly to be a Land of Bliss without animal rebirths.[29]

As I will argue below, this is one of the major clues that this description of the Land of Bliss is based on reworking earlier accounts of perfect cities—and gardens—found in our world. In these descriptions of the perfect, garden-like city—as seen in the *Perfection of Wisdom in 8,000 Lines* and in even older Buddhist texts—one finds the same descriptions of the jeweled items, the magical winds, and the wondrous birds, and yet the birds are not said to be magical creations since they are simply part of a wonderful landscape in our world where animal rebirth is completely normal. In sum, here is important evidence that, while there is not exactly trouble in paradise, there is trouble getting paradise set up such that it can conceal the ad-hoc process by which prior elements of the wider Indian cultural tradition were recycled in that construction process.[30]

The Winds

The treatment of the winds through the trees in the Land of Bliss is a good bit simpler and doesn't involve the creation of faux animals:[31]

> Furthermore, Śāriputra, when the rows of palm trees and nets of tinkling bells in that buddha-field sway in the wind, a sweet and enrapturing sound issues from them. This concert of sounds is, Śāriputra, like a set of heavenly cymbals, with a hundred, thousand, million playing parts—when these cymbals are played by expert musicians, a sweet and enrapturing sound issues from them. In exactly the same way, a sweet and enrapturing sound proceeds from those rows of palm trees and those nets of tinkling bells when they sway in the wind. When human beings in that world hear this sound, they remember the Buddha and feel his presence in their whole body, they remember the dharma and

feel its presence in their whole body, and they remember the sangha and feel its presence in their whole body.

With the regular delivery of this kind of surround-sound dharma, the Land of Bliss provides tradition directly and spontaneously, without the intervening problems of interpretation or boredom, and all those complicated intersubjective elements that usually exist between a discourse and its audience. Moreover, as with the birds, the wind discourse arrives as pure, unadulterated pleasure—something that few speakers or texts can supply.

Remembering that numerous Mahāyāna texts promote the idea that in other lands, Buddhist teaching is accomplished by nonhuman entities, I think it is worth wondering if our author isn't working to interest the reader in the promise that this natural "music"—surely an essentially non-linguistic entity—could completely replace the troubling play of language which, though made of sound, involves all sorts of complex interactions as words, ideas, histories, and desires combine in the construction of meaning. Reflecting on how the text has constructed this kind of perfect non-linguistic transmission of the linguistic items of tradition, I wonder if we might not have another seductive bargain offered here: read this text in an open and accepting manner, akin to the way the inhabitants of the Land of Bliss listen to the birds sing, and in time those birds will indeed sing for you. It seems to me that if one ignores this tension between these two modes of Buddhist communication—the textuality of our fallen world and the natural transmission of tradition via birds and wind in the Land of Bliss—one loses sight of what appears to be one of the main thematics of the work.

A Word about Names

These two zones of communication—the troubled one between text and reader and the effortless one between the Land of Bliss and its inhabitants—are linked up in the way that the text fetishizes itself. Avoiding "the cult of the text" rhetoric that calls for the reader to treat the text as a buddha-substitute—as seen, for example, in the *Perfection of Wisdom in 8,000 Lines* or the *Lotus Sūtra*—the *Land of Bliss* simply claims that taking hold of Amitāyus's name will finalize one's relationship with the text and its contents, and it will also lead to rebirth in the Land of Bliss at death. Thus, in organizing the reader's desire for the Land of Bliss's perfected form of communication, the text first pares itself down to a single name that is offered to the reader as the point of contact that will first cover one's relationship to the entire text and, second, will serve as the gateway into the Land of Bliss where the transmission of tradition will finally be accomplished.[32]

In that sense the text, as an long series of complex sentences, first defines the powers of Amitāyus's name and the rules for engaging that name, but then effectively disappears, leaving the reader with just Amitāyus's name as the effective icon for the totality of the text, even as all those textual promises presumably linger in the reader's imagination. In other words, the text makes Amitāyus's name appear purer and more powerful than itself when, in fact, our impressions of the name are all formulated by the text. In this dialectic between the magical name and its supporting body of explanation, the name without the supporting text would be worth nothing, and yet the text, by packing all its value into the name, invites the believing reader to look past the bulkiness of the text's prose to see, in its place, only the pure simplicity of Amitāyus's name, just as it asks the reader to look past the text and its place in the messiness of the Buddhist tradition to "see" the Land of Bliss, with its oh-so-simple and "natural" form of tradition.

The salvific powers of Amitāyus's name are made clear midway through the text when the Buddha Śākyamuni explains to Śāriputra how faith in Amitāyus's name will draw Amitāyus and his retinue to the believer at death.

> Śāriputra, those sons or daughters of good families who will hear the name of the blessed Amitāyus, the Tathāgata, and then bring it to mind, and will keep it in mind without distraction for one night, or two, or three, four, five, six, or seven nights—they will be met by the Tathāgata at the moment of their death. When the moment of death approaches for one of these sons or daughters of good families, Amitāyus the Tathāgata, surrounded by an assembly of disciples and at the head of a host of bodhisattvas will stand before this son or daughter, and this son or daughter will die with a mind that is free from distorted views. After they die, they will be reborn in the Land of Bliss, in the buddhafield of Amitāyus the Tathāgata.

With this involved promise in place, it's clear that the author is enticing the reader with the idea that accepting Amitāyus's name with single-minded devotion will lead on to a final kind of union with the truth-father since the truth-father will arrive to greet the dying son or daughter of good family and whisk him or her off to his land to enjoy the company of like-minded practitioners. Then, once there, a final rebirth can be expected and it is one in which the devotee will become the same as the truth-father. As the

Buddha is made to say: "Furthermore, Śāriputra, those sentient beings who are reborn in the buddha-field of the Tathāgata Amitāyus are pure bodhisattvas who will not fall back and will be separated from awakening by only one rebirth."[33] This final rebirth isn't described, but it surely occurs without sex or assistance from women. Thus, though the text doesn't metaphorize one's relationship with Amitāyus in a father-son manner, it still seems clear that the text works to convince the believer that he or she can join with the deepest kind of patriarch in the universe in the form of Amitāyus—the Buddha of "measureless lifespan"—who has created just this place where one's final identity as a double of the truth-father will be accomplished.[34] Amitāyus, in short, promises to be one's final parent in that postmortem land where the believer supposedly joins ranks with the truth-fathers.

Here, There, and the Enormous Tongues of Truth

To get a better sense of the seduction that the *Land of Bliss* offers, we will do well to follow the basic "here-there" structure of the narrative. For the purposes of this discussion, the "there" is defined by the vision of all the other buddhas in the universe, including Amitāyus, who look from their buddhalands back "here" at our world, at our Buddha, and at this text, all in order to offer encouragement and legitimizing commentary. Besides these functions, the text also claims that all the other buddhas in the universe are in their respective buddhalands preaching the dharma by extending their tongues to cover their realms in order to teach their limitless disciples, disciples who apparently don't need texts, and who don't need to hear other buddhas explain the truthfulness of the discourses that their buddha gives them. As the Buddha of our world puts it, "Each one of these buddhas covers his own buddha-field with his tongue and then reveals all that is in it."[35] In short, in those perfect lands there is no gap between the buddha's tongue—which covers the land—and the inhabitants. Truth flows perfectly from the buddha to the inhabitants without ever requiring any mediation—literary or otherwise—and without ever generating any resistance. The situation, obviously, is quite different in our world where the gap between the Buddha's tongue and his disciples is quite significant. In fact, it would seem that the text is making clear that in our world this gap is defined by this text itself, since it is obviously the item that conveys our Buddha's teaching to the reader qua disciple. Put that way, the text seems to be acknowledging that having textuality intervene in that space between the Buddha's tongue and the disciples is far from ideal; in fact, in the conclusion the author has the cosmic buddhas applaud our Buddha for his success in achieving unsurpassed enlightenment in this world and for teaching this sūtra which is a "dharma that the whole world was reluctant to accept."[36] In short, the direct, oral dispensation of truth in the buddhalands of the cosmic buddhas—delivered via their massive tongues—is a far cry from the gritty work of getting the disciples of our world to believe this discourse—the *Land of Bliss*—a discourse that seems to have come out of the sophisticated literary experiments that are so characteristic of early Mahāyāna Buddhism.[37]

Expected resistance to the text also appears when the author has these cosmic buddhas say to the inhabitants of our world, "You should place your trust in this discourse on the dharma, called 'Embraced by All Buddhas,' which extols inconceivable qualities."[38] One might think at first that these buddhas were addressing their own disciples with this advice, but since the text, as we have seen, has gone out of its way to say that what is unique about our Buddha's land is his resistant audience, and since the title "Embraced by All Buddhas" is the secondary title that the *Land of Bliss* gives to itself, this exhortation by the cosmic buddhas is surely directed back to beings in our world, back to the reader, in other words, the one who needs to overcome his or her resistance to this text in order to put his faith in Amitāyus's name and get to the Land of Bliss at death. In this way, the "there" of the cosmic buddhas is depicted as a perfect zone of transmitting tradition, one where there are no texts and only those enormous tradition-giving tongues, and where the buddhas look back at our fallen situation and urge us to trust this text that promises to take us to a place where there will be no encumbering texts hindering the transmission of tradition. In short, the text seems to be involved in a complex act of self-overcoming as it works to get the reader to love the text for the way that it will get rid of texts in a final manner.

Likewise, having the reader imagine that his gaze "into" the text and then "out" into the universe is reflected by the cosmic buddhas gazing back at him as he reads this very text is a pretty clever rhetorical figure, and for several reasons. First, it tempts the reader with the possibility that he and the text are at the center of the universe; certainly the cosmic buddhas aren't shown interested in other activities, and thus there is an immense narcissism implicit in the structure of the situation.[39] Second, since those buddhas are acknowledging that this discourse is hard to believe, the text is articulating and then normalizing the resistance that it hopes to overcome—these cosmic buddhas already know about the reader's resistance and have appropriate things to say about overcoming that resistance. Thus, any reluctance on the part of the reader to duck these claims immediately gets referred to this gallery of know-it-all buddhas who understand, supposedly, the reading subject better than himself. Likewise, in a fully circular manner, the text explains that that very resistance proves why the text shouldn't be resisted. In short, we live in a defiled world where bad views and bad readers are the norm, and it is this very badness that is to be overcome—by the text, itself. Consequently, in overcoming one's resistance to the text, one overcomes the defilement of our world in an act which again aggrandizes the reader.

Third, the text is essentially requiring the reader to denounce not just this world, but Buddhism as he or she might have known it. Thus, the text works to cut itself away from the supposedly defiled nature of contemporaneous Buddhism, offering itself as the singular way to gain real tradition, even as its gesture of defining the present as "defiled" generated the very need to escape current forms of tradition.[40] In sum, the text has brilliantly insinuated itself into the reader's relationship with: 1) past tradition and the defiled world that supposedly defines both that past tradition and the current reading moment; 2) all the current buddhas in the universe who are at this very moment looking on and urging conversion to the text; and 3) the future which, with a moment of faith in Amitāyus, or rather his name, is to be defined by rebirth in the Land of Bliss.

On another level, the construction of this vision that moves out into the universe and then back to our reading moment ought to remind us of that parallel to-and-fro motion that characterizes the inhabitants' daily routine in the Land of Bliss whereby they leave to worship these same cosmic buddhas and then return in time for lunch. As mentioned above, no one seems to worship locally in the Land of Bliss, and instead has to exit to worship countless *other* buddhas in *their* lands. Thus, in either situation the author has constructed an exchange between an empty center and hallowed periphery—defined in both cases by the gallery of cosmic buddhas—which secures the value and legitimacy of that center, be it the text or Amitāyus's Land of Bliss. In all these structures, one sees the author working with a tension between a tightly defined Something—Amitāyus's name, the text, the Land of Bliss—and the matrix of supporting powers-that-be located outside those icons, powers that need to be in place to supply the icons with content and legitimacy and which, nonetheless, aren't very useful on their own until they can be compressed into these icons and offered to the believer who understands them to be useful precisely for that power to fetishize all the supporting powers-that-be into a singularly handy and desirable item.

Part II: The Textual Genesis of the Land of Bliss

Seeking the literary antecedents of the *Land of Bliss* requires a good bit of audacity since there are very few secure historical facts for this period of Indian Buddhism.[41] Despite the significant uncertainties involved, I think we can begin to sketch a rudimentary outline of what happened in the genesis of the *Land of Bliss*. Even if this minimalist history remains conjectural, I think the project has value since it will require clarifying a number of unique elements and dynamics in the *Land of Bliss*. To build this history, we need to see that several pre-Mahāyāna Buddhist accounts of perfect cities closely match the details of the Land of Bliss. For instance, in what most likely is a pre-Mahāyānic text from the Pali Canon, the *Mahāsudassanasutta*, one finds a description of the ancient city of Kusavati that lies, mysteriously, behind the current rundown city of Kusinara.[42] Though currently invisible, the Buddha explains that Kusavati is made of jewels, surrounded by seven rows of palm trees, with lotus ponds, and with a lovely wind that blows through the trees' leaves, making a symphonic sound that rivals what skilled musicians could achieve.

In order to show how much continuity there is between these descriptions and those of later Mahāyāna texts, I will cite the full passage in which the Buddha is explaining to Ananda why it is alright for the Buddha to die in Kusinara, whereas in Ananda's eyes, it appears as but a grubby little town not fit to be the site of the Buddha's demise. The Buddha says,[43]

> Ananda, don't call it a miserable little town of wattle-and-daub, right in the jungle in the back of beyond! Once upon a time, Ananda, King Mahāsudassana was a wheel-turning monarch, a rightful and righteous king, who had conquered the land in four directions and ensured the security of his realm. And this King Mahāsudassana had this very [city of] Kusinara, under the name of Kusavati, for his capital. And it was twelve yojanas long from east to west, and seven yojanas wide from north to south. Kusavati was rich, prosperous and well-populated, crowded with people and well-stocked . . . And the city of Kusavati was never free of the ten sounds by day or night: the sound of elephants, horses, carriages, kettle-drums, side-drums, lutes, singing, cymbals, and gongs, with cries of "Eat, drink and be merry," as tenth.
>
> The royal city of Kusavati was surrounded by seven encircling walls. One was of gold, one silver, one beryl, one crystal, one ruby, one emerald, and one of all sorts of gems.

> And the gates of Kusavati were of four colors: one of gold, one silver, one beryl, one crystal. And before each gate were set seven pillars, three or four times a man's height. One was gold, one silver, one beryl, one crystal, one ruby, one emerald, and one of all sorts of gems.
>
> Kusavati was surrounded by seven rows of palm-trees, of the same [precious] materials. The gold trees had gold trunks with silver leaves and fruit, the silver trees had silver trunks. . . . The sound of the leaves stirred by the wind was lovely, delightful, sweet, and intoxicating, just like that of the five kinds of musical instruments played in concert by well-trained and skillful players. And, Ananda, those who were libertines and drunkards in Kusavati had their desires assuaged by the sound of the leaves in the wind.

Obviously there is much here that appears to be quite parallel to the description of the Land of Bliss.[44] And in terms of structure, this text, like the *Land of Bliss*, works up a vision of perfect and imperfect examples of tradition since the author appears intent on a kind of apologetics in which the Buddha's death is relocated to this perfected city, Kusavati, and away from the apparently lackluster, wattle-and-daub town of Kusinara.

There is a curious detail in this description that warrants special attention. Though the author clearly wanted this newly revealed glorious city to be happy and full of pleasure, as the tenth of the unceasing sounds "Eat, drink and be merry" promises, the final line in this section undermines that direct approach to pleasure by stipulating that the "libertines and drunkards" in this happy city actually get their satisfaction not from sex and alcohol, but from the "sound of the leaves in the wind." Thus, in organizing pleasure and consumption in Kusavati, our author insisted that the city is incomparable in its ability to satisfy its inhabitants, and yet the fulfillment of baser desires occurs through a pronounced displacement, with the wind in the trees providing the needed stimulus, all in order that the city's inhabitants live in accord with basic Buddhist ethics. Catching sight of this technique for allowing technically unacceptable elements onto a Buddhist landscape— sex and alcohol—is useful for understanding how the author of the *Land of Bliss* likewise relied on the wind (and the birds) to funnel pleasure into a landscape devoted to producing Buddhist content. Hence, it would seem that as the author of the *Land of Bliss* chose to rely on the birds and wind to blend pleasure and the Buddhist tradition into a harmonious whole, he reveals his familiarity with this earlier literary trope—taken from this text or one like it—and reapplies it in a parallel manner.

Leaving aside, for the moment, the implications of this repeated trope that uses the wind-through-the-trees to deliver lawful pleasure, we can say that similar descriptions of perfect Buddhist cities can be found in other pre-Mahayanic works such as the *Legend of King Aśoka, (Aśokāvadana)*[45] and the *Prediction of Maitreya (Aryamaitreya vyakaraṇa)*.[46] Hence it seems safe to conclude that various pre-Mahāyāna authors constructed magical landscapes to house Buddhist truth and tradition, and did so by recycling these descriptions of perfect cities, regularly imagined to be twelve leagues by seven, housing wondrous music, jewels, and birds, and all set on flat landscapes. Crucial to note in these pre-Mahāyāna examples is that the presentation of the perfect Buddhist city is never directly related to the text presenting that description; nor is the perfect city directly implicated in the seduction of the reader. Instead, the point seems to be that buddhas deserve to live in these wonderful places, and thus wherever a buddha is, one ought to suspect that there will be such a city, almost as part of his entourage.

A good example of how a buddha and this kind of landscape are imagined to exist in unison is found in the *Prediction of Maitreya* where the Buddha explains to Śāriputra that when the future buddha Maitreya comes, the world will be magically transformed and, in particular, a certain city named Ketumati will appear.[47]

> At that time [when Maitreya comes], for many leagues around, the oceans will dry up; the roads will become easily passable for cakravartin kings, and Jambudvipa [India] will be flat like a field extending in every direction for ten thousand leagues, a dwelling place for all creatures. And the human beings in those various regions will do good deeds, they will be nonviolent, nonvengeful, very prosperous, and happy. And the surface of the ground will be even, free from thorns and covered with green grass that yields gently when one jumps onto it and is soft like cotton. It will be sweet-smelling, and a delicious rice will grow there without any labor. And the trees will have garments of different colors hanging down from them. . . . And the beings will have good skin and large bodies and be very strong; and they will be intelligent, free from defilements, without fault, and long-lived. They will suffer only from three troubles: desires, old

age, and indigestion. Women will get married only when they are five hundred years old.

And at that time there will be a city called Ketumati. It will be the residence of beings who work for the welfare of all creatures, and will be twelve leagues in length and seven leagues wide, a delightful, meritorious, pure city. . . . It will have a resplendent king named Sanka, a powerful cakravartin ruler over four continents, endowed with the seven jewels of kingship and have a four-fold army.

In this presentation we see that the author wanted to convincingly depict the arrival of Maitreya, and did so by describing a corresponding city of ease and order that would house this buddha and, of course, thereby confirm his power and benevolence. In short, in these pre-Mahayanic depictions of the perfect city, the city is a visual representative of the moral powers of the residing buddha, powers that produce fertility, ease, order, and pleasure.

This arrangement seems to have been radically shifted in the *Perfection of Wisdom in 8,000 Lines*, considered to be one of the earliest Mahāyāna sūtras, where we find the perfect city housing not a buddha but a text, and, no surprise, it is the text that one is reading—the *Perfection of Wisdom in 8,000 Lines*. The obvious implication is that this text—as container of tradition—is equal in grandeur to the buddhas and thus warrants an equally marvelous host city to prove that grandeur. And yet just as this development separated the perfect city from the buddhas, it also opened the door for complex self-referential narratives that made use of the perfect city to mediate reader-text relations in a manner that appears unexplored in the earlier, non-Mahāyāna works.

City of Narrative, City of Love

The *Perfection of Wisdom in 8,000 Lines* is a long and baffling work that remains little digested in Buddhist studies. The finale, however, seems more readable since it develops a fairly straightforward narrative that recounts the wondrous attributes of a perfect city, named Gandhavati, where one can find this very *Perfection of Wisdom* text. Moreover, the narrative cleverly aligns one's movement trent through the narrative with physical movement toward Gandhavati by recounting the travails of a bodhisattva named Ever Wailing (Sadaprarudita) who is desperately searching for this text, a search that of course leads him (and the reader) to the magical city of Gandhavati. Once in Gandhavati, he discovers, along with the reader, that this very narrative, in both oral and literary forms, is celebrated at the center of this delightful city where there also are ample boating opportunities and, apparently, a lot of sex.

In short, one is reading over Ever Wailing's shoulder as he seeks out the text one is reading, with the important difference that Ever Wailing's implacable longing for the text will deliver him to the land of Gandhavati with all its splashy pleasures, whereas the reader of the text will only arrive at a *description of Gandhavati*. Thus, with his or her pleasures deferred, the reader is left to find satisfaction in worshipping the text in the standard form detailed above in the case of the *Lotus Sūtra*: one is expected to read, recite, copy, and explain the text. In brief, the text has sought to generate desire for itself by demonstrating just how strong that desire for the text ought to be—as demonstrated by the indefatigable Ever Wailing—and, correspondingly, just how pleasurable the completion of the journey/narrative will be when one really gets "to" the text. That is, desire for this text has become the main theme of the narrative as Ever Wailing is presented as the perfect reader, ready and willing to die to get a hold of this text which he takes to be the essence of Buddhism and the universe.[48]

And to be very clear about the earthy nature of this city, let me emphasize that in Gandhavati there are real animals, women, commerce, boating, and a whole lot of cavorting about. The key to this literary seduction is that the reader is promised that he will, like Ever Wailing, win access to this city of various pleasures, provided that he reads devotedly about that city and the rules to get there. In short, here is that familiar dialectic in which the more one steps into the narrative, the more one will want to step into the narrative, since the text is both the promise of bliss and the rules for getting that bliss, with the two wrapped around one another such that imagining the effect of inspired reading—the bliss of receiving the discourse in that far away, sexed-up city—helps you accept the text that is offering you the deal in the first place.

Reading from Edward Conze's translation of the *Perfection of Wisdom*, we find Ever Wailing traveling east in search of the *Perfection of Wisdom*, but currently in anguish over his inability to arrive at the promised locale. For clarity's sake, I have italicized the elements that appear in the *Land of Bliss* and included enough of the narrative to show how the *Perfection of Wisdom* has designed its relationship to the reader:[49]

When Ever Wailing thus sorrowed and pined away, a buddha-figure [suddenly] stood before him, gave his approval and said:

Well spoken, son of good family! For the Tathāgatas [buddhas] of the past, when they were the Bodhisattvas, have also searched for the perfect wisdom in the same spirit in which you just now search for it. In this same spirit of vigor and determination, of zeal and zest—do you go East! There, five hundred leagues away from here is a town called Gandhavati. It is build of the seven precious things. It is twelve leagues long and twelve leagues broad, and enclosed by seven walls, seven moats and seven rows of palm trees. It is prosperous and flourishing, secure from attack, contains abundant provisions and is full of beasts and men.

Five hundred rows of shops run through the town from one end to the other, beautiful to behold like a well-colored painting, arranged one by one in regular succession, and in between them well-constructed sites and passages are erected, respectively for vehicles drawn by animals, for palanquins, and for pedestrians, so that there is plenty of room for all. There well-founded copings slope into the golden river Jampu. And on each coping grows a *tree, made of the seven precious things*, laden with various fruits, also made of precious things. *All around, between each tree and the next, hangs a string, also made of precious substances. A network of small bells is fastened on the strings,* and thus surrounds the entire city. *When stirred by the wind, the small bells give out a sweet, charming and delightful sound, just like the sound from the five musical instruments when they are played in harmony by the Gandharvas, skilled in songs.* And that sound causes those beings to divert, enjoy and amuse themselves.

The moats all around the city are full of water which flows gently along, neither too cold nor too hot. The boats on that river are brilliant with the seven precious things, beautiful to behold, and their existence is a reward for the past deeds of the inhabitants who, aboard them, divert, enjoy, and amuse themselves. *The water is everywhere covered with blossoms of the blue lotus, of the pink lotus, of the white lotus, and with other most beautiful and fragrant flowers.* There is no species of flowers in the great trichiliocosm that is not found there.

All around that city there are five hundred parks, beautiful to behold, brilliant with the seven precious things. Each park has five times five hundred large lotus ponds, *covered with beautiful blossoms, each of the size of a cartwheel, fragrant,—blue, yellow, red and white. The sounds of geese, cranes, ducks, curlews, and other birds fill the air over the ponds.* And the existence of those parks which they do not regard as their own private property is a reward for the past deeds of those beings, for they had coursed for a long time in the perfection of wisdom, their minds faithfully devoted to the Guide of the Buddhas and bent on listening to the perfection of wisdom and understanding the perfection of wisdom, and for a long time they had been intent on deep dharmas.

And there, in that city of Gandhavati, at a place where four roads meet, is the house of the Bodhisattva Dharmodgata—one league all round, bright with the seven precious things, beautiful to behold, enclosed by seven walls and seven rows of palm trees. There are four parks near the house, for the enjoyment of those who live in it. They are called Nityapramudita, Asoka, Sokavigata, and Pushpacitra. Each park has eight lotus ponds. . . . One side of each pond is of gold, the second of silver, the third of vaid-urya, the fourth of crystal. The ground of the bottom consists of quartz. Each pond has eight stairs to it, decorated with steps, made of variegated jewels. In the gaps between the steps, inside the river Jambu, grows a plantain tree. The ponds are covered with various kinds of water flowers, and the air above them is filled with the sounds of various birds. Round these ponds grow various flowering trees, and when they are stirred by the wind, their flowers drop into the ponds. The water in the ponds has the scent, color, taste, and feel of sandalwood.

In this mansion lives the Bodhisattva Dharmodgata, with his retinue, among them sixty-eight thousand women. He diverts, enjoys and amuses himself, he feels and tastes the five kinds of sense-pleasure. All the inhabitants of that city, both women and men, divert, enjoy and amuse themselves, they have constant joy in the parks and on the ponds and they feel and taste the five kinds of sense-pleasure. *The Bodhisattva Dharmodgata, however, with his retinue, diverts, enjoys and amuses himself only for a certain time, and thereafter he always demonstrates the Perfection of Wisdom.*

And all the citizens of that town built a pulpit for the Bodhisattva Dharmodgata in the central square of the town. It has a golden base, then a cotton mattress is spread on that, then a woolen cover, a cushion and a silken cloth are put on top of that. High up in the air, half a mile high (half a *ko* high), there is an awning, shining with pearls, even and firm. All round that pulpit flowers of the five colors are strewed and scattered, and the pulpit itself is scented with various perfumes. So pure is the heart of Dharmodgata, so great the respect of his hearers for dharma. Seated on the pulpit, the Bodhisattva Dharmodgata demonstrates the Perfection of Wisdom. The citizens of that town listen to his teaching with great respect for the dharma, with trust in dharma, faith in what is worthy of faith, with minds that are lifted up in faith.

In addition many hundreds, many thousands, many hundred of thousands of living beings, Gods and men, assemble there to listen. Some of them explain the perfection of wisdom, some repeat it, some copy it, some follow it with wise attention.

With all these shared details, it is obviously worth wondering if there might not be some kind of connection between this section of the *Perfection of Wisdom in 8,000 Lines* and the *Land of Bliss.*

In fact, let's note that there are six types of parallels between the paradises presented in the two texts. First, in both texts, the perfect sites are defined by their directionality vis-à-vis the reader: thus, just as this city Gandhavati is a long way off to the east, so too is the Land of Bliss a long way off to the west. Second, both lands are made of the seven precious jewels. Third, they are arranged in an orderly fashion based on a rectangle or a square. Fourth, they share a range of enticing elements that include palm trees in rows, netting in jeweled trees which produces symphonic music when the wind blows, a variety of lovely birds, enticing water in ponds with gold sand on the bottom and multicolored lotus flowers the size of cartwheels on their surfaces. Fifth, both lands are organized around pleasure, even if that pleasure is treated differently in either land. And, last, the two lands have parallel names: Gandhavati and Sukhāvatī.

Despite these significant parallels that suggest some basic template at work in the presentation of Buddhist paradises, there are also important differences. For instance, we can see that in the *Land of Bliss* the site seems more like a garden and less like a city. More importantly the template has been monasticized, and thus the shops, boats, women, and sex have been excluded in the *Land of Bliss.* Likewise, in the *Land of Bliss* pleasure has been harmonized with the goal of delivering Buddhist truth. Pleasure in Gandhavati was described in order to draw Ever Wailing, and the reader, into this wonderful place where the text is housed and humanly preached, but it had also lingered as a somewhat disruptive element that had to be withdrawn in order for the public teaching of the Perfection of Wisdom to go forward. Thus we read above that Bodhisattva Dharmodgata "diverts, enjoys and amuses himself *only for a certain time, and thereafter* he always demonstrates the Perfection of Wisdom." I should add that Kumārajīva's early fifth century translation of this section of the *Perfection of Wisdom* specifies that it is three times a day that Dharmodgata, after having taken his pleasure with the various palace women, teaches the Perfection of Wisdom. If Kumārajīva's rendering accurately represents the scheduling of pleasure and teaching in an Indian version of the *Perfection of Wisdom*, then perhaps this timing was used to similarly structure the Land of Bliss's dispensation of dharma via the magical birds. Actually, Xuanzang's later translation of the *Perfection of Wisdom* in the seventh century basically follows Kumārajīva's but clarifies that it is three times, night and day, that Dharmodgata performs this cycle of sex and teaching, thereby matching the schedule of the birds singing in the Pure Land as found in the Sanskrit.[50]

The parallel timing here is tantalizing, but it shouldn't cover up the basic point that the author of the *Perfection of Wisdom* wasn't bashful about showing the reader how much pleasure the bodhisattva Dharmodgata enjoyed with the sixty-eight thousand maidens, and that that pleasure *wasn't harmonized* with the teaching of the *Perfection of Wisdom*, since the two activities had to alternate. In Gandhavati pleasure isn't as yet folded into the reader's contact with tradition; instead, it lingers simply as an enticement for the reader to get to the *scene* of tradition. In the *Land of Bliss*, on the other hand, pleasure and teachings have been fully combined so that they arrive in conjunction. Thus, the inhabitants of the Land of Bliss receive their quotas of pleasure precisely when they receive the dharma teachings in the form of the winds and the birds singing. Of course, by turning the reception of tradition into pleasure, the *Land of Bliss* had no reason to keep women or sex on site. In short, the author of the *Land of Bliss* has cleverly reified pleasure and, lifting it free from any connection to the body and sex, lodged it directly between tradition and its recipient, where it became the very substance of transmission. It is just this kind of ingenious reworking of details that makes it likely that the *Land of Bliss* comes late in this cycle of redesigning the perfect Buddhist landscape.

Another key difference in these two paradises has to do, again, with *the medium* of truth and tradition. The *Perfection of Wisdom*, in the above passage and throughout its other chapters, speaks of itself regularly as a text, as some *thing* to be desired, copied, and shared; likewise, the narrative explains its full book-form presence in Gandhavati where it is locked up in a case sealed with seven seals. The *Land of Bliss*, on the other hand, has purified the Land of Bliss of all textuality and thus of all visible forms of the cult of the text. Hence, whereas the *Perfection of Wisdom* sought to seduce the reader by creating a full double of itself in a cityscape of pleasure and harmony, the *Land of Bliss* seduces the reader by offering a fetishized version of itself in two forms: first, it seems to disappear into itself under the form of Amitāyus's name; and, then, in a similar move to condense and purify the reader-text relationship, the *Land of Bliss* explains that its final work of transmitting tradition is accomplished not in a city of pleasure built around itself as visible, physical presence, but rather in a place where texts—and their masters—disappear altogether, leaving only their effects: pleasure, truth, and the direct and endless reception of tradition. Looked at this way, it makes sense to say that the *Land of Bliss* has rather cleverly redesigned the perfect Buddhist city-garden *as something like a text*; thus, as one enters the Land of Bliss, the land now is the perfect conveyor of tradition and there is no longer any need for a functioning buddha or a Mahāyāna text. Consequently, the city of pleasure, with its long history of *supporting* the spokespersons of tradition—be it a buddha or a Mahāyāna text—has become, itself, the spokesperson of tradition.[51]

In this way it seems that the *Land of Bliss* represents a brilliant improvement on the "cult of the text" in which, via the fetish of the name Amitāyus that leads one to the tradition-promoting landscape of the Land of Bliss, the transmission of tradition is now promised completely free of texts and language, even though the whole scenario came out of the literary tradition that was very much aware of the cult of the text and its risks. And here it isn't just that the medium has become the message, but rather that the message is about getting the message. Framed that way, the *Land of Bliss* looks much more logical: it is a work largely uninterested in the content of (old) tradition and instead appears obsessed with delivering the image of tradition's most delightful delivery.

Conclusions

One could profitably reflect on the billions of lives touched by this doctrine of Amitāyus and his Land of Bliss to again appreciate the power of religious inventions to shape lives, generation after generation. Certainly, we don't think about this enough, and definitely not from the point of view of noting how the content of tradition developed under the pressures of making images of the transcendent look desirable and legitimate, while also making the delivery system for that content appear desirable and legitimate. In terms of being a fine example of fetishizing tradition, we can briefly note six things about the *Land of Bliss*. First, obviously, the effort to reinvent tradition ended up again relying on a kind of belief in belief, here based on a simple faith that faith in the text, and the name that it offers, will deliver one to the Land of Bliss where tradition will, finally, be delivered. Thus, without the Manichaean drama of the gospel narratives and without the interiorized self-crucifixion that Paul set forth, the believer in the *Land of Bliss* simply has the name of Amitāyus and the supporting text that provides convincing "legality" for this kind of faith.

Second, and again obviously, content has disappeared in the efforts to make believers believe that content really can be recovered later. Hence, the Buddha has been reduced to a signpost for Amitāyus and the Land of Bliss, while the more customary forms of Buddhist practice—ethics, meditation, monasticism, and so on—have slipped from view, and all that is left is that directive to wait for death when one's faith will effect one's transfer to the zone of real tradition. Third, to make all these inventions look traditional, the author both recycled key elements from tradition and then invented new versions of the truth-fathers—all those cosmic buddhas in the cardinal directions—in order to legitimate the arrangement. Fourth, desire seems to have taken center stage in the reconfiguration of tradition. The *Land of Bliss*, besides offering rather attractive terms for winning salvation, devotes a large section of its discourse to describing the gem-land, with the trees, the ponds, and so on, all carefully described in their resplendent glory. Likewise, one can expect personal contact with Buddha Amitāyus as he comes to the rescue of each believer as he or she dies—a rather amazing promise within traditional Buddhist cosmology. Too, once in this distant land, life is no more complicated than collecting flowers and offering them to all the buddhas, with plenty of time for naps afterwards. Clearly, then, the author's need for the reader's desire has shaped what this revised form of tradition offers back to the reader: tradition, then, has become an image of the reader's desire, or at least what the author imagined the reader's desire to be.

Fifth, if I am right about placing the *Land of Bliss* at the end of a track of literary experimentation with the Mahāyāna "cult of the text," then the Land of Bliss ends up looking like a very ironic figure, since it appears to be a perfectly invisible text where highly stylized versions of tradition, beauty, pleasure, and ease are seamlessly intertwined, while textuality, and even the language of tradition, have been banished. Thus it seems worth saying that the early Mahāyāna texts that fetishized tradition have, themselves, been subject to a fetishization project, and all that remains in their wake are those lovable birds and the sonic breezes which now perform textual functions. Who needs Bodhisattva Dharmodgata and his textual version of the *Perfection of Wisdom*—however golden and bejeweled that text might have been in Gandhavati—when one could more perfectly receive tradition from the most natural elements of the perfect garden: the singing birds and the breezes? Put that way, one senses that the traditional Buddhist desire to make the monastery into a pleasure grove—a desire well established in the Vinaya—has won out since in the final phase of the dialectic, Buddhism disappears, and all that remains is the garden, and yet all of the Buddhist tradition is present and totally effective, albeit in a totally invisible form that in no way obstructs the gentle grandeur of the perfect garden. Arguably, then, with the *Land of Bliss*, Buddhism fetishized itself in a most thoroughgoing and charming manner until it was practically nonexistent.

The final conclusion is simply that with the *Land of Bliss*, worlds have been turned into tools for the transmission of tradition. That is, tradition is no longer a simple human thing that one finds in this world or in another; instead, traditions *are* worlds since the two have become indistinguishable. Thus, according to the *Land of Bliss*, our world is degraded and limited, just as traditional Buddhism is degraded and limited. Likewise, the Land of Bliss is perfect, beautiful, and thoroughly effective because that is the kind of Buddhist tradition that "lives" there. In effect, in this text, and the same goes for Paul and Mark, the author has expanded the "ontic power" of religious discourse such that it is coterminous with the world. *Doctrine is no longer a piece of the world, it is the stuff that worlds are made of.* Hence, when we try to situate the practice of fetishizing tradition within a larger history of the human ability to objectify and represent the world, we shouldn't miss that the *Land of Bliss* is an excellent example of an account of the world turning into the world.[52] Thus, just as Paul explained the world as afflicted with a pregnancy that only our faith could deliver, and just as Mark has an apocalyptic end-of-the-world finalizing his plot, so too do we see here that doctrine has become world in the sense that the world is no longer a non-human thing out there, but instead is formally constructed as the house of tradition, a house that is, literally, made of the tradition we live in. Obviously, in this light, we are looking at clear evidence that these cycles of fetishizing tradition belong within the much larger project of domesticating the universe, one in which the essences of the traditions we invent are to be read in (and out of) the visible facticity of lived reality—be it in our degraded world or in the glamour of the Land of Bliss.

Not surprisingly, since it is tradition that now creates worlds, we can see too that language has become the thing that makes these worlds. Or, more exactly, in the case of the Land of Bliss, the entire land is but one big symphonic entity, dedicated to regularly broadcasting the perfect form of tradition and in a manner that rhymes with all the other similarly constructed lands in the universe. Of course, too, it is language—the text and the name of Amitāyus that it delivers—that allows one to move between our world and the Land of Bliss, implying, of course, that one is what one believes, with language performing an ontic function in world- and self-creation.

In the centuries that followed the writing of the *Land of Bliss*, the literary processes by which the Buddhist tradition was overcome and rewritten continued to develop in both India and China. In the following chapter I will consider how one of these developments took form in China when the Mahāyāna world of textuality was overcome by a theory explaining how tradition was directly inherited, man-to-man, a theory that in time gave birth to the Chan (Zen) genealogies that claimed that the Buddhist masters of East Asia were, in fact, buddha replicas; thus it was said that one need not rely on Mahāyāna sūtras anymore and would do better to read the writings of East Asian buddhas, writings which, of course, became sūtra-like in function. In short, the fetishizing work of the Mahāyāna sūtras would, itself, soon be fetishized in this new format, with important implications for how one was to find the essence of tradition.

5

The *Platform Sūtra of the Sixth Patriarch*, or Paternal Truth for the Masses

Introduction

Contrary to popular impressions that Chan and Zen aren't really religions, and thus certainly not to be drawn into discussions of fetishizing tradition, the eighth century *Platform Sūtra* and other early Chan texts represent unusually good examples of just these religious dynamics. That we haven't noticed this before is simply due to the fact that we haven't read these texts in a way that would make their construction of desire and authority available for this kind of critique.[1] Though Chan studies has become notably more critical and self-aware in the past twenty-five years, the rather limited application of literary criticism in Chan studies has produced a limited and skewed view of Chan texts and the literary talents that went into their composition. In place of a more balanced account of how these texts function *as texts*, twentieth-century scholarship seemed largely obsessed with extracting "philosophy" from these texts. Thus, reading these texts for their multisided narratives, complicated intersubjectivity, and rich intertextuality didn't happen. Instead, scholars and enthusiasts extracted what they took to be particularly "zenny" passages from these texts, hoping thereby to grasp the supposed essence of Chan/Zen philosophy. While fetishizing Chan/Zen in this manner makes it easier to compare Chan and Zen to twentieth-century philosophic movements—with a noted preference for phenomenology, existentialism, and deconstruction—this style of reading seems to miss the real "philosophy" of these texts—a philosophy that can only be appreciated when we read these texts for their narrative programs

163

and ideological ventures. Ironically, we can only see how these texts fetishize tradition when we stop fetishizing them.

To begin to get a fuller account of how the *Platform Sūtra* works as a religious text, I have organized this chapter into three sections. The first section provides context for reading the *Platform Sūtra* by locating it in a brief history of early Chan. The second section presents a close reading of the *Platform Sūtra*, with a focus on the first third of the text—the narrative part of the work—that explains the identity of Chan Master Huineng (n.d.), the figure who speaks most of the text's discourse and is put forward as the sixth patriarch in the family of truth-fathers that take Bodhidharma (n.d.) to be their progenitor. The third section of the chapter moves to consider the content of Huineng's supposed teachings while also exploring the problems involved in the text's various promises regarding a kind of final paternity that is everyone's birthright, but only Huineng's to give.

A Real Find

The *Platform Sūtra* exists in several versions, with the oldest version dating roughly to the 780s. In the centuries after its composition it was edited and rewritten in important ways, with later editors smoothing out the text's rough grammar and removing some troubling content, while also molding it so that it came to reflect the ideological contours of Chan Buddhism as it took form in the Song Dynasty (960–1279). It was one of these later, revised versions that was included in the official Buddhist canon and that remains an important part of modern Chan and Zen traditions.[2] Despite the delay in letting the text into the Chinese Buddhist canon, certain narrative elements regarding Huineng's identity seem to have been extracted from the earlier version of the *Platform Sūtra* and redeployed in a number of high-profile Chan and Zen texts dating from the second half of the Tang Dynasty (618–907) and into the Song. In particular, it was the image of Huineng as a Chinese buddha who never relied on texts, or on the elements of tradition imported from India, that would be central in establishing the logic and appeal of the Chan and Zen traditions.

The earliest extant version of the *Platform Sūtra*, which is the one I will be reading from, would never have been known to us were it not for a lost "library" that came to light in 1907. In that year, Hungarian-British archeologist and adventurer Sir Aurel Stein paid the Daoist priest Wang Yuanlu a small sum of money to take down a wall blocking off one of the niches in the Mogao caves at Dunhuang, an oasis town on the Silk Route. Behind this wall was a large cache of texts, monastic documents, and artifacts of various kinds—elements that appeared to have been haphazardly collected early in the eleventh century and sealed behind this wall. This trove of texts and art, mysterious and jumbled as it was, has given scholars access to a range of texts that later tradition seems to have been quite happy to ignore. In the case of the Chan and Zen traditions, the Dunhuang texts include a number of genealogies from the eighth and ninth centuries—including this early version of the *Platform Sūtra*—which explain why certain Chinese men should be considered enlightened buddhas, since they supposedly stood in a family of truth-fathers reaching back to Bodhidharma and, ultimately, the Indian Buddha. The problem with these genealogies is that they are mutually contradictory and, equally troubling, they don't match the genealogies that the modern Chan and Zen traditions rely on for explaining how enlightenment moved from the Indian Buddha to East Asia and into the present.

In taking stock of these long-lost genealogies, it seems we ought to conclude that the Tang dynasty was notable for a kind of literary competition in which various authors sought to establish their preferred figures— and sometimes the preferred figure was the author himself—as the singular representative of the Buddhist tradition. Though we are far from being sure that we know all the "warring" genealogies that circulated during the Tang dynasty, it is quite clear that the *Platform Sūtra* appeared fairly late in this cycle of rewriting the past. Actually, the central narrative in the *Platform Sūtra* is a complicated story explaining how the essence of tradition had wrongly been thought to have been in the possession of a certain famous monk named Shenxiu (d. 706) when in fact Huineng was the legitimate owner of tradition. Shenxiu, in fact, is identified as the inheritor of total tradition in several early genealogies, and thus it seems clear that the *Platform Sūtra* is working to undermine a certain fetishization of tradition that had already taken form several decades earlier.

The Early Bodhidharma Lineages

The earliest "freestanding" version of the Bodhidharma lineage is found on a stone stele carved in 690, on the grounds of Shaolin monastery, just outside of the capital city of Loyang.[3] In this narrative, we learn that a certain master Faru (d. 689) was the disciple of master Hongren of East Mountain (located in Huangmei, in modern day Hubei province) and that he received from Hongren, suddenly and in a private event, the totality of the Buddhist tradition. He then came to Shaolin where he lived for a while and then died, whereupon he was buried and honored with this stele. To solidify these claims, the narrative explains how Hongren had inherited tradition from Bodhidharma, via the intervening masters Huike, Sengcan, and Daoxin, and how the Buddha, back in India, had initiated such a practice of transmission by secretly giving tradition to Ananda who then passed it on in a similarly clandestine manner.

Though the Indian side of the story is left vague and incomplete, Faru is sumptuously presented as the most recent owner of tradition. Hoping to demonstrate that his identity as the owner of tradition was already widely accepted, the narrative turns to explain how a large number of monks from all over China supposedly came to Faru to request his dharma teaching in 686. Once on site at Shaolin monastery, they supposedly recited a condensed version of the entire Buddha-to-Bodhidharma-to-Faru narrative that the stele had been working up, adding that this genealogy of Bodhidharma descendants had been widely recognized from the [Northern] Wei dynasty (386–534) onward. With this brief account of the visiting monks' thorough knowledge of Faru's genealogy, the narrative has doubled itself such that a condensed version of itself appears to arrive from off-stage where it supposedly had already been accurately known and accepted. Naturally, this gives the impression that Faru's genealogy was, in fact, not the recent creation of Shaolin monastery since, supposedly, this narrative had been well known and accepted by the general public. This rather sophisticated narrative device also suggests that the Shaolin author/s very much knew what they were doing as they crafted this Bodhidharma-to-Faru narrative and sought to hide their invention by pretending that it was, in fact, not their creation at all.

What seems undeniable in this earliest Bodhidharma lineage is that it was designed to convince all and sundry—the public, other Buddhist leaders, and the court—that Shaolin monastery was recently the host of a Chinese buddha (Faru) who, as a buddha, was naturally in full possession of tradition. Though Faru was, admittedly, dead and gone, the narrative makes clear that while alive he had graced Shaolin with his buddha presence and his thoroughly authoritative teaching, thereby marking Shaolin as the preeminent monastery in the land. Given this claim that so effectively fetishizes tradition, one can imagine the effect it had on other Buddhist leaders who had hitherto attached themselves to the Indian tradition in much less direct ways. In particular, one can imagine other Buddhists thinking: Why bother with translated sūtras and their endless commentaries when a living buddha has been discovered in China, and his disciples can still be found at Shaolin monastery?

Though we don't have specific evidence reflecting how this genealogy was received by the throne, the public, or other Buddhist leaders, we do find several slightly later genealogies of the Bodhidharma lineage that claim that though Faru died at Shaolin, the totality of tradition that had been his inheritance lived on in master Shenxiu. Thus, whereas the Shaolin narrative leaves Faru with no heir, these later reinterpretations provide the lineage Bodhidharma with living descendants and even specific "rules" for reproducing the totality of tradition in the chosen figures of the next generation. The genealogy that seems to come most directly after the Faru stele is the *Record of the Transmission of the Dharma-Jewel* (*Chuan fabao ji*), written by Du Fei in the decade after Shenxiu's death in 706. Reading Du Fei's text carefully, it becomes clear that it has the specific goal of co-opting the genealogy that Shaolin had recently invented. Du Fei accomplishes this heist by arguing that Hongren in fact transmitted total tradition to two disciples—Faru and Shenxiu—and then when Faru died, Shenxiu took over as the living representative of the Bodhidharma lineage. It was supposedly in this capacity, then, that Shenxiu received imperial recognition as "Teacher of the Nation" (國師) while also serving as a personal teacher to Empress Wu and her sons, Emperors Ruizong and Zhongzong.

While it seems true that Shenxiu was, in fact, an imperially recognized master and likely did instruct the empress and her sons, his connection to Hongren, along with his place in this recently constructed Bodhidharma lineage, seems completely fabricated. The details of Du Fei's narrative are quite involved, but what matters for this chapter is simply to see that in the early eighth century, shortly after Shenxiu died, other leading monks at the capital wanted to identify new figures in the Bodhidharma family-of-truth, and to do so they first wrote Shenxiu into the lineage and then presented this or that living master as Shenxiu's descendent.[4] Thus, in a short while, two monks—Yifu (d. 736) and Puji (d. 739)—both claimed to have inherited tradition from Shenxiu and were, in time, imperially recognized in this way and granted the same title of "Teacher of the Nation."

Though modern readers might find this zeal for creatively rewriting the Bodhidharma family odd and disturbing, and certainly far from the imagined cool transcendence that we have come to associate with Chan and Zen, it is hard to read these dueling genealogies without noting significant levels of craft and calculation. I should add, too, that this process of rewriting the past to win the present and future is quite visible throughout the eighth century. In fact, parallel literary inventions occurred on and off throughout the rest of Chan and Zen's history, and even up into the present. This suggests that these writing strategies were not only an essential element in the life of tradition, but also that they were consciously recognized as such, which is to say that the Chan and Zen traditions carry within themselves just this knowledge of how to reinvent tradition as need be.

In the decades after Shenxiu's death it seems clear that the claim that Shenxiu (and not Faru) was the real inheritor of Hongren's special transmission came to be taken as an accurate historical claim. Thus, besides various narratives found at Dunhuang that assume this to be the case, there are also several early eighth-century steles that present Shenxiu as the sixth patriarch in the lineage of Bodhidharma. Likewise, slightly later there appear steles for Shenxiu's disciples—Yifu and Puji—and both recount how they received tradition from Shenxiu and that he belonged to the Bodhidharma lineage. Generalizing from this evidence it would seem that at this period in Chinese history, elite Buddhists were on their way, at least on the level of narrative, to creating something like a papal system that centralized Buddhist authority around Shenxiu and his family of "descendants."

Such a papal system, however, never took hold. Instead, centralized governmental power, which was absolutely critical for anchoring and maintaining this kind of centralized Buddhist leadership, suffered a notable collapse in the 750s when China slipped into a decade of civil war, a war that led to a marked deterioration of State power for the next two centuries. Roughly at the same time alternative accounts of the Bodhidharma lineage appeared, accounts that, directly or indirectly, sought to disenfranchise Shenxiu and his legacy. Thus, though it seems likely that the earliest lineages were intent on fixing the identity of a single Buddhist leader for the nation, once the religious and political center no longer held, authors far from court redefined the family of Bodhidharma as they wished. In fact, as we will see, the *Platform Sūtra* represents a key piece of evidence in establishing this shift in genealogical writing from "papal politics" to something perhaps more aptly called "legitimizing the local master."

The Earliest Account of Huineng

The oldest surviving narrative that worked to undermine the Hongren-Shenxiu connection is the funeral stele for master Huineng, written by the poet-artist Wang Wei (701–61) at the behest of Shenhui (d. 758—not to be confused with *Shenxiu*).[5] In this narrative we are introduced to the remarkable figure of Huineng, who is completely the opposite of Shenxiu: instead of being an elite monk, well trained in Buddhist and non-Buddhist literature as Shenxiu seems to have been, Huineng is rustic figure, a stranger to literature and learning, and even a stranger to Buddhism. Nevertheless he spontaneously achieves enlightenment and then is recognized as a living buddha by Hongren, who then formally installs him in the Bodhidharma lineage. Not too surprisingly, this narrative also explains that, despite these humble origins, Huineng then received imperial recognition (in the form of an invitation to come to court, which he supposedly refused). Then, with his buddhahood confirmed by Hongren and the throne, Huineng supposedly gave transmission to Shenhui. While the text makes no direct attack on Shenxiu's supposed inheritance from Hongren, it presents Huineng as the uniquely outstanding student in the mass of Hongren's disciples, and it concludes with Hongren passing on his robe and bowl to Huineng—items that of course make Huineng appear as Hongren's chosen descendent. In short, the narrative completely upsets the claims made on behalf of Shenxiu since suddenly we "see" Hongren give his singular transmission to Huineng, with Shenxiu nowhere in sight.

Key to note is that in the inscription Wang Wei has created his account of this untutored buddha with a raft of quotes from Buddhist and Confucian classics. In fact, practically the entirety of Huineng's life is written with snippets drawn from a range of Chinese classics.[6] In taking stock of Wang Wei's writing, it is clear that Huineng's unlettered simplicity is based on a complex collage of literary allusions generated by one of the most educated writers of the era who wrote Huineng into existence by stitching together a staggeringly diverse set of quotations from Chinese literature, Buddhist and non-Buddhist. This means that there is a funny mismatch between form and content here: Huineng is presented as an all-natural, backwoods, illiterate buddha, but this image is evoked with quotations from a wide range of sophisticated books, lightly alluded to, in an elegant and learned eulogy. Similarly, there is a tension between observer and spectacle. Wang Wei's dense writing is accessible only to those literati for whom the figure of super-simple Huineng stands as a kind of polar opposite, and thus to get the literary references about Huineng's down-home innocence is already to find oneself on the wrong side of the fence. By locating pure Buddhism in this rural and completely unadorned figure, far from court and high culture, Wang Wei has given Shenhui a heavy stick to beat the establishment with since Shenhui has positioned himself to inherit perfection from one who apparently never sought confirmation of his perfect status from the public or from the Buddhist hierarchy. Thus, though appearing contentedly unwashed and completely uninvolved with institutional status, Wang Wei's Huineng is turned into a site for collecting a spectrum of Chinese values and organizing them so that they can be "harvested" by his son, Shenhui, for some rather institutional purposes.

In short, Huineng as a historical figure was immaculately produced by gathering up literary references and putting them into the image of a body. Thus, Wang Wei's fathering of Huineng involved creating a perimeter, notably sealed off from any natal lineage and injecting that circumscribed space with the literary tropes that the literati generally cared about. In this displacement, the literary chunks don't exactly change their meaning, but their context now is defined as living through a real body and not through mere words and the encumbering physicality of texts. Similarly, in receiving this literary content as his interior and as the basis for his life, Huineng is purified of being ordinary and particular, since now his person is the quilting point for the cachet associated with these various literary allusions of "universal" acclaim. Thus, there is an interesting dialectic at work here: literature, after chosen pieces of it have been recombined and injected into the body of the rustic, shines back to the literati as an image of itself housed in a zone most distant from itself, thereby purifying itself of itself, even as it has manufactured a new literary form qua container for focusing desire on itself.

Of course, something else has happened. With this immaculate relocation of literature in a man's body, Wang Wei easily moves that perfection forward into Shenhui's body, and with the most partisan of intentions, one suspects. Thus, the dialectic of recombining Chinese literary values with its opposite—Huineng's smelly body—comes hand in hand with the most private kind of self-aggrandizement: Shenhui is now the sole inheritor of this repackaged image of tradition that holds Confucian, Daoist, and Buddhist values in a new synthetic totality. Put otherwise, the whole maneuver focuses desire for tradition onto the figure of a single man, a gesture that is exciting for the immediacy and intensity it promises, even though this gesture is also the one that will keep those desires from doing anything other than appreciating those elements from afar, since, according to the logic of inheritance, only Shenhui will come to fully own them. In sum, Wang Wei's account of the Huineng-to-Shenhui transmission transforms literary values into human perfection and establishes this amalgam in a historical framework that, once it looks historical, erases Wang Wei's role in just this creation and thereby allows for new levels of desire for these forms of perfection that are captivating precisely for the series of purification that they incarnate: literature purified of itself, humanity purified of itself, the writing of history purified of itself, and, perhaps most important, polemics purified of itself.

It isn't clear when this stele was cut, but it likely was after the death of Puji in 739.[7] This supposition would make sense insofar as it was only in the 740s/50s that we have evidence that Shenhui was called to court to serve as a barker of sorts—selling Buddhist ordination certificates in public auctions orchestrated to generate capital for the throne which was sorely in need of money to raise armies to beat back the An Lushan Rebellion. Though the evidence is only circumstantial, it would seem that in the wake of Puji's death there was a kind of power vacuum as the nascent "papal system," based on the throne selecting the next "Teacher of the Nation," faltered. Shenhui appears to have sought to fill that void by putting forward several texts that announced his identity as the real seventh patriarch—instead of Puji and Yifu—with Huineng and not Shenxiu counted as the sixth patriarch. Despite these efforts, and his evident charisma as a public speaker, Shenhui apparently ran afoul of imperial powers, and was temporarily banished from the capital. Likewise, he seems not to have received formal imperial recognition during his life; nor is there evidence that his death was honored with any imperial action. Though his recently discovered funeral stele speaks of Shenhui as "Teacher of the Nation" and the "Seventh Patriarch," these titles aren't reported in any other contemporary non-Shenhui source and are likely the exaggerations of the author of the stele.[8]

While the details regarding Shenhui's life remain largely unknown, it is clear, from the ongoing process of rewriting the Bodhidharma lineage that followed, that he, with the aid of Wang Wei, had given birth to a most productive father in the form of this uncanny, all-natural buddha called Huineng. In fact, three texts soon took up this figure of Huineng for their own purposes: 1) the *Unofficial Biography of Huineng*—what's referred to as Huineng's *Biezhuan*; 2) the *Lidai fabao ji*; and, 3) the *Platform Sūtra*. What needs to be underscored, though, is that all three of these texts, though eager to take hold of the newly fabricated truth-father Huineng, work in different ways to push his "son," Shenhui, aside so that other want-to-be inheritors can receive tradition from Huineng. Thus, the cycle of ancestor thieving continued as various Buddhist authors eagerly adopted each other's narratives, and especially those narratives that presented an image of owning tradition in a manner far from the hands of clever authors.

With these background details in view, let's turn to a close reading of the *Platform Sūtra* and its construction of Huineng as the owner of total tradition.

Overview of the Narrative

The *Platform Sūtra*, despite resting on an account of Huineng's sudden and effortless enlightenment, is a long, chaotic text.[9] The first third of the text, which explains the details of this enlightenment, is fairly carefully written, though there are also some glaring problems in the narrative's logic. The second phase of the text has Huineng lead the internal audience in a standard ritual sequence involving repentance and the taking of vows, and so on. The flow of this ritual procedure, however, is regularly taken over by Huineng's long and meandering commentaries on the Indian sūtras that had over the centuries most interested Chinese readers. The final phase recounts Huineng's death and is rather ragged and seems dedicated to presenting various fetish items that promise to deliver the payload of Huineng's spiritual achievements. Thus, for instance, in this final section various poems are presented as containing the totality of tradition and the essence of Huineng's teaching. Likewise, it is three times claimed that the *Platform Sūtra* itself is the essence of Huineng's teaching and that tradition henceforth will be regenerated by transmitting this text, with the added detail given that the transmitter of the text should write the name of the recipient on the back of the text to finalize the act of transmission. Other matters regarding the inheritance of tradition are also sorted out in this final section, such as a second demonstration of the shortcomings of Shenxiu and his school (now called the Northern School) and the demotion of Shenhui who, though he invented this Huineng figure, is presented as a secondary disciple in this text. Most interesting in this section is the intriguing effort to identify an otherwise unknown Fahai as Huineng's best disciple. In short, in this section an author is clearly working to do what all the other preceding genealogists sought to do: attach new figures to the ever-expanding Bodhidharma genealogy of perfect tradition.

Setting the Scene

The *Platform Sūtra* opens by replaying the standard format of the Indian sūtra: the audience and setting are first identified, the request for the teaching is then articulated, and so on. Of course, setting up Huineng's discourse in this manner gently implies to the reader that Huineng is going to perform as a buddha. While the formal characteristics have been taken from the Indian sūtra setting, everything about this stock scene is sinified so that the teaching is given in a Chinese town, by a Chinese master, who is surrounded by important figures from Chinese society, including government officials and Confucian scholars. Moreover, we learn that Fahai was designated as the recorder of the event and that this was done explicitly so that Huineng's articulation of tradition could be transmitted to later generations: "The prefect then had the monk-disciple Fahai record his (Huineng's) words so that they might become known to later generations and be of benefit to students of the Way, in order that they might receive the pivot of the teaching and transmit it among themselves, taking these words as their authority" (126).[10]

In this initial statement regarding the production, value, and future of this teaching "event," we can already see how the narrative is preparing the reader to accept the text containing Huineng and his speech as the new essence of tradition: the text is to be that pivot where the past, present, and future are fruitfully combined, and in an authoritative manner. Not to be missed, either, is the way the text has explained its own textuality: supposedly, the written version of these events is but a direct duplication of Huineng's orality, prepared by the loyal Fahai, who was simply following the orders of the local prefect who wished that this writing would aid future students of Buddhism. With this chain of command explaining its genesis, the text has prepared a triple innocence for itself: 1) Huineng's discourse on this day wasn't, at least according to this statement, presented with the intention to refigure tradition—he simply was teaching on this day; and, 2) Fahai wasn't in anyway responsible for inventing this discourse since he was serving as a simple secretary for the event and thus likewise had no desire to reinvent tradition; and 3) even Fahai's act of turning orality into textuality was only enacted in accord with the wishes of a non-Buddhist figure—the local prefect—who, somewhat oddly it must be admitted, appears to be the only one on stage with practical Buddhist goals in mind.

This last point is doubly interesting because as the text finds its origins in the command of a governmental leader, it seems to rely on State forms of authority to justify itself. Presumably this makes its religious agenda appear innocent of polemics, as if to say, "See, the origins of this discourse aren't in the various lineage battles fought between dueling religious authors, but rather in the generous and visionary instructions of a local official who was simply interested in ensuring the life of the Buddhist tradition." Naturally, too, this claim, along with the mention of the numerous Confucian officials in attendance, gives the impression that the entire affair was conducted with governmental approval. In sum, it would seem that this prefect has, with his hopes to generate this text as the pivot of tradition for future generations, become a double of the author—expressing, in a distinctly disinterested manner, the desires of the author, who, as we will see, is precisely interested in making this text the fetish of tradition in just such a manner that future students of the Way "might receive the pivot of the teaching and transmit it among themselves, taking these words as their authority."

With this sanctifying backdrop in place, Huineng begins to explain his past—and, of course, his connection to Hongren—to the audience in the text and, naturally, the reader. As the figure of Huineng sketches this short autobiography we have to recognize how the text is working to blend two histories. The first history is simply the account that Huineng is putting forward regarding his contact with the lineage (his relationship with Hongren, that is); but this history is part of another history that recounts how Huineng gave this history on this particular day—that public moment captured when Fahai supposedly wrote down everything that Huineng said, thereby generating this text. Of course, these two histories fit together in the sense that one needs to believe the text's account of its own history in order to believe Huineng's account of his own history.

Presumably, the influence goes in the other direction too since as the reader gets involved in Huineng's account of his humble, literature-less life, it becomes harder to see that Huineng, in fact, only lives in literature. In fact, the whole text is designed to effect just that movement from life into literature so that in the future, tradition can be made to live with the mere presence of this text. In short, we are beginning to witness a three-step motion: 1) tradition is gathered up and *installed in Huineng*; 2) Huineng, and his tradition-evoking language is gathered up and *installed in this text*; and 3) the text then explains *how to get tradition out of this text*. Consequently, the concocted image of Huineng's pure, uninflected, unmotivated orality appears as the text's chosen route for accomplishing its basic task of becoming the living source of tradition for future "students of the Way"—readers, that is.

Huineng's illiteracy also works to cloak the fact that the text, and especially its various claims about the inheritance of enlightenment, is intimately involved in the snowballing literary efforts to lay hold of the splendor of the newly invented buddha lineage. That is, whereas the text evokes the pure interior of Huineng as the origin of the discourse, a closer look shows that the real "fathers" of his discourse are to be found in that welter of lineage claims that had been made in the eighth century. This dependence on prior lineage claims appears all the clearer when we see that Huineng's enlightenment is produced in the narrative only when he finally trounces Shenxiu, the prior claimant to the Bodhidharma mantle. In terms of narrative logic, it was those texts that had fetishized Shenxiu as the essence of tradition that, in turn, gave the author of the *Platform Sūtra* the material he needed to refetishize tradition in the figure of Huineng. As we will see, Huineng's identity as a perfect buddha is generated in the symbolic execution of Shenxiu—the one previously known as the reigning Chinese buddha—with that "death" opening up the space for Huineng to be, in the eyes of the reader, who he's supposed to be.

The Action

The action starts when, having asked his audience to purify their thoughts, Huineng begins to explain how he got to be the sixth patriarch in Bodhidharma's lineage by first providing some details about his impoverished childhood. Huineng explains that he was, originally, the son of an official who served in Fanyang (in modern day Hubei), in central China. For unexplained reasons his father was banished to the south, to Xinzhou in Lingnan (roughly the area around Guangdong), where he died, leaving Huineng fatherless at a young age. His mother then moved them to Nanhai (also near modern day Guangdong), where Huineng earned a meager living selling firewood in the marketplace. Right after these details are given we learn how in an accidental manner Huineng came into contact with the Buddhist tradition and immediately penetrated to its core, with no preparation or effort.

Before considering this magical moment, let's gather up the implications of the first part of this supposed autobiography. As we sort through these details we have essentially three hermeneutical choices: we can simply take these details as: 1) inconsequential, assuming that they are basically random elements of storytelling designed to make the narrative more interesting in a generic way; or, 2) interesting for historical reasons insofar as they represent the remains of historical facts, but again inconsequential for reading the narrative since they are in the narrative through the force of real history and not because they are part of a seduction organized by the author; or, 3) and this is obviously my preference, that these details were carefully created by the author to fit with other details, all in the effort to make this presentation of Huineng, and the text he lives in, more desirable in the eyes of the external audience.

The first thing to notice about these brief autobiographic details is that Huineng presents himself as one whose origins are quite ambiguous. His southernness—so crucial to his identity in this text and in particular for his coming discussions with Hongren—appears to be a somewhat superficial reality, generated as it was by his father's recent fall from grace that occasioned the move down south from Fanyang in Hubei. We can't assume that his father was originally from Hubei—he might have just been temporarily posted there—but it is still the case that the move to the south is explained as the result of a punishment and isn't marked as a homecoming or a return to the family's roots; in fact it seems that the move was a kind of forced exile. The story doesn't specify if Huineng was born before or after his father moved the family down south, but at any rate in terms of traditional Chinese logic regarding homesteads, Huineng would have typically identified with his father's hometown, presumably in the central, more sinified part of the Tang empire, instead of his new place of residence in the "barbarian" deep south. In fact, many elite families that moved to the south at this period of Chinese history regularly identified themselves as northerns—for centuries—and thus an eighth-century Chinese reader likely would see Huineng not as from the south, since his family so recently arrived from a locale to the north (Hubei or elsewhere). To really lean on this point, we shouldn't forget about the differences in local Chinese dialects. Presumably, the people of Lingnan would have spoken a Chinese quite different from Huineng's since, regardless of his birthplace, he would have presumably followed his parents in speaking a dialectic from Hubei or some other nonsouthern dialect.[11]

A parallel ambiguity organizes Huineng's commoner status: the narrative makes clear that despite ending up completely impoverished, he actually really is of good birth; it is just that his father lost the high status that comes with being an official, and thus, *now*, Huineng is but a commoner, an identity further thrust upon him by his father's death. Again, according to traditional Chinese logic, the son of an official is still a son of an official regardless of where the family moves, regardless of the current financial situation of the family, and, of course, regardless of the death of the father-official.

Summing up these two ambiguities that are introduced to explain his identity, Huineng appears as one who is inhabiting more than one site since his current southernness and his impoverished conditions are complicated by a narrative that suggests that he actually has the rights to an identity made up of the opposite elements since he is, after all, the son of an official who used to be posted in Hubei. Added to this kind of confusion in his character profile, we shouldn't miss that Huineng fails to give his pre-Buddhist name. His name, "Huineng," is a Buddhist name that he would only have received upon his formal induction into the Buddhist order, one that in no way connects him to his natal family. Thus, unlike the standard biography of an eminent monk, which normally gives the birthplace, family name, and given name of the monk, here Huineng's origins remain vague and multiform. Or better, without giving us his pre-Buddhist surname, there's a certain untraceability to Huineng's account of his origins.

In the next piece of action, Huineng, while selling firewood in the marketplace, bumps into a man who takes him to a "lodging house for officials." Here, as he is about to exit the house, he happens to notice another man who is reciting the *Diamond Sūtra* by the gate. Huineng explains, "Upon hearing it [the *Diamond Sūtra*] my mind became clear and I was awakened" (127). So, with this vignette, the downward spiral that had hitherto defined his life is reversed, and he is brought back up into the zone of respectability, finding himself in the officials' residence which was but the backdrop for an even greater leap upward: he hears the *Diamond Sūtra* and attains awakening. This sequence, however unlikely (Chinese literature, including Buddhist texts like the *Diamond Sūtra*, are completely incomprehensible when recited to illiterates) sets Huineng on track for a move not just upward, but towards the center of tradition, as manifest in the figure of Hongren.[12]

For those readers who might have thought that I exaggerated the importance of the opening detail regarding the prefect's role in commanding Fahai to write the text, here is another moment when the author preferred to have Buddhist "work" handled, not by professional Buddhists of any stripe, but by a figure who is presented without any Buddhist credentials or affiliations—just a man reciting the *Diamond Sūtra* in the officials' residence. In fact, this man's likely lay status is underscored when he explains that Hongren had taught him that monks and lay persons alike could attain enlightenment from reciting the *Diamond Sūtra*. Thus, just as the composition of the *Platform Sūtra* was supposedly commanded by an impartial non-Buddhist official, so too is Huineng's entry into the Buddhist tradition generated by contact with a nondescript man with some vague connection to governmental authority and definitely no specific Buddhist status. One can easily imagine that if our author had provided Huineng with a Buddhist mentor at this point this would have confused and diluted Huineng's heritage, while also opening him up to charges of partisanship.

It is worth noting, too, that the *Diamond Sūtra* would have been doubly unintelligible to the uninitiated listener such as Huineng since the *Diamond Sūtra* is fundamentally a kind of commentary on (old) tradition. It only has meaning and appeal for those who already know tradition and have some prior allegiance to key elements of tradition such as the dharma, the transmission of buddha-identity between Dīpankara and Śākyamuni Buddha, the bodhisattva ideal, and so on, since these are the items that are negated, overcome, and absorbed by the text.[13] In short, the *Diamond Sūtra*, as a piece of writing *completely* dedicated to negating tradition on one level, and then of course subsuming tradition into itself on another level, represents an impossible point of entry into tradition since without (old) tradition standing at its back, the text's endless negations would mean nothing. Presumably these technical problems couldn't hold our author back from selecting the *Diamond Sūtra* as the cause of Huineng's enlightenment since it was, in China, so regularly taken to be the best articulation of the Buddhist truth.

The magical reaction that Huineng has to this reading of the *Diamond Sūtra* comes with the subtle implication that the *Platform Sūtra* is identifying the *Diamond Sūtra* as a father of sorts for Huineng. Perhaps we even ought to say that the *Diamond Sūtra* functions in the narrative as Huineng's realest father, with this moment of aural contact effecting a full dissemination of tradition in such a manner that Huineng's later engagement with Hongren appears more as a formality. At any rate, it seems that the *Platform Sūtra* is turning Huineng into a walking, talking version of the *Diamond Sūtra*, and some coming details in the narrative are going to reinforce this perspective.[14]

After this awakening, Huineng asks the man where he got this sūtra and learns that master Hongren gave it to him and that it is supposedly the key to enlightenment and becoming a buddha. With this piece of news, the reader now has been informed that Huineng's singular comprehension of the *Diamond Sūtra* is to be taken as a legitimate reception of the totality of tradition since the other wing of legitimacy in this story—the Bodhidharma lineage, as represented by Hongren—confirms that the *Diamond Sūtra* is the magic talisman that does everything a fetish of tradition is supposed to do: it makes the whole of tradition present and likewise allows the "owner" of the fetish access to that whole.[15] The following events will work to bring these two wings of authority together in the figure of Huineng, who, in time, will have the mutually confirming dyad of the *Diamond Sūtra* and the Bodhidharma lineage firmly installed in his being, with the narrative offering "visible" proof of this installation in two crucial ways: Huineng will "spontaneously" speak the negative dialectics of the *Diamond Sūtra* in public, with that language recorded for posterity, even as he also comes to carry the robe of Bodhidharma.

At the end of this sequence in which Huineng magically gained the whole of tradition, we learn that Huineng also realized that he had a karmic connection with Hongren and that he needed to go visit him. With this claim—a common enough claim in early Chan narratives, actually—the story has invoked an invisible karmic past to sanctify its explanation of "current" events. In short, just as with Jesus thrice mentioning his awareness of the divinely ordained narrative of sacrifice that he was living in, here Huineng makes his life-choices with the supposed knowledge that it was all already written in the past, with that "karmic connection" functioning as something like a ghost writer for Huineng's coming coronation as the "king of Buddhism." Apparently confident of the pre-ordained quality of his life, he takes leave of his mother, and heads off to Hongren's monastery where he immediately finds himself discussing buddhahood with Hongren, on East Mountain, in Huangmei.

Before considering that conversation, let's note that the narrative, sketched in terms of descent and ascent, has just described a "V" of sorts: Huineng's family started "high" with official status in middle China, fell to the south and poverty, and then Huineng, without meaning too, is whisked back upward, first into the company of officials, then into an enlightenment won through magically comprehending a favorite Buddhist sūtra, and then off to the north for a private conversation with a living buddha, Hongren. Catching sight of this "V" motion is useful for several reasons, not the least of which is that just this gesture will be repeated in describing the action that follows the conversation with Hongren.

In an event that was presumably as unlikely as understanding the *Diamond Sūtra* without any education, Huineng presents himself to Hongren, bows, and has the following conversation in which he holds a position that is typically Buddhist while Hongren is shown advancing a racism regarding Chineseness and non-Chineseness that is fundamentally at odds with very basic tenets that structure the Buddhist tradition. In this exchange Hongreng is, obviously, referred to as "the Master" even though everything about this encounter suggests Huineng is the real holder of tradition. (And, it is useful to remember that this conversation is being related by Huineng to his patient audience back in Shaozhou where Fahai is supposedly faithfully writing all this verbiage down.) Huineng explains to his audience:

> Master Hongren asked me: "Where are you from that you come to this mountain to make obeisance to me? Just what is it that you are looking for from me?"
>
> I replied: "I am from Lingnan, a commoner from Xinzhou. I have come this long distance only to make obeisance to you. I am seeking no particular thing, but only the buddhadharma."
>
> The Master then reproved me, saying: "If you're from Lingnan then you're a barbarian. How can you become a buddha?"

I replied: "Although people from the south and people from the north differ, there is no north and south in buddha nature. Although my barbarian's body and your body are not the same, what difference is there in our buddha nature?"

The Master wished to continue his discussion with me; however, seeing that there were other people nearby, he said no more. Then he sent me to work with the assembly. Later a lay disciple had me go to the threshing room where I spent over eight months treading the pestle.

The first thing to note in this exchange is that it initiates a second "V" movement in the narrative: after Huineng had been brought up to the pinnacle of Buddhist value and authority—defined by the figure of Hongren—he is immediately cast back down the register of social standing as Hongren sends him off to work with the assembly, whereupon another man leads him off to a presumably even more plebian locale in the threshing room. Thus, just one moment after debating the essence of Buddhism with a living buddha he is now "treading the pestle," presumably preparing the rice that all in the monastery are to eat, and in that sense he is intimately involved in the lowest common denominator of the social group—their daily gruel.

This demotion in social status is made clearer with the detail that a "lay disciple had me go to the threshing room," implying that now he is taking orders from those who themselves have low status. In short, as the narrative moves Huineng around in this yo-yo fashion, the reader seems invited to conclude that Huineng is master wherever he is because, in a sense, he *always also belongs somewhere else,* and at any rate can effortlessly take on the tasks and talents required in high or low zones of activity. Talk tough with the buddha-master? Not a problem. Grind the daily rice at the behest of a peon? What could be easier? Or put another way, the "V" motion appears as a narrative technique for expressing a complex and contradictory identity that the author wanted to install "in" Huineng, an identity based on simultaneously attributing to him incompatible qualities: he is both a plebian and a buddha, just as he is both from central China and from the South, just as he is both Chinese and barbarian, just as he is both the "son" of Hongren and yet also his teacher, and, most importantly, he is both illiterate and yet the best reader of tradition.

Crucial to note in that initial conversation with Hongren is that hierarchy is being reversed. That is, though the narrative made clear that Huineng was drawn up suddenly to the peak of symbolic value where he claims to be seeking only "buddhadharma," in fact he is not shown asking for any information or guidance at all. Actually, he is clearly *giving* Hongren a lesson in what most readers would consider a very basic point in Buddhist thought: that truth and enlightenment are available to all humans, regardless of their origins, and, of course, regardless of their bodies. In short, Huineng appears to already have tradition and, conversely, Hongren, as the place where perfect tradition supposedly was to be found, is shown holding tenets that are quite at odds with basic Buddhist principles. Hongren's problematic qualities are underscored by having him "scold" Huineng. Normally buddhas don't scold anyone.

A third detail leaves little doubt about the negativity that is being generated around Hongren: we see Hongren closing out the conversation because he notes others were watching; a real buddha, of course, wouldn't be influenced by the presence or absence of the public and could be counted on to do as he pleased, especially in terms of clarifying truth in tradition. This point is strengthened when we remember that the image of the Chan master taking form in the eighth century was based on the claim that the master was totally impervious to precisely this kind of intersubjective pressure. Next to these points regarding Hongren's problematic profile in this initial encounter, we ought to add one more: it is Huineng and not Hongren who knows that they have a karmic connection from the past. Thus it is, ironically, the son and not the father who knows the past that they have shared and, presumably, the future that they will again share. Or put more starkly, here it is the son instead of the father who knows where he has come from, a position that is decidedly the inverse of how knowledge of the past is usually distributed from fathers to sons.

To begin assessing other aspects of this important conversation, we should note that this is the first of two places in Huineng's account where he engages Hongren in discussions of dharma. The second occurs when Hongren gives him dharma transmission and his robe, telling him to flee the monastery. Thus, these two discussions serve as bookends for Huineng's relationship to tradition, or at least tradition as it was imagined lodged in the Bodhidharma lineage (as opposed to being in the *Diamond Sūtra*), and thus ought to be read with special care. In this first conversation, Huineng appears to be hitting a brick wall: he is in the presence of what is supposed to be total tradition—Hongren—but he is rebuffed and sent back down the social hierarchy, having gained nothing. Worse, Hongren as the font of tradition looks rather unattractive, while Huineng glows with a kind of innocence and integrity.

Though this encounter serves primarily to defer the final connection that will be established between these two figures, it also promotes a number of things about Huineng's multiform identity and his "visible" grandeur vis-à-vis the current owner of tradition. For instance, though the narrative is designed to overcome not just Shenxiu and the prior Bodhidharma lineages, it also seems interested in implicitly belittling the whole lineage system since in this exchange Huineng appears as a self-enlightened figure standing taller than Hongren.[16] Actually, this seems to be part of Huineng's enduring charm and why he is a crucial node in the Chan/Zen genealogies: he was the master who even mastered the masters since he was the son who was more legitimate than the father who legitimized him. This is just the kind of detail that modern readers of the text miss, overlooking how Huineng's mastery of tradition is best read neither as a historical fact, nor as a simple lineage claim, but rather as a complex recipe for desire for the reader. In effect, the text seems to be inviting the reader to generate something of a narcissistic identification with Huineng along the lines of, "Hey, Huineng was really great, but maybe I could be great someday, too. After all, Huineng didn't have any status and yet made it to the top . . . and, anyway, I can see what's going on in this debate and probably would have handled it just as well." Or put another way, Huineng seems designed as a kind of Cinderella figure—temporarily stuck in poverty but destined to be set at the peak of the symbolic order.

To get at the details regarding race in this encounter we need to admit that the content of this conversation is not so straightforward, especially in light of Huineng's complex origins. The key problem in the debate is that Huineng doesn't correct Hongren's mistaken assumption that if he is from Lingnan, he is a non-Chinese barbarian and therefore must have a "barbarian's body" and, worse, that somehow with such a barbarian body, buddhahood won't be possible. And to be clear: the term used here for "barbarian," *ge lao*, isn't just derogatory but also serves as a fixed category since Hongren's basic point is that one can't stop being *ge lao* no matter what one tries to do culturally since, for Hongren, *ge lao* is body and mind and is in no way amenable to Buddhist refathering. However, the reader knows very well that Huineng will be refathered since Huineng has from the beginning of the text been presented as the sixth patriarch who had of course been refathered by Hongren, the fifth patriarch. More complicated, though, is the fact that the reader also knows that Huineng *isn't* really a barbarian to begin with, and thus has neither a barbarian's body or mind, or the problems that Hongren attributes to him. He is after all the son of an official most recently from Hubei, who just happened to end up in the southern "barbarian" zone of Lingnan. Thus, while Huineng gave *us*, the reading audience, clear details about his multilocale origins, he lets Hongren take the phrase *from Lingnan* in its simplest sense, thereby drawing conclusions about Huineng's identity that the reader knows to be false. Then with these misunderstandings left uncorrected, Hongren launches into a kind of Buddhist racism that, again, the normal Buddhist reader would know to be wrong-headed.

Given this complex parceling out of information, one has to ask: Why does our author set up this situation that presents both Huineng and Hongren in a troubling light—the first for allowing a gross misinterpretation of his identity; the second for his bad assumption about Huineng's identity and for his misguided notions regarding race in Buddhist teachings? In a very basic sense, it would seem that the author has made us witness a bad reading of Huineng that we, the readers, know to be incorrect and in need of restitution. Then, and moving to a layer slightly below the surface, this initial encounter seems designed to put in play issues regarding the gap between physical origins and real "internal" identity, issues that of course are at the heart of the entire Chan genealogical effort to convincingly install Indian Buddhism in Chinese men. In this light we might be right in suspecting that this conversation built around clarifying the universal, nonracial nature of internal identity is set here to provide a kind of trampoline for the coming revelation of Huineng's other real identity—his buddhahood. That is, just as he is a man of good Chinese stock, mistaken for a barbarian from Lingnan, so too is he a fully enlightened buddha just like the one in India, temporarily taken to be nothing more than a Chinese wannabe.

Likewise, in this initial conversation, Huineng is given lines that demonstrate that he has already mastered the logic that is at the heart of how truth-fathers make their descendants. Huineng is, in effect, arguing: "Yes, we have different bodies, but we share an invisible nature that is beyond bodies and temporal/spatial origins, a buddha-nature that is supposedly at the basis of all the fathers and sons in Buddhism." In short, Huineng, as the son, understands the logic of refathering, and it is by wielding just this logic that he is going to extract this fatherhood from his father-to-be.[17]

To try to make more sense of this rather curious exchange, I suggest we look back to the earliest account of Huineng (Wang Wei's) where Huineng is clearly designed to play a mediating role between India and China. Thus while Wang Wei presented Huineng as Chinese (his surname Lu presumably secured this identity in that narrative), Wang Wei claimed that Huineng wasn't limited by country or region and didn't only abide in China.[18] The implication seemed to be that he was somewhat multicultural and thus a fine candidate for reaching the essence of foreign Buddhism while also being completely able to bring it "home" to his native China. In this sense, just as the "V" motion works to move Huineng up and down the scale of symbolic values, his nomadic multicultural qualities allow him to zigzag between Indian items and the Chinese homeland, with these two motions—vertical and horizontal—crucial to the creation of his identity that will henceforth sink Indian perfection perfectly into the isness of China and her men.

In the *Platform Sutra*, as in Wang Wei's stele, Huineng appears mediating the race problem but in a somewhat different way. Here, though he is first identified as a Chinese figure, he works on Hongren in the guise of being a barbarian—a figure who is neither Chinese nor Indian—and in these interactions proves in word and deed that enlightenment can jump racial categories. In this sense, the narrative works up the race-and-enlightenment debate in a zone defined by the polarity of Chinese versus barbarian, and when that polarity is dissolved in favor of an enlightenment that transcends race, the conclusion seems to slide back onto the real problem which is the divide between India and China. In short, though it is in the guise of being a barbarian that Huineng wins the right to enlightenment, this newly won right isn't for barbarians but for Chinese, and this conclusion hits all the harder since the reader knows all along that Huineng is Chinese.

So, as Huineng obliterates Hongren's racist logic about barbarian limitations—and his eventual reception of the Bodhidharma legacy from Hongren is proof of his victory—the Chinese reader concludes that it is both theoretically and practically possible that Indian Buddhism be installed in a Chinese body. Or, rather, it is precisely by upholding his *theory* of nonracial enlightenment that Huineng proves to the reader that both he and the reader are candidates for nonracial enlightenment. In short, Huineng is shown winning enlightenment with his more acceptable *theory of enlightenment*—that is, he wins actual access to buddhahood by winning arguments in the narrative (and in the reader's eyes) regarding access to buddhahood. Naturally this works to convince the reader because the reader is expected to have just these traditional notions regarding access to buddhahood and not those put forward by Hongren. In sum, the reader sides with Huineng from the outset, and is just waiting for the logic of Huineng's position, which is none other than the logic of tradition, to push its way past Hongren's resistance and to lodge itself, *relodge* itself actually, in the perfect interior of tradition where it belongs.

In a certain sense, in this complex set-up Hongren is positioned to play the role of "India," and he is being "opened up" and universalized by Huineng posing as a barbarian and yet being more Buddhist than the supposed owner of tradition. Then, once enlightenment is extracted from the "racist" Hongren—and note that the text has poised the reader to be the judge in this encounter—tradition is taken to be a Thing that could be rightfully owned by the Chinese. Clearly the point of the encounter isn't to explain why barbarians (vis-à-vis the Chinese) are now rightful claimants to buddhahood. Instead it is China's "barbarianness" vis-à-vis India that is getting resolved, with the logic presumably being that once one kind of barbarianness vis-à-vis the owner of tradition has been overcome, then all kinds of barbarianness can likewise be vanquished. Or perhaps we should say that the framing works by getting the reader to see that if even a "barbarian" from Lingnan has rights to enlightenment and tradition, so much more should fully Chinese readers, from more "cultural" parts of China, have just these same rights.

Considering how this conversation ends so inconclusively with Huineng sent off to the threshing room, it would seem that the author has turned Huineng into something like a resident time bomb, now ticking away in the bowels of this monastery where he just happened to have landed. Huineng entered Hongren's monastery in search of enlightenment, and yet he is already enlightened in some manner (from his first contact with the *Diamond Sūtra*), and he has shown himself to be wiser, by far, than the resident buddha, and thus his ongoing presence in the threshing room appears as something of a threat: When will the correct vision of tradition, so amply portrayed in this figure, burst through the shroudings of hierarchy and fear? And, obviously, the narrative has arranged the reader to completely side with Huineng against just that misaligned social order.

Despite working up this tension between Huineng's new social status as a menial labor in the monastery and the buddha status that the reader suspects is his due, this tension isn't admitted into the interior of the figure of Huineng—his ascent to the peak of Buddhist value is made to appear accidental, unmotivated, and uncolored by pleasure or surprise, just as his demotion to the threshing room is received without a word of bitterness or disappointment. Huineng simply goes where he is told to go.

The Poetry Contest

Directly following the above account of Huineng's move down into the threshing room, we learn that Hongren is hosting a poetry contest in which anyone can offer a poem that demonstrates his enlightenment, and, if the master is suitably impressed, he will bestow on that person "dharma transmission" and the title of "sixth patriarch." Thus, having just installed Huineng in the lowest place in the monastery, the narrative suddenly jumps to the top of the symbolic order to depict a public poetry contest in which a winning poem will move one from being a nobody to being the son of the truth-father.[19] To make sense of this event, which, like Huineng's account of himself, is full of reversals and duplicity, we need to follow two themes that the author seems intent on developing: 1) explaining how it was that Huineng, in fact, got transmission instead of Shenxiu; and 2) explaining why stories that highlight the *Laṅkāvatāra Sūtra* in the dharma-transmission process are not to be trusted.[20]

The action starts when, after learning of Hongren's announcement, the monks conclude that the head monk Shenxiu really is their leader, so there's no point in participating in the contest since surely he is to win the competition. In this brief passage, the monks are depicted as lazy and indifferent. Shenxiu, for his part, appears quite unnerved. Speaking as an omniscient narrator, Huineng explains to his current audience what Shenxiu was thinking back in those days. First it seems that Shenxiu has no idea if he is enlightened or not, and, worse, he finds himself in a double-bind since if he competes by offering a poem it would seem that he is doing so out of personal ambition, and yet without offering a poem he has no chance to win the status of buddhahood. Huineng explains: "The head monk Shenxiu thought: 'The others won't present mind-verses because I am their teacher. If I don't offer a mind-verse, how can the fifth patriarch estimate the degree of understanding within my mind? If I offer my mind to the fifth patriarch with the intention of gaining the dharma, it is justifiable; however, if I am seeking the patriarchship, then it cannot be justified. Then it would be like a common man usurping the saintly position. But if I don't offer my mind then I cannot learn the dharma.' For a long time he thought about it and was very much perplexed" (129, with slight changes). Shenxiu's solution to this impasse was, supposedly, to secretively offer his poem and then wait to see if Hongren accepted it before claiming it as his own. Huineng quotes Shenxiu's thinking on the matter: "If the fifth patriarch sees the verse tomorrow and is pleased with it, then I shall come forward and say that I wrote it. If he tells me that it is not worthwhile, then I shall know that the homage I have received for these several years on this mountain has been in vain, and that I have no hope of learning the Dao" (129n.29—this passage is taken from the Koshoji manuscript because the Dunhuang text is clearly corrupt here).

With this duplicitous plan in place, we have clear "evidence" of how different Shenxiu is from Huineng. Huineng, with his accidental enlightenment from the *Diamond Sūtra*, moved up in Buddhist status naturally, effortlessly, and with no thought—in fact, we never hear a word of what Huineng was thinking, and certainly he is never shown debating with himself over how to influence the Other's opinion of him. Shenxiu, on the other hand, is presented as a developed site of intersubjectivity since he is carefully considering how to control how those above and below him in the social hierarchy view him, and he is quite willing to employ deception to arrange things to his liking. Likewise, whereas Huineng's commoner status appears as an asset—a wholesome simplicity and a natural innocence—Shenxiu's internal reflections show him considering that his ambition is the very thing that makes him a commoner since he says to himself: "If I am seeking the patriarchship, then it cannot be justified. Then it would be like a common man usurping the saintly position." In short, Shenxiu is Huineng's opposite in terms of identity and motion: Shenxiu is at the top where he has been receiving worship for the past couple of years (weirdly, since the monks should have been worshipping Hongren), and yet any action that he might take to solidify that privilege in terms of becoming the new truth-father will cast him down to commoner status. Huineng, for his part, is at the bottom of all relevant hierarchies, takes no action—with one exception being granted so that he can offer his own poem sometime later—and yet will find himself at the top.

Seeing how well Shenxiu's "interior" is being developed in this passage—with this monologue rendered verbatim, years later—warrants some reflection. If the *Platform Sūtra* was written around 780, then Shenxiu has been dead for seventy-five years, and this scene with Hongren would have had to occur in an even more distant past since Hongren died in 674. There is, as far as we know, no prior textual source, or hint of a source, for these events, much less Shenxiu's intimate reflections on his bid to be the sixth patriarch. In fact, connecting Shenxiu with Hongren only appeared in narratives written after Shenxiu's death when various authors had reason to attach him to Hongren and the Bodhidharma lineage. Thus, we have to wonder where this rich and detailed interior monologue came from. If it hasn't come to the author from the literary record—and all the preceding accounts of Shenxiu present a completely positive image of him—my guess is that in Shenxiu's Hamlet-style ruminations we see the author of the *Platform Sūtra* foisting a portion of his own subjectivity onto Shenxiu since Shenxiu is doing, in a simple way, what the *Platform Sūtra* is designed to do: take hold of the Bodhidharma inheritance by manipulating public opinion, through inserting unsigned and misrecognized literature into the public sphere. Below, I will consider more closely what it means that the text has presented Shenxiu in this manner, but for now let's move forward in the narrative having noted that our author seems rather familiar with the dilemma that he has injected into Shenxiu, a familiarity that presumably renders our author far from innocent.

Resolved to follow his ruse, Shenxiu writes his poem in the middle of the night on the wall outside the master's hall. This wall, it turns out, is presented as something of a public canvas since we learn that it had been divided into three sections and had been designated as the site for painting scenes from the *Laṇkāvatāra Sūtra*, along with scenes from the coming transmission moment when Hongren will crown one of his disciples as the sixth patriarch. Hongren had supposedly already invited a painter to come to paint these scenes, presumably to thereby formally inscribe in public space the reality of the transmission while also underscoring the central role that the *Laṇkāvatāra Sūtra* was expected to have in that moment. Since several early Bodhidharma genealogies claimed that the totality of tradition was to be found in the *Laṇkāvatāra Sūtra*, the narrative, for the moment, appears to be developing in accord with those older versions of the Bodhidharma lineage. However, once these expectations are established in the story, they soon will be radically reversed.

In the morning, when Hongren sees Shenxiu's unsigned poem written on the central panel of the triptych on the wall—intruding exactly where he had planned to have the scenes from the *Laṇkāvatāra Sūtra* painted—he cancels his plan to have the paintings done. Explaining his course of action to the painter, he quotes from the *Diamond Sūtra* saying: "It is said in the *Diamond Sūtra*: All forms everywhere are unreal and false" (130). Now one might rightly wonder why Hongren is thinking in *Diamond Sūtra* terms about the unreality of forms only *now* at the very end of his career. In short, what is an enlightened buddha doing changing sūtras at this very late hour? The oddness of this detail is all the clearer when we remember that when Huineng first bumped into the *Diamond Sūtra* back down south in Nanhai, the man reciting the text told him that he had received the text from Hongren with the advice that this text, the *Diamond Sūtra* (and *not* the *Laṇkāvatāra Sūtra*), was the ticket to salvation. In short, if we were to take the narrative as account of real history, the scene would make no sense at all.

However, once we begin to focus on the art of the text, this moment makes perfect sense and even perhaps qualifies as a masterful palace coup, since both prior claimants—the *Laṇkāvatāra Sūtra* and Shenxiu—have been "invited" to this wall, a wall which in fact is a kind of killing floor, since Hongren will soon symbolically execute them both.[21] Once we realize that the narrative is designed to overcome prior claims to own tradition, Hongren's abrupt and unexplained shifts in allegiance read out easily as explanations for why there are these earlier texts that explain how Hongren took the *Laṇkāvatāra Sūtra* and Shenxiu to be icons of total content even though, now, we readers of the *Platform Sūtra* understand that those two items were never really legitimate.

The complexities in Hongren's attitude toward truth and tradition densify when the narrative has Hongren announce that he plans to leave Shenxiu's poem on the wall since it will, supposedly, aid practitioners and keep them from falling into bad rebirths. As Hongren says, "It would be best to leave this verse here and to have the deluded ones recite it. If they practice in accordance with it, they will not fall into the three evil ways. Those who practice by it will gain great benefit" (130). Hongren then goes a step further, burning incense in front of the poem and encouraging the monks—the "deluded ones"—to have faith in it, now publicly claiming that it will keep them out of bad rebirths *and* give them insight into their fundamental natures. Once instructed in this recitation, the monks were delighted and cried out, "How excellent!" (130). Given how Hongren is shown temporarily supporting the two icons found in the older genealogies, we have to say that the text is presenting Hongren as that complicated site where good and bad versions of tradition coexisted in a manner that, now years after the events, needs to be correctly understood, a task, of course, that the narrative of the *Platform Sūtra* takes as its *raison d'être*. Or put in other terms: the text is working up a complex conspiracy theory with Hongren set up as the main conspirator.[22]

Continuing in this charade, Hongren has Shenxiu come to his room to ask him if he is the author of this poem. Once Shenxiu arrives, Hongren first explains that whoever wrote this poem will get to be the sixth patriarch—a bald lie, of course. Given that pretext, Shenxiu naturally claims the poem as his own and begs Hongren to tell him if he has any understanding or not. Once again, then, Shenxiu is stuck in intersubjective no-man's land since he is begging the Other to define his own interior. After Shenxiu confesses to Hongren that he is the author of this poem, Hongren tells him directly that he doesn't have understanding and that he stands outside the house of patriarchs. Hongren reiterates that what Shenxiu has is a second-rate form of tradition that is useful for aiding the deluded but useless for seeing "ultimate enlightenment." The poem, however, stays on the wall.

Some Time Later

The effects of these various deceptions become clearer when, some time later, a novice monk passes by the threshing room reciting Shenxiu's poem. When Huineng hears the novice recite the poem, he immediately knows it to be a second-rate statement of enlightenment and "that the person who had written it had yet to know his own nature and to discern the cardinal meaning (大意)" (131). That is, the narrative unflinchingly shows us that Huineng has the eyes and ears of the confirmed master, Hongren, since they both instantaneously recognize the poem for what it is: junk. And yet in a moment Huineng will lie and tell this passing monk to take him to the poem so that he can worship it with incense. And yet before that moment of duplicity, the narrative has the poem-reciting monk repeat everything that has happened regarding the poetry contest, since Huineng, off in the threshing room as he has been, apparently hasn't heard anything about it.

In the monk's recounting of the poetry contest, the reader gets a vision of how the (bad) version of tradition that took Shenxiu to be the sixth patriarch has thoroughly seeped into the collective memory of the monastery. Thus, this monk's version of events, given in the narrative to inform the otherwise clueless Huineng, works well to prove that Shenxiu was, in fact, taken to be the sixth patriarch and that tradition was wrongly imagined to flow into him. Thus, as in all conspiracy theories, the "true account" of the matter also contains an explanation for how and why the false version of events was put into the public sphere and taken to be accurate. In response to this information about the poetry contest and its implications, Huineng insists on his total ignorance of the affair since after all he has been treading the pestle for the past eight months and hasn't even been to the great hall.[23] Given all this news, Huineng tells this monk that he would like to go to the hall and pay obeisance to Shenxiu's poem hoping, thereby, to win rebirth in a buddhaland—a motivation that he has, of course, never announced before. In fact, he declared the opposite in his first interview with Hongren where he said he wasn't searching for anything, just "buddhadharma"—the essence of tradition.[24]

Thus, for the first time in the narrative, Huineng is shown having emotions and desires, desires even for Buddhism, something that was completely absent from the profile offered earlier when he was both empty of intention and completely brazen and unyielding in the opening conversation with Hongren. Now, suddenly, he is supposedly eager to worship Shenxiu's poem with the hope of obtaining the decidedly second-rate goal of rebirth in a buddhaland. Likewise, insofar as Huineng has already been shown challenging Hongren over the hard-core issue of buddhanature and barbarian bodies, not to mention having been initially enlightened by hearing the *Diamond Sūtra*, we haven't been prepared to imagine a craven Huineng eager to follow the herd in reciting what Hongren and Huineng (!) know to be an invalid articulation of tradition. What might explain this new profile of Huineng that is so at odds with other elements in the text?

As usual, these supposed "historical" details don't make sense until one shifts to the text-as-art model. Once in that mind-set, it is not too hard to see what is going on: the narrative has to get Huineng to the poetry contest—in order that he can win the title of "sixth patriarch" from Hongren—but, given the larger demand that Huineng also be an accidental buddha, his arrival at the scene of the competition has to be motivated by something besides ambition. To balance these two requirements our author first kept Huineng away from the contest, away from the halls of power, and totally ignorant of the whole affair, which supposedly has now been concluded. Then, when Huineng does enter into contact with the competition, our author emphasizes that this contact occurred accidentally since, after all, it was supposedly only by chance that the no-name novice happened to be reciting the "winning" poem as he passed the threshing room, with this happenstance contact being the hook that brought Huineng to the wall—that vexed place where tradition's ownership was to be finalized.

Our author further emphasizes Huineng's lack of ambition by having Huineng claim that he wants to go to the wall, and the poem that it holds, because he wants to worship it. Thus Huineng moves upward to the place where tradition is to be reproduced with the simple desires of a common monk, completely uninterested in the leadership position. In short, in a text full of overt lies and subterfuge, these narrative foils work to maintain a sheen of innocence around Huineng and, of course, the whole narrative itself. The problem, of course, is that the more the narrative works to generate this image of how Huineng came to so innocently own tradition, the more it has to indulge in a variety of mini-plots that strain credibility in several directions.

In fact there is another narrative problem that is equally glaring: the whole story of the poetry contest, including the omniscient narration of Shenxiu's thoughts, has been part of an account that Huineng is relating in the first-person. That is, everything that has happened so far regarding the competition has come forth from Huineng's mouth as he sits at the head of this great gathering in Shaozhou in the real time of the text. Of course, then, we have to ask how Huineng could have been off in the threshing room, completely ignorant of the poetry contest *and* also completely privy not just to the conversations between Hongren and Shenxiu—private conversations that were specifically kept from the other monks—but also privy to Shenxiu's interior reflections and his secretive nighttime actions. Now one might think that Huineng simply learned of all these events later from other monks; however, this isn't explained by the narrative which seems to hope that we don't notice the problem. In fact, it is just this information that the other monks would have lacked if they were worshipping Shenxiu's poem and taking him to be the sixth patriarch.

This narrative awkwardness results, it would seem, from the fact that the key to the *Platform Sūtra's* success is that it must, in the guise of pure history, show how the transmission of pure tradition didn't in fact go to Shenxiu but instead went to Huineng, who in fact never wanted it. Hence, Huineng can only be who he claims to be if he can "prove" that Shenxiu isn't who he was taken to be, since they are claiming the same singular identity of being the sixth patriarch. Thus, as mentioned at the outset of this chapter, the symbolic death of Shenxiu is the only place where Huineng's identity as the sixth patriarch can be born. Hence, Huineng's story of himself is really the story of Shenxiu's failure, with Huineng weirdly inside Shenxiu's head, giving us the information that absolutely destroys Shenxiu's identity as the proper holder of tradition.

Sonship 2.0

On another level, this set-up makes good sense if we return to the arguments made about sonship in chapter 3. There, in the context of explaining the various narrative ploys in the Gospel of Mark, I argued that sonship resides not in the private rapport between father and son, but in the *public acceptance* of the father-son narrative that joins the two together. Thus, in this case, if the public took Shenxiu to be the sixth patriarch, then the only way Huineng can take hold of that identity is to "prove" to the public that that attribution was mistaken. Thus, the claim that Huineng is the sixth patriarch—and that's the point of the whole narrative—must include within it three things: 1) the history of why Shenxiu wasn't the real "truth-son" of Hongren; 2) the history of why this attribution was, mistakenly, given to him by the public; and, 3) the history of how real sonship went from Hongren to Huineng.

Given these three structural demands, it isn't surprising that up to this point the narrative has been working to hollow out the older father-son narrative linking Hongren and Shenxiu, while *also* showing how that sham transmission had been established and widely recognized by the public. Of course, once these two sides of the triangle are sufficiently explained, the narrative will turn to finalize the figure with a history of how Hongren's real paternity was given to Huineng. And, to finesse this complicated play of dependence and (imagined) independence in the establishment of sonship, the narrative has Huineng blindly nudging his way into his sonship role with no notion that his actions and their assessment in the eyes of the public are the key to owning this identity. In fact, it seems he doesn't even know that this spectacular form of sonship is an identity that could be won; in coming to meet Hongren, he identifies his agenda with a denial: "I am seeking no particular thing, but only the buddhadharma"—a bold claim that removes the possibility that Huineng arrived with plans to be recognized as Hongren's truth-son.

A similar kind of authorial acumen is visible in the way that the narrative prepares snapshots of Huineng's sonship taking form in private or unofficial zones. Thus, the enlightenment via the *Diamond Sūtra* back in Lingnan and the first conversation with Hongren appear as clear "proofs" of Huineng's identity as the rightful sixth patriarch, but the narrative doesn't immediately cash in on these proofs, saving them up instead for the moment when these accumulated "savings" are turned into a perfect purchase when Hongren officially coronates Huineng as the sixth patriarch. The logic at work here is simple enough: while identity is a brutal yes-no matter, public assent to identity is always partial, changeable, and organic in the sense of existing on a scale of probability: one thinks, "Yeah, I bet this Huineng is the real sixth patriarch and not Shenxiu, or at least it's really starting to look that way. I wonder what others think." Given this tension, the reader is slowly given reasons (and desires) to accept the suddenness of the coming coronation, since this magical moment will only succeed if the reading public has been suitably prepared with the various "silent changes" in which Huineng's sonship is constructed and Shenxiu's is destroyed. In short, Huineng's identity is made of the reader's desire, and this desire has to be evoked and then managed in certain ways to get it to turn into a quasi-juridical declaration: "Yes, I hereby assent to the claim that Huineng is the sixth patriarch."

Of course within this dialect between desire and the granting of identity, public recognition of Huineng's sonship *inside the text*—as performed by Hongren and others—functions to persuade the reading audience *outside of the text*, who, in good mimetic fashion, are asked to draw the same conclusions as those inside the text. Thus, though the final transmission of identity between Hongren and Huineng will happen secretly in the narrative, it is of course happening in plain view of the public who reads this narrative and is being asked to be the guarantors of Huineng's sonship, confirming this particular father-son pair and the sacred essence that supposedly has passed between them. Thus, to make the father-son double look convincing—and here "convincing" always means for the public—another set of doubles has to be invoked: the public inside the text which is manipulated as needed by the author in order that the real public outside of the text can, after a fashion, be manipulated as well. Arguably, we are squarely in the zone that determined the writing of the Gospel of Mark where similar writing strategies arranged claims regarding Jesus' sonship, and, in particular, the way internal audiences were deployed to work on external audiences.

Overwriting the Past

Once in front of the wall where Shenxiu has written his poem, Huineng worships the bad poem. But, then, presumably in an effort to emphasize how removed Huineng is from literature, the poetry contest, and the pyramid of Buddhist social status, Huineng asks that the poem be read to him since he is illiterate. Of course, a minute earlier he had heard the poem down in the threshing room, understood it completely, and judged it to be an inferior work. Thus, just as Huineng is both completely clairvoyant regarding Shenxiu's life *and* absolutely ignorant of it all, so too can Huineng offer an effortless and penetrating critique of the poem and yet claim a moment later that he needs someone to read it to him (again). So, there stands Huineng in front of the item that, according to the public, has made Shenxiu into Hongren's truth-son, and he supposedly can't recognize it for what it is or for what it has done. Naturally, this reinforces the narrative's point that Huineng is completely innocent of the symbolic economy that has to be engaged in the process of making such a son since, as argued above, it is precisely the image of this kind of innocence that makes the public more liable to accept a new narrative of sonship. Again, if one reads these events without a sense for the dynamics involved in making sons, none of this would make much sense.

What happens next at first seems even stranger but in fact fits the pattern. Huineng, upon hearing Shenxiu's poem recited, suddenly comes to understand the "cardinal meaning." This phrase seems to imply that Huineng is, ironically, getting enlightened and fathered by the failed son's effort to get fathered. On the surface this hardly seems reasonable, especially when we remember that his initial reaction to the poem down in the thresh-ing room was to think to himself "that the person who had written it had yet to know his own nature and to discern *the cardinal meaning*." Staying on the surface of this situation, it seems that in this moment Huineng receives from *this failed poem* the enlightenment that would turn him into Hongren's legitimate truth-son—that is, he is getting his sonship precisely from the place where Shenxiu's sonship had failed. This, of course makes sense given that only one of them can be accorded the title of "sixth patriarch," and thus Huineng's sonship can only occur in the space created when Shenxiu's sonship is voided. Focusing on questions of ownership and not on supposed wisdom issues makes the whole arrangement seem more sensible. In fact, considering the details more closely, below, reveals that the sequence is best treated as a kind of sacrifice with Huineng's poem being no more or less than the controlled execution of Shenxiu's poem—and thus his identity as the temporary holder of the title of the "sixth patriarch"—in just such a manner that Huineng's identity takes form in its place.

Having just been enlightened to the "cardinal meaning" when Shenxiu's bad poem was read to him, Huineng has a literate person write Huineng's own poem on the wall. In a real glitch in editing, two poems are given in the *Platform Sūtra*, as if the author couldn't decide which looked most convincing.[25]

Shenxiu's poem reads:

> The body is the Bodhi tree,
> The mind is like a clear mirror.
> At all times we must strive to polish it,
> And must not let the dust collect.

Huineng's poems read:

> Bodhi originally has no tree,
> The mirror also has no stand.
> Buddha nature is always clean and pure;
> Where is there room for dust?

> The mind is the Bodhi tree,
> The body is the mirror stand.
> The mirror is originally clean and pure;
> Where can it be stained by dust?

Though different in mode of attack, each of Huineng's poems culminates in the basic negation of the two concluding lines in Shenxiu's poem. Thus, whereas Shenxiu's poem calls for the purification of mind—keeping dust off the mirror of buddhahood—Huineng's poems deny that buddhahood could ever be tainted by the dust of afflictions. The evident effect of this negation, which would seem to negate Buddhist practice, is that Huineng appears much more intimate with buddhahood. Thus, Huineng seems to inhabit a zone where the normal logic of Buddhism is confounded by a perspective that is perhaps best defined as being "so Buddhist it doesn't need Buddhism." Of course the clear implication here is that as a buddha, Huineng not only has no use for Buddhism—he has after all become the site of Buddhist perfection and purity—and now can see that the prior state of delusion and imperfection was completely misguided and fundamentally "impossible" vis-à-vis the now omnipresent reality of his buddhahood.

Despite signaling his mastery of buddhahood, Huineng's two poems as literature are obviously parasitic on Shenxiu's content; that is, one comes to see Huineng's supposed mastery of buddhahood only by juxtaposing it with Shenxiu's poem which *now* appears to have been written by one located at a good distance from the goal of enlightenment and ignorant of its radical immanence. In short, the content of Huineng's poem, and its winning nature, are only "visible" via the negation of Shenxiu's poem; presumably if Shenxiu hadn't been set up to play the straight man and had instead written a more radical poem, Huineng's two poems would look rather shabby. More exactly, it is precisely that gap of difference, created by giving Shenxiu a poem that looks like Buddhism 101, that makes Huineng appear to be the buddha who possesses tradition. Of course this dependence on Shenxiu's poem corresponds with the entire issue of Huineng's sonship, which takes form in the execution of Shenxiu, who needs to die as Hongren's truth-son *and yet in that dying transfer that identity to Huineng.* In this sense, Huineng isn't getting transmission from Hongren; rather, he is getting it from Shenxiu, since that sonship must leave Shenxiu's body and land on Huineng's. Or in terms of social recognition, the whole scene must gather up past social recognition of Shenxiu's sonship and deposit it, innocently and naturally, on Huineng's body. In this sense, Huineng is condemned to carry around the symbolic corpse of Shenxiu's sonship, just as his poems must always be read against Shenxiu's to have their intended meaning and effect.

In all this, we shouldn't overlook that the *Platform Sūtra* is minting a moment of perfect writing by constructing its opposite: an unmotivated, untutored orality happens to arrive at the scene of writing and transmission, and, once there, perfectly overcomes the iconic writing of the supposed heir to tradition—Shenxiu. In sum, our author has worked hard to give the impression that the literary tradition has been bested from below—superseded by an underground and innocent Something that renders old literature defunct, even as it is, itself, new literature, written in public, in a manner that encases within it the carcass of the old literature. In effect, this is the moment when the time bomb that the narrative had installed explodes, and upsets all prior forms of order and hierarchy, save for the pivotal father who must now regive his heritage. In sum, our author apparently decided to present Huineng as the proper inheritor of tradition by demonstrating his perfection in terms of absolute simplicity: no education, no ambition, no pedigree, no Buddhist training, no status, and so on. Ironically, though, this perfection of simplicity and innocence has to be "harvested" within the literary tradition in the double sense of showing Huineng winning the poetry contest and then lodging him in the *Platform Sūtra* which will soon put itself, as text, forward as the essence of the Buddhist tradition.

The Death and Rebirth of Sonship

Once Huineng's poem is written on the wall (and I will be referring to it in the singular for simplicity's sake), everyone is amazed, and here obviously our author is giving the reading audience a basic clue about how to respond to the poem. Despite all the hoopla over his poem, Huineng goes back down the social register, returning to the threshing room, with that up-and-down "V" movement continuing to organize action in the story. Then, despite the out-of-context quality of Huineng's "writing"—the competition was officially over—the truth-father becomes aware of this newly tendered "son-making" literature, recognizes it as a mark of perfect sonship, and secretly calls Huineng to his room for a midnight transmission ceremony in which he recites the *Diamond Sūtra* to him, a reading which again enlightens Huineng. Hongren then hands over to him his robe, the robe that supposedly had been the property of every prior member of the lineage. However, he does all this while saying in public that the poem is "not complete understanding," and this he does supposedly out of fear, a fear that presumably is designed to match the fear he manifested after his first conversation with Huineng at the beginning of their relationship. Apparently both of these details—Hongren's public rejection of Huineng's poem and his supposed fear of the public—are included to explain why the accurate version of sonship wasn't publicly installed in Huineng in a way that would have made it widely known to history. Presumably too it implicitly stigmatizes Shenxiu supporters as violent.

With this clear account of Hongren's secret transmission of tradition to Huineng now in full view for the reader, and set against the false one publicly granted to Shenxiu, it seems clear that the text is dedicated to winning the reader's conversion to a new notion of tradition by showing two versions of tradition—the old and new—along with correct and incorrect readings of those two versions. Thus, just like the split-screen situation in Mark, here too we have been given a series of scenes where supposedly real and unreal (even if widely accepted) versions of tradition are paraded in front of us, and we have been given many reasons to side with the supposedly real version and against the older, established version. In fact, the whole logic of the poetry contest seems designed to put before the reader a kind of externalization of sonship in which normally invisible sonship finds an icon of readability, not just in the odd notion that poems can be taken as proof of one's interior, but also in the gap between Huineng's antinomian poem/s and Shenxiu's white-bread ditty, with this gap in "profundity" presented to the reader as obvious proof of their respective identities.

To get a sense of how truth, enlightenment, and tradition are getting culturally fabricated here one could imagine that buddhahood might not result in wonderful and self-revealing poetic skills, and thus the winner of the poetry contest might be the better poet and not necessarily the buddha who should inherit the patriarchy. And yet the author trusts that the reader will believe that poems are windows into the soul that allow legitimate sonship to be read out of that interior. What might not seem obvious at first though is that the whole set-up of taking poems to be the indicator of one's interior is occurring because the entire event is a literary fabrication destined for the reader who naturally needs his "evidence" of buddhahood to come in a literary mode. This isn't to say that during the Tang there wasn't a developed code for interpreting poems in terms of their supposed sincerity and authenticity—there was—but this background cultural logic provides no more than the material for arranging the event.[26]

The heart of the matter is the text-as-public-art problem: as our author generates his text for the reader, it is the author-reader relationship that defines the form and content of the relationship between Hongren and Huineng—a relationship that will only be meaningful in the narrative if it can be read *outward* in an obvious and "natural" manner. To really get at why this has to be a literary contest, consider the pitfalls of having Hongren demand paintings instead of poems from his entourage: in that case, the narrative would be able to *say* that Huineng's painting was the better, more enlightened painting, but it wouldn't be able to *show* this difference in writing. On the other hand, with the two poems back to back "on the wall," the reader can, finally, "see" the difference between the two combatting sons and naturally side with the owner of the better poem, with "better" meaning apparently more intimate with buddhahood and more in line with chosen Indian Buddhist texts that emphasized the negation-of-tradition as proof of owning tradition, texts such as the *Diamond Sūtra* and the *Vimalakīti*.

Truth and Violence

Thinking through the logic of the poetry context in this manner helps makes sense of another element in the narrative that might at first appear arbitrary but isn't: abundant violence. As seen above, threats of violence appeared in the first moment of contact between Huineng and Hongren. In that moment when Hongren doesn't want to continue the conversation because others are around, we are given the impression that the truth-father knows that joining (this) son to the Bodhidharma lineage will result in public outrage. This menace is evoked again when Hongren is afraid to reveal his choice of Huineng following his belated entry into the poetry contest. This fear is repeated in their nighttime transmission moment when Hongren makes clear that the dharma transmission is always at risk and that Huineng's life is now in danger. Hongren explains, "From ancient times the transmission of the dharma has been as tenuous as a dangling thread. If you stay here there are people who will harm you. You must leave at once" (133). Of course, this comment works to demonize any opposition to the text's claim about Huineng, but it also rather handily gets Huineng out of sight of the local community who presumably will remain duped about the real recipient of tradition. Thus having Huineng run away not only explains why no one knew about this transmission—it was never publicly recognized by Hongren's monastery—it also explains why Huineng had nothing to do with Hongren's death rituals—a key sequence of events that inheritors normally are supposed to take part in. However, in addition to solving these somewhat technical matters in the narrative, this theme of public violence will soon have other roles to play, and in the next set of events it functions more elegantly to solidify a number of the text's claims.

On that very same night of the dangerous dharma transmission, Hongren escorts Huineng part of the way down the road to see him off in an event that culminates in another enlightenment experience for Huineng. In saying goodbye, Hongren also councils him to stay incognito for three years to avoid being attacked. Huineng then sets off on his long trip south when, en route, he discovers that he is being followed by hundreds of people who want to kill him "and steal his robe and dharma" (134). After two months of travel, a particularly rude and aggressive general of the third rank, Huiming, catches up with Huineng on the peak of a mountain (the other malefactors had turned away by now) and demands the transmission that Huineng supposedly received from Hongren. Huineng offers him the robe, but Huiming wants the dharma, so Huineng transmits the dharma to him and, when Huiming hears it—and we readers get to hear nothing—he is immediately enlightened. Then Huineng instructs him to go north and convert the people.

Looking at the broad outlines of this mini-story that concludes Huineng's account of his life, one might find it, along with the other events in this narrative, bizarre and of little import. What, after all, is the point of narrating this chase scene and then having Huineng suddenly give General Huiming dharma transmission, but without the robe? Actually, as with the other odd things in the narrative, I believe that this mini-story proves a number of useful points and works to resolve some doubts, too. First, the mass of people chasing Huineng functions as a general public who want what Huineng now supposedly has—the dharma and the robe. Thus, the crazed mob in the story functions to "prove," again visibly, that Huineng actually has the dharma transmission and the robe: "seeing" this mad horde chase after him makes clear to the reader that, in a sense, Huineng has been publicly recognized as the sixth patriarch since now all these people look to him as the owner of just these items. And, as usual in this type of story, the trope of violence works to mask this newly won recognition with a kind of innocence. Huineng never wanted this kind of recognition—who would, given that it leads to these mortally dangerous situations? And likewise, with this violent mob chasing after Huineng, the author has managed to generate for the reader the image of total public recognition—surely with this kind of fervor, no one had any doubts about the real owner of tradition—and yet has the reader absorb this fact indirectly, under the banner of negation: no one ever desired this outcome inside the narrative since in fact this appears to be a rather negative outcome. And yet in good fairytale fashion, this negativity turns out to be toothless—the mob never gets a hold of Huineng—and instead the author has positioned this mini-story so that the reader is left with the force of these narrative claims and concludes: "Wow, everyone must have really been convinced of this Hongren-Huineng father-son connection. If not, why would they go charging after Huineng for months?"

Proving the ownership of tradition seems to be the point, too, of that sudden transmission to the general. Though, Huineng has absolutely no history with this man, he is shown handing off *half* of the transmission—giving him the dharma but not the robe. Thus as we watch Huineng enlighten Huiming, we again gain confidence in Huineng's ownership of tradition since we see that he is, in fact, capable of giving it to Huiming.[27] And despite the logical desire to want to know what became of this general, we learn nothing more about him. I would suggest that the episode functions as a dummy transmission in the sense that the author has no interest in the general or the transmission that he now been given, since the point of the episode is just to prove Huineng's functioning ownership of tradition. This reading seems worthwhile because the next thing that happens is a jump into "real time" where Huineng returns to talking to his audience in the southern town of Shaozhou, in the "present." That is, this dummy transmission to the general is the final piece of the puzzle that proves that Huineng is fully endowed with the essence of tradition from Hongren and is ready to go to work on the tasks that the rest of the narrative will set before him.[28]

Resetting the *Diamond Sūtra,* or Refetishizing a Fetish

Once the narrative has returned to the present, the action turns from history to ritual since in this section of the text, the audience-in-the-text is asked to participate in a traditional procedure of taking refuge, confessing their sins, taking vows, and so on. In effect, then, in terms of narrative development, the author first established Huineng as Hongren's sole heir—and thus a living buddha of sorts—and then presents Huineng leading the public through these ritual acts as though tradition were born anew that day. Thus, whether we say the historical Buddha has been "front-loaded" into the present of Tang China or that the audience has been thrust back into the historical moment of the Indian Buddha who now appears as Huineng, the result is the same: total tradition is present and is effectively doing what tradition must do—replicate itself. More exactly, in a manner that fulfills Bourdieu's model of religious authority to a "T," original tradition has been shown to live in real time, in the form of Huineng who, due to his direct contact with the origins of tradition—via his enlightenment/s and his place in the lineage of truth-fathers—is now legally authorized to dispense tradition to the public who, provided they believe this history, are now confident that they will come in contact with real tradition in the present.

Before moving into this section of the text, let's stand back from the history that Huineng has presented of himself to assess how the content of tradition has been handled. First, it seems fair to say that content, in the sense of specific Buddhist teachings, has largely been missing in the story. Thus, in each of the moments when one would hope that the content of the dharma might be revealed, there is little or nothing said that would allow the reader to "see" inside the tube of transmission. Of course this fits with the overall agenda of the narrative which is dedicated to explaining why it is that only the masters in the Bodhidharma lineage have the full and perfect version of tradition. And yet there is a sliver of content to be reckoned, and it centers on the *Diamond Sūtra* and a style of negation that is the main element in that sūtra. We first saw this in that moment when Huineng hears the *Diamond Sūtra* recited, gets enlightened, and goes to see Hongren. Then, in a more explicit moment, Hongren explains his choice to dismiss the painter and the plans for painting the *Laṅkāvatāra Sūtra* by citing a line from the *Diamond Sūtra*. Shortly thereafter, Huineng's "attack" poem works in a manner consistent with the rhetoric of the *Diamond Sūtra*, negating the building blocks of the Buddhist tradition in order to prove a higher/deeper understanding of tradition. Presumably for readers familiar with the *Diamond Sūtra*, this negation of cause and effect in the practice of Buddhism would have been read in line with the passages in the *Diamond Sūtra* where the Indian Buddha is made to negate the existence of any specific dharma as well as all the levels of practical achievement. Finally, in his last night with Hongren, Huineng receives from him an explanation of the *Diamond Sūtra,* and "hearing it but once, I was immediately awakened" (133).

If one is unfamiliar with the *Diamond Sūtra* and how its rhetoric of negation is designed to overcome old tradition, one will miss what the *Diamond Sūtra* is doing in the *Platform Sūtra's* narrative. Likewise, one will also miss a chance to appreciate the layers of commentary that are at work here as our author tries to give the reader the impression that tradition really is present here in the hands of a totally unschooled illiterate. To begin to appreciate these larger continuities in the literary effort to make the past of a tradition seem present, we need to understand how Chan texts represent a second-order effort to fetish tradition, one that follows on the heels of the Mahāyāna effort to fetishize tradition back in India. In China, Chan writers drew on these earlier rhetorical strategies but were also completely at odds with them since they wanted to fetishize tradition into a Chinese man and not an Indian sūtra. In short, we need to briefly return to India to first see how a text like the *Diamond Sūtra* worked to fetishize tradition and then move back to China to see how this sūtra is being positioned to effect a new fetishization of tradition that takes up many of the *Diamond Sūtra's* gestures but, in effect, turns those gestures on the text itself in order to draw the marrow out of that work and lodge it in the Chinese masters and the texts that they lived in.

To understand Chan as a second-order overcoming of tradition, we need to remember, as mentioned in the last chapter, that roughly at the beginning of the Common Era there appeared a number of texts that sought to advance the claim that the totality of the Buddhist tradition was to be found within their own borders. The *Diamond Sūtra's* technique for stealing tradition from the Buddha, and the living tradition that he had inaugurated, was to negate the items that appeared to have been fundamental to the standard form of tradition. Thus, the *Diamond Sūtra* presents a new version of the Buddha who rather clumsily goes through a list of key elements in (old) tradition and negates them. Of course, many elements from (old) tradition don't get negated, and, in particular, the text never allows its discourse to ruin the sanctity of the Buddha's identity, the power of Buddhist truth, or the text's own project of moving "tradition" forward. In short, the negation of (old) tradition is partial and functions in the text to prove that there really is a "speaking" Buddha present in this new literary form, and thus his negation of tradition proves, in several ways, his ownership of tradition and therefore his right to declare what is and isn't tradition. In short, the negation of (old) tradition is *not* to be seen as a simple attack on tradition but rather an effective manner to deracinate it and prepare it to be lodged elsewhere. In fact, that is exactly what happens since after negating the various traditional Buddhist items, the Buddha-in-the-text turns to explain that the total content of tradition is to be found in the physical presence of the *Diamond Sūtra*. Likewise, he adds that all buddhas "come out" of the *Diamond Sūtra*, and thus the text functions to capture the beginning and end of all the buddhas, and thus all possible forms of tradition.[29]

What modern readers of the *Diamond Sūtra* have been slow to realize is that the radical negation of various elements of tradition isn't a philosophical position that ought to be treated apart from the "narrative" role that that negation plays in the text. In short, the negations can't be separated from the creation of new authority and tradition. Just as Jesus, in the Gospel of Mark, negates essential elements of the Jewish tradition—the Torah, the priestly representatives of the law, the purity laws, and so on—in a manner that proves to the believing reader that he has the Father-given right to legislate tradition, so too the Mahāyāna authors figured out similar uses for negative rhetoric in their effort to front-load tradition into the newly invented cult of the text where tradition would be endlessly available in the worship (and reproduction) of these strange texts-of-tradition. It turns out that these Indian sūtras that fetishized tradition via a process of negation were often those favored by the Chinese, and in fact, the *Diamond Sūtra* likely is China's best-loved sūtra of all time.

What happened with the advent of the Chan tradition was that the *Diamond Sūtra* and its sister texts were, in a sense, uploaded into Chinese bodies. In that repositioning, the negative rhetoric of the sūtras was first cut away from the matrix of the cult of the text and then put in the mouths of certain Chinese masters, thereby giving the impression that this beloved rhetoric was now coming forth from local figures, implying thereby that these local figures were, in essence, no different from the distant Indian Buddha. This fusion of local masters with the Indian Buddha was, of course, enhanced by giving them Bodhidharma pedigrees to prove that they were direct inheritors of the historical Buddha and thus had a kind of "genetic right" to own and manipulate tradition in these ways.

In the case of the *Platform Sūtra*, we have just seen the author's careful and extended effort to inscribe Huineng in the Bodhidharma lineage and, ultimately, to present him as a living Chinese buddha by working on three themes: 1) attaching Huineng to Hongren and the Bodhidharma lineage, at large; 2) presenting Huineng as magically gifted in his sudden and total comprehension of the *Diamond Sūtra*; and 3) giving Huineng lines—in particular the negation of Shenxiu's poem—that mirror the rhetorical strategies of the *Diamond Sūtra* and win the day for him. With these three literary techniques working in tandem, the author is about to turn to three other projects. First, he is going to have Huineng teach like a Buddha, and to do this he is going to give Huineng a body of recycled language drawn from the sūtras and from earlier Chan texts. Second, he will have this newly minted buddha perform in public space (within the narrative) and induct the imaginary audience into the essence of Buddhism in a gesture that, again, mimics developments in earlier Chan texts. And, then third, and most interesting, he has this buddha refetishize tradition into several long and rambling poems, and then into the whole text itself. Thus, after all the effort that went into getting tradition out of the sūtras and into Chinese bodies, this text ends up having one of these virtual Chinese bodies—Huineng's—relocate tradition back in a text to reinstitute the cult of the text, with the only difference being that inside this text-that-holds-tradition we now find a Chinese buddha, and not Śākyamuni Buddha. Of course, given that from the outset the text presented itself, literally, as a sūtra, this circuitous return to cult of the text shouldn't be too shocking.

The Teachings

Most readers moving into the teaching section of the *Platform Sūtra* will quickly find themselves overwhelmed. Topics come and go, themes seem to start to develop but then are quickly dropped, ritual action is commanded only to be followed by long unrelated dharma discussions, and so on. Then, suddenly, the text jumps ahead forty years to narrate Huineng's death and in doing so clearly leaves the teaching site at Shaozhou, and, more surprisingly, drops Huineng as the narrator, without explaining who is taking over in his place. Thus, after a fairly well-crafted introduction that gave us Huineng recounting his accidental attainment of buddhahood, the text suddenly loses its focus and splinters in various directions. Given this chaos in the text, and the sheer quantity of material in this section, I will present a general strategy for reading it and then focus on the opening section to demonstrate how my reading approach handles this more "philosophic" content.

To begin organizing an interpretation of this section of the *Platform Sūtra*, we can note three basic agendas that are getting worked on. First, as just mentioned, the text gives us a ritual sequence in which the audience inside the text is inducted or reinducted into Buddhism. This procedure seems to echo the title of the text since it appears that the audience is being brought to an ordination platform-of-sorts where they are to make contact with tradition and be formally reinstalled in their Buddhist identities. That is, the text, from its title on down, functions as a textual (and virtual) version of the totality of tradition in which an image of the perfect past proves its perfection in the present and then goes about the traditional task of inducting believers into the interior of tradition. However, it isn't exactly clear what we should make of this structure in which reading the text stands in for attendance at a real ceremony. Is the text promoting a kind of internal ritual in which the reader is invited to join in this Huineng-led rite in a kind of "as if" manner, with the motion of reading implicitly made equivalent to processing through a public ritual sequence? Or, on the other hand, is the detailed sequence something like a "manual" for Buddhist masters to read and emulate as they incarnate the role of Huineng and then actually lead audiences through these steps? Evidence for this second possibility comes from occasional comments to the reader such as: "What follows is the dharma" (134), comments that seem to function as stage-directives.

To best weigh these possibilities we should turn to a text associated with Shenhui (not Shenxiu!), the *Platform Sermon* (*Tanyu*), that appears to have been in circulation a decade or two before the *Platform Sūtra* was written. This text, besides suggesting a title for the *Platform Sūtra*, also seems to have provided a template for this kind of virtual ritual sequence. In fact, we wouldn't be far wrong in imagining that the *Platform Sūtra* is an innovative attempt to absorb and redirect the *Platform Sermon* for new purposes. Shenhui's version of this sequence, instead of representing a kind of ritual for the reader that concludes in a cult-of-the-text program as the *Platform Sūtra* does, reads more like a manual-for-master, and thus the reader comes to understand how to perform these public rites. Yet this, too, isn't so cut and dried.[30]

Seeing both texts as somewhat indeterminate, I would favor an explanation that allows for both functions. Thus, given that three times figures in the *Platform Sūtra* explicitly explain how it is to be passed from master to disciple in the act of rebirthing tradition (173, 180, and 182), we have to assume that it was designed to be a text *for* masters—self-proclaimed elites who, with this text in hand, claimed to own tradition. For such a reader, the ritual sequence would be read first as an induction into tradition—led by the timeless master Huineng who "lives" inside the narrative—*and* then as the template for that reader's own future actions as he repeats the gesture on others. The text, then, seems designed to function in two distinct ways: 1) it makes new masters who, with this text, have "proof" of their "family descent" from Huineng, Bodhidharma, and the Indian Buddha; and 2) it provides such a newly generated master with a way to perform as a mini-Huineng, in public, mimicking his words and actions as he adopts the leadership role and leads the congregation through these rituals.

Seeing in the *Platform Sūtra* this double-edged function matches, in a rough way, how Mahāyāna sūtras work on readers since in developing the cult of the text in a work such as the *Diamond Sūtra*, the reader learns, in reading the text, both how to properly receive it—to participate in its sequence as a neophyte—and then how to copy and transmit it to the next reader, with these two functions wrapped around one another. Thus, though the figure of Huineng is clearly designed to overcome the cult of the text, or rather the cult of the Indian text, it seems hard to avoid the conclusion that the *Platform Sūtra* is still operating with very similar assumptions insofar as it arranges for the reader's seduction and then puts the believing reader to work producing new converts.

The second basic agenda in Huineng's discourse provides an arc that moves from the teaching and the rituals into several discussions in which Huineng is shown creating and validating a number of fetishes for tradition. Besides the text explaining itself as the new fetish of tradition, there are three long poems (159, 175, 180) that Huineng recites for his audience, and each of these poems comes with the explicit promise that after his death, if one recites these poems, it will be as though he is still present. Given these poems and their promises, it would seem reasonable to argue that Huineng's dharma teachings can't read apart from their role in preparing for these later fetish items, which is to say that at least part of the meaning of these dharma discourses is to be found in their destination—the three poems promising the presence of the master. At the very least one ought to see a basic consonance between the heavy-hitting negations in the teaching section and the reassuring promises of presence, security, and continuity that are given in the poems.

The third basic agenda in this section is to demonstrate how Huineng dominated the competition. Huineng's dominance over various figures takes several forms but most basically has Huineng "correcting" misunderstandings regarding meditation and wisdom. In one rather protracted episode (165–68), Huineng is shown instructing, and ultimately enlightening, a deluded monk who had, hitherto, dedicated himself to the *Lotus Sūtra*. In the course of their exchange, the reader comes to see how much more potent Huineng's version of tradition is compared to this older version of the cult of the text, as found in the *Lotus Sūtra*. In the same vein, aspirations for the Land of Bliss, and buddhalands in general, which were quite widespread at the time, are debunked and relegated to secondary measures that lack the essence of tradition (156–59). Then, in a more poignant episode, Shenxiu is dealt with in a manner that clarifies his second-rate status. Thus, in this zone, dharma instruction morphs into well-aimed polemics, and a take-no-prisoners style of sectarianism.

Though other scores are settled in this section of the text, we shouldn't miss that Shenhui (not Shenxiu!) is also getting demoted.[31] In the Shenhui material that the *Platform Sūtra* clearly is drawing from, it is Shenhui who is the veritable master on stage, the one who claims his buddha status publicly and leads the congregation through the rites. Here in the *Platform Sūtra*, Shenhui is given a much smaller role, and in the end, is overshadowed by Fahai, the monk supposedly recording the text as Huineng speaks it, and more explicitly winning his legacy (180, 182). Thus, though Shenhui is included among Huineng's chosen ten disciples (170)—albeit last on the list—and is shown receiving a beating from Huineng that suggests a special intimacy (169–70), and though Shenhui is singled out as the only one who doesn't cry on the eve of Huineng's death (174), these special moments aren't harvested in any way. Hence, while the narrative works at breaking the Hongren-Shenxiu (not Shenhui) link that had been established in the older genealogies, the text is also trying to break into the newly wrought Huineng-Shenhui link that had been put into public with the Shenhui material. In this sense, just as Shenhui tried to steal Shenxiu's truth-father, Hongren—by creating Huineng—so too is this text trying to steal Shenhui's truth-father, Huineng, by creating this teaching moment so ably "recorded" and absorbed by Fahai.

Learning to Say "No" in a Positive Way

Having clarified the basic thematics structuring Huineng's dharma "talk," let's turn to briefly consider its literary and philosophic qualities. The first thing to note is that Huineng's discourse—however, negative and unthinkable—is authoritative, and in several ways. Huineng never is shown doubting himself, admitting that language might not work that well for describing the world, or that it is completely futile to try to transmit Buddhist wisdom via language, and so on. Instead Huineng is shown ever confident in his handling of language, and his wild-sounding negations never get in the way of the forward motion of the narrative as it tracks through the ritual structure and heads off to ratify the various fetish items that Huineng claims will contain his buddha-essence after he has passed on. Without these self-imposed guardrails of confidence and authority in place, one could easily imagine the discourse exploding into dadaesque silliness, with Huineng perhaps falling into a self-induced trance by talking about no-thought for several minutes too long.[32] Of course, that's not what happens.

Likewise, Huineng's alarming negations never obstruct the ongoing clarification of identity and status. Thus, no-thought never turns into no-differentiation in terms of who is the master and who is the student, even as Huineng explains that there is, ultimately, no difference between the two. In fact, even the act of claiming a deep sameness between buddhas and ordinary beings is proof of one's manifest buddhahood—proof of one's difference from the masses, that is.[33] In short, this kind of antinomian rhetoric that asserts a *theoretical sameness* between master and disciple never jumps track to derail the basic effort to inscribe one sole figure at the head of the Buddhist community. Moreover, there is never a hint of rebellion or resistance in the audience: there are no hecklers, and the auditors are perfectly docile as they are informed about what is and isn't true in tradition.

Besides these conservative trends in Huineng's discourse, we can see that Huineng's negations, like the *Diamond Sūtra's*, are applied to certain categories of items and not others. Of course, what is "attacked" are the old pillars of Buddhist thought, such as meditation, wisdom, and so on, and the logic that held them in place. These elements are upended by Huineng's commentary as he insists, for instance, that meditation and wisdom are one thing or that sentient beings and buddhas are fundamentally the same. This kind of confusion of categories is, nonetheless, applied in a careful, *categorical* manner. Thus, just as Jesus's various critiques of purity, the Sabbath, and the Torah are best read as set pieces proving his mastery of (old) tradition, and not at all separable from the articulation of the new form of tradition, I think we should read Huineng's attacks on these building blocks of Buddhism in a similar vein: the point isn't to destroy tradition in its form and content, but rather to present the image of one who is above it all and can prove this superiority by denigrating what everyone else respects. In short, we are looking at a standard "transgression-as-proof-of-transcendence" strategy in which the act of negating (old) tradition "proves" one's right to articulate (new) tradition.

Though seeing how useful and foundational (!) this negative language is, we also have to admit that there is little that is practical in Huineng's discussion of (new) tradition. For instance, even though the topic of meditation will come and go, it isn't clear that this discussion of meditation is really about meditation. As Huineng claims that meditation is the same as wisdom (they are traditionally understood as abiding in a cause and effect relationship), the point doesn't seem to be to get the reader to change his style of meditation; in fact, the reader and his reeducation aren't in view since this language just spills out of Huineng with little indication that it is to land on anyone in order to shift his or her notions of meditation or the practice of Buddhism. Certainly, Huineng is never shown saying, "Hey, forget about all my wild talk for a minute, and let me give you some pointers on practice." Rather, it is the talk as "wild talk" that matters to the text; it is language whose meaning isn't so much in its didactic content as in its ability to transmit *the image* of the master as the one who lives and thinks beyond the confines of is and isn't. In this light, it is hard not to suspect that Chan's rhetoric on the unthinkability of meditation or truth is performative in a large measure and in that sense is about the master's status, not about the student's practice of Buddhism.

Finally, as we try to interpret Huineng's supposedly "wild talk," we have to see that it is hardly original. Thus, Huineng is made to recite language that had been established in Indian sūtras and more recently in Shenhui's (not Shenxiu's) writing. In either case, the naturally enlightened Huineng—supposedly so unique and independent in his untutored brilliance—appears to know the literary sources very well. Thus, not only does the figure of Huineng borrow Shenhui's rhetoric in many places, but he also borrows Shenhui's view of the Indian sūtras, and even he comments on the same passages from them as well—a real neat trick for a supposedly illiterate master.[34]

To get at how indebted Huineng's language is to prior sources, let's consider his very first comments as the narrative turns from his personal history to his teaching:

"I was predestined to come to live here and to preach to you officials, monks, and laymen. My teaching has been handed down from the sages of the past; it is not my own personal knowledge. If you wish to hear the teachings of the sages of the past, each of you must quiet his mind and hear me to the end. Please cast aside your own delusions; then you will be no different from the sages of the past." (What follows below is the dharma.)

The Master Huineng called, saying: "Good friends, enlightenment *(bodhi)* and intuitive wisdom *(prajña)* are from the outset possessed by men of this world themselves. It is just because the mind is deluded that men cannot attain awakening to themselves. They must seek a good teacher to show them how to see into their own natures. Good friends, if you meet awakening, [buddha]-wisdom will be achieved.

"Good friends, my teaching of the dharma takes meditation *(ding)* and wisdom *(hui)* as its basis. Never under any circumstances say mistakenly that meditation and wisdom are different; they are a unity, not two things. Meditation itself is the substance of wisdom; wisdom itself is the function of meditation. At the very moment when there is wisdom, then meditation exists in wisdom; at the very moment when there is meditation, then wisdom exists in meditation. Good friends, this means that meditation and wisdom are alike. Students, be careful not to say that meditation gives rise to wisdom, or that wisdom gives rise to meditation, or that meditation and wisdom are different from each other. To hold this view implies that things have duality—if good is spoken while the mind is not good, meditation and wisdom will not be alike. If mind and speech are both good, then the internal and the external are the same and meditation and wisdom are alike. The practice of self-awakening does not lie in verbal arguments. If you argue—which comes first, meditation or wisdom, you are deluded people. You won't be able to settle the argument and instead will cling to objective things, and will never escape from the four states of phenomena."

This passage opens by clarifying that what Huineng is "saying" is not really his own creation and has to be received within two kinds of historical understanding. The first of these "histories" is none other than the claim that Huineng's teaching is to be trusted because it is that which "has been handed down from the sages of the past." This claim of inheriting the wisdom of the previous sages presumably also works to show that Huineng's teaching stands above and beyond the typical literature-of-tradition that was available to any literate Buddhist. The second history in the above passage is a karmic narrative that is invoked when Huineng says, "I was predestined to come to live here and to preach to you." With this line, the reader is invited to believe that everything in Huineng's "history" of his coronation as the sixth patriarch and his subsequent teaching on this particular day is nothing more than the working out of a deeper karmic "history," one "written" elsewhere in a manner completely unavailable to the reader. In short, just as with the Gospel of Mark, we have several layers of history balancing against each other in order to give the reader the sense that nothing in the story of perfect truth was invented or accidental.

A second theme in the above passage is crucial to all Chan arrangements and is a central theme in practically all the Chan texts that predate the *Platform Sūtra*: Huineng claims that all people already have truth and tradition within them. The problem is that they can't get at it, and thus "They must seek a good teacher to show them how to see into their own natures." Thus, according to Huineng, truth and tradition are quite alive and well, and are to be found in two places: inside the master—the "good teacher," in the line above—and inside every other human. The snag, of course, is that the student's innate possession of truth and tradition is out of reach, and thus he needs to find a master to gain access to what he supposedly already has. In short, while this rhetoric of internal buddhahood appears tantalizing for the way it *theoretically* levels all hierarchies, it in no way shifts the master-disciple dialectic that the Chan system of lineages is designed to produce.[35]

In another sense, this means that all the nonmasters live in a state of self-alienation, never being able to become the natural buddhas that Huineng, alone, knows them to be. This self-alienation also implies that the ordinary Buddhist isn't in touch with reality since his mode of being in Being is, in a Sartrean sense, completely inauthentic. In short, the rhetoric of internal buddhahood works to generate a gap between the reader and his or her authentic "self," just as it serves to separate the master from the masses. As I'll explore below, this essentially means that the master—Huineng and all the other members of the Bodhidharma lineage—represent that singular place where humanity touches reality, the place where language, culture, and contingency supposedly melt away and all that remains is that perfect fusion between the enlightened mind and the final version of reality. Of course this magical node beyond language then becomes the place where final language describing reality and humanity can be generated and shared out to all those who lack access to just this node. Put that way, it is a lot easier to see why Chan rhetoric worked to fetishize truth and tradition into the masters of the lineage, since in so doing Chan authors had solved the basic problem of religion: establishing a final ground for deciding truth and tradition while also producing convincing logic about why this version of truth and tradition should be accepted. Or put more fully, the Chan lineage system produced an image of the total ownership of truth and tradition in order that truth and tradition could be *partially* shared out to those excluded from the lineages.

A third important theme in the above passage is that fairly long riff on the nonduality of meditation and wisdom, a motif that we see repeated several times in Huineng's "teachings." Reading this riff without knowing the earlier Chan literature, and especially the Shenhui texts, one might think that there is something new, rich, and truly "zenny" being said here. After all, it does sound rather radical to claim that wisdom and meditation are fundamentally one and never dissociable, since normally Buddhist rhetoric assumes that meditation leads to wisdom. However, once we locate this statement in the wake of other similar statements, we see that Huineng's speechifying is derivative, and even a bit hackneyed. In the Shenhui material, especially in the final parts of the *Treatise Defining the True and the False*, one finds similar statements regarding the essence of tradition in which cause and effect are collapsed into one item.[36] Thus, Shenhui argues at one point that meditation and sitting aren't two practices and should never be separated, invoking a similar kind of nondualism. To really make this point, the Shenhui material then explicitly points back to an Indian text, the *Vimalakīti*, where defining meditation in this unthinkable manner is the key point in Vimalakīti's attack on Śāriputra, a figure standing in for pre-Mahāyāna, Buddhism.[37] In that discussion, the figure of Vimalakīti works to show that Śāriputra, though meditating, doesn't know what he is doing and certainly shouldn't count himself as an inheritor of tradition. The technique that the author of the *Vimalakīti* uses to demonstrate Śāriputra's distance from tradition is precisely this collapse of cause and effect. Thus Vimalakīti keeps asking Śāriputra if he can, in his meditations, achieve wisdom, equanimity, liberation, and so on while also maintaining their opposites: ignorance, desire, bondage, and so on.[38] Since this is logically impossible, Śāriputra has nothing to say back to Vimalakīti who, of course, is poised to look as though he is the grand master of tradition. With these precedents in view, Huineng's "speech" appears altogether indebted to the literary record. He has, in effect, become the new mouthpiece for these well-established literary precedents and that, of course, is the basis of his charm.

Conclusions: Being There

As I have been arguing throughout this chapter, and those that precede it, one of the characteristics of these Buddhist and Christian texts that fetishize tradition is the way they artfully redefine history in order to make final statements about the nature of truth, tradition, and authority. Thus, for example, the *Platform Sūtra* gives the impression that Huineng's language isn't shaped by the narrator and his desires, by the recent series of lineage disputes in the eighth century, or by the long arc of Indian Buddhist literature—with its own styles and stratagems for overcoming older forms of tradition. Instead, with the illiterate Huineng purified of literature, desire, and normal humanity, the author makes it seem as though Huineng is speaking from that impossible place within the human subject where we are asked to believe that there could be meaning and truth without history, culture, or commentary. This is, of course, identified as his buddha nature, that final blend of consciousness and Being that all humans supposedly possess but which only Huineng and those within the Bodhidharma lineage have accessed. At one with his original perfection and finding therein the totality of tradition, Huineng can do the impossible: he can articulate tradition from that Archimedean place beyond time and particularity, and free of desire and doubt; he has become a perfect universal, and thus all this language that is shown spilling out of him isn't language in any ordinary sense. Far from it. It is, literally, the stuff of tradition and thus Huineng's oral teachings—as presented in the text—are given to the reader as though these articulations carried the unthinkable essence of the final truth of tradition and, by implication, the truth of the universe at large.

To get a better sense for this fantasy that lodges tradition in a man—truly an exquisite example of fetishizing tradition—let's consider how this arrangement handles three crucial elements: humanity, Being, and language. First, in terms of humanity, we are asked to believe that Huineng is the one man who can represent the essence of all humans. This fetishization of humanity into the singular master requires that Huineng, or any other absolute master, be refathered in a transcendental manner. Thus, like

Jesus, Huineng needed to have a second, otherworldly patriarch standing behind him—Hongren and the Bodhidharma lineage back to the Indian Buddha—and it was his induction into that track of pure patriarchy that gives him his new identity, along with direct access to total tradition. Ironically, it is only by being refathered in this totally *unique* manner that Huineng (or Jesus) can stand as the final or consummated version of all humans. According to this logic, Huineng, as a living Buddha, is us, and we are him, and any perceived mismatch is just a temporary lack of clarity due to our non-buddha status. In short, Huineng's refathered identity as the master-of-us-all means that our own *partial* refathering can only be effected by worshipping him and his teachings, and the text that he lives in, just as worship of Jesus's inexplicable and unique sonship, and the texts that he lives in, becomes our means for transforming ourselves into "sons of God," as Paul put it.

Read this way it is clear that the *Platform Sūtra*—and Chan, in general—represents yet another example of the fantasy that a deep patriline of truth comes out of the stuff of reality. In this case, the perfect patriline begins with the Indian Buddha who supposedly reproduced one real descendent, who then reproduced one real descendent and so on up to Huineng.[39] Each of these singular men not only produces the next descendent, but he also offers his language to the masses, promising to give them access to their deepest patriarchy, that place where reality and the human subject are one. In effect, just as with Jesus as the Son of God, we have in Huineng and the *Platform Sūtra* a very obvious literary effort to domesticize the universe such that a final version of fathers and son appears to emerge from reality, offering us—for unclear reasons—perfect language about themselves and their singular patriline, while also promising us that if we take this language-of-patriarchy seriously, we will get refathered and thereby gain abiding confidence in the reality of our deepest patrilineal identity.

The key theoretical point is that this process of fetishizing the text, tradition, and the master-of-reality is but one side of the equation since all of that only matters if one treats one's self in a similar fetishistic manner. Thus there's a fundamental correspondence at work here: by getting involved in a text's fetishization of the master, tradition, language, truth, and so on, one naturally engages in a parallel project that is directed toward transcendentalizing one's own identity—building one's personal Eiffel Tower, as it were. Thus, whether it is New Testament writing, the early Mahāyāna texts, or the Chan texts, the fetishization of tradition intimately involves the fetishization of the self into the form of the Spirit, the internal buddhahood, or that crucial moment of faith that will take one to the Land of Bliss. As though tracing down both wings of a "V," one comes to the point where fetishized tradition and fetishized self touch: this perfect master is me, and I am the master—or at least we share a truth-father, in the figure of God or the Buddha—and even if proof of our inclusion in the final form of patriarchy eludes us for the moment, we believe that we must accept our participation in that paternal sameness on faith because, after all, the master-who-knows-reality has said that just this sameness is ineluctably true. Without confidence in this final point of union where the perfectly condensed self finally meets the already-fetishized perfect master who owns tradition, truth, reality, and so on, there would be no reason to get involved with any of this language.

With this notion of how fetishizing tradition involves fetishizing the self, we begin to get a sense for why these texts were, in their various ways, so terribly successful: they provide, in their various fetishizing functions, powerful rhetoric that allows believers to inhabit a world that now seems logical, readable, legal, and familiar—in the double sense of the word. Reality, it turns out, isn't a vast desert of meaningless matter hung, temporarily, in the truly endless expanse of black nothingness. Instead, reality has a distinctly human aspect to it since in the final analysis, reality and these male divinities—Jesus, God, the Buddha, and Huineng—are inseparable. In fact, and only bowdlerizing slightly, it turns out that in each of these texts, truth-fathers and their sons are the final version of reality such that reality, when read in this manner, is just one huge, invisible-but-real, ribbon of patriarchy waiting to regather and finalize otherwise distant and alienated subjects—as though patriarchy were an aching Möbius strip located beyond time and space that, again for reasons none of these authors cared to explain, simply wants to regather his "children."

In sum, the Buddhist and Christian texts considered above have to be read as subject-generating ventures that rely on seductive discourses in which desire for accessing a final form of truth and patriarchy is relied upon to draw readers into new and complex relations with this very language offering final patriarchy—language that, of course, promises that it is of the truth-father and can take one back to the truth-father. The art of these texts, besides the standard trick of disappearing as art, is to fetishize truth, tradition and the reading subject, so that the subject can take hold of the text and believe that he is getting access to the final version of the universe and himself, a promise that, in one way or another, each of these texts tenders. Why, exactly, this rhetorical gesture has had so much appeal over the past two millennia and why we are still so taken with these projects is a topic that what I will try to address in the conclusion.

Conclusions

The Limits of Fetishizing Tradition

Since I began this book with a children's story it seems appropriate to end with one. In Crockett Johnson's *Harold and the Purple Crayon* (1955) we meet a youngster named Harold who at first wanders about a dull and empty space until, realizing that the art that he sketches with his crayon turns into reality, he begins to create the things he would like to have in his life. Thus, when Harold needs a pathway to walk on, he draws it; when he feels hungry, he sketches himself a picnic; and so on. In time, he has constructed a whole city. Looking at the city, and now feeling somewhat tired, he begins to wonder how he can get home, so he simply draws his own room, with his bed by the window, and then sleeps in it. With his home-coming accomplished, we leave the story with the sense that Harold can comfortably come and go from his self-sketched reality, and that his night's sleep will most likely be followed by another round of world-invention.

Such a playful vision of desire, art, and an augmented version of reality is of course quite different from the narratives considered in the preceding chapters. Even though the narratives of Buddhism and Christianity are also intent on redesigning the world and rendering it, thereby, domesticated and more livable, as soon as one enters these imaginary worlds, one discovers that someone else is always holding the purple crayon. Thus, even though one *is* invited into a process of re-sketching one's world in accord with this or that Buddhist or Christian cosmology, the problem is that this new form of the world—however enticing—comes prefabricated in a terribly limited and limiting manner. In short, whereas the narrative of *Harold and the Purple Crayon* is dedicated to celebrating the open-ended process of self- and world-reconfiguration, in the case of Buddhism or Christianity, the newly proffered story explaining one's self and the world is written elsewhere and given to the reader/listener as fait accompli.

Similarly, the believer who comes to live in this religiously reconfigured version of reality has to misrecognize this version of the world as something that was there all along, before the believer got involved in the narrative and before anyone got clever about world-refashioning. In short, the embellished version of reality, in which theology comes to be taken for reliable ontology, requires that the believer ignore the human powers of world-reinvention that made this new version of the world possible, while also renouncing one's own potential role in future world-reinventions. Harold, on the other hand, seems to be quite aware of where all these new items are coming from and, better, delights in his role in the process of world re-creation. Of course, this is what is so appealing about *Harold and the Purple Crayon*: the oh-so-simple narrative reawakens in us appreciation for this most ordinary dialectic whereby we, to a significant degree, live in the world that we artfully or, more often, less artfully, construct. Besides being reminded of our *potential* role in this refashioning of the world—a rather Sartrean realization, to be sure—we also get to enjoy the figure of Harold who so innocently does just this kind of world-construction, and with a good bit more joy than the rest of us do.[1]

The key question, then, is this: What chance, really, does anyone have to exercise these creative powers involved in the reconfiguration of the world? Now one might at first think that *Harold and the Purple Crayon*, Sartre's writing, and books like this one are simply examples of a very recently won form of freedom and artistic self-awareness. However, the point of *Fetishizing Tradition* has been to show that, back in ancient and medieval periods, one can find similar talents for world-critique and world-reconfiguration in the very texts that, in fact, took such powers away from those who later consumed them. Thus, what appears to me distinctly ironic in recognizing certain Buddhist and Christian narratives as efforts to fetishize tradition is that we come to see that *some people* have been exercising their capacity to reinvent tradition and to redraw the world as they saw fit. Hence, this book has sought to show that at several key moments in Buddhism and Christianity, inventive narratives appeared that bear the mark of some rather impressive manipulation of the reigning symbolic order, and thus it would seem most reasonable to attribute to these authors a high degree of awareness regarding the form and function of religious logic. In short, there would seem to have been a fair number of "Harolds" in either tradition.

The further irony, though, is that once this talent was exercised, and the products of such creativity were shared around, those who consumed these narratives forfeited their own rights to similar re-creations, and even lost the ability to recognize these art products for what they are. This, in fact, isn't an accidental outcome, since I've tried to show that part of the art talent on display in these religious narratives is the higher order talent that knows how to hide that very talent for remaking the symbolic worlds of those who would consume them. Whether or not one ultimately concludes that it is the nature of religious narrative to demand this kind of blindness and submission, it seems to me, as an academic in the field of religious studies, important to first articulate what it is that has happened before drawing conclusions about its necessity or appropriateness.

In a similar vein, it seems to me important to situate the above analysis of Buddhist and Christian narratives in a larger context in which we ask about the limits of applying this kind of reading. To address this issue of limits, which I believe belongs at the end of a book such as this, let me briefly enumerate several other zones, ancient and modern, that likely would benefit from this perspective. I should add that I have in no way done a systematic survey to decide what texts and/or traditions might warrant a fetishizing-tradition analysis. Instead, I have simply noted, over the years, several texts and traditions that stand out as likely candidates for this kind of reading. My objective in mentioning several of these cases is simply to promote the value of this perspective on fetishizing tradition, while also suggesting that it is a rather common historical reality.

Beginning with the Chinese traditions, the *Daode jing*—dated roughly to the third century BCE—seems to develop a rhetoric that both overcomes prior positions and then offers itself as a totalizing replacement; in fact, it offers the specific promise that the very removal of the prior articulations of tradition—presumably those made by the early Confucians and the Mohists—will in fact be the mechanism by which real tradition will arrive, especially in terms of delivering righteousness, harmony, filial piety, and social order in the kingdom.[2] In short, the *Daode jing* puts itself forward, as doctrine, technique, and text, as the sole item needed for reestablishing all previously established cultural values.

Actually, the early Confucian tradition—dated to the fifth or fourth century BCE—can also be read as working to subsume tradition in a fetishizing manner, with the Confucians focusing on certain icons of reference—most notably the Odes (詩) and the Rites (裡)—that supposedly held the essence of the beloved Zhou dynasty and could, when given the right care, be relied on to bring the essence of the Zhou dynasty into the Warring States period.[3] Then, once the Confucian tradition began to solidify in the early Han dynasty, Confucius himself was positioned to function in a highly iconic manner. In fact, he was turned into the fount of tradition, since it was claimed that he composed or edited most of the literary classics of the pre-Confucian tradition—the Odes, the *Yijing*, the Histories, and so on. Then, with Confucius set up as the (new) author of tradition, the Confucian texts that claimed to hold his teachings were fetishized as the essence of tradition and then memorized for two millennia.[4]

Moving to religious texts from ancient India, there are plenty of passages in the Upanishads that suggest a process of fetishizing tradition was at work as authors claimed that yoga or the mystical syllable "Om" summed up and surpassed all the older Vedic practices.[5] More striking is the example of the *Bhagavad Gītā* which is a prime candidate for this kind of analysis since it explicitly argues that all the prior forms of tradition are to be found within itself and then offers belief in belief as the technique for recovering all of tradition. Thus one is to believe in Krishna as the newly revealed "father of the universe" (11:43) and to dedicate all works to him, knowing that with such a gesture of devotion and submission all other religious goals will be accomplished, with yoga and Vedic ritual explicitly relegated to second-rate activities. Krishna even explains that those who have been engaged in other non-Krishna-focused practices have been, in fact, worshipping him all along (9:15). This new form of belief in Krishna is itself called a *yoga*, making clear that the terms of the older system have been fully overhauled.[6] Notable too is the way that the *Gītā* opens such a practice up to all members of society, including women and untouchables (9:32), and thus represents a striking example of the priestification of the masses somewhat parallel to what was implicit in early Christian practices. Equally worth noting is that the text also takes itself, as a teaching, to be the repository of the totality of truth and tradition, and thus we can see that the Buddhist cult of the text, so evident in early Mahāyāna literature, had something of a counterpart in contemporaneous Hinduism.[7]

Another striking example of fetishizing tradition is Mormonism, which presents a newly invented genealogy to perform that standard end-run on (old) tradition, one that absorbs and overcomes those prior elements of (old) tradition. So, as usual, suddenly an established tradition (it is Christianity that is to be overcome this time) is undermined by a newly revealed backstory that renders (old) tradition secondary and insufficient. In this case, the key to the story of overcoming is that some citizens of Jerusalem were led by God to America, circa 600 BCE. Once in-country, their final prophet, Moroni, wrote/edited the Mormon Bible, buried it on a hill in upstate New York, and then some two millennia later returned to the site as a spirit and revealed the text to Joseph Smith in 1830. With this text supposedly then translated by Smith, a new religion was born that claimed to be Christian even as it made clear that (old) Christianity was to be abandoned.

Other modern cases of fetishizing tradition appear when we look at how communism played out in China and Russia. As most commentators have noted, both Russian and Chinese styles of communism worked to divinize their founders; thus, Lenin and Mao appear as impossibly wonderful fathers of the nation, while enjoying the religious-themed cults of personality that were orchestrated around them. In both cases, older forms of religious tradition were invoked and put to use "demonstrating" the authority and deep legitimacy of either political figure. Nina Tumarkin highlights this dialectic between (old) tradition and the iconization of Lenin, arguing, "The Russian revolution was a process of mounting anarchy that called for new symbols to confer meaning upon the chaos, and as the Communist Party moved to dominate Russia it increasingly centered its claims to legitimate rule on an idealization of Lenin as the revolution's author and guiding force. . . . The full-blown cult of Lenin was an organized system of rites and symbols whose collective function was to arouse in the cult's participants and spectators the reverential mood necessary to create an emotional bond between them and the party personified by Lenin. Stylized portraits and busts of Lenin were its icons, his idealized biography its gospel, and Leninism its sacred writings."[8] Likewise, she points out that this "shows how the new Bolshevik order, seeking to impose itself upon Russia, was itself *molded by precisely those elements of old Russian culture that Lenin so desperately sought to destroy.*"[9]

This perspective works also well for the case of Chairman Mao, though Mao's cult of personality is particularly colorful given the vast efforts put into iconizing Mao on billions of aluminum badges.[10] Likewise his sayings were gathered up, as a kind of gospel, in the "Little Red Book" that was memorized and regularly bandied about by millions. At the height of the Cultural Revolution, Mao was explicitly identified as embodying the essence of the nation and thus we find popular statements such as "Chairman Mao is the very red sun that shines most brightly in our hearts."[11] When Mao died in 1976, he was mummified and then set up in the newly built Memorial Hall on Tiananmen Square, arguably at the symbolic heart of China; on the south wall of the hall was carved the phrase: "Forever eternal, without corrupting."[12] In a sense this claim to immortality might have some truth to it. For instance, Ian Buruma, while visiting Mao's hometown in 2001, was much impressed by the ongoing effort to preserve Mao as a perfect container of tradition. As he put it, "Shaoshan, the birthplace of the greatest wrecker of Chinese tradition, has become, in many ways, a repository of it."[13] In short, for the twentieth-century communist experiments in Russia and China, the thematic of fetishizing tradition provides a useful and even unavoidable angle of analysis.

In thinking more broadly about twentieth-century political moments it would seem fair to say that fascism in general—be it Italian, German, Romanian, French, or Indian—can be usefully read as a form of fetishizing tradition. In each case the supposed essence of the nation is suddenly just within reach, and everywhere there are flags, parades, and theatrical speeches evoking over and over how the imagined nation, and its glorious past (and future), can be won once one commits oneself to a politics of violence and hysteria.[14] While in a way fascism simply represents an extreme version of what Eric Hobsbawm dubbed "The Invention of Tradition"—a modern practice found throughout Europe and beyond—in another sense the fascist examples are particularly instructive cases of fetishizing tradition given the intensity of the pageantry and the density of the iconic programs.

Besides these examples drawn from ancient and modern religious and political movements, I would like to conclude by suggesting that there is another zone, one much closer to my own locale, where the lens of fetishizing tradition is useful: the twentieth-century discussion of religion and truth. In particular it seems that some of the "stars" of twentieth-century thought—Carl Jung, Martin Heidegger, and Mircea Eliade—wrote in ways that very much fall within the category of fetishizing tradition. In the case of Jung, Jungian analysis promised to recover the essences of various archaic Western traditions, including the Mithraic mysteries and the equally obscure Teutonic traditions that seemed to have obsessed Jung. By arguing that all this past religiosity was currently present in the collective unconscious located at the base of each person's normal consciousness, the point of therapy was to make contact with that traditional religiosity and make it one's own in a more conscious and wholesome manner.[15] Of course, this put Jung in charge of transmitting the entirety of the Western tradition, and in that role he and his writing served to perpetuate a new gospel of sorts. Thus, with or without accepting arguments regarding Jung's self-deification in 1916, it is clear that he organized the typical end-run on tradition, one that explained how one could and should regather the essence of past tradition/s through belief in Jung, his narratives of the past, and his newly developed psychoanalytic practices.[16] Clearly this basic structure in Jungian thought and practice accords well with the dynamics of fetishizing tradition.

Heidegger's writing works in a parallel manner though with a focus on the Western philosophic traditions instead of religion. Claiming that he had recovered the lost vision of the pre-Socratics who supposedly had glimpsed the fullness of Being, Heidegger set himself up as the figure who would overcome and authenticate the Western tradition. Framed that way, Heidegger's gestures share much with the Buddhist and Christian narratives treated here in terms of: 1) laying claim to a new origin (the pre-Socratics) that is supposedly more original than the one that initiated tradition (Plato and the Judeo-Christian tradition) and claiming it in such a way that this origin appears naturally so and not part of a recently devised polemical program; and 2) maintaining that the reader could inherit the wonders of that recently discovered origin via Heidegger's own writing.[17]

Eliade's academic writing functions similarly, though his goal was to gather up and offer to the reader what he took to be the essence of world religiosity. Thus, regularly drifting away from trying to explain the actual forms of religious activity in specific historical settings, Eliade selectively shaped his material so as to essentialize religious life into the ideal figure of "homo religiosus"—a faceless, timeless man who, we were told, practiced religion in a very stylized way that neatly demonstrated the key elements of Eliade's definition of religion, with a notable focus on overcoming history, reclaiming the center of the cosmos, fusing symbolic opposites, and so on. With the sprawling and heterogeneous nature of religious life thusly condensed into his chosen fetish topics, Eliade sought to instill in his readers a heady excitement over re-contacting this supposed essence of religion. In fact, he rather explicitly claimed that the very reading of his research should have religious effects on the reader.[18]

In reviewing each of these twentieth-century cases, we see that even for scholars who have made it their business, literarily, to make sense of the history and play of symbolic orders—be they religious or philosophic—the will to fetishize (and appropriate) tradition seems hard to resist. For my part, though I recognize the deep and abiding appeal of these rhetorics of overcoming, I hope in giving a non-religious account of these narratives of desire and reinvention in Buddhism and Christianity, I have offered the reader new perspectives for reconsidering not just the past, but the future as well. Surely coming to recognize these narratives of overcoming for what they are offers us a chance to reevaluate our "spiritual" ancestry, while also inviting us to ask if there aren't other, less antagonistic, ways to secure a sense of belonging in the universe.

Notes

Preface

1. Jean Baudrillard's first two books, *Le Système des objects* and *La Société de consommation,* explore a similar logic and were, looking back on this project, a major influence on my thinking. For Baudrillard's specific arguments about fetishism, see chapter 3, "Fetishism and Ideology" in his *For a Critique of the Political Economy of the Sign.* What is crucial in his work is the effort to shift the meaning of the term *fetish* away from referring to a specific object toward seeing the fetish-object as a place where the whole symbolic order is articulated, managed, and desired.

2. *Jesus: A New Vision: Spirit, Culture and the Life of Discipleship,* ix.

3. I will regularly return to this problem in the chapters ahead. For now it is enough to point out that the confessional aspect of religious studies been well documented over the past thirty years; for recent reflections on the matter, see Bruce Lincoln, *Gods and Demons, Priests and Scholars: Critical Explorations in the History of Religions;* for an early discussion of the problem, see Donald Wiebe, "The Failure of Nerve in the Academic Study of Religion"; Wiebe then developed this argument in *The Politics of Religious Studies: The Continuing Conflict with Theology in the Modern University;* more recently, Wiebe, with Luther Martin, took stock of the problem in "Religious Studies as a Scientific Discipline: The Persistence of a Delusion"; for an international perspective on the problem, see Gregory Alles, *Religious Studies: A Global View.*

4. Those familiar with the hilarious second chapter of the *Zhuangzi* will no doubt recognize here his influence on my position. For translation and commentary, see Brook Ziporyn, *Zhuangzi: The Essential Writings.*

5. Nietzsche presents a somewhat similar view in "Truth and Lies in an Extra-Moral Sense" where he invites the reader to reconsider, from a very distant point of view, the "star on which clever beasts invented knowing"; see Walter Kaufmann's translation in *The Portable Nietzsche,* 42–47.

Introduction

1. Charles de Brosses's, *Du culte des dieux fétisches ou Parallèle de l'ancienne religion de l'Egypte avec la religion actuelle de Nigritie* (1760) regularly gets credit for first using the term *fétische* in this ethnographic way. His text is available through Gallica Bibliothèque Numérique, http://gallica.bnf.fr/ark:/12148/bpt6k106440f.

2. For discussion of the history of the term *fetish*, and its place in Christian discussions of idolatry, see the three classic essays by William Pietz: "The Problem of the Fetish, I"; "The Problem of the Fetish, II: The Origin of the Fetish"; and "The Problem of the Fetish, III: Bosman's Guinea and the Enlightenment Theory of Fetishism." For an equally useful account of the history of the term with a focus on the nineteenth century, see Peter Melville Logan, *Victorian Fetishism: Intellectuals and Primitives*, especially the introduction and first chapter. For a more anthropological account of the term, see Roy Ellen, "Fetishism"; in a similar vein, see Robert Miklitsch, "The Commodity-Body-Sign: Toward a General Economy of 'Commodity Fetishism.'"

For a fine essay considering the connection between fetishes and narrative, see Paul Christopher Johnson, "The Fetish and McGwire's Balls." For reflections on the problem of fetishizing the Other, especially in construction of museums, see James Clifford, *The Predicament of Culture: Twentieth-Century Ethnography, Literature, and Art*, esp. chapter 9. For reflections on fetish theory in a similarly modern, or rather postmodern, vein, see Tomaz Tadeu da Silva, "The Curriculum as Fetish." Other useful discussions include: E. L. McCallum, *Object Lessons: How to Do Things with Fetishism*; L. Mulvey, *Fetishism and Curiosity*; A. Shelton ed., *Fetishism: Visualizing Power and Desire*.

3. Writing in *Victorian Fetishism* (7) about how the term *fetish* functioned to divide Europe from Africa in the second half of the nineteenth century, Peter Melville Logan argues, "Ultimately it [fetish] was always a European artifact, rather than an African condition; it was a projection of European assumptions onto African social practices, and so the concept of religious fetishism ultimately had little to do with African spiritualism as such. . . . For the European idea of the fetish was itself a fetish and thus an example of the thing it claimed to describe."

4. Marx's discussion of "the fetishism of commodities" appears in section four of the first volume of *Capital*; for an English translation, see Robert C. Tucker ed., *The Marx-Engels Reader*, 319–323; for an internet text, see https://www.marxists.org/archive/marx/works/1867-c1/ch01.htm#S4.

5. It turns out that Marx was interested in the term *fetish* in an earlier phase of his career, in the early 1840's when he was writing his "Wood Theft" articles. For discussion of Marx's use of *fetish* in these essays, see Erica Sherover, "The Virtue of Poverty: Marx's Transformation of Hegel's Concept of the Poor."

6. See his *Three Essays on the Theory of Sexuality*. Actually, the term *fetishisme* had already, in 1867, been used in this sexualized sense by Albert Binet in his "Le fétichisme dans l'amour: la vie psychique des micro-organismes, l'intensité

des images mentales, etc."; this essay, along with others, was recently republished in book-form as: *Le fétichisme dans l'amour*.

7. This passage is taken from Freud's brief 1927 essay, "Fetishism," in *Freud: Sexuality and the Psychology of Love*, 216; italics added.

8. And here we aren't too far from Schopenhauer's account of how the Will-as-desire is responsible for the process of "individuation" in the sense that objects only come to consciousness through the function of desire, or in his terms, the will.

9. Thinking about fetish-functions in this manner, one might be tempted to argue that all language is basically fetishistic vis-à-vis reality, with words such as *table* and *chair* representing handy abstractions of endlessly complex items. This is true in a sense, and yet if we put *fetish* to work in this more generalized sense, it would come to cover the same semantic domain as "signifier," and thereby cease to indicate the particular way that fetishes produce desire in the very act of condensing the Real of an item into an iconic-something. Hearing the word *chair* does little to one's circuits of desire, but mention *Marilyn* or *JFK* and whole vistas appear and linger.

10. For a wide-ranging account of Western attempts to make language and objects represent reality in a final manner, see Susan Stewart, *On Longing: Narratives of the Miniature, the Gigantic, the Souvenir, the Collection*.

11. For a translation of Barthes's "The Eiffel Tower," see Susan Sontag ed., *A Barthes Reader*.

12. Andrew S. Jacobs develops a similar theoretical point of view in the introduction to his *Christ Circumcised: A Study in Early Christian History and Difference*. Jacobs (4) draws on Terry Eagleton's useful discussion of Lacan and identity formation in Eagleton, *Literary Theory: An Introduction*, 142–67.

13. Though Buddhist thought, in general, is an excellent source for this kind of analysis that leads to a vision of no-self, one finds it appearing in modern literature as well, often described with a kind of vividness that is missing in Buddhist writing. For instance, Nabokov's short story "Terror" (1926) presents a harrowing account of what happens when the patina of reification is removed: "I understood the horror of a human face. Anatomy, sexual distinctions, the notion of 'legs,' 'arms,' 'clothes'—all that was abolished, and there remained in front of me a mere *something*—not even a creature, for that too is a human concept, but merely *something* moving past."

14. Ludwig Feuerbach, in *The Essence of Christianity* (1841), pioneered this perspective of self-projection and self-reclamation. More recently, Louis Althusser has an insightful discussion of how this relay process of identification works in Christianity; see his "Ideology and Ideological State Apparatuses," esp. 179ff.

15. I note that the analytic philosopher Daniel Dennett has recently used the phrase "belief in belief" in a somewhat similar manner. For his discussion, see his *Breaking the Spell: Religion as a Natural Phenomenon*.

16. The phrase "Jesus is Lord" appears in Paul's Letter to the Romans 10:9 in a passage that reads: "because if you confess with your lips that Jesus is Lord and

believe in your heart that God has raised him from the dead, you will be saved." More recently, it has been taken to be the litmus test of Christian identity by the World Council of Churches, which claims to have 340 million members. All Bible quotes are taken from the New Revised Standard Version. In places where the NRSV editors shifted gender-specific phrases such as "brothers" to "friends" (Rom 7:4), or "sons of God" to "children of God" (Rom. 8:14), I have, based on other translations, returned the passages to their original gender-specific forms.

17. Guy G. Stroumsa presents a somewhat parallel argument in his *The End of Sacrifice: Religious Transformations in Late Antiquity*. Marie-Zoe Petropoulou also has touched on related themes in her *Animal Sacrifice in Ancient Greek Religion, Judaism, and Christianity, 100 BC to AD 200*, 240ff, where she writes of "the undermining role of metaphor in Paul" as he refigured sacrifice in new imaginary ways. In 2006, Jonathan Klawans published *Purity, Sacrifice and the Temple: Symbolism and Supersessionism in the Study of Ancient Judaism*, which offers a number of important insights regarding the forces shaping modern discourse on sacrifice, and is particularly useful in urging us to avoid a kind of evolutionary triumphalism, with Christianity touted as the culmination of Jewish sacrificial traditions. I should add, however, that one can argue, as I am, that sacrifice moved from a hands-on practice to a metaphoric presence in narrative, and yet *not see that as some improvement or laudable "spiritualization" of sacrifice*. There is, *pace* John Gager (see the final section of chapter 2 for more discussion of his position), a supercessionist perspective built squarely into various Christian discourses—in Paul's letters, in the gospels, and in the later pseudo-Pauline works such as Hebrews—and it involves just this movement from real sacrifice to metaphoric forms of sacrifice. And yet, again, to point this out in no way commits one to the opinion that Christianity is somehow an improvement over prior forms of religiosity.

18. Some readers might look askance at a buddhologist getting involved in Christian studies and, yet, it is precisely this resistance to compare, and the resultant insularity of Christian studies, that makes such a foray worthwhile. Certainly Frank Kermode's *The Genesis of Secrecy: On the Interpretation of Narrative* stands as a fine example of the richness that can be found when an outsider reads Christian texts. For my part, though I can't deliver Kermode's shimmering prose, I would suggest that the Buddhist-Christian comparison brings several important issues to the fore, issues that have been ignored in more traditional discussions of either tradition. Of course this is just a polite way of saying that to compare traditions is to interrupt the fetishizing processes that organize the scholarship that focuses on each of these traditions. For an argument promoting comparison in religious studies, see Jonathan Z. Smith's *Drudgery Divine*.

19. Here my comments owe much to Freud's *Wit and Its Relationship to the Unconscious*; see also Mary Douglas's essay, "Jokes."

20. Here the work of Russell McCutcheon is most apropos; see, among other useful essays, his "The Myth of the Apolitical Scholar: The Life and Works of Mircea Eliade."

21. Jonathan Z. Smith attempts to make sense of this history in his essay, "The Devil in Mr. Jones." For more recent accounts, see Samuel Preus, *Explaining*

Religion: Criticism and Theory from Bodin to Freud; see also Guy Stroumsa, *A New Science: The Discovery of Religion in the Age of Reason*. Russell McCutcheon presents a particularly trenchant discussion of the problem in his "The Costs of Discipleship: On the Limits of the Humanistic Study of Religion."

22. Explaining the history of *how* Christian studies, with its various conservative faith-commitments and fear of theory, got itself wedged into the American university system would require another book—and it would be a very interesting one at that. Again, McCutcheon offers us an excellent place to start this inquiry with his "Just Follow the Money: The Cold War, the Humanistic Study of Religion and the Fallacy of Insufficient Cynicism."

Chapter 1

1. For Jonathan Z. Smith's comments on the primacy of commentary, see his essay, "The Domestication of Sacrifice."

2. Though I believe it useful to imagine that these texts were often received aurally, I will at different points in my discussion speak of the texts' audience as "readers" for simplicity's sake.

3. And, given that the texts addressed here are all statements of new forms of cosmic law, and since laws are always for a community of one kind or another, we have even more reason to insist on their public nature.

4. Anthony Grafton develops a somewhat similar perspective as he tries to theorize the intersubjective creativity necessary for generating confidence in forged religious, legal, and literary documents, a creativity that always has to integrate several zones of perception and, in particular, the public sense of a prior historical moment; for his position, see *Forgers and Critics: Creativity and Duplicity in Western Scholarship*, 49–50: the forger "must give his text the appearance—the linguistic appearance as a text and the physical appearance as a document—of something from a period dramatically earlier than and different from his own. He must, in other words, imagine two things: what a text would have looked like when it was written and what it should look like now that he has found it. Two forms of imagination should lead to two different, complementary acts of falsification: he must produce a text that seems distant from the present day and an object that seems distant from its purported time of origin." Slightly later, 62, he extends this perspective to forgers who try, in a wholesale manner, to shift their audiences' sense of the past by blending the familiar and the recently invented: "The most ambitious forger imaginable, then, the one who seeks to reorient his contemporaries' mental maps of a whole sector of the past, must apparently depict many familiar landmarks even when he insists that he is not doing so."

5. I will regularly qualify tradition as "old" in this ambiguous, parenthetical manner to emphasize that the tradition in question isn't "old" until one accepts the perspective of the new text that fetishizes tradition into some novel form.

6. This perspective works well with the arguments in Bart Ehrman's most recent book, *Forgery and Counterforgery: The Use of Literary Deceit in Early Christian*

Polemics; see esp. 128–132 for a discussion of the literary intention to manipulate and deceive.

7. The past fifty years have seen the slow emergence of a consensus in Christian studies that the gospel writers were actually authors. This point of view began to gain traction when significant scholars in the field moved away from the paradigm of "source" and "form" criticism to opt for "redaction" criticism that focused on the specific ways that gospel writers shaped received material. Later, in the 1980s and 90s, another step was taken when well-respected New Testament scholars argued that each gospel, in its entirety, was a work of literature, controlled by guiding principles and artistic choices. It seems to me, though, that the implications of reading the gospels as literature haven't been fully drawn out, especially in terms of the intersubjectivity that the category of text-as-art demands. Burton Mack, arguably one of the more inventive and intrepid scholars in New Testament studies, comes close to setting up this model for reading the Gospel of Mark in *A Myth of Innocence: Mark and Christian Origins*, esp., chapters 11–13; and yet while he is wonderfully precise in showing how the Markan narrative works to overcome and appropriate (old) tradition, he doesn't attempt to theorize *how* Mark's author worked up such a complex literary experience for his reading/listening public. Arguably, it is reckoning just this talent for reinventing tradition *for the reader* that spells the end of what Mack calls "a myth of innocence" in conceptualizing the composition of the gospel narratives.

8. While one might feel, as many do, that this kind of questioning is impolite and even indecent, it seems just as easy to argue that the very fact that all these pious people, with their diehard beliefs and extravagant commitments, have rudely and inconveniently prefigured one's present ability to think critically about these texts. That is, paradoxically, belief and commitment are also a kind of rudeness, though we usually chose not to see it that way.

9. And, for the more philosophically minded, I should add that this gesture of both belonging to an active matrix, and yet finding a space or a platform to turn around to face the forces of that matrix, presents an image of human agency parallel to the one found in a moment of decision-making when the subject is surrounded by the pressures of preordained things that push one to action, and yet still maintains a quantum of autonomy for choosing a course of action not fully determined by the past and its present representatives. Far from seeing here a kind of absolute freedom from determination, I would argue instead for a sliver of reflexivity vis-à-vis one's historical position, a reflexivity which also has a very modest margin for maneuvering.

10. The final complexity arrives when we realize that the narratives explored here are themselves quasi-histories designed to explain why one needs to shift from old tradition to new tradition. None of the texts simply says: "Dear audience, please give up your commitments to the historical view that informed the old version of tradition and accept this new version." Instead audiences are treated to supposedly historical events that prove why this shift in histories is legitimate and necessary.

11. Daniel Sibony, little read in the Anglo-Saxon world, is a useful resource for thinking about these problems. Many of his works deal with the process of "coming second" in a sequence of claims to own authenticity. His *Les trois monothé-*

ismes: Juifs, Chrétiens, Musulmans entre leurs sources et leurs destins presents useful perspectives on this problem of traditions built on the dynamics of overcoming their predecessor. Though I am impressed with many of Sibony's discussions, I am less taken with the quasi-theological assumptions regarding Being—in a Heideggerian sense—that often animate his analyses.

12. Equally interesting, the seductive narrative strategies offered to incite movement from old tradition to new tradition will remain present long after this conflict between old and new tradition has disappeared. In this sense, the narratives considered here can appear as odd vestiges of their moment-of-origin when their right to exist still had to be fought for—as though one was proposing to one's wife every day of the marriage.

13. In arguing for desire's place in religious life, and having emphasized doubles above, I should add that my position is quite at odds with René Girard's theory of mimesis, violence, and scapegoating. The hermeneutical mistakes that he makes are many, but the one that makes his work useless in my eyes is that he assumes that violence in narratives can and should be explained with models of real violence. Thus he relies on studies of the "physiology of violence" by Anthony Storr and Konrad Lorenz to set up his reading of narrative accounts of violence such as found in the gospels; see his *Violence and the Sacred*, 2. Later (23), he argues, "Religion in its broadest sense, then, must be another term for that obscurity that surrounds man's efforts to defend himself by curative or preventative means against his own violence." Girard, though trained in literary studies, seems to have forgotten that narratives function on their own terms and vibrate according to logics that are rather different from the "physiology of violence" that animates decision-making and action in the real world. For example, while video games such as Grand Theft Auto IV likely increase a tendency for violence (of various kinds) in the real world, the organization of violence *in the video* works according to logics defined by what we could call a "sympathetic connection" that must be maintained between the game and the player. Thus, narrative violence, in religion or in game form, ends up being user-friendly and integrated into the subject's symbolic order in a manner that radically shifts how it is to be interpreted.

For a different critique of Girard, see Jonathan Klawans' *Purity, Sacrifice, and the Temple*, 22–26.

14. For more discussion on the art of disappearing-as-art, see my *Fathering Your Father*, esp. the introduction and the conclusion.

15. Those familiar with the work of John G. Gager, and in particular his position in *Reinventing Paul*, needn't worry that I haven't taken account of his arguments against reading Paul's position as one of "refute and replace." My arguments in the following chapter deal with his position and others like it.

16. Ben Witherington III makes a similar case in his *Paul's Narrative Thought World: The Tapestry of Tragedy and Triumph*, though he takes this narrative world to be truth and not just a human creation.

17. Here, readers familiar with the argument that Mark's Christology lacks this element of sacrifice shouldn't be tempted to turn away from this framing; chapter 3 presents solid reasons for insisting on this sacrificial theme.

18. I am happy to note that several other readers of Mark have tried out versions of this approach. See, for instance, Stephen D. Moore's essay, "Deconstructive Criticism: Turning Mark Inside-Out," 105. As I will mention below, there are other things that make less sense in Moore's essay. For general reflections on the problem of antisemitism in Christianity, see Gavin Langmuir, *History, Religion and Antisemitism*, esp. chapter 2; Langmuir's position is usefully critiqued (and appreciated) by Hyam Maccoby in his *Antisemitism and Modernity*, 159–60. For a wide-ranging discussion of the role anti-Judaism has played in the West, see David Nirenberg's, *Anti-Judaism: The Western Tradition*.

19. For a succinct statement of his position, see his "Rites of Institution" in *Language and Symbolic Power*. The following two paragraphs are taken from my essay, "Simplicity for the Sophisticated: Rereading the *Daode Jing* for the Polemics of Ease and Innocence."

Chapter 2

1. Jonathan Klawans presents somewhat parallel arguments in his *Purity, Sacrifice, and the Temple*, esp. chapter 7. However, Klawans, in fighting so hard against pro-Christian presentations of Paul's "spiritualization of sacrifice," ends up in the awkward place of saying, "[W]e are to understand Jesus's sacrificial metaphors as we understand Paul's: not as a spiritualization of, or a critique of, the cult but as an appropriation of, a borrowing from, the cult" (223). I translate this sentence to say, in effect, "Yes, Paul stole Temple sacrifice and gave it to his readers *as metaphor*, but that doesn't mean he didn't appreciate and respect Temple sacrifice." What Klawans's position seems to overlook is that the very *relocation* of traditional items into a new space—a space defined by a new rhetoric, a new authority structure, a new system of meaning, and, most obviously the new mode of metaphor—is itself a most thorough-going usurpation of (old) tradition's *raison d'être*. As in the bumper sticker that reads: "Suburbia is where they cut down all the trees and name the streets after them," a dialectic of overcoming can still salute the very thing that it laid to waste—in fact, that is exactly what one would expect.

2. Readers familiar with the scholarly movement named "The New Perspective on Paul" that first appeared in the 1980s needn't worry that I am overlooking this recent trend in scholarship that argues for a place for ethics and moral action in Paul's notion of "salvation by faith." In the final section of this chapter I offer some reflections, from an outsider's point of view, on the work of E. P. Sanders, James D. G. Dunn, John G. Gager, N. T. Wright, and the other figures in this new version of Pauline studies.

3. A classic example of this gesture is from chapter 3 of Letter to the Romans: "For we hold that a person is justified by faith apart from works prescribed by the law. Or is God the God of Jews only? Is he not the God of Gentiles also? Yes, of Gentiles also, since God is one; and he will justify the circumcised on the ground of faith and the uncircumcised through that same faith. Do we

then overthrow the law by this faith? By no means! On the contrary, we uphold the law" (3:28–31).

4. While I agree with Krister Stendahl that we moderns likely read into Paul's writing more psychology than is actually there, and especially that peculiar form of Augustinian self-introspection, I don't think that insight prohibits appreciating the rather powerful role that emotions and "interiority" play in Paul's explanation of personal salvation; for Stendahl's argument, see his famous essay, "The Apostle Paul and the Introspective Conscience of the West."

5. Though below I criticize E. P. Sanders's approach to reading the gospel narratives, his discussion of Paul's efforts to suture together the old and new forms of the law is quite useful. For a condensed presentation of his position, see *Paul: A Very Short Introduction*, esp. chapters 9 and 11.

6. For general (and useful) comments on battling over ancestors, see Bruce Lincoln, *Discourse and the Construction of Society: Comparative Studies of Myth, Ritual, and Classification*, 18–21. As he puts it, "it is not enough to observe blandly that the various groups and subgroups are defined by reference to apical ancestors: Rather, they are constructed, literally *called into being* by ancestral invocation . . ." (20). Mary Douglas makes a similar point: "When ancestors intervene they are usually part of a system that confirms local inheritance laws. Anyone wanting to validate his own claims has to trace his descent; anyone interested in contesting the claim has to question the genealogy." See her *How Institutions Think*, 51.

7. For a readable approach to assessing this kind of anti-Judaism in Paul and the New Testament, see Amy-Jill Levine, *The Misunderstood Jew: The Church and the Scandal of the Jewish Jesus*, esp. chapter 3; for a more technical presentation of her position that focuses on the Gospel of Matthew, see "Anti-Judaism and the Gospel of Matthew."

8. I hasten to add that I am not promoting a "mythicist" position in what follows; that is, I am not claiming that Jesus never existed. In fact, I believe there are good reasons to believe that a man named Jesus lived in the first third of the first century and taught some version of Judaism that captivated a number of people, including his brother James, and then was executed by the Romans. G. A. Wells is often cited as the most thoughtful of the so-called mythicists, but he has, since the mid-1990's, shifted his views to allow that a man named Jesus lived and taught in the first century. For his reflections on his shifting position, see his *Can We Trust the New Testament? Thoughts on the Reliability of Early Christian Testimony*, 49–50. Recently Bart Ehrman has done his best to counter the fundamental doubts Wells and others, myself included, have about the historical reliability of the various presentations of Jesus, but his arguments seem far from being conclusive; for Ehrman's discussion of the mythicist position, see his *Did Jesus Exist? The Historical Argument for Jesus of Nazareth*. To get a taste of Ehrman's logic—which is altogether normal within New Testament studies—consider his claim that since the Gospel of Matthew has material in it that isn't found elsewhere, the author must have had some as yet unknown source. Thus he writes: "These [stories] then must have come from Matthew's special source, which scholars have therefore labeled *M*" (69–70). He then

treats this hypothetical source *M*—and one that he conjures up to stand behind the Gospel of Luke—as solid sources such that: "When dealing only with Matthew, Mark, and Luke, the synoptic Gospels, then, we are talking not just about three books written late in the first century. We are talking about at least four sources: Mark, Q, M, and L, the latter two of which could easily have represented several, or even many, other written sources" (70). This of course isn't a good argument since obviously Matthew (or Luke) could have simply made up the material that is unique to their gospels without any recourse to some unknown source labeled *M* (or *L*). How to know either way? More troubling is the circularity of the reasoning: Ehrman assumes that the gospel writers didn't make up their material since, whenever they have material that is unique or idiosyncratic, he assumes that it must have been taken from some other source, and therefore there can never be any evidence that they made up their material.

9. It is worth asking if the endless stream of publications on early Christianity, produced in this pro-Christian mode, might not be best characterized as the beginnings of a Second Protestant Reformation in which academic authors attempt, in good Protestant fashion, to take readers back to Paul and Jesus, while carefully slipping around the traditional points of reference such as Luther, Calvin, and Augustine. In this sense the heaps of books, articles, reviews, and interviews on Paul and the gospels appear as modern-day pamphlets—not too different from the ones that the earliest Protestant authors relied on in the sixteenth century in Northern Europe—that promise to symbolically kill off current religious structures and assumptions in order to get, once again, at the original essence of tradition, untainted by its later historical manifestations. It is no surprise, then, that one regularly finds in these studies (and their reception) a jittery enthusiasm for this project of moving around traditional interpretations to begin the exciting work of getting at the "real" Paul or the "real" Jesus of the gospels. For reflections on this modern enthusiasm for books on early Christianity, see Adam Gopnik, "What Did Jesus Do? Reading and Unreading the Gospels."

10. I will refer to the Gospel of Mark, as "Mark" though this name only came to be associated with the anonymous gospel in the second and third centuries.

11. See her *From Jesus to Christ: The Origins of the New Testament Images of Jesus*, 3–4; italics added. For those who might have hoped that New Testament studies was a field experimenting with new ideas, it hardly gives one confidence to notice that Fredriksen's position is nearly identical to that of Martin Dibelius who, writing in the early decades of the twentieth century, did much to establish form criticism; see his *From Tradition to Gospel*, 3: "The literary understanding of the synoptics begins with the recognition that they are collections of material. *The composers are only to the smallest extent authors. They are principally collectors, vehicles of tradition, editors*" (italics added; cited in Michael J. Cook, *Mark's Treatment of the Jewish Leaders*, 8, n.12). That Fredriksen champions such a position in the late 1980s means she decided to ignore narrative studies of the Gospel of Mark that emerged in the late 1970s and early 1980s and that, in various ways, disrupt Fredriksen's paradigm. Not surprisingly, books and articles from this subfield are missing from

her bibliography. Next to these problems we also need to ask how, in the passage cited above, Fredriksen can so conclusively state that the author of Mark was a Gentile. In *Augustine and the Jews: A Christian Defense of Jews and Judaism*, xiv, she appears to have changed her mind on this matter.

12. Some ten years after writing *From Jesus to Christ*, Fredriksen, in her *Jesus of Nazareth, King of the Jews: A Jewish Life and the Emergence of Christianity*, steps away from some of her arguments in *From Jesus to Christ*, (see, for instance, 9–10), and, in particular, begins treating Mark as an author, 34, 107–9, while also taking up the issue of the effect of the fall of the Temple on gospel writing; for instance, see 10–11, 38–39. That seems all to the good, but what is unfortunate in the newer study is that she still hasn't settled on a strategy for reading narrative and, worse, has come to favor the possibility that the narrative in the Gospel of John is more historically reliable than the Synoptics. Thus she writes: "When I began to conceive that the Gospel of John might in some way surpass the Synoptics as historical evidence for the shape of Jesus's mission, I was abetted in my heresy by the valuable insights, knowledge, and wisdom of John Ashton and Brian Rice McCarthy. Ed Sanders interrupted his prodigious schedule of research and writing to read the penultimate version of my entire manuscript: he saved me from many errors, and forced me to sharpen my arguments" xiv–xv. In short, whether it is the Gospel of Mark or John, Fredriksen still thinks real historical events are behind the scenes crafted in the gospels.

Finally, I should add that given Sanders's close involvement with the final shaping of this book, some might find problematic his glowing review of Fredriksen's book in the *New York Review of Books*, especially since his role in the project wasn't mentioned. See *New York Review of Books*, Nov. 15, 2001, p. 33.

13. See his *The Historical Figure of Jesus*, 10–11. Bart Ehrman presents a similar list in his *Did Jesus Exist? The Historical Argument for Jesus of Nazareth*; see, in particular, 210–11, where he also adds that "virtually all critical scholars" agree on these basic elements in Jesus's life.

14. This statement comes from his *Jesus and Judaism*, 16, where Sanders is trying to establish criteria, via "double dissimilarity" from Judaism and "later church material," for accepting Jesus as the authentic spokesperson of various passages in early Christian documents. This discussion flows from an earlier list of "several facts about Jesus's career *and its aftermath* which can be known beyond doubt" (11). There follow eight "facts" such as Jesus's baptism by John the Baptist and his "controversy with the temple" that match substantially those mentioned above, as taken from his later work, *The Historical Figure of Jesus*. In a longer effort to clarify his reading strategy, which is basically redaction criticism, see his *Studying the Synoptic Gospels*, esp. chapters 20 and 21.

15. *The Historical Figure of Jesus*, 5; italics added.

16. Burton Mack has a useful discussion of the fetishistic search for the historical Jesus; see the introduction to his *The Myth of Innocence*, 1–24.

17. It wasn't until the early 1990s that Chan/Zen studies began to articulate a similar problem vis-à-vis the supposed historicity of teachings from various Chan/

Zen masters. For a discussion of the issues, see T. Griffith Foulk's "Myth, Ritual, and Monastic Practice in Sung Ch'an Buddhism."

18. The first-century historian Josephus claimed that 1.1 million Jews were killed in the massacre and that Jerusalem and other major cities around Jerusalem were razed to the ground. For reflections on the implications of this destruction, see Mireille Hadas-Lebel, "La destruction du Temple et ses conséquences."

19. Sanders merely points out the need to establish two *other* contexts: 1) the general "Jewish theological" constructs from the Hebrew Bible that gospel writers would have been accustomed to; and, 2) the more particular context of Jesus's life; for more discussion, see his *The Historical Figure of Jesus*, chapter 7, entitled "Two Contexts."

20. For Sanders's account of how this conflict between Jesus and the Jewish authorities in the gospels supposedly reflects real historical events from Jesus's era, see chapter 10 of *Jesus and Judaism*.

21. "If Jerusalem Stood: The Destruction of Jerusalem and Christian Anti-Judaism," 203.

22. Ibid., 204. Several decades ago, S.G.F. Brandon, then professor of comparative religion at the University of Manchester, also put forward arguments regarding the impact that the fall of the Temple had on Mark's narrative. For a brief version of his position, taken from his *The Trial of Jesus of Nazareth*, see "History or Theology? The Basic Problems of the Evidence of the Trial of Jesus." I find some of the orienting questions in Brandon's approach attractive—especially his reflections on the impetus to rewrite Jesus's identity in the wake of the Jewish-Roman War—but he completely overreaches when he tries to read real history out of the gospel material, especially in developing his theory that Jesus and his followers were violent revolutionaries intent on a messianic coup d'etat.

23. Here I am following scholarly opinion which takes the controversial passage in 1 Thessalonians 2:14–16 about Jesus's murder by the Jews to be a later addition to this letter. For more discussion of this problem, see Mack, *Who Wrote the New Testament?*, 113. For a similar opinion, see Jon Levenson, *The Death and Resurrection of the Beloved Son*, 230, 250n.13. The final phrase in the suspect passage suggests that it was written after the fall of the Temple and therefore must be an interpolation: "Thus they [the Jews] have constantly been filling up the measure of their sins; but God's wrath has overtaken them at last." Even if this passage accusing the Jews of killing Jesus was original to the letter, its generic identification of the "Jews, who killed both the Lord Jesus and the prophets" is a far cry from the details of the Passion narrative which so thoroughly indicts Jewish religious authorities and the Jewish tradition itself. It would seem, too, that this line doesn't necessarily imply that Jesus's teachings or actions were anti-Judaic and thus the cause of his execution.

For my part, I would agree with Gary Greenburg and others who argue that this passage needs to be read against 1 Cor. 2: 6–8 where Paul discusses Jesus's death and doesn't mention that the Jews were responsible. Paul writes only, "None of the rulers of this age understood this [God's wisdom]; for if they had, they would not have crucified the Lord of glory." Clearly here was a moment to assign blame, and yet Paul instead chose to speak vaguely of "rulers of this age." For Gary Greenberg's position, see his *The Judas Brief: Who Really Killed Jesus*, 59. In concluding that this passage is an interpolation, I am not trying to purge Paul of one of his more flagrant moments of anti-Judaism; rather, it simply seems that this passage is out of keeping with the rest of his writing.

24. Against this claim some might think of the "Eucharist" passage: "For I received from the Lord what I also handed on to you, that the Lord Jesus on the night when he was betrayed took a loaf of bread. . . ." (1 Cor. 11:23). The basic problem here, as many scholars have noted, is that the phrase translated as "betrayed" really means something more like "handed over" (*paradidonai*); for more discussion, see Burton Mack, *The Myth of Innocence*, 299. For a parallel discussion that argues more strongly that this "handing over" is actually to be understood as the hand of God at work and not a betrayal at all, see Bart Ehrman, *The Lost Gospel of Judas Iscariot: A New Look at Betrayer and Betrayed*, 15–16; see also Ehrman's parallel comments on the phrase in *Did Jesus Exist?*, 97.

25. Paul mentions that he traveled to Jerusalem twice: first to consult with Cephas (Peter) and James, the supposed brother of Jesus (Gal. 1:18), and then fourteen years later when he met with the "acknowledged leaders" (Gal. 2:2). He claims that during this second visit, his gospel was ratified by James, Cephas, and John "who were acknowledged pillars" (Gal. 2:9).

26. I believe Burton Mack is right in claiming that Paul completely lacks the anti-Temple animus that organizes Mark's narrative: "There is not the slightest hint in any text of the Pauline corpus that he or the Christians to which he was converted thought of Jesus or themselves in opposition to the temple establishment in Jerusalem, as Mark will say in his gospel." See his *Who Wrote the New Testament*, 87.

27. For a brief discussion of this problem, see Elaine Pagels, *The Origin of Satan: How Christians Demonized Jews, Pagans, and Heretics*, 25–28.

28. See Pagels, 29–33, for first-century sources that depict Pilate as stubborn and cruel.

29. In the next chapter I detail the narrative construction of anti-Judaism in the Gospel of Mark; for now it is enough to mention six crucial elements in the story: 1) Jesus's various conflicts with temple authorities on matters of tradition, authority, and the law, with the authorities shown to be petty, conniving, hard-hearted, and vicious; 2) the failure of the disciples to understand and protect Jesus, a tendency heightened in the portrayal of Peter's lassitude and his dramatic denial of Jesus during the trial, and of course Judas's betrayal; 3) Jesus's hasty and unfair trial by the Sanhedrin; 4) the crowd of Jerusalemites calling for Jesus's execution and asking Pilate to free Barabbas instead of Jesus; 5) Jesus's humiliation at the hands of the Jerusalem population who mocked him on the cross; and 6) the way that his execution magically rent the Temple curtain. Given these rather obvious themes, I find it unusual that Adela Yarbro Collins' review of Mack's *A Myth of Innocence* expresses the opinion that: "Mack presents Mark as apocalypse in a negative light. He is able to do so in large part because *he finds anti-Judaism*

and a sectarian mentality in Mark. The presence of these qualities is debatable." One wonders what it would take for Collins to conclude that a narrative develops anti-Judaism themes (729).

30. I believe Burton Mack would agree with *some* aspects of this perspective. For a useful history of twentieth-century scholarship on Mark that is *slowly* coming to the opinion that Mark invented the Passion narrative, see his *A Myth of Innocence*, chapter 9. Despite this (happy) concordance on some matters, I disagree with Mack on four important points: 1) I don't assume that Mark's gospel can be read to reflect community concerns: the narrative doesn't appear to be written by committee, and it is surprisingly free of the normal items one expects to find in a document designed to organize group membership in a real community setting; 2) I don't assume that Mark's narrative is the result of a steady process of experimentation in the decades that followed Jesus's death—in fact, as noted below, the narrative seems dedicated to disenfranchising previous efforts to define a Jesus-tradition; 3) I don't assume that various "pronouncement stories" in Mark go back to Jesus and the early phases of the Jesus-movement; they could just as likely be those of another prophet-teacher, such as John the Baptist, which were then tucked into Mark's narrative in order to develop an image of Jesus that Mark preferred—we simply have no way of knowing, though it is clear that Mark used Hebrew Bible material in a very self-serving manner, a fact that, in itself, should temper assumptions about the credibility of his narrative material; and, finally, 4) Mack doesn't explore the possibility that Mark's narrative also represents a radical shift in which belief in belief overrides any prior form of religiosity. For a very readable introduction to Mack's thought, and the problem of the Q Gospel, see Charlotte Allen, "The Search for a No-Frills Jesus."

31. By the mid-1970s a new wave of scholarship argued that form criticism can't take one back "behind" the Passion narrative as Mark has constructed it; for instance, see Werner Kelber, "Mark 14: 32–42: Gethsemane, Passion Christology and Discipleship Failure"; see also his "The Hour of the Son of Man and the Temptation of the Disciples."

32. For a discussion of the problem of the Q Gospel, see John S. Kloppenborg's detailed review of M. S. Goodacre, *The Case Against Q: Studies in Markan Priority and the Synoptic Problem*. Kloppenborg, the scholar perhaps most involved in recent attempts to reconstruct Q, does his theory a favor by working through what he takes to be the strong and weak points of Goodacre's effort to prove that Q is unnecessary in explaining the synoptic gospels' various forms of overlap. That Q studies is a North American obsession little shared in England and on the European continent, and that it is often pursued by those also hell-bent on recovering a new version of the historical Jesus, might, on its own, suggest that there is more than a little bit of religious ideology at work in shaping the arguments in favor of Q's existence. For a useful essay on this North American phenomenon, see British scholar Michael Goulder, "Is Q a Juggernaut?"; see also his review of R. A. Piper, ed., *The Gospel Behind the Gospels: Current Studies on Q in Novum Testamentum*.

33. Hypothetical Q does have some passages critical of the Jewish establishment, and these are consigned to the supposed third layer of Q; see, for instance,

the Jerusalem Lament found in Luke 13:34–35. Burton Mack, in his *Who Wrote the New Testament*, 52–53, gives a brief discussion of such passages.

34. For his discussion of the hypothetical "Cross Gospel," see *Who Killed Jesus?*, 223–27.

35. Trying to figure out why the disciples look so bad in Mark has brought forth a number of interesting articles in the past thirty-some years; see for instance, the classic piece by Robert C. Tannehill, "The Disciples in Mark: The Function of a Narrative Role"; Samuel Sandmel has interesting points on the matter in *Anti-Semitism in the New Testament?*, esp. 46–48; more recently, see Elizabeth Struthers Malbon's thoughtful analyses in *In the Company of Jesus: Characters in Mark's Gospel*, esp. chapters 2–4.

36. At the beginning of this encounter, Jesus explains, quoting Isaiah 6:9–10, that in fact he fully intends that his audience not receive his message: "And he said to them, 'To you has been given the secret of the kingdom of God, but for those outside, everything comes in parables; in order that

> they may indeed look, but not perceive,
> and may indeed listen, but not understand;
> so that they may not turn again and be forgiven.'" (Mark 4:11–12)

37. Though his reading strategy is different, and his overall conclusions quite different, I should note that John Shelby Spong makes some of these points regarding the invention of Judas in his popular book, *The Sins of Scripture: Exposing the Bible's Texts of Hate to Reveal the God of Love*.

38. The overall disappointing quality of the disciples had, of course, been demonstrated on the night of Jesus's arrest when, instead of following his command to stay awake, they all feel asleep—three times (14:32–42).

39. The selfish and foolish nature of the disciples is reinforced as we watch James and John impudently ask to be placed at the left and right hands of Jesus after the resurrection (Mark 10:35ff). This lampooning of the disciples for their unbounded egotism is presumably the second phase of a problem that surfaces in 9:33 when Jesus finds out that his disciples, having just learned of his imminent demise, were still interested in establishing who would be "the greatest." Their guilt and shame in holding these conversations is presumably proven when they refuse to answer Jesus's question regarding the content of their discussions (9:34).

40. In explaining how Jesus appeared, post-resurrection, Paul mentions that Jesus first appeared to Cephas (Peter) and then to the other disciples (1 Cor. 15:5), but then he also privileges James when he writes slightly later, "Then he appeared to James, then to all the apostles" (1 Cor. 15:7). In any case, despite his admitted theological differences with the Jerusalem church, especially his dislike of their supposed "Judaizing" tendencies, Paul has nothing particularly bad to say about the twelve disciples; likewise here, and in other places, Paul assumes that James was an important authority figure. See, for instance, Paul's account of his two visits to Jerusalem.(Gal. 1:18–2:14, esp. 2:9).

41. Josephus's passage explains how a particular Sadducee priest, Ananus, recently installed in the position of high priest, seemed to have a special animus for James and company and "thought he had now a proper opportunity [to exercise his authority.] Festus was now dead, and Albinus [the replacement procurator sent from Rome] was but upon the road; so he assembled the Sanhedrin of judges, and brought before them the brother of Jesus, who was called Christ, whose name was James, and some others, [or, some of his companions]; and when he had formed an accusation against them as breakers of the law, he delivered them to be stoned; but as for those who seemed the most equitable of the citizens, and such as were the most uneasy at the breach of the laws, they disliked what was done; they also sent to the king [Agrippa], desiring him to send to Ananus that he should act so no more, for that what he had already done was not to be justified." See William Whiston's translation in *The Works of Josephus, Complete and Unabridged*, 538.

The details here suggest that Ananus is acting more or less alone and against the will of the public. For a useful discussion of Jesus's brother, James, see Andre Lemair's "Jacques et les Chrétiens de Jerusalem."

42. For a detailed account of various kinds of pro-Torah Christianity, see Joel Marcus, "Jewish Christianity."

43. For a translation of Josephus's account of James's execution, and reflections on the Jesus-James parallels, see Craig Evans, "Jesus and James: Martyrs of the Temple," 233–34. I should add that Evans does not speculate, as I am, that the historical event of James's execution provided material for Mark's construction of the Passion narrative. Instead, his position is that both figures actually struggled with Temple authorities in a parallel manner and then met parallel fates (see esp. 249), a position that requires treating the gospel narrative of Jesus's trial as historically reliable.

44. I am happy to see that the work of Thomas L. Brodie on literary mimesis in the writing of the New Testament continues to draw interest and support. I believe just this perspective should be expanded to include other historical elements—such as the real world executions of John the Baptist and James—that appear to be shaping the form and content of the gospel narratives. For an example of his work, see his *Beyond the Quest for the Historical Jesus: Memoir of a Discovery*.

45. For this line of analysis and other interesting details on the construction of the martyrdom of James, see Bauckham, "For What Offence Was James Put to Death?"

46. These dates appear secure since Josephus connects these events to Tiberius' reign: "Philip, Herod's brother, departed this life, in the twentieth year of the reign of Tiberius" (*Jewish Antiquities*, 18:4.6, 483; Tiberius rule began on 8/19/14, so this puts Philip's death in 34). Tiberius then dies two years later "after he had held the government twenty-two years five months and three days" (18:6.10, 491), just as the war between Herod and Aretas is getting underway in what must have been 36 (18:5.3, 485).

47. The problems involved in Josephus's dating of John the Baptist's death have been noted since the turn of the last century. The *Catholic Encyclopedia* (1902),

for instance, simply claims, not surprisingly, that this is yet another example of how unreliable Josephus's accounts are in comparison to the gospels. Historians, of course, would assume the opposite. For a webpage devoted to this problem, see G. J. Goldberg, "John the Baptist and Josephus," http://www.josephus.org/JohnTBaptist. htm. Christine Saulnier has tried to argue for a different rendering of Josephus's dates that would resolve the problem; see her "Hérode Antipas et Jean le Baptiste: Quelques remarques sur les confusions chronologique de Flavius Josèphe." Goldberg reviews her argument at the above mentioned website.

48. Though wrapped up in twentieth-century German theological debates about the origins of Christian doctrine, Martin Hengel's *The Son of God* still provides a useful framing of the problem of Paul's use of this term "Son of God." This essay is also reprinted in the first section of Hengel's *The Cross of the Son of God.*

49. There is, of course, another dialectic here since the new law is, in part, shaped by the way that the new law is said to be fulfilled by accepting it as the final version of tradition—that is to say, the new law is fulfilled when one takes the new law as legitimate.

50. As attentive readers will notice, I believe Paul's position on the eternal availability of divine patriarchy is a good bit like the one organizing Mark's narrative.

51. J. D. G. Dunn presents a rather interesting, and in some ways parallel, assessment of the importance of blood sacrifice in understanding Paul's theology. See his "Paul's Understanding of the Death of Jesus as Sacrifice." See, in particular, his discussion of what is implied by having God be the "subject of the action" in the sacrificial deed; see 48–49.

52. It needs to be pointed out that creating this status reversal for God, however implicit, is altogether different from the way Jesus is later depicted in the gospels as the king who dies so piteously and powerlessly. However, it may be that the two status reversals are complimentary in the narrow sense that once one gets used to the idea that God's Son is an "upside-down king," one is much less bothered by the implication that his Father has also been presented as an upside-down figure.

53. It is worth wondering if part of the appeal of Paul's message derives from the reader thinking, consciously or unconsciously, that God is just like him—suffering in an unresolved manner that he finally got a hold of by offering a sacrifice that, though a terrible loss, restores some sense of acceptability in the universe. In short, God appears as a schemer who looks for ruses to get around current obstacles, and presumably this image of God would have been particularly attractive to one getting involved in Paul's rhetoric since, in the end, this too is what Paul's rhetoric offers: a new way to get around the old law.

54. For an account of the development of the theme of firstborn sacrifices, see Jon Levenson, *The Death and Resurrection of the Beloved Son*, especially chapters 15 and 16. In pointing out the power of recycling the story of Abraham and Isaac, Levenson writes: "Once Jesus has displaced Isaac, it follows that the promises and blessings that had been associated with the beloved son par excellence in Genesis must be available instead through the Christian messiah" (211). Even though the paschal lamb and the offering of Jesus as God's firstborn would become stock items in later

Christian rhetoric, I believe Paul only once uses this terminology: "For our paschal lamb, Christ, has been sacrificed" (1 Cor. 5:7). Though mention of "our paschal lamb" suggests a connection between Jesus's death and the festival of Passover when paschal lambs are offered, such a connection with Passover isn't, to my knowledge, made anywhere else in Paul's writing—a key point in assessing the origins of the Passion narrative which, of course, is said to have taken place on Passover.

55. In fact, as I will argue below, even this "killing" of the old law is folded back into a sacrificial logic that is both from the old law and at war with it. For more reflections on how the motifs of blood and sacrifice were exchanged by Jewish and Christian authors, see David Biale, *Blood and Belief: The Circulation of a Symbol between Jews and Christians*.

56. In presenting himself in such close proximity to Jesus and God the Father, perhaps it isn't too shocking that Paul likewise presents himself as Christlike. Hence, Paul makes the basic claim that it is Christ who lives within him: "I have been crucified with Christ; and it is no longer I who live, but it is Christ who lives in me" (Gal. 2:19–20). However, he pushes this claim of internal christhood even further with the vague claim that he is also physically like Christ. He writes, "From now on, let no one make trouble for me; for I carry the marks of Jesus branded on my body" (Gal. 6:17). Paul's eagerness to slip into the Christ position appears, as well, in that odd passage in which he explains how the community at Galatia took him in despite his physical infirmities and "welcomed me as an angel of God, as Christ Jesus" (Gal. 4:14).

57. Besides this highly selective reading of tradition, we shouldn't miss that Paul has decided to treat tradition as something that is, by definition, readable and recoverable in language. Consequently, he has no interest in (old) tradition as an institution, sacred item/icon, or as a practice, or again as found in a genealogy of real human beings. In effect, Paul is terribly Protestant, *avant la lettre*.

To get a sense of the audacity and irony here, one might imagine Lenin quoting the New Testament to validate the communist revolution, a revolution which of course is dedicated to completely overcoming Christianity. This comparison is rich because just as Paul's rhetoric that argues for the overcoming of traditional Judaism relies on the rhetoric of Judaism, so too does communism carry within it elements that it seems to have inherited from Christianity and Judaism, especially in terms of imagining an imminent apocalypse that leads on to a utopia won through sacrifice and death. Assuming this connection between Christianity and Marxism makes sense in a genealogical manner too since, if Marxism is Hegel turned upside down, with capital replacing Spirit, and if Hegel is, in a very general sense, an effort to historicize Christianity in a new manner, then Marxism has to be read as bearing the imprint of Hegel's historicized Christianity. Also, one tends to forget that Lenin was fluent in German and had a Lutheran mother.

58. The manner in which Paul takes over tradition's literature is also apparent in his explicit allegorization of biblical stories, as in the case of claiming that the descendants of Abraham's two wives—Hagar and Sarah—represent those to whom higher and lower forms of the law are given (Gal. 4:21ff).

59. Understanding this tension helps explain Paul's fury in his Letter to the Galatians over their interest in circumcision: insofar as they wanted to involve themselves in the particulars of the (old) law they were, by definition, negating the very gesture of overcoming the law that is the modus operandi of Paul's theology. Counting his version of the law as Spirit that could be won through belief and not works, he berates them for slipping backwards toward the "flesh" of the old law: "Did you receive the Spirit by doing the works of the law or by believing what you heard? Are you so foolish? Having started with the Spirit, are you now ending with the flesh?" (Gal. 3:2–3).

60. In another such passage that casts the individual as the temple, he writes, "What agreement has the temple of God with idols? For we are the temple of the living God" (2 Cor. 6:16).

61. Not to be missed is that the phrase "circumcision of the heart" can be found in Deuteronomy 10:16, suggesting that Paul's metaphorization of (old) tradition can be seen to have had some clear traditional antecedents.

62. In a parallel gesture, Paul presents Jesus as the sole inheritor of Abraham in Gal. 3:16.

63. Paul provides a parallel argument in Gal. 3: 6–15.

64. For a parallel gesture in the *Lotus Sūtra*, see my *Text as Father*, chapters 2 and 3.

65. Put this way we aren't too far from the analogy of video soccer that I proposed in the introduction since the new form of the law (the new game) is built around playing the old game but now on a console far from the field of the old game, in a manner that, in effect, threatens the survival of the old game.

66. For Dunn's understanding of the "lifelong process" of self-crucifixion, see "Paul's Understanding of the Death of Jesus as Sacrifice," 47.

67. Slavoj Žižek describes Paul's Jesus in a similar manner but doesn't locate that profile within the sacrificial logic that seems to be animating Paul's christology. For Žižek's discussion, see *The Puppet and the Dwarf: The Perverse Core of Christianity*, 9.

68. The key passage that explains dying to both the passions and the old law reads: "In the same way, my brothers, you have died to the law through the body of Christ, so that you may belong to another, to him who has been raised from the dead in order that we may bear fruit for God. While we were living in the flesh, our sinful passions, aroused by the law, were at work in our members to bear fruit for death. But now we are discharged from the law, dead to that which held us captive, so that we are slaves not under the old written code but in the new life of the Spirit" (Rom. 7:4–6).

69. I have added in the two literal phrases from the Scripture4All: Greek Interlinear Bible, available at http://www.scripture4all.org/OnlineInterlinear/Greek_Index.htm. All subsequent literal translations, placed in parenthesis, are from this source.

70. Here I suspect I have been influenced by Žižek's essay, "The Wound Is Healed Only by the Spear That Smote You."

71. A similar logic seems to be at work in the pseudo-Pauline Letter to the Hebrews, 6:6.

72. It is worth pointing out that one of the better ways to understand circumcision is that it identifies the penis as something like "God's rod," thereby making the reproduction of God's People occur under the sign of the covenant with God and, of course, rendering more visible the claim that the Jews are God's children. Fertility, once signified in this manner, isn't a natural phenomenon but instead only arrives via the organ marked by God's presence, a presence that was established in that first covenant, arranged with Abraham, in which God offered endless fertility in exchange for obedience to his law, and, in particular, submission to God's law of circumcision (Gen. 17:9ff). Understanding circumcision as a visible indicator that God was present at the beginning of life, and by implication was the "real" father, helps explain the trope that the firstborn be returned to God since it was his all along according to the logic of this arrangement. Remembering that God was positioned to be the ultimate source of fertility also helps to make sense of the way Leviticus explains that all blood from sacrificed animals must be brought to God "at the entrance of the tent of meeting" and not consumed by humans (Lev. 17:3ff). Thus, at both ends of life—conception and execution—God is positioned to be the Real behind it all: the place from whence fertility arrives and the place to which it ought to return.

73. The phrase "to be made sons" is taken from the *Complete Jewish Bible*.

74. Paul seems to hold a straightforward, Genesis-style notion of God's role in creation. For example he writes, "Ever since the creation of the world his eternal power and divine nature, invisible though they are, have been understood and seen through the things he has made" (Rom. 1:20).

75. For an equally important passage on Christ as God's firstborn who unifies all of reality, see Col. 1:15ff.

76. For useful reflections on sacrifice, paternity, and the exclusion of women in defining identity, see Jay's *Throughout Your Generations Forever: Sacrifice, Religion, and Paternity*.

77. Once we begin to glimpse *how* the production of the image of Spirit is such an interesting linguistic and historical invention, we can return to the works of Marcus Borg and others to conclude that assuming Spirit to be a pre-existent Real behind religious traditions and their various inventions isn't simply to turn religious studies into theology, but also supplies the blinders that will, by design, conceal the really stunning process by which the image of Spirit was manufactured in history.

78. For a historian's reflections on this tension, see Gavin Langmuir, *History, Religion and Antisemitism*, esp. chapter 14.

79. The prayer published in 2007 reads, "Let us also pray for the Jews: That our God and Lord may illuminate their hearts, that they acknowledge that Jesus Christ is the Savior of all men." The more traditional prayer, from the sixteenth-century prayer, reads, "Let us pray also for the faithless Jews: that almighty God may remove the veil from their hearts; so that they too may acknowledge Jesus Christ our Lord." The intervening, toned-down, Vatican II version of 1970 reads,

"Let us pray for the Jewish people, the first to hear the word of God, that they may continue to grow in the love of his name and in faithfulness to his covenant." Prayers translated from Latin in "Insulting to Jews: Leading German Rabbi Condemns Pope's Good Friday Prayer," in *Der Speigel Online*, 3/21/2008.

80. It could be argued that just as we are all vaguely Freudian in the twentieth and twenty-first centuries—given how much psychoanalytic language has entered modern lexicons—we are all also somewhat Lutheran given the lasting force of his discourse. And yet for someone like me who is reading Paul from a non-theological point of view that simply asks, "How does Paul's writing interact with older forms of Jewish tradition?" the power of Luther is arguably minimal.

81. This is claimed in the *Diamond Sūtra* and other Mahāyāna works. For a discussion of this dynamic see my *Text as Father*.

82. Recent historical research on Christianity under the Third Reich has produced some surprising results, results that suggest that the standard denial of any substantial connection between German Christianity and Nazism needs to be rethought. For useful discussions, see Richard Steigmann-Gall, *The Holy Reich: Nazi Conceptions of Christianity, 1919–1945;* see also, Matthew D. Kockenos, *A Church Divided: German Protestants Confront the Nazi Past*, and, Susannah Heschel, *The Aryan Jesus: Christian Theologians and the Bible in Nazi Germany*.

83. At this point I need to address, however briefly, John Gager's claim that Paul's writing doesn't represent a "rejection-replacement" view of Judaism. Gager's position, as he presents it in *Reinventing Paul*, builds on the work of Lloyd Gaston and others, and has two key components: first, he claims that Paul's comments about Jews, Judaism, and, especially the validity of the Torah were all made in letters to Gentile groups, and thus whatever negativity was expressed there has to be read in that special context (see 38–39, and 44). Thus, that Paul told Gentiles that they didn't need to concern themselves with the Torah, in Gager's reading, tells us nothing about what Paul thought about the Torah for Jews; and here, too, Gager often argues that Paul's more specific targets within the Gentile community were the "Judaizers" within the Jesus movement, that is, those who wanted Gentiles to convert to Judaism within the context of believing in Jesus as Christ. Second, Gager argues that one can't speak of the early Jesus movement as being outside the pale of Judaism, and thus it would be anachronistic to speak of Paul's writing as anti-Judaic.

I believe at least five important points could be made against Gager's position:

1. A rhetoric of overcoming the (old) law needn't totally refute the (old) law. In fact, according to my model, it will need to build with elements and icons-of-authority of that older tradition, and this seems very much to be Paul's modus operandi; that is, it is precisely with positive (old) Jewish things that Paul is constructing the new covenant, and thus, depending on the occasion, valorizing various aspects of (old) tradition is completely useful to his program of overcoming the (old) law; Gager's discussion, unfortunately doesn't allow for this kind of dialectic.

2. One can't read Paul without noticing that key figures and terms are shifting their meaning, function, and locale—the law, Abraham, the covenant, the chosen people, and so on—all these terms are being redefined; thus, one can't point to a passage like "Do we overthrow the law through faith? By no means. On the contrary, we uphold the law" (Rom. 3:31) without suspecting that Paul is expanding and redefining what "law" means here, as he does with other important terms.

3. It is undeniable that Paul has reconstructed authority in tradition. His authority comes from his vision of Jesus and from some kind of direct contact with God. He in no way subordinates himself to the Hebrew Bible (more on this below), to Jerusalem Temple authorities, or to traditional practices. Likewise when he has doubts about his mission to the Gentiles it is to the "pillars" of the Jesus movement—James and Peter—that he goes for support. Clearly if he was still living his life under the (old) law he would have sought the sanctification of traditional authorities—the priests and/or Pharisees.

4. I don't think Gager has given enough weight to the way horizons-of-tradition work in religion: if you live under a law or tradition it is, by definition, totalizing; thus whether the (old) law is good or bad isn't as important a question as whether it is whole or partial. And here there is little doubt what Paul has in mind: the (old) law is insufficient and needs to be supplemented by Paul's program. Thus, it doesn't help to point out that Paul brandishes his Pharisee background and circumcision in a passage or two since these "boasts" do nothing to shift the fact that Paul has stepped outside the horizon of (old) tradition, objectified (old) tradition, and now speaks back to it from a position of supposed superiority that is *far* beyond the zone of traditional authority. With his direct assumption of God's (new) law, Paul alone is in charge of what is and isn't legal—end of discussion.

5. Gager avoids passages where Paul explicitly presents a supercessionist model to explain the relationship of his law to (old) law. For instance, Gager doesn't discuss Paul's example of the widow marrying anew (Rom. 7:1–6), or the way the gardener grafts new limbs onto a plant in the places where older limbs had been broken off (Rom. 11:17); both analogies leave little doubt about Paul's commitment to overcoming (rejecting and replacing) the old form/s of tradition.

In sum, Gager's position that Paul might have supported the view that Jews had better uphold the (old) law is *not* incompatible with Paul's more general supercessionist agenda. It simply means that Paul seems to have believed that if you had, by birth or historical accident, entered into that older form of covenant with God, you had better continue with it; you just shouldn't think, though, that that is the final form of your religious obligations since Jews, like Gentiles, have to "graduate" to Paul's notion of salvation through faith in Jesus Christ. What is strictly anti-Judaic here is that Paul took the finality of Jewish law and made it partial, incomplete, and in dire need of a supplement which, of course, Paul provides through the new dispensations from God, his Son, and God's Gospel which Paul is uniquely in charge of.

84. This is Sanders's basic point in *Jesus and Judaism.*

Chapter 3

1. Richard A. Horsley likewise argues for this antagonistic struggle structuring the plot but then much too quickly moves from the narrative world into the real world, thereby taking the narrative as an account of Jesus leading a people's rebellion against the powers that be. Thus, in his *Hearing the Whole Story: The Politics of Plot in Mark's Gospel,* xiii, Horsely argues,"Almost from the beginning of the story, moreover, he [Jesus] carries out his renewal of Israel in pointed opposition to, and with the opposition of, the Pharisaic and scribal representatives of the Jerusalem rulers of Israel." Of course, in arguing in this manner Horsley has forgotten that Mark's narrative most certainly was written after the fall of the Temple and the destruction of Jerusalem, a fact that renders useless his arguments that the narrative reflects Galilean popular religionists rising up against Jerusalem's religious elite during Jesus's lifetime. For an attempt to work the fall of the Temple into a Galilee-versus-Jerusalem approach to Mark, see Edwin K. Broadhead, "Jesus and the Priests of Israel," 133–34. I don't find Broadhead's approach or conclusions convincing, but I am happy to see that he is trying to think about the construction of Jesus's identity in a supersessionist mode; see ibid., esp. 144.

2. Throughout this chapter I refer to the text's audience as "reader" though I would agree that in many cases the "reader" was in fact a "listener," with someone else doing the reading, publicly or privately. On the other hand, we shouldn't overlook that odd comment when Mark writes, "let the reader understand" (13:14). For discussion of this problem of readership, see Mary Ann Tolbert, *Sowing the Gospel,* 304–306.

3. Burton Mack shares some of these views. In summing up his conclusions regarding the "mythmaking" in Mark, in *A Christian Myth of Innocence,* Mack argues that a conflict between Jesus and the Jerusalem authorities was invented and inserted back into Jesus's life story to explain the sacking of the city and to likewise presage the coming apocalypse: "Another observation is that the crucifixion is viewed as a violence perpetrated in the city that thereby sealed its own destruction. *This was achieved by relating the crucifixion of Jesus (30 C.E) to the destruction of the temple (70 C.E.) and casting both as the first two battles in an elongated apocalyptic scenario. . . .* For Mark, Jesus's crucifixion was not a sign of powerlessness, not an event of redemption, and not the end of the story. It was only the first in a series

of violent reciprocities" (144–45, italics added). Obviously, there is much here that I would agree with, and Mack even has something of a fetish theory in view when he argues, "Power, purity, and innocence had been collapsed in the single figure of Jesus as the son of God who, from Mark's perspective, had every right to violate the temple and challenge the sovereignty of the Second Temple state" (145; for a somewhat parallel comment regarding the narrative construction of a new symbolic whole around the messiah, see 132). What I can't accept in Mack's argument is his passion for resurrecting yet another historical Jesus who—guess what?—looks like a late twentieth-century hipster, straight out of central casting. This new Jesus, found in hypothetical Q, fuses easy-going cynicism with crazy wisdom and a 1968-style Marxism lite, all mellowed with a commitment to universal benevolence. Though Mack is quite aware of the perils of such a construction, it seems he is proving Albert Schweister right again.

4. Mack, 145.

5. It is useful to note, in addition to my comments in the previous chapter about how the deaths of James and John the Baptist were taken to be the causes of subsequent political catastrophes, that the Roman conquest of Jerusalem in 63 BCE gave rise to a similar kind of rhetoric of divine retribution as found in the Psalm of Solomon which casts the pre-invasion Jewish leaders as completely sinful and depraved. I think E. P. Sanders is right on target to bring this kind of evidence into the discussion of anti-Judaism in Christian material, but I don't think he has seen the full implications of this parallel since he treats both the Psalm of Solomon and Christian literature as partially accurate in depicting real events. For his comments, see "Reflections on Anti-Judaism in the New Testament and in Christianity," esp., 268–69.

6. Presumably the 1979 publication of Frank Kermode's *The Genesis of Secrecy: On the Interpretation of Secrecy* contributed to this trend.

7. See, for instance, the collection of essays edited by Norman R. Petersen, *Semia: Perspectives on Mark's Gospel.* Within that collection, see, in particular, Robert Tannehill's "The Gospel of Mark as Narrative Christology."

8. While not identifying the narrative as the presentation of the new law, Mary Ann Tolbert explores how the story positions readers to realize that their reaction to the narrative is determinant of their salvation; see her *Sowing the Gospel,* 296–99. For a somewhat parallel discussion of the demands that the narrative makes on readers, see Edwin K. Broadhead, *Prophet, Son, Messiah: Narrative Form and Function in Mark 14–16,* 25–27.

9. Tolbert also argues for a position parallel to this one; see her *Sowing the Gospel,* 306. John Dominic Crossan also seems close to holding this position in *Who Killed Jesus* when he criticizes Raymond Brown for assuming the gospel narrative to be representative of real historical events and not the effect of carefully chosen tropes that were expected to resonate with readers familiar with older examples of similar tropes that Crossan refers to as "prophecy." Thus, I completely agree with Crossan's effort to treat the supposed real history *inside the narrative* as nothing but

a literary contrivance: "Hence the first thesis of this book: the units, sequences, and frames of the passion narrative were derived not from history remembered but from prophecy historicized." (4) Crossan is also, in my opinion, wise in pointing out that Mark seems intent on disenfranchising Jesus's closest disciples and their "descendants" (16). This, by the way, means that the narrative's version of "history" is poised to overtake any community-based memory of historical events. Where Crossan doesn't go far enough is in his notion of "narrative override," a phrase he uses to explain how gospel "history" is made up with pieces of the past to produce "apologetic or polemical" effects (98). What he doesn't consider is that these pieces of the past were selected not just for the process of making the image of history, but for making the *account of that past, that is, the narrative itself,* look desirable. That is, Crossan has no place for the medium shaping the message. Similarly, he misses the narrative value of creating the Jewish sin against Jesus. Thus, though he sees this antagonistic element in Mark, he thinks it is due to some real first-century sectarianism, whereas I see it as a narrative invention that was designed to turn the catastrophic loss of the Temple into a deserved divine retribution that can be pulled into the seduction schema of the narrative.

10. For instance, Richard A. Burridge's *What Are the Gospels?: A Comparison with Graeco-Roman Biography* is useful for a history of how the question of the gospel-genre has been treated in the past century, but, in the end, his discussion founders since the fundamental law-giving function of the gospel narratives is overlooked. For a thoughtful review of the problem of Mark's literary genre, see Adela Yarbro Collins, *Is Mark's Gospel a Life of Jesus?: The Question of Genre.* I think she has good reasons for arguing that "[t]he fundamental purpose of Mark does not then seem to be to depict the essence or character of Jesus Christ, to present Jesus as a model, to indicate who possesses the true tradition at the time the gospel was written, or to synthesize the various literary forms taken by the tradition about Jesus and their theologies. I would like to suggest that the primary intention of the author of Mark was to write history" (44–45). To this I would add that this is a history of correct and incorrect readings of Jesus's identity, with the consequences of those readings made abundantly clear for the reader, who, of course, is confronted with just this task of reading Jesus.

11. For an alternative attempt to get at the issues of medium and message in Mark, see Werner Kelber, *The Oral and the Written Gospel.*

12. For a discussion of why it isn't a good idea to assume that the gospels came out of religious communities—communities that have never been proven to have existed—see Tolbert, *Sowing the Gospel,* 303. For different criticism of this assumption of the gospel's original community, see *The Postmodern Bible,* 42–43. For more recent critiques of this assumption, see Dwight N. Peterson, *The Origins of Mark: The Markan Community in Current Debate.*

13. That the narrative is designed to involve the reader is well accepted in Markan studies; see, for instance, David Rhoads, Joanna Dewy, and Donald Michie, *Mark as Story: An Introduction to the Narrative of a Gospel,* esp. 39–43.

14. It is, of course, true that some seductions still work perfectly well even when they are recognized as seductions. However, in other cases, especially where the Thing being offered in the seduction is only desirable when it is assumed to be unconstructed and uninflected by human machinations, awareness of the seduction ruins the adventure, like realizing a history book is just part of a government program to organize popular support for a particular agenda.

15. This self-effacement of the narrative has hardly lost its force in the modern era, and a review of New Testament studies suggests that this arrangement has been little understood, presumably because New Testament studies has been conducted almost exclusively by those for whom just this literary gesture of narrative self-effacement has succeeded. David Rhoads, Joanna Dewy, and Donald Michie's *Mark as Story*, 46, briefly mention how the narrative "keeps the focus on the story itself without drawing attention to the storytelling." While I find Tolbert's *Sowing the Gospel* a real *tour de force* for many reasons, she doesn't explore this angle of the narrative's need to disappear behind the story it is telling.

16. For reflections on Kähler's influence on the field of Markan studies, see Edwin K. Broadhead *Prophet, Son, Messiah*, 12–13. Broadhead provides excellent details pointing out why, despite this divide in the narrative, the two pieces need to be seen as a coherent whole (see, 273–96); surprisingly, given his sense for unity in the narrative, he then claims that Mark was written by a community of disciples, a process that would, one imagines, have resulted in a much rougher final product: "The form, content and function of the Gospel of Mark are best explained as the work of a larger community operating over a longer period of time" (290).

17. For Tolbert's discussion of this structure, see her *Sowing the Gospel*, 113ff.

18. For Adela Yarbro Collins's useful reflections on the meaning of the phrase "Son of God," see her "Mark and His Readers: The Son of God among Jews" and "Mark and His Readers: The Son of God among Greeks and Romans."

19. Throughout *Sowing the Gospel* Tolbert wisely focuses on the centrality of faith in the narrative's promises but doesn't clarify that this faith is none other than faith in the narrative of Jesus-as-Son-of-God, and thus is inseparable from faith in the Gospel of Mark as a whole. In fact, Tolbert never addresses what Jesus's divine sonship entails in terms of owning tradition in a new and commanding manner; nor does she address the basic problem that sonship is always a narrative claim designed to be accepted by the Other in a manner that hopes to turn that narrative claim into the appearance of substance—the reproduced substance of the father.

20. Adela Yarbro Collins explores a number of ways to read Mark's construction of Jesus's death as a sacrifice; see her "The Meaning of the Death of Jesus."

21. Tolbert argues against this position, claiming that Jesus's death in the narrative is not presented as a divine sacrifice; however, as I will try to point out, various kinds of evidence suggest otherwise. For Tolbert's position, see *Sowing the Gospel*, 203, 237, 262. Tolbert develops her treatment of the narrative focusing on two themes: "The first emphasizes his [Jesus's] task and the second his identity, together they make up the Gospel's basic narrative Christology" (122). Different

versions of this approach can be found throughout her *Sowing the Gospel*, 107, 115, 231, 238, 271. Identifying the two parts this way means Tolbert misses the point that Jesus's death is presented as a sacrifice of sorts and that this sacrifice is to be read in conjunction with his murder by the Jewish authorities. I should add that this oversight goes hand in hand with the way she avoids the question of the new law overcoming the old, a question that presumably doesn't come up since she assumes that Mark was written for a "predominantly Gentile audience" (36) and thus not designed to work on Jewish assumptions about the law.

22. Creatively redesigning Jesus's death within a pattern of replicating *and* overcoming older Jewish models of sacrifice is also central to the pseudo-Pauline Letter to the Hebrews. See especially chapters 8 and 9 where the author interlaces old and new versions of tradition and their respective covenants in order to make Jesus the ultimate Jewish blood-sacrifice that renders old-style sacrifice obsolete (Heb. 8:13). For instance, consider this striking passage: "But when Christ came as a high priest of the good things that have come, then through the greater and perfect tent (not made with hands, that is, not of this creation), he entered once for all into the Holy Place, not with the blood of goats and calves, but with his own blood, thus obtaining eternal redemption. For if the blood of goats and bulls, with the sprinkling of the ashes of a heifer, sanctifies those who have been defiled so that their flesh is purified, how much more will the blood of Christ, who through the eternal Spirit offered himself without blemish to God, purify our conscience from dead works to worship the living God!" (9:11–14)

23. See his discussion in *A Brief Introduction to the New Testament*, 58–60; Sanders has a parallel discussion in *The Historical Figure of Jesus*, 72.

24. Bart Ehrman works hard to render the entirety of Mark's account historically plausible—including assuming that there really was a figure Judas who betrayed Jesus to the Jewish authorities right at Passover. And, yet, he has to admit that the various elements and actions in the story don't add up that well as reflective of a historical reality. For his discussion, see *The Lost Gospel of Judas*, 164–69.

25. I owe this insight, in part, to Jon Levenson's thoughtful discussion in *The Death and Resurrection of the Beloved Son*, 206–7.

26. And here again Jon Levenson's work is useful since he points out that combining the narrative of Abraham-nearly-sacrificing-Isaac with Passover, and with the paschal lamb in general, was already established in pre-Christian texts; see 176–77 and 184–85. Thus, once Jesus was identified as God's only Son, and thus an Isaac of sorts, it is easy to see how the scripting of Jesus's death on Passover would have seemed natural enough. For an interesting essay exploring whether the Last Supper should be read as a Seder, see Johnathan Klawans, "Was Jesus' Last Supper a Seder?"; see also his "Interpreting the Last Supper: Sacrifice, Spiritualization, and Anti-Sacrifice." Petropoulou, in her *Animal Sacrifice 100BC to AD 200*, fails to mention that part of the constellation of metaphors used by Mark to explain Jesus's death include placing it on the Passover weekend, a fact that anchors Jesus's "Eucharist" comments fully in the zone of an atonement sacrifice; for her position, see 244–46.

27. For Kelber's discussion of the likely dispersal and/or destruction of the early Christians in Jerusalem during the Jewish-Roman War, see his *Mark's Story of Jesus*, 88–95.

28. Reading Mark's narrative construction of secrecy goes back more than a century to William Wrede's insightful *Messianic Secret* of 1901. For a parallel discussion of how conspiracy theories work in establishing new versions of sacred paternity in Chan/Zen Buddhism, see my forthcoming *Patriarchs on Paper: A Brief History of Chan (Zen) Literature from 600 to 1300*, chapter 5.

29. And, given that there are several commands in the narrative to spread the gospel, the reader also has the related task to produce just this relationship between the narrative and the reader in all those who haven't already been convinced of the narrative's legitimacy. Obviously this secondary command has important sociological implications, but I count it as the same basic work of becoming convinced that the narrative of divine-patriarchy—the gospel itself, that is—comes from, and returns one to, divine patriarchy. This is because, in a sense, convincing the Other that the narrative of divine patriarchy is made out of the stuff of patriarchy is not different from doing this to oneself since arguably generating conviction where there didn't used to be conviction on one's own home ground is not different from doing similarly to the Other.

30. For more discussion of the transcendental qualities of sonship, see my *Text as Father*, especially the Introduction.

31. Arguably the other paradox at work here is that ownership, in general, is an externally constructed social reality: I only own my things if you, the public, agree; the same goes for my name, my social status, and so on. Presumably this paradox explains why movies such as *The Return of Martin Guerre* and *Broken Flowers* are so intriguing.

32. For more discussion of patriarchy as a fetishizing system, see my *Fathering Your Father*. As already mentioned in the introduction, all identity is basically fetish-like in format with the proper name invoking a supposed essence or substance that stands behind or beyond the mass of elements—physical and mental—that actually make up the individual. The case of identity-through-patriarchy is simply more visibly fetishistic since it has to work to get rid of the mother's contribution to one's identity.

33. This state of conviction regarding Jesus's divine paternity arrives simultaneously with the conclusion that what is obviously a well-wrought story—and obviously inventive and ideological in all sorts of ways—is actually no more than the innocent assimilation of real historical events.

34. One of the many strengths of Tolbert's *Sowing the Gospel* is her choice to read the parable of the sower and the parable of the tenants as condensations of the two parts of the narrative.

35. It is worth pointing out that in a slightly later healing sequence (1:40), Jesus heals a leper—cleanses, actually—and then, having bid him be silent about the matter, also instructs him to go "show yourself to the priest, and offer for your

cleansing what Moses commanded, as a testimony to them" (1:44). For some reason many scholars take this little episode as proof that Jesus was pro-Temple. I think we can construct a better reading that makes sense of the details of the vignette and also fits them into the logic of the entire narrative: Jesus is commanding the man to go and introduce Jesus's magical handiwork into the old authority structure in a manner that hollows it out and proves that it is superfluous. True, the ex-leper is instructed to make the regular offering to the priest, but, of course, the healing purification has already been effected elsewhere and by one who stands completely clear of the normal chain of command, and clear too of the quid-pro-quo economy to which Jesus is sending the man back to. Thus, having mastered the healing process on his own, which is essentially illegal or extralegal at best, Jesus appears interested in presenting that *fait accompli* back into the zone where that healing power *ought to have been found*. And, depending on how one reads the line "as a testimony to them," the demonstration might have been expected to have been a warning of sorts, as though to say: "How does this sit with you? You see, now, what I'm capable of, yes? And, of course, I know what Moses commanded regarded healing and payment, and I can instruct those around me to follow those commands, but take note that I represent this whole new channel of power and authority that makes allegiance to those Mosaic commands optional and redundant."

The most important point, though, is that this sequence presents a pattern that maps very well onto Mark's whole narrative since, later, Jesus's death functions as a new kind of atonement that is found *precisely* in the midst of the old ritual form of atonement—Passover. In both cases, then, the real power of tradition is located in Jesus's person, proven to be effective, and then put back in the (old) traditional slot in a manner that allows for Jesus to look somewhat traditional even as his presence there casts doubts on the enduring validity of (old) tradition. It is just this "way better but still the same" kind of value claim that modern scholarship has, wrongly, tried to wedge into a strictly pro-Temple or anti-Temple position. I take it to be, ultimately, anti-Temple, but it built the image of its own reliability by using aspects of traditions which, in their role as supporting cast, have to retain some positive qualities.

36. Tolbert has useful comments on the limits of Jesus's power (it is always the effect of belief, and it is nothing that he can deliver unilaterally) but this problem of recognition needs to be conjoined to the more basic problem of Jesus's sonship, an issue that Tolbert ignores.

37. It might seem like a minor point at first, but it is quite telling nonetheless: there is a fundamental parallel between the suddenness of the healings that Jesus performs and the suddenness of identity-recognition. That is, Jesus is either taken to be ordinary or divine, and that either-or quality of his identity is mirrored in the health-illness dyad which doesn't allow the possibility of gradual healing. The case of Jesus healing a blind man in two stages—the man at first sees people, but thinks they look like walking trees (8:24)—still proceeds suddenly, with both stages of the healing being effected more or less instantaneously. For

more discussion of the connection between paternal identity and things sudden, see my *Fathering Your Father*.

38. Pushing on the details of this scene, it would seem that the coming catastrophic conflict between Jesus's tradition and the authority-less "scribe" tradition is also announced in the unclean spirit's additional comment, "Have you come to destroy us?" (1:24)—a comment that certainly can be read as predicting the arc of the entire narrative which will fold the actual destruction of (old) tradition into its own plot about Jesus's arrival in history.

39. Tolbert assumes, unwisely I think, that the reader was convinced by the initial statements regarding Jesus's divine sonship. Instead, I believe that these set pieces which make up the first part of the text are designed to supplement those initial statements and gradually build pressure on the reader to accept those otherwise baffling statements. For her position, see *Sowing the Gospel*, 204. It is also worth mentioning that though Tolbert will on occasion speak of how the narrative is designed to persuade the reader (125, 288, 303), she presents no model for explaining how the reader is seduced by the narrative or what that seduction is ultimately made of—a rather difficult but unavoidable question.

40. Simon's mother-in-law gets healed and serves the disciples (1:30), but it certainly isn't implied that she joined the twelve disciples whose number remains inviolable. Also, Bartimaeus, the last to be healed in the narrative, regains his sight and, as the exception that proves the rule, follows Jesus, 10:52, but again it is never said that he thereby enters into the category of the disciples.

41. This sense that Jesus operates on another plan of legality is also manifest in his "healing" of Jairus's daughter, who, apparently, was dead (5:21ff). That is, Jesus is shown more or less reversing time so that the dead can live again.

42. Though I am using the New Revised Standard Version of the Bible, here it seems unhelpful to follow their editing choice to insert "and sister" into this passage.

43. It is hard to avoid the conclusion that the author purposefully left out mention of Jesus's Nazarene father. Presumably with Jesus's earthly father absent, there was more symbolic space to develop his transcendental father. The tension regarding Jesus's natal family's rights to intimacy with him—rights that would ruin the entire package of this new form of "family through faith"—has to be kept in mind for parsing Mark's conclusion where it is precisely familiar women—the two Marys, one presumably being his mother—who come to mourn him and yet are driven away in fear (16:1).

44. I am assuming that the different titles that Jesus is given throughout the narrative—Son of God, Son of Man, King of the Jews, messiah, Christ—are of little importance. In terms of the narrative's basic claims regarding the effects of faith in Jesus's identity as a divine figure capable of reconfiguring (old) tradition, these variant appellations seem to matter not at all. And, presumably after God was quoted as saying "You are my Son," the variants mouthed by various figures in the story don't carry much weight. Also, during the trial, the author has Jesus using these terms with a clear sense of interchangability: "Again, the high priest asked, Are you the Messiah (the Christ), the Son of the Blessed One?" Jesus said,

"I am; and 'you will see the Son of Man seated at the right hand of the Power,' and 'coming with the clouds of heaven'" (14:61–62). For more discussion of the matter, see Adela Yarbro Collins and John Joseph Collins, *King and Messiah as Son of God: Divine, Human, and Angelic Messianic Figures*, 126–34.

45. This is another good example of the inexact nature of the nomenclature used to identify Jesus. Here, in the middle of the sentence Jesus refers to himself as "Son of Man" but at the end of the sentence he promises to return with "his Father," thereby implying that he is the Son of God who expected to be resurrected and returned to his Father, as well.

46. Not to be missed here is that the postmortem appearance of Jesus is promised to be an event in which his sonship is going to be *visibly apparent* since he arrives "in the glory of his Father with the holy angels." Of course, in the first swoop into history his sonship isn't visible at all, with the result that one has to rely on language and belief to secure the reality of this sonship. Thus, the second "visible" appearance of pure tradition, while but nothing more than another linguistic fantasy within the text, works to create a double of itself in which language can finally rest by pretending that vision will finally take over: Jesus's identity will be visibly evident as Father and Son arrive together in the company of angels, with that very togetherness taken to be proof of their always-invisible familial relationship.

47. In another sense, this mimesis can also be read in the opposite direction with the prediction of what is to happen *outside* the narrative in real history—the persecution of Jesus-believers—proving the reality of the divine promises made *inside* the narrative. In this light, just as the author has apparently threaded the destruction of the Temple into both Jesus's teaching and the logic of the narrative that he lives in, so too it seems that in this passage the historical mistreatment of Jesus-believers (of whatever type) is being put to work in the narrative.

48. The identity of this young man has perplexed many readers. For my part, I would side with those who believe that there seems to be an implied connection between him and the young man who runs naked from Gethsemane in chapter 13 since they are described with the same term *neaniskos*. And given Mark's overall narrative sophistication, I suspect our author is working up an important parallel that works as follows: the previously mentioned young man was notable for being with Jesus and then without clothes. The second young man is notable for being with Jesus but with clothes, with the added detail that he now is wearing a white robe. So if we take them to be the same young man, then there now is a robe where there once was none, and thus it would seem we are being invited to reason: "Right, we did just have a naked young man in need of clothes, and now we've got a young man with some notable robe on who seems to have just been in intimate contact with Jesus, so I wonder where he got that robe? Oh, that's it! It must have been what Jesus was magically wearing just prior to the resurrection and which he bequeathed to him in exiting our world . . ." This connection appears stronger when we remember that Jesus is presented in a dazzling white robe in the Transfiguration—a similarly magical moment when he seems to have stepped out of time.

We shouldn't miss, too, that connecting the two young men in this manner provides more continuity to the narrative since, if the reader takes them to be one and the same person, then we have someone: 1) who was with the disciples back in Gethsemane—his sudden and dramatic exit from their company is but his entrance into a new way of being with Jesus; 2) who then witnessed the resurrection, whereas the disciples didn't; and, finally, 3) who provides the directions for sending this finalizing piece of the story back to the disciples even if it never arrives. In short, the nameless young man is the holder of the narrative that seals the deal, the narrative that the reader needs, but which the author doesn't want to give to the disciples given his general disparaging treatment of them. As holder of the final narrative chunk that is supposed to legitimize the whole narrative, the young man is then made to give it to the women, who, just like the disciples then run away. Thus, the narrative within the narrative is fully announced to the reader, even as the author has again produced reasons why no one knew about this.

49. I should alert the reader to the fact that the Catholic priest, John P. Meier, in his very well received book, *A Marginal Jew, Volume 4: Law and Love*, holds a completely different view of these debates, since he believes that they reflect the historical reality of Jesus arguing legal matters with the authorities of his day.

50. The phrase "hardening of the heart" is, of course, a phrase often used in the Hebrew Bible where it means turning away from God and his commands. That Jesus is made to use this phrase to describe resistance to him matches all the other various claims regarding his divinity.

51. This sense of immanent evil competing with things divine seems to be at play, too, when Jesus calls Peter "Satan," when Peter won't accept Jesus's account of the divine narrative that he is living in. Jesus yells at him: "Get behind me, Satan! For you are setting your mind not on divine things but on human things" (8:33).

52. In some statements Jesus is shown simply calling for the audience to have faith in God; see, for example, 11:22 and 12:29. However, this in no way eclipses the primacy of the good news which, of course, is that God reproduced himself in the form of Jesus and then sent Jesus, and his law about himself, into our world.

53. The scene just before this statement is telling. A man runs up and asks Jesus what he must do to inherit "eternal life." Jesus first says, "You know the commandments" (10:19) and then lists a short version of them, but then requires the man to sell all his possessions and then give the proceeds to the poor, and "Then come, follow me" (10:21). This exchanges makes clear, again, how Mark so comfortably puts Jesus in charge of the rules for salvation and in a manner that explicitly supersedes prior forms of tradition—here defined as keeping "the commandments"—since keeping company with Jesus is identified as the culmination of this new code of ethics.

54. Likewise, we shouldn't miss the point that as Jesus and the disciples are shown sharing Passover together, instead of with their families, the narrative is generating a kind of hyper-family that stands over and against family values as they were articulated in (old) tradition.

55. For a discussion of this parable that explores its reworking of the vineyard song in Isaiah: 5 and sets that reworking in the context of the destruction of Jerusalem, see Joel Marcus, "The Intertextual Polemic of the Markan Vineyard Parable."

56. Adela Yarbro Collins presents evidence that the mockery of a king was an established trope in first-century literature; see her "Mark's Interpretation of the Death of Jesus," 552ff. This is a useful perspective but doesn't undermine the argument I'm presenting here about the prophetic quality of the mockery.

57. Morna Hooker's reflections on how the end of Mark is designed to confront the reader are helpful here; see her *Endings: Invitations to Discipleship*, chapter 2. The classic essay exploring how Mark's finale is designed to work on the reader is Norman R. Petersen, "When Is the End Not the End?: Literary Reflections on the Ending of Mark's Narrative."

Chapter 4

1. Kumārajīva translated the text into Chinese in 402 (T. no. 366); it was then translated again by Xuanzang in 650 (T. no. 367). There is another equally famous text that goes by the title "The Longer Sūtra on the Land of Bliss." The relationship between these two texts is quite unclear. The "Longer Sūtra" was translated into Chinese by the early third century, suggesting that it is the older of the two; and, as we will see, there are also several aspects of its presentation of Buddhism and the Land of Bliss that give the impression that it is an earlier and less radical attempt to build tradition around the Land of Bliss. For a brief note on the translation of the longer *Land of Bliss* into Chinese, see Jan Nattier's, "The Realm of Akṣobhya: A Missing Piece in the History of Indian Buddhism," 76, n.13.

2. The text refers to this buddha as "Amitāyus," meaning "measureless lifespan," but there is also a passage that seems to identify him as "Amitābha" which means "measureless light."

3. For a careful translation that makes use of the Sanskrit, Chinese, and Tibetan versions of the text, see Luis O. Gómez, *The Land of Bliss: The Paradise of the Buddha of Measureless Light: Sanskrit and Chinese Versions of the Sukhāvatīvyūha Sutras.*

4. The "Longer Sūtra," while also celebrating the salvific power to be won from worshipping the name of Amitābha—and the text that he lives in—spends considerable time encouraging readers/listeners to engage in a range of traditional Buddhist practices. Thus, the "Longer Sūtra" positions itself as gentle supplement to tradition. In comparison, the "Shorter" *Land of Bliss* is more radical in its fetishization of tradition and also seems to work up a much more involved text-reader relationship.

5. Gómez, *The Land of Bliss*, 18. Without delving too far into the history of the text, I should alert readers to the fact that the surviving Sanskrit manu-

script of the text is not necessarily the oldest version of the work. In general, it is very clear that Indian Buddhist texts were often edited, expanded, rewritten, or reorganized after they were put in circulation. This means that early translations of these works into Chinese—a process that begins roughly at the end of the second century of the Common Era—often present versions that appear older than those that survive in Sanskrit.

6. For discussion of the emergence of Mahāyānic ideas regarding buddha-lands, see Jan Nattier, "Indian Roots of Pure Land Buddhism: Insights from the Oldest Chinese Version of the Larger *Sukhāvatī*."

7. In the "Longer Sūtra," Śākyamuni Buddha very much maintains his traditional role as a full-fledged teacher of truth and tradition, again making the "Longer Sūtra" appear much less radical vis-à-vis established tradition.

8. The full passage is: "After he awakened to unsurpassable, perfect and full enlightenment in this Saha world, he taught a dharma that the whole world was reluctant to accept, at a time when the cosmos was in a period of decay, when living beings were in a period of decay, when views and opinions corrupted human beings, when the length of human life had declined, when the afflictions vitiated human beings" (Gómez, 21).

9. The "Longer Sūtra" presents, at length, a discourse on the five afflictions found in our world; it also explains, in its concluding remarks, that accepting its teaching is the hardest thing to do in the world. However, it doesn't link these two discourses. Likewise the list of five afflictions in the "Longer Sūtra" appear quite different from the five that are so quickly enumerated in the "Shorter Sūtra."

10. For a discussion of lands of bliss in a range of Mahāyāna works, see Gregory Schopen, "*Sukhāvatī* as a Generalized Religious Goal in Sanskrit Mahāyāna Sūtra Literature."

11. In East Asian Buddhism, the following three Land of Bliss texts are often grouped together: 1) The *Land of Bliss*, treated here; 2) the "Longer" *Land of Bliss*; and, 3) *The Sūtra on Contemplation of Amitāyus* (*Amitāyardhyāna Sūtra*) which seems to have been composed outside of India, perhaps in a Central Asian kingdom. For translation of these works, see Hisao Inagaki, *The Three Pure Land Sūtras*. For a collection of essays on how the Land of Bliss figures in various Buddhist traditions, see Richard K. Payne and Kenneth K. Tanaka eds., *Approaching the Land of Bliss: Religious Praxis in the Cult of Amitābha*.

12. For brief history of Buddhist funerals in China that demonstrates the predominance of the Land of Bliss in East Asian conceptions of the afterlife, see my "Upside Down/Right Side Up: A Revisionist History of Buddhist Funerals in China."

13. Several other Mahāyāna texts evoke magical lands where the Buddha's teachings, or "the work of the Buddhas," are provided by non-humans. See, for instance, the brief passage in the *Vimalakīrti*, where we learn that in Akṣobhya's Land of Bliss there are "bodhi trees and wonderful lotus blossoms that are able to carry out the buddha's work in the ten directions" (Watson, trans., 133). Earlier

in the *Vimalakīrti* we find a list of non-human entities that can, in various buddhalands, do a "buddha's work"; this list includes: light, fragrance, gardens, groves, pavilions, towers, the Buddha's garments, his bedding and food, and so on (Watson, trans., 123). Similarly, in the *Tathāgatagarbha Sūtra*, the Buddha of our world is made to describe a buddha from the very distant past, named the Eternally Light-Bestowing King, who produced a magical light that covered his land and made the wind through the trees articulate "soft, subtle sounds that expounded freely and unrestrainedly the three jewels, the bodhisattva virtues, the power of good roots, the study of the path, meditation, and liberation. Beings who heard it all attained joy in the dharma. Their faith was made firm, and they were forever freed from the realms of evil rebirth. Vajramati, because all the beings of the ten directions were instantly enveloped in light, at six o'clock every morning and evening they joined their palms together and offered worship" (Grosnick trans., 105).

14. For a overview of what is known about the genesis of the Mahāyāna traditions, see Richard Gombrich's "How the Mahāyāna Began."

15. Gregory Schopen makes this point quite convincingly in his "The Buddhist 'Monastery' and the Indian Garden: Aesthetics, Assimilations, and the Siting of Monastic Establishments."

16. For more discussion of the symbiotic relationship between the Buddhist monasteries and the reproductive family, see my essay, "Buddhism."

17. For discussion of the way the Vinaya was likely expanded and reworked, at the beginning of the Common Era, in response to the growing complexity of monastic architecture and administration, see Gregory Schopen, *Buddhist Monks and Business: Still More Papers on Monastic Buddhism in India*, 73–80.

18. See Gregory Schopen, "The Phrase '*sa pṛthivīpradeśaś caityabhūto bhavet*' in the *Vajracchedikā*: Notes on the Cult of the Book in Mahāyāna." For more reflections on the invention of Mahāyāna texts, see Jan Nattier, *A Few Good Men: The Bodhisattva Path according to the Inquiry of Ugra (Ugraparipṛcchā)*,; see also, Daniel Boucher, *Bodhisattvas of the Forest and the Formation of the Mahāyāna: A Study and Translation of the Rāṣṭrapālaparipṛcchā-sūtra*.

19. Translation from Burton Watson, *The Lotus Sūtra*, 161, with minor changes; T.9.30c.7.

20. This paragraph and the preceding one are taken from the preface to *Text as Father*, with slight changes.

21. Jan Nattier and others have argued that the Land of Bliss texts were composed largely due to the visions that their authors had gained through meditation; for her comments, see "Indian Roots of Pure Land Buddhism," 184–85. This may have been the case in some instances; however, it seems to me that we could just as easily imagine "literary genius" producing some of these texts, with authors reading each other's descriptions and thinking of ways to shift and improve the presentations of these paradises. Of course, once we see that the Lands of Bliss often parallel other culturally produced items—such as images of the perfect garden or city—it becomes increasingly hard to posit meditation as the origin of these "visions."

22. The "Longer Sūtra" lacks just this kind of clever trope of self-validation. Though there is a kind of intergalactic vision mentioned, with the inhabitants of the Land of Bliss at one point looking at Ananda and the other monks in India, and vice-versa, the cosmic buddhas in the "Longer Sūtra" aren't employed to endorse the text itself.

23. The *Vimalakīrti* works up a parallel attack on traditional Buddhism, claiming that when cosmos-tripping Buddhists arrive in our world, they are astounded at the primitive nature of our "local" Buddhism. See, chapter 10 of the *Vimalakīrti*, Watson, trans., esp. 117–18.

24. The Chinese translation reads clearly enough and leaves no doubt that the Buddha is being made to talk about the powers of the very talk that he is supposedly currently giving to Śāriputra.

25. Gómez, 16.

26. I am quite happy to discover, thanks to Prof. Charles Jones of Catholic University, that a version of this problem was addressed in the *Prajñāpāramitāśastra*—an encyclopedic work compiled in China, roughly in the late fourth or early fifth century. The relevant passage tries to explain why it is that, if buddhas are as omnipotent as they are supposed to be, they don't just manifest themselves everywhere and why they would, likewise, rely on animals and winds to do their teaching for them. See T.25.712a.17–712b.2.

27. Gómez, 17. Gómez also translates Kumārjīva's fifth-century rendering of the Sanskrit into Chinese, which is slightly different (T.12.347a.12); see 145–51: "Moreover, Śāriputra, in that land you will always see many flocks of rare and exquisite birds of many colors—white egrets, peacocks, parrots, shari, and kalavinka birds, and those birds called 'Living Together.' Droves of these birds gather to sing with soothing, exquisite voices six times a day, exactly on the hour, day, and night. Their voices proclaim the tenets of the Buddha's teaching—for instance, they sing of the five spiritual faculties, of the five spiritual powers, of the seven aspects of awakening, of the Eightfold Path that is followed by those of spiritual nobility, and of many other aspects of the Buddha's dharma. When the living beings in that buddha-field hear such song, they all immediately enjoy thoughts of the Buddha, of his dharma, and of his order, and keep these three in mind incessantly."

28. Gómez, 17.

29. In other contemporaneous descriptions of these buddhalands, it is normal to insist that there are no animals; see, for instance, the *Lotus Sūtra* (Watson trans., 113, 145).

30. Jan Nattier makes nearly the same point in her "The Realm of Akṣobhya," 75 n.9: "There was clearly a widely accepted body of ideas in India about what an ideal world should be, for the same attributes—soft earth, golden color, pleasant breezes, fragrant scents, easily accessible food and clothing, abundant pools, flowers and fruit, a large population, and so on—recur in a wide range of literature." Many of these items were also regarded as essential in a classical Indian garden. For discussion of these details, see Daud Ali, "Gardens in Early Indian Court Life," *Studies in History*, 19.2.

31. Gómez, 18. For a translation of Kumārajīva's Chinese translation, see Gómez, 147: "Śāriputra, in that buddha-land, a subtle breeze blows, swaying the rows of jeweled trees and the jeweled nets, so that they emit an exquisite sound, like that of hundreds of thousands of diverse kinds of musical instruments playing together at the same time. All those who hear this sound enjoy spontaneously (*zi ran*) and immediately thoughts of the Buddha, of his dharma, and of his order, and keep these three in mind incessantly, bringing to mind the Buddha, bringing to mind his dharma, bringing to mind his Order" (T.12.147a.21).

32. Actually, a number of other Mahāyāna texts—such as the *Diamond Sūtra*—claim that accepting, upholding, and teaching as little as four lines of their discourse is sufficient to fulfill the text's demand to be worshipped, so that the *Land of Bliss* has boiled that requirement down to one single name shouldn't be seen as that extraordinary.

33. Gómez, p. 18.

34. The "Longer Sūtra" uses terms such as "sons of the Buddha [Sugata]" (Gómez, 62), along with presenting a developed patriline that explains how the Land of Bliss was created by a certain Dharmakara—soon to be Amitāyus—who figures in a long lineage of buddhas qua truth-fathers. (See 64–65.) Given the prominence of this lineage, it's not surprising that Dharmakara's vows include the wish to be just like his truth-father, Lokeshvararaja (66). The mimesis between the inhabitants in the land and their truth-father is made visible, too, in the detail that all inhabitants of the land will have the thirty-two marks of a buddha-body (71).

35. Gómez, 19.

36. Ibid., 21.

37. The "Longer Sūtra" seems to lack this motif regarding the hyper-orality of the buddhas teaching in their respective lands of bliss.

38. Gomez, 20.

39. Equally telling, the "Longer Sūtra" doesn't set up the reading moment as a pivot in the universe where all these cosmic buddhas are looking back at the reader. Instead in the "Longer Sūtra" the cosmic focus is on Amitāyus and his Land of Bliss, which was appreciated by all the cosmic buddhas as the best buddhaland ever.

40. The "Longer Sūtra" doesn't advance this trope at all and instead claims that the Buddha was completely successful as a teacher, and wherever he went, he magically purified the country. It is, supposedly, only after he dies that the world takes on the aspects characterized as the "five sins."

41. For reflections on the problems involved in writing a history of early Mahāyāna Buddhism, see Gregory Schopen, "The Mahāyāna and the Middle Period of Indian Buddhism: Through a Chinese Looking-glass."

42. For some time scholars have been suggesting a parallel between pre-Mahāyānic descriptions of perfect cities and the details in the *Land of Bliss*; see Gómez, 271; see also Maurice Walshe, in his *The Long Discourses of the Buddha: A Translation of the Dīghanikāya*, 576 n. 468, where he cites T. W. Rhys Davids'

translation of the same passage and adds that Rhys Davids saw a connection between this passage and the descriptions of the Land of Bliss.

43. Translation by Maurice Walshe in *The Long Discourses of the Buddha*, 279–80. In fact, this account of the city is repeated in the *Mahāparinibbāna sutta* as well (see Walshe, 266); however, given its awkward placement in the *Mahāparinibbāna sutta*, this description could have been interpolated from the *Mahāsudassāna sutta*. At any rate, its presence in these two works shows the level of interest in this cityscape and its place in prominent pre-Mahāyānic works.

44. Later in the *Mahāsudassāna sutta* the jeweled ponds are described.

45. For a translation, see John S. Strong, *The Legend of King Aśoka*, 198–99.

46. Translated by John S. Strong in *The Experience of Buddhism*, 42–43.

47. Ibid.

48. This convoluted figure of an art-form articulating the proper desire that one should have for it, while perhaps not widely recognized in the world of religious studies, has many parallels in pop culture. Rappers rap, endlessly, about how great their rap is, just as blues singers give us similarly self-promoting rhapsodies on the soulful quality of the blues that they are, in fact, playing.

49. Edward Conze trans., *Perfection of Wisdom in 8,000 Lines & Its Verse Summary*, chapter 30, 277ff, with small stylistic changes. It is worth noting that just before this long description of Gandhavati, in chapter 28 (269–70), one finds a vision of the buddhaland of Akṣobhya, a buddhaland usually situated in the east, which some scholars take to be one of the earliest buddhalands mentioned in the literary record. However, in this vision, which focuses on the inhabitants of this buddhaland, no specific architectural details are given, and thus one might wonder if the author of the *Land of Bliss* didn't take the concept of a buddhaland from chapter 28 and flesh it out with these details from chapter 30 that describe Gandhavati, thereby mapping the details of the perfect city onto the otherwise barren buddhaland of Akṣobhya. Some minimalist details are given from Akṣobhya's buddhaland earlier in the text (220), but they in no way match the presentation of Gandhavati or Amitāyus's Land of Bliss. One final detail to note: the buddha Akṣobhya appears in another section, this time chapter 27 (261), where the author explains how the buddhas in various buddhalands look at each other and discourse on each other's accomplishments. As seen above, the *Land of Bliss* also relies on just this mutual vision between buddhas.

50. For Kumārajīva's translation, see T.8.581a.29ff; for Xuanzang's, see T.6.1061a.23.

51. There are hints of this dynamic coming to the fore in several of the details in the "Longer" *Land of Bliss*, but arguably the strategy was only fully developed in the "Shorter" *Land of Bliss*. Thus, in the "Shorter" *Land of Bliss*, pleasure isn't tradition's handmaiden—pleasure and tradition are one entity and *it* arrives in an automatic way that can't be resisted. That is, as the birds sing, as the wind rustles through the trees, tradition and pleasure are inevitably transferred to the listener, making it seem as though the author is seducing the reader with an image of a future seduction into tradition, one that will be automatic, and one in which all

culture disappears with only nature remaining—or at least facsimiles of nature. In short, seduction, as a human enterprise—or, rather, a literary enterprise—has itself been purified of its dialectical and contingent nature.

52. Thinking about the text in this manner is far from being a modern conceit. Another Mahāyāna text roughly contemporaneous with the *Land of Bliss* built its entire discourse around the audacious claim that it was, as text, coterminous with the universe. For discussion and a translation, see Luis O. Gómez, "The Whole Universe as a Sūtra."

Chapter 5

1. Recently Stephen F. Teiser and Morten Schlütter published a collection of useful of essays, *Readings of the Platform Sūtra*. Another important study is John Jorgensen, *Inventing Hui-neng, the Sixth Patriarch: Hagiography and Biography in Early Chan*; see also his "*The Platform Sūtra* and the Corpus of Shenhui: Recent Critical Text Editions and Studies." See also Morten Schlütter, "Transmission and Enlightenment in Chan Buddhism Seen through the *Platform Sūtra* (*Liuzu tanjing*), and "A Study in the Genealogy of the *Platform Sūtra*." Besides these sources, Carl Bielefeldt and Lewis Lancaster published an important overview of the text: "*T'an Ching* (Platform Scripture)." Behind these efforts is Philip Yampolsky's monumental study of the text, *The Platform Sūtra of the Sixth Patriarch*, which though far ahead of its time and still a very fine translation, offers a somewhat credulous reading of the text that the past forty years of research have, increasingly, put in doubt.

2. For a detailed account of the evolution of the manuscripts of the text, see Morten Schlütter's two essays cited above.

3. There is a slightly older and much less developed version of Bodhidharma's Chinese descendants in two places in the important encyclopedia of Daoxuan, *Continued Biographies of Eminent Monks*: in the entry for Huike, and then again in the entry for Fachong. Both entries present fairly crude narratives that have clearly been reworked—presumably in the years after the encyclopedia was finished in 645—in order to advance the hazy claim that master Fachong was a direct descendent of Huike and thus a descendent of Bodhidharma, since Huike's biography presents Huike as Bodhidharma's disciple. For more discussion, see my *Fathering Your Father*, chapter 3.

4. For more discussion of this text and its relationship to the Faru biography, see my *Fathering Your Father*, chapter 4.

5. For more details regarding this stele for Huineng, see my *Fathering Your Father*, chapter 6.

6. This paragraph and the next three are taken from *Fathering Your Father*, 217–18, with small changes.

7. In *Fathering Your Father*, 234ff, I explain why the regularly cited date of 732 for Shenhui's supposed first attack on Puji isn't reliable.

8. For the stele, see Wen Yucheng, "*Ji xin chu tu de Heze Dashi Shenhui taming.*" As Wen notes, this stele seems to have been carved over an older stele and seven characters from the older narrative are still legible—ground (地), patriarch (祖), and Śākyamuni (釋, twice) and Monastery of Ten Thousand Treasures (萬珍寺)—suggesting in a more concrete way the rewriting of tradition in a palimpsest manner.

9. The text's formal title promises the doctrine of sudden enlightenment, but it too is a sprawling piece of verbiage: "Southern School Sudden Doctrine, Supreme Mahāyāna Great Perfection of Wisdom: The Platform Sūtra Preached by the Sixth Patriarch Huineng at the Dafan Temple in Shaozhou, one roll, recorded by the spreader of the dharma, the disciple Fahai, who at the same time received the Precepts of Formlessness."

10. All quotations will be taken from Yampolsky's translation, unless otherwise noted; in this case what Yampolsky translated as "pivot of the teaching" could have been better rendered as "essence of the lineage" (宗旨).

11. As far as I know, none of the early Chan texts addresses the problem of local dialects, which underscores that the *mise en scène* of these texts remains completely literary, with the "conversations" between figures never having to face the real problems of orality in multi-dialect China.

12. And here, again, it is worth noting how regional dialects are being ignored in the narrative. The text, obviously, gives no thought to this problem, but if this official is a local official, he is presumably reciting the *Diamond Sūtra* in some southern dialect of the Guangdong area, a dialect that, most likely, would be incomprehensible to someone from Hubei. Of course, regardless of where Huineng was supposedly born, a reader might imagine that he had mastered the local dialect as he made himself at home in the south, but then again he has had two residences in the south—one in Lingnan and one in Nanhai—and one might rightly wonder if they spoke different dialects in these different locales. Of course, the text is content to avoid these details, giving the sense that the author's presentation of "orality" in the text is, in fact, still fully literary.

13. See my *Text as Father*, chapter 4 for more discussion of this problem.

14. In the texts associated with Shenhui, which slightly predate the *Platform Sūtra*, we find clear instances of authors trying to turn Shenhui into something like a human version of the *Diamond Sūtra* such that when he speaks only that text comes out of him but in a manner that, literally, breathes life into the text and, by implication, makes him appear as a buddha since the Buddha's voice and his own are now so mixed. For more discussion of this issue, see my *Fathering Your Father*, chapter 6.

15. The relationship between the *Diamond Sūtra* and the Bodhidharma lineage—as manifest in Hongren—suggests that it takes a fetish-of-tradition to make a fetish-of-tradition since one needs a singular point of authority to ratify another singular point of authority. One need only consider the opposite to see the logic here: imagine what would happen if an open ballot were given to all living members

of the Buddhist tradition, asking them to pencil in their candidate for fetish-of-tradition. The One must be made by another One.

16. In the biography that Wang Wei crafted for Huineng we learn that Huineng was enlightened "in the tall grasses" on his own, and later simply received transmission from Hongren as a kind of after-the-fact formality.

17. Presumably this claim of a transcendental sameness with the master is aided by the fact that Huineng has no competing father already claiming such a sameness. Huineng isn't simply a fatherless child, he also has no surname, as mentioned above, and thus this process of refathering him in no way requires a "de-fathering," as most such acts would.

18. The *Platform Sūtra* seems to have developed several themes from Wang Wei's stele; thus, Wang Wei's vague comment that Huineng was from "such and such region and province" and that he "did not only dwell in China" appears to have developed into this complex identity of being from the south, but not really. Likewise, Wang Wei's point that Huineng wasn't from "an aristocratic" family is now amply developed in Huineng's poverty. And, finally, Wang Wei's comment that at Huangmei, Huineng was "installed in the [work of] the well and pestle" is taken up and amplified in the *Platform Sūtra's* account of his "more than eight months" of labor in the threshing room. For more discussion of Wang Wei's biography for Huineng, see my *Fathering Your Father*, 215–21.

19. In terms of the Cinderella comparison, this poetry contest is much like the ball when the prince's wife is to be selected: in either case it is a matter of publicly selecting the figure who will allow for the legitimate reproduction of the system, while also filling the audience with a sense of fairness and respect for tradition which, in properly reproducing itself, overcomes some injustice.

20. To round out the above argument about the author's construction of Hongren's racism in that initial conversation with Huineng, we should note that in this scene, Hongren is shown promoting a race-blind competition in which a poem by anyone, presumably even by a "barbarian," could win the day. Seeing this flip-flop—and more are coming—makes Hongren appear as a malleable puppet brought on stage at different times to do and say symbolically useful things that advance the narrative. Of course, the same could be said of Huineng.

21. In Du Fei's *Chuan fabao ji* we see a fine example of just this gesture of partially validating the *Laṅkāvatāra Sūtra* as the fetish-of-tradition and then, conclusively and authoritatively, relegating it to a half-measure for beginners. See my *Fathering Your Father*, chapter 4, for more discussion of the matter.

22. For a reading of the *Platform Sūtra* that focuses on the conspiracy-theory theme, see my "Conspiracy's Truth: The Zen of Narrative Cunning in the *Platform Sūtra*," *AsiaMajor*, vol. 28, part 1, 2015.

23. That Huineng twice mentions (128, 131) that it was more than eight months that he spent in the threshing room might suggest that the author wanted to make his stay there comparable to the time a fetus would gestate in the womb. Thus though the "more than eight months" doesn't match the standard Chinese

phrasing of "ten months" in the womb, it is after this time that he is refathered and assumes his new identity.

24. And, certainly, this goal of seeking buddhadharma would have been read as more noble than the pedestrian desire to be reborn in a buddhaland, a desire that had already been associated with the monastery's monks who, accused of "seeking after fields of merit," were implicitly put in the category of laity who in normal Buddhist discourse are expected to seek after the monkly "fields of merit." Thus, though Huineng is so clearly already marked by the narrative as a master, various details are provided that cast him as an unmotivated commoner, accidently heading towards the peak of symbolic power and value.

25. Hu Shi thought that this doubling of the winning poems reflected how the "unknown author of this fictionalized autobiography of Huineng was evidently experimenting with his verse writing and was not sure which verse was better." (This quote is given by Yampolsky, 133n39.)

26. For discussion of poetry and selfhood, see Stephen Owen, "The Self's Perfect Mirror: Poetry as Autobiography."

27. Inventing this general who shares Huineng's first name adds to the sense of continuity between these two figures since it was common for disciples to take the first character of their master's dharma name as the first character in their own names.

28. What I take to be "dummy transmissions" proving the ownership of tradition are also findable in Mahāyāna sūtras, such as the *Lotus Sūtra*. For more discussion, see my *Text as Father*, chapter 2.

29. For more discussion of the *Diamond Sūtra's* negative dialectics, see my *Text as Father*, chapter 4.

30. For arguments regarding the use of Shenhui's *Platform Sermon*, see chapter 6 of *Fathering Your Father*.

31. For more discussion of Shenhui's writing, see chapter 6 of my *Fathering Your Father*.

32. Themes of self-doubt are fairly well known in high Chinese literature: both the *Zhuangzi* and the *Daode jing* represent authorial voices quiet unsure of themselves at times.

33. I develop this argument in chapters 5 and 6 of *Fathering Your Father*; a parallel argument can be found in my treatment of the *Tathāgatagarbha Sūtra* in *Text as Father*, chapter 5.

34. There is another irony here: Shenhui, in the texts associated with him, never quotes his supposed master, Huineng, a fact that is odd in itself. Actually, of the four texts in the Shenhui corpus, there is hardly any mention of Huineng, with the *Treatise on Defining the True and False* providing but a line here and there on him, and then only in a later section that seems to have been added at a later date. In short, Shenhui never details his relationship with Huineng, the historicity of their contact, or his reception of Huineng's teachings. Arguably, then, Huineng stands as Shenhui's imaginary point of contact with the imaginary Bodhidharma lineage.

35. I consider this problematic at length in chapter 5 of *Fathering Your Father*.

36. For a discussion of Shenhui's treatment of meditation, see my *Fathering Your Father*, 274–80.

37. This discussion is found at the opening of chapter 3 of the *Vimalakīti*; see Watson, trans., *The Vimalakīti Sūtra*, 37.

38. For discussion of these issues, see chapter 6 of *Fathering Your Father*.

39. Actually, when the full lineage back to India is given late in the text, the Buddha Śākyamuni is, himself, given six preceding buddha truth-fathers. (179)

Conclusion

1. The second chapter of Jean-Paul Sartre's *What Is Literature?*, titled "Why Write?," is particularly worth reading on just this theme of narratizing the world for one's self and/or the Other.

2. I argued for such a reading of the *Daode jing* in "Simplicity for the Sophisticated: Rereading the *Daode jing* for the Polemics of Ease and Innocence."

3. Throughout the *Analects* one sees such claims; a particularly clear example is found in 16.13 where Boyu, Confucius's son, recounts how his father asked him if he had learned the Odes and Rites yet, because if he hadn't, then he would have "nothing to say" and "no where to stand."

4. For discussion of the various ways that Confucius has been refigured throughout Chinese history, see Michael Nylan and Thomas Wilson, *The Lives of Confucius*.

5. The Katha, Prasna, and Kena Upanishads present just these claims.

6. For examples of this new kind of yoga that renders daily life into a form of asceticism that surpasses Vedic practices and old-style yoga, see the *Gītā*, 2.36ff.

7. See the final section of the *Gītā*, 18.64ff.

8. Nina Tumarkin, *Lenin Lives: The Lenin Cult in Soviet Russia*, 2.

9. Ibid., 3, italics added.

10. For an effort to make sense at the iconicization of Mao, see Melissa Schrift, *Biography of a Chairman Mao Badge*. For other theoretical reflections on the Mao badges as fetishes, see Jennifer Hubbert, "(Re)collecting Mao: Memory and Fetish in Contemporary China."

11. For exploring the logic of this claim, see chapter 2 of Fredrick Wakeman, *History and Will: Philosophical Perspectives of Mao Tse-tung's Thought*.

12. This detail is taken from an excellent account of the traditional elements and logics in Mao's funeral and mummification in Fredrick Wakeman, Jr., "Mao's Remains."

13. See Buruma's "Cult of the Chairman" in the *Guardian*, March 7, 2001.

14. The literature on fascism as a quasi-religious sociopolitical formation is voluminous. For an introductory essay, see Robert Ellwood, "Nazism as a Millennialist Movement."

15. Though his modern advocates try to avoid discussing it, let's not overlook that for Jung the collective unconscious supposedly came in Aryan and Jewish forms, with the latter being decidedly weak, overly cultured, and rootless. Jung also argued that non-Jewish Europeans should move away from Freudian analysis in order to get a psychoanalysis more suited to their Aryan psyches. For these antisemitic comments, see his "The Unconscious" (1916), esp. 12–14.

16. See Richard Noll, *The Aryan Christ: The Secret Life of Carl Jung*, for details regarding this phase of Jung's life.

17. Richard Rorty's discussion of Heidegger's effort to fashion a "final language" gets at some of these issues; see his "Heidegger, contingency, and pragmatism"; see also Charles Bambach, *Heidegger's Roots: Nietzsche, National Socialism, and the Greeks* for discussion of how Heidegger sought to overcome and revivify the Western tradition.

18. For an account of the seductive strategies at work in Eliade's prose, see Daniel Dubuisson, "The Poetical and Rhetorical Structure of the Eliadean Text." Dubuisson also takes up the problematic figure of Eliade's "homo religiosus" in his *Impostures et pseudo-science. L'œuvre de Mircea Eliade.*

Bibliography

Aichele, G. ed. *The Postmodern Bible: The Bible and Culture Collective*. New Haven: Yale University Press, 1997.

Ali, Daud. "Gardens in Early Indian Court Life." *Studies in History* 19, no. 2 (2003): 221–52.

Allen, Charlotte. "The Search for a No-Frills Jesus." *Atlantic Monthly* 278, no. 6 (Dec., 1996): 51–68.

Alles, Gregory. *Religious Studies: A Global View*. London: Routlege, 2007.

Althusser, Louis. "Ideology and Ideological State Apparatuses." In *Lenin and Philosophy*, 127–186. New York: Monthly Review Press, 1978.

Bambach, Charles. *Heidegger's Roots: Nietzsche, National Socialism, and the Greeks*. Ithaca: Cornell University Press, 2003.

Barthes, Roland. "The Eiffel Tower." In *A Barthes Reader*, edited by Susan Sontag, 236–250. New York: Hill and Wang, 1982.

Bauckham, Richard. "For What Offence Was James Put to Death?" In *James the Just and Christian Origins*, edited by Chilton and Evans, 199–232. Leiden: Brill, 1999.

Baudrillard, Jean. *For a Critique of the Political Economy of the Sign*. New York: Telos Press, 1981.

———. *La Société de consommation*. Paris: Gallimard, 1970.

———. *Le Système des objects*. Paris: Gallimard, 1968.

Biale, David. *Blood and Belief: The Circulation of a Symbol between Jews and Christians*. Berkeley: University of California Press, 2007.

Bielefeldt, Carl, and Lewis Lancaster. "*T'an Ching* (Platform Scripture)." *Philosophy East and West* 25, no. 2 (April, 1975): 197–212.

———. "Ch'ang-lu Tsung-tse's *Tso-Ch'an I* and the 'Secret' of Zen Meditation." In *Traditions of Meditation in Chinese Buddhism*, edited by Peter Gregory, 129–161. Honolulu: University of Hawai'i Press, 1986.

Binet, Albert. "Le fétichisme dans l'amour: la vie psychique des micro-organismes, l'intensité des images mentales, etc." *Le fétichisme dans l'amour*. Paris: Payot, 2000 [1887].

Borg, Marcus. *Jesus: A New Vision: Spirit, Culture and the Life of Discipleship*. New York: HarperCollins, 1987.

Boucher, Daniel. *Bodhisattvas of the Forest and the Formation of the Mahāyāna: A Study and Translation of the Rāṣṭrapālaparipṛcchā-sūtra*. Honolulu: University of Hawaii Press, 2008.

Bourdieu, Pierre. "Rites of Institution." In *Language and Symbolic Power*, 117–126. Cambridge, MA: Harvard University Press, 1991.

Boyer, Peter J. "The Jesus War." *The New Yorker* Sept. 15, 2003.

Brandon, S. G. F. "History or Theology? The Basic Problems of the Evidence of the Trial of Jesus." In *Essential Papers on Judaism and Christianity in Conflict*, edited by Jeremy Cohen, 114–130. New York: New York University Press, 1991.

Broadhead, Edwin K. "Jesus and the Priests of Israel." In *Jesus from Judaism to Christianity: Continuum Approaches to the Historical Jesus*, edited by Tom Holmén, 125–44. London: T&T Clark, 2007.

———. *Prophet, Son, Messiah: Narrative Form and Function in Mark 14–16*. Sheffield: Journal for the Study of the New Testament, Supplement Series 97, 1994.

Brodie, Thomas L. *Beyond the Quest for the Historical Jesus: Memoir of a Discovery*. Sheffield: Sheffield Phoenix Press, 2012.

Burridge, Richard A. *What Are the Gospels? A Comparison with Graeco-Roman Biography*. Grand Rapids, MI: Eerdmans Publishing Co.; 2nd edition, 2004.

Clifford, James. *The Predicament of Culture: Twentieth-Century Ethnography, Literature, and Art*. Cambridge, MA: Harvard University Press, 1988.

Cole, Alan. "Buddhism." In *Sex, Marriage, and Family in the World Religions*. edited by Don Browning, 299–366. New York: Columbia University Press, 2005.

———. "Conspiracy's Truth: The Zen of Narrative Cunning in the *Platform Sūtra*." *AsiaMajor*, vol. 28, part 1, 2015.

———. *Fathering Your Father: The Zen of Fabrication in Tang Buddhism*. Berkeley: University of California Press, 2009.

———. *Patriarchs on Paper: A Brief History of Chan (Zen) Literature from 600 to 1300*. University of California Press, 2016.

———. "Simplicity for the Sophisticated: Rereading the *Daode Jing* for the Polemics of Ease and Innocence." *History of Religions* 46 (2006): 1–49.

———. *Text as Father: Paternal Seductions in Early Mahāyāna Buddhist Literature*. Berkeley: University of California Press, 2005.

———. "Upside Down/Right Side Up: A Revisionist History of Buddhist Funerals in China." *History of Religions* 35, no. 4 (1996): 307–338.

Collins, Adela Yarbro. "Mark and His Readers: The Son of God among Greeks and Romans." *Harvard Theological Review* 93 (2000): 85–100.

———. "Mark and His Readers: The Son of God among Jews." *Harvard Theological Review* 92 (1999): 393–408.

———. *Is Mark's Gospel a Life of Jesus?: The Question of Genre*. Milwaukee: Marquette University Press, 1990.

————. "The Meaning of the Death of Jesus." *The Journal of Religion* 78, no. 2 (Apr., 1998): 175–196.

————. "Review of *A Myth of Innocence*, by Burton Mack." *The Society of Biblical Literature* 108, no. 4, (Winter, 1989): 726–729.

Collins, Adela Yarbro, and John Joseph Collins. *King and Messiah as Son of God: Divine, Human, and Angelic Messianic Figures in Biblical and Related Literature.* Grand Rapids, MI: Eerdmans, 2008.

Cook, Michael J. *Mark's Treatment of the Jewish Leaders.* Leiden: Brill, 1978.

da Silva, Tomaz Tadeu. "The Curriculum as Fetish." *Taboo: The Journal of Culture and Education* 4, no. 1 (Spring–Summer, 2000): 19–44.

de Brosses, Charles. *Du culte des dieux fétische ou Parallelel de l'ancienne religion de l'Egypte avec la religion actuelle de Nigritie*, 1760. On line: http://gallica.bnf.fr/ark:/12148/bpt6k106440f.

Dennett, Daniel. *Breaking the Spell: Religion as a Natural Phenomenon.* New York: Viking, 2006.

Dibelius, Martin. *From Tradition to Gospel.* Translated by B.L. Woolf. New York: Scribner, 1935 [1919].

Douglas, Mary. *How Institutions Think.* Syracuse, NY: Syracuse University Press, 1986.

————. "Jokes." In *Rethinking Popular Culture: Contemporary Perspectives in Cultural Studies*, edited by Chandra Mukerji and Michael Schudson, 291–310. Berkeley: University of California Press, 1991.

Dubuisson, Daniel. *Impostures et pseudo-science. L'œuvre de Mircea Eliade.* Villeneuve d'Ascq: Presses Universitaires du Septentrion, 2005.

————. "The Poetical and Rhetorical Structure of the Eliadean Text." In *Hermeneutics, Politics, and the History of Religions: The Contested Legacies of Joachim Wach and Mircea Eliade*, edited by Christian Wedemeyer et Wendy Doniger, 133–146. New York: Oxford University Press, 2010.

Dunn, J. D. G. "Paul's Understanding of the Death of Jesus as Sacrifice." In *Sacrifice and Redemption: Durham Essays in Theology*, edited by S. W. Sykes, 35–56. Cambridge: Cambridge University Press, 1991.

Eagleton, Terry. *Literary Theory: An Introduction.* Missoula: University of Minnesota Press, 1983.

Ellen, Roy. 1988 "Fetishism." *Man* (n.s.) 23, no. 2, (1988): 213–235.

Ellwood, Robert. "Nazism as a Millennialist Movement." In *Millenianism, Persecution & Violence: Historical Cases*, edited by Catherine Wessinger, 241–60. Syracuse University Press, 2000.

Ehrman, Bart. *A Brief Introduction to the New Testament.* Oxford: Oxford University Press, 2004.

————. *Did Jesus Exist? The Historical Argument for Jesus of Nazareth.* New York: HarperOne, 2012.

————. *Forgery and Counterforgery: The Use of Literary Deceit in Early Christian Polemics.* Oxford: Oxford University Press, 2012.

————. *The Lost Gospel of Judas Iscariot: A New Look at Betrayer and Betrayed.* Oxford: Oxford University Press, 2006.

Evans, Craig. "Jesus and James: Martyrs of the Temple." In *James the Just and Christian Origins*, edited by Bruce Chilton and Craig Evans, 233–50. Leiden: Brill, 1999.

Feuerbach, Ludwig. *The Essence of Christianity*. 1841. Available online: http://www.marxists.org/reference/archive/feuerbach/works/essence/.

Foulk, T. Griffith. "Myth, Ritual, and Monastic Practice in Sung Ch'an Buddhism." In *Religion and Society in T'ang and Sung China*, edited by Patricia Buckley Ebrey and Peter N. Gregory, 147–208. Honolulu: University of Hawai'i Press, 1993.

Fredriksen, Paula. *Augustine and the Jews: A Christian Defense of Jews and Judaism*. New Haven: Yale University Press, 2010.

———. *From Jesus to Christ: The Origins of the New Testament Images of Jesus*. New Haven: Yale University Press, 1988.

———. *Jesus of Nazareth, King of the Jews: A Jewish Life and the Emergence of Christianity*. New York: Vintage Books, 1999.

Freud, Sigmund. "Fetishism." In *Freud: Sexuality and the Psychology of Love*. New York: Collier Books, 1963.

———. *Three Essays on the Theory of Sexuality*. Translated by James Strachey. New York: Basic Books, 1962.

———. *Wit and Its Relationship to the Unconscious*. Translated by A. A. Brill. New York: Moffat, Yard & Co., 1916.

Gager, John G. *Reinventing Paul*. Oxford: Oxford University Press, 2000.

Goldberg, G. J. "John the Baptist and Josephus." On line: http://www.josephus.org/JohnTBaptist.htm.

Gopnik, Adam. "What Did Jesus Do? Reading and Unreading the Gospels." *The New Yorker*, May 24th, 2010.

Girard, René. *Violence and the Sacred*. Baltimore, MD: Johns Hopkins University Press, 1977.

Gómez, Luis O. *The Land of Bliss: The Paradise of the Buddha of Measureless Light: Sanskrit and Chinese Versions of the Sukhāvatīvyūha Sutras*. Honolulu: University of Hawai'i Press, 1996.

———. "The Whole Universe as a Sūtra." In *Buddhism in Practice*, edited by Donald S. Lopez Jr., 107–111. Princeton: Princeton University Press, 1995.

Goulder, Michael. "Is Q a Juggernaut." *Journal of Biblical Literature* 115, no. 4 (1996): 667–681.

———. Review of R. A. Piper ed., *The Gospel Behind the Gospels: Current Studies on Q*. *Novum Testamentum* 38, no. 2 (1996): 194–196.

Grafton, Anthony. *Forgers and Critics: Creativity and Duplicity in Western Scholarship*. Princeton: Princeton University Press, 1990.

Greek Interlinear Bible, available on line at Scripture4All: http://www.scripture4all.org/OnlineInterlinear/Greek_Index.htm.

Greenberg, Gary. *The Judas Brief: Who Really Killed Jesus*. New York: Continuum, 2007.

Grosnick, William H. "The *Tathāgatagarbha Sūtra*." In *Buddhism in Practice*, edited by Donald S. Lopez Jr., 92–106. Princeton: Princeton University Press, 1995.

Kaufmann, Walter. *The Portable Nietzsche*. New York: Viking Press, 1976.

Hadas-Lebel, Mireille. "La destruction du Temple et ses conséquences." In *Les Premiers temps de l'Église: de Saint Paul à Augustine*, edited by Marie-Francoise Baslez, 363–371. Paris: Folio, 2004.

Hengel, Martin. *The Cross of the Son of God*. London: SCM Press, 1986.

———. *The Son of God*. London: SCM Press, 1976.

Heschel, Susannah. *The Aryan Jesus: Christian Theologians and the Bible in Nazi Germany*. Princeton: Princeton University Press, 2008.

Hooker, Morna. *Endings: Invitations to Discipleship*. Peabody, MA: Hendrickson Publishers, 2003.

Horsley, Richard. *Hearing the Whole Story: The Politics of Plot in Mark's Gospel*. Louisville: Westminster John Knox Press, 2001.

Hubbert, Jennifer. "(Re)collecting Mao: Memory and Fetish in Contemporary China." *American Ethnologist* 33, no. 2 (May, 2006): 145–161.

Inagaki, Hisao. *The Three Pure Land Sutras*. Berkeley: Numata Center for Buddhist Translation and Research, 2003.

Jacobs, Andrew S. *Christ Circumcised: A Study in Early Christian History and Difference*. Philadelphia: University of Pennsylvania Press, 2012.

Jay, Nancy. *Throughout Your Generations Forever: Sacrifice, Religion, and Paternity*. Chicago: University of Chicago Press, 1994.

Johnson, Paul Christopher. "The Fetish and McGwire's Balls." *Journal of American Academy of Religion* 68, no. 2 (June, 2000): 243–264.

Jorgensen, John. *Inventing Hui-neng, the Sixth Patriarch: Hagiography and Biography in Early Chan*. Leiden: Brill, 2005.

———. "*The Platform Sūtra* and the Corpus of Shenhui: Recent Critical Text Editions and Studies." *Revue Bibliographique de Sinologie* 20 (2002): 399–438.

Josephus, Flavius. *The Works of Josephus, Complete and Unabridged, New Updated Edition*. Translated by William Whiston. Peabody, MA: Hendrickson Publishers, 1987. Available on line: http://www.biblestudytools.com/history/flavius-josephus/.

Jung, Carl G. "The Unconscious." In *Civilization in Transition (The Collected Works C. G. Jung, vol. 10)*, 3–28. Princeton: Princeton University Press, 1970.

Kelber, Werner. "The Hour of the Son of Man and the Temptation of the Disciples." In *The Passion in Mark: Studies on Mark 14–16*, edited by Werner Kelber, 41–60. Philadelphia: Fortress Press, 1976.

———. "Mark 14: 32–42: Gethsemane, Passion Christology and Discipleship Failure." *Zeitschrift für neuentestamentliche Wissenschaft* 63 (1972): 166–187.

———. *The Oral and the Written Gospel: The Hermeneutics of Speaking and Writing in the Synoptic Tradition, Mark, Paul, and Q*. Bloomington: Indiana University Press, 1997.

Kermode, Frank. *The Genesis of Secrecy: On the Interpretation of Narrative*. Cambridge, MA: Harvard University Press, 1979.

Klawans, Jonathan. "Interpreting the Last Supper: Sacrifice, Spiritualization, and Anti-Sacrifice." *New Testament Studies* 48, no. 1 (2002): 1–17.

———. *Purity, Sacrifice and the Temple: Symbolism and Supersessionism in the Study of Ancient Judaism*. Oxford: Oxford University Press, 2005.

———. "Was Jesus' Last Supper a Seder?" *Bible Review* 17:05 (2001): 24–33.

Kloppenborg, John. "On Dispensing with Q? Goodacre on the Relation of Luke to Matthew." *New Testament Studies* 49, no. 2 (2003): 210–236.

Kockenos, Matthew D. *A Church Divided: German Protestants Confront the Nazi Past*. Bloomington: Indiana University Press, 2004.

Langmuir, Gavin. *History, Religion, and Antisemitism*. Berkeley: University of California Press, 1990.

Lau, D. C., trans. *The Analects*. London: Penguin Books, 1979.

Lemair, Andre. "Jacques et les Chrétiens de Jerusalem." In *Les premiers temps de l'Église: de saint Paul à saint Augustin*, edited by Marie-Françoise Baslez, 375–380. Paris: Gallimard, 2004.

Levine, AmyJill. "Anti-Judaism and the Gospel of Matthew." In *Anti-Judaism and the Gospels*, edited by William R. Farmer, 9–36. Harrisburg, PA: Trinity Press, 1999.

———. *The Misunderstood Jew: The Church and the Scandal of the Jewish Jesus*. New York: HarperCollins, 2006.

Levenson, Jon. *The Death and Resurrection of the Beloved Son: The Transformation of Child Sacrifice in Judaism and Christianity*. New Haven: Yale University Press, 1993.

Lincoln, Bruce. *Discourse and the Construction of Society: Comparative Studies of Myth, Ritual, and Classification*. Oxford: Oxford University Press, 1989.

———. *Gods and Demons, Priests and Scholars: Critical Explorations in the History of Religions*. Chicago: University of Chicago Press, 2012.

Logan, Peter Melville. *Victorian Fetishism: Intellectuals and Primitives*. Albany: State University of New York Press, 2008.

Maccoby, Hyam. *Antisemitism and Modernity: Innovation and Continuity*. New York: Routledge, 2006.

Mack, Burton. *A Myth of Innocence: Mark and Christian Origins*. Minneapolis: Fortress Press, 1991.

———. *Who Wrote the New Testament?: The Making of the Christian Myth*. San Francisco: HarperCollins, 1996.

Malbon, Elizabeth Struthers. *In the Company of Jesus: Characters in Mark's Gospel*. Louisville: Westminster John Knox Press, 2000.

Marcus, Joel. "The Intertextual Polemic of the Markan Vineyard Parable." In *Tolerance and Intolerance in Early Judaism and Christianity*, edited by Graham N. Stanton and Guy G. Stroumsa, 211–227. Cambridge: Cambridge University Press, 1998.

————. "Jewish Christianity." In *Cambridge History of Christianity, vol. 1: Origins to Constantine*, edited by Margaret Mitchell and Frances Young, 87–102. Cambridge: Cambridge University Press, 2006.

Marx, Karl. *Capital, vol. 1.* In *The Marx-Engels Reader, 2ⁿᵈ edition*, edited by Robert C. Tucker, 294–438. New York: W. W. Norton, 1978. https://www.marxists. org/archive/marx/works/1867-c1/ch01.htm#S4.

McCallum, E. L. *Object Lessons: How to Do Things with Fetishism.* Albany: State University of New York Press, 1999.

McCutcheon, Russell. "The Costs of Discipleship: On the Limits of the Humanistic Study of Religion." http://religion.ua.edu/pdf/mccutchdiscipleship.pdf.

————. "Just Follow the Money: The Cold War, the Humanistic Study of Religion and the Fallacy of Insufficient Cynicism." *Culture and Religion* 5, no. 1 (2004): 41–69.

————. "The Myth of the Apolitical Scholar: The Life and Works of Mircea Eliade." *Queen's Quarterly* 100, no. 3 (1993): 642–663.

Meier, John P. *A Marginal Jew, Volume 4: Law and Love.* New Haven: Yale University Press, 2009.

Miklitsch, Robert. "The Commodity-Body-Sign: Toward a General Economy of 'Commodity Fetishism.'" *Cultural Critique* (Spring, 1996): 5–40.

Moore, Stephen D. "Deconstructive Criticism: Turning Mark Inside-Out." In *Mark and Method: New Approaches in Biblical Studies*, 2ⁿᵈ edition, edited by Janice Capel Anderson and Stephen D. Moore, 95–110. Minneapolis: Fortress Press, 2008.

Mulvey, L. *Fetishism and Curiosity.* Bloomington: Indiana University Press, 1996.

Nattier, Jan. *A Few Good Men: The Bodhisattva Path according to the Inquiry of Ugra (Ugraparipṛcchā).* Honolulu: University of Hawai'i Press, 2003.

————. "Indian Roots of Pure Land Buddhism: Insights from the Oldest Chinese Version of the *Larger Sukhāvatīvyūha*." *Pacific World: Journal of the Institute of Buddhist Studies* (2003): 179–201.

————. "The Realm of Akṣobhya: A Missing Piece in the History of Indian Buddhism." *Journal of the International Association of Buddhist Studies* 23, no. 1 (2000): 71–102.

Nietzsche, Friedrich. "Truth and Lies in an Extra-Moral Sense." In *The Portable Nietzsche*, translated by Walter Kaufmann, 42–47. New York: Viking Press, 1976.

Noll, Richard. *The Aryan Christ: The Secret Life of Carl Jung.* New York: Random House, 1997.

Nylan, Michael, and Thomas Wilson. *The Lives of Confucius: Civilization's Greatest Sage through the Ages.* New York: Doubleday, 2010.

Owen, Stephen. "The Self's Perfect Mirror: Poetry as Autobiography." In *The Vitality of the Lyric Voice*, edited by Stephen Owen and Lin Shuen-fu, 71–85. Princeton: Princeton University Press, 1986.

Pagels, Elaine. *The Origin of Satan: How Christians Demonized Jews, Pagans and Heretics.* New York: Vintage Press, 1996.

Payne, Richard K., and Kenneth K. Tanaka, eds. *Approaching the Land of Bliss: Religious Praxis in the Cult of Amitābha*. Honolulu: University of Hawai'i Press, 2003.

Petropoulou, Marie-Zoe. *Animal Sacrifice in Ancient Greek Religion, Judaism, and Christianity, 100 BC to AD 200*. Oxford: Oxford University Press, 2008.

Perkins, Pheme. "If Jerusalem Stood: The Destruction of Jerusalem and Christian Anti-Judaism." *Biblical Interpretation* 8:1–2 (2000): 194–204.

Peterson, Dwight N. *The Origins of Mark: The Markan Community in Current Debate*. Leiden: Brill, 2000.

Petersen, Norman R. *Semia 16: Perspectives on Mark's Gospel*, Society of Biblical Literature. Atlanta, GA, 1980.

———. "When Is the End Not the End?: Literary Reflections on the Ending of Mark's Narrative." *Interpretation* 34 (1980): 151–166.

Pietz, William. "The Problem of the Fetish, I." *Res* 9 (Spring 1985): 5–17.

———. "The Problem of the Fetish, II: The Origin of the Fetish," *Res* 13 (Spring 1987): 23–45.

———. "The Problem of the Fetish, III: Bosman's Guinea and the Enlightenment Theory of Fetishism," *Res* 16 (Autumn 1988): 105–123.

Preus, Samuel. *Explaining Religion: Criticism and Theory from Bodin to Freud*. Oxford: Oxford University Press, 1987.

Rhoads, David, Joanna Dewey, and Donald Michie. *Mark as Story: An Introduction to the Narrative of a Gospel*. Philadelphia: Fortress Press, 1999.

Rorty, Richard. "Heidegger, Contingency, and Pragmatism." In *Essays on Heidegger and Others*, 27–49. Cambridge: Cambridge University Press, 1991.

Sanders, E. P. "In Quest of the Historical Jesus." *The New York Review of Books* 48, no. 18, Nov. 15, 2001.

———. *The Historical Figure of Jesus*. London: Penguin Books, 1996.

———. *Jesus and Judaism*. Philadelphia: Fortress Press, 1985.

———. *Paul: A Very Short Introduction*. Oxford: Oxford University Press, 2001.

———. "Reflections on Anti-Judaism in the New Testament and in Christianity." In *Anti-Judaism and the Gospels*, edited by William R. Farmer, 265–286. Harrisburg, PA: Trinity Press, 1999.

———. *Studying the Synoptic Gospels*. London: SCM Press, 1989.

Sandmel, Samuel. *Anti-Semitism in the New Testament?* Philadelphia: Fortress Press, 1978.

Sartre, Jean-Paul. *"What Is Literature?" And Other Essays*. Cambridge, MA: Harvard University Press, 1988.

Saulnier, Christine. "Hérode Antipas et Jean le Baptiste: Quelques remarques sur les confusions chronologique de Flavius Josèphe." *Revue Biblique* 91 (1984): 362–376.

Schlütter, Morten. "A Study in the Genealogy of the *Platform Sūtra*." *Studies in Central and East Asian Religions* 2 (1989): 53–114.

———. "Transmission and Enlightenment in Chan Buddhism Seen through the *Platform Sūtra (Liuzu tanjing)*." *Chung-Hwa Buddhist Journal* 20 (2007): 379–410.

Schopen, Gregory. "The Buddhist 'Monastery' and the Indian Garden: Aesthetics, Assimilations, and the Siting of Monastic Establishments." *Journal of the American Oriental Society* 126, no. 4 (Oct–Dec., 2006): 487–505.

———. *Buddhist Monks and Business: Still More Papers on Monastic Buddhism in India*. Honolulu: University of Hawai'i Press, 2004.

———. "The Mahāyāna and the Middle Period of Indian Buddhism: Through a Chinese Looking-glass." *The Eastern Buddhist* 32, no. 2 (2000): 1–26.

———. "The Phrase '*sa pṛthivīpradeśaś caityabhūto bhavet*' in the *Vajracchedikā*: Notes on the Cult of the Book in Mahāyāna." *Indo-Iranian Journal* 17 (1975): 148–181.

———. "*Sukhāvatī* as a Generalized Religious Goal in Sanskrit Mahāyāna Sūtra Literature." *Indo-Iranian Journal* 19 (1977): 177–210.

Schrift, Melissa. *Biography of a Chairman Mao Badge: The Creation and Mass Consumption of a Personality Cult*. Newark, NJ: Rutgers University Press, 2001.

Shelton, A., ed. *Fetishism: Visualizing Power and Desire*. London: Lund Humphries, 1995.

Sherover, Erica. "The Virtue of Poverty: Marx's Transformation of Hegel's Concept of the Poor." *Canadian Journal of Political Theory* 3, no. 1 (Winter, 1979): 53–66.

Sibony, Daniel. *Les trois monothéismes: Juifs, Chrétiens, Musulmans entre leurs sources et leurs destins*. Paris: Seuil, 1992.

Smith, Jonathan Z. Smith. "The Devil in Mr. Jones." In *Imagining Religion: From Babylon to Jonestown*, 102–120. Chicago: University of Chicago Press, 1982.

———. "The Domestication of Sacrifice." In *Violent Origins: Walter Burkert, Rene Girard, and Jonathan Z. Smith on Ritual Killing and Cultural Formation*, edited by Robert G. Hamerton-Kelly, 191–205. Stanford University Press, 1987.

———. *Drudgery Divine: On the Comparison of Early Christianities and the Religions of Late Antiquity*. Chicago: University of Chicago Press, 1994.

Spong, John Shelby. *The Sins of Scripture: Exposing the Bible's Texts of Hate to Reveal the God of Love*. New York: HarperOne, 2005.

Steigmann-Gall, Richard. *The Holy Reich: Nazi Conceptions of Christianity, 1919–1945*. Cambridge: Cambridge University Press, 2003.

Stendahl, Krister. "The Apostle Paul and the Introspective Conscience of the West." *The Harvard Theological Review* 56, no. 3 (July, 1963): 199–215.

Stewart, Susan. *On Longing: Narratives of the Miniature, the Gigantic, the Souvenir, the Collection*. Baltimore, MD: Johns Hopkins University Press, 1984.

Stroumsa, Guy G. *A New Science: The Discovery of Religion in the Age of Reason*. Cambridge, MA: Harvard University Press, 2010.

———. *The End of Sacrifice: Religious Transformations in Late Antiquity*. Translated by Susan Emanuel. Chicago: University of Chicago Press, 2009.

Tannehill, Robert C. "The Disciples in Mark: The Function of a Narrative Role." *The Journal of Religion* 57, no. 4 (Oct., 1977): 386–405.

———. "The Gospel of Mark as Narrative Christology." In *Semia 16: Perspectives on Mark's Gospel*, edited by Norman R. Petersen, 57–95. Society of Biblical Literature, 1980.

Teiser, Stephen F., and Morten Schlütter. *Readings of the Platform Sūtra*. New York: Columbia University Press, 2012.

Tolbert, Mary Ann. *Sowing the Gospel: Mark's Work in Literary-Historical Perspective.* Philadelphia: Augsburg Fortress, 1996.

Tumarkin, Nina. *Lenin Lives: The Lenin Cult in Soviet Russia.* Harvard University Press, 1983.

Wakeman, Fredrick. *History and Will: Philosophical Perspectives of Mao Tse-tung's Thought.* Berkeley: University of California Press, 1973.

———. "Mao's Remains." In *Death Rituals in Late Imperial and Modern China,* edited by James L. Watson and Evelyn S. Rawski, 254–288. Berkeley: University of California Press, 1988.

Watson, Burton, trans. *The Vimalakīrti Sūtra.* New York: Columbia University Press, 1997.

———, trans. *The Lotus Sutra.* New York: Columbia University Press, 1993.

Wells, G. A. *Can We Trust the New Testament? Thoughts on the Reliability of Early Christian Testimony.* Chicago: Open Court, 2003.

Wen Yucheng. *"Ji xin chu tu de Heze Dashi Shenhui taming." Shijie zongjiao yanjiu* 2 (1984): 78–79.

Wiebe, Donald. "The Failure of Nerve in the Academic Study of Religion." 1984.

———. *The Politics of Religious Studies: The Continuing Conflict with Theology in the Modern University.* New York: St. Martin's Press, 1991.

Wiebe, Donald, with Martin Luther. "Religious Studies as a Scientific Discipline: The Persistence of a Delusion." *Journal of the American Academy of Religion* 80 (2012): 1–11.

Witherington III, Ben. *Paul's Narrative Thought World: The Tapestry of Tragedy and Triumph.* Louisville, KY: Westminster John Knox Press, 1994.

Wrede, William. *Messianic Secret.* Translated by J. C. G. Grieg. Cambridge: James Clarke & Co., 1971 [1901].

Yampolsky, Philip B., trans. *The Platform Sūtra of the Sixth Patriarch.* New York: Columbia University Press, 1967.

Ziporyn, Brook, trans. *Zhuangzi: The Essential Writings.* New York: Hackett, 2008.

Žižek, Slavoj. *The Puppet and the Dwarf: The Perverse Core of Christianity.* Cambridge, MA: MIT Press, 2003.

———. "The Wound Is Healed Only by the Spear That Smote You." In *Tarrying with the Negative: Kant, Hegel and the Critique of Ideology,* 165–199. Durham, NC: Duke University Press, 1993.

Index